Pro CSS for High Traffic Websites

Antony Kennedy
Inayaili de León

Apress®

Pro CSS for High Traffic Websites

President and Publisher: Paul Manning
Lead Editor: Ben Renow-Clarke
Technical Reviewer: David Storey
Editorial Board: Steve Anglin, Mark Beckner, Ewan Buckingham, Gary Cornell, Jonathan Gennick, Jonathan Hassell, Michelle Lowman, Matthew Moodie, Jeff Olson, Jeffrey Pepper, Frank Pohlmann, Douglas Pundick, Ben Renow-Clarke, Dominic Shakeshaft, Matt Wade, Tom Welsh
Coordinating Editor: Mary Tobin
Copy Editor: Nancy Sixsmith
Compositor: Bytheway Publishing Services
Indexer: John Collin
Artist: April Milne
Cover Designer: Anna Ishchenko

Distributed to the book trade worldwide by Springer Science+Business Media, LLC., 233 Spring Street, 6th Floor, New York, NY 10013. Phone 1-800-SPRINGER, fax (201) 348-4505, e-mail orders-ny@springer-sbm.com, or visit www.springeronline.com.

For information on translations, please e-mail rights@apress.com, or visit www.apress.com.

Apress and friends of ED books may be purchased in bulk for academic, corporate, or promotional use. eBook versions and licenses are also available for most titles. For more information, reference our Special Bulk Sales–eBook Licensing web page at www.apress.com/info/bulksales.

The source code for this book is available to readers at www.apress.com, and from www.procssforhightrafficwebsites.com.

Contents at a Glance

Contents

Foreword

These days, everyone is trying to drive a revolution against older browsers and toward new technologies. Although embracing new methods is a good and commendable thing to do, many developers simply need to support older browsers or cut corners to meet their deadlines and the expectations of their managers. Particularly in high-traffic environments, compromises have to be made.

From this perspective, this book is a breath of fresh air. Rather than scolding you for doing what your business needs to be done, Antony and Inayaili attempt to explain how best to make these compromises and which battles to choose. Writing CSS is about more than just the code—to be a great developer, you need to understand what's going on under the hood, the way different browsers process and render websites, the different environments you might be in, performance, accessibility, semantics, usability…

Too often, in large businesses, the developers put their convenience first and the user second. This book advises you against that and helps you deliver something you and your business can be proud of, without going too far in either direction. It's CSS for the real world.

Bruce Lawson, co-author of *Introducing HTML5*
(`http://introducinghtml5.com`); Open Standards Evangelist at Opera

About the Authors

Antony Kennedy currently describes himself as a senior front-end engineer. He has worked on many high-traffic sites for companies such as the BBC, BSkyB, Tesco, Disney, and Channel4. He is an advocate of good processes and agile development, and writes (infrequently) about them and web development on his blog Zeroed and Noughted (`http://zeroedandnoughted.com/`). He recently released an album on iTunes (`http://itunes.apple.com/gb/album/clawsality/id401976277`), which is in absolutely no danger of threatening the charts any time soon.

In addition to once working as a sound engineer for a travelling pantomime, Antony has been working in web and development technologies for more than 14 years (and remembers Internet Explorer 3 and Xara 3D fondly). He particularly enjoys arguing, fixing broken processes, and demonstrating that you *can* be agile in a waterfall business environment. His doorbell tweets him pictures of people that ring it. Antony lives in a half-finished house in North East London and complains about it a lot. He can't cook (except for sushi and pot noodles). He is very difficult to buy presents for.

Inayaili de León is a London-based web designer from Portugal who currently works for Canonical (the creators of Ubuntu). She loves and lives the Web and her job; she loves that there is no time to teach herself everything and that she can learn something new every day.

Self-taught when it comes to web design, Inayaili has a degree in Communications Design. Working on content-heavy web applications is a challenge and a pleasure that she will happily take on, transforming what could easily look like a mess into user-friendly designs. Clean, semantic, and efficient HTML and CSS are a must when converting those designs into the Web, and it is a subject that she is passionate about.

Sundays are dedicated to reading and writing about design, web standards, CSS and HTML. Inayaili speaks at conferences when she can and writes for 24 Ways, Smashing Magazine, and .net magazine as well as on her own blog, Web Designer Notebook (`http://webdesignernotebook.com`).

Chocolate, pizza, and pancakes make Inayaili's days happier, and she is open to online stalking via `http://yaili.com/`.

About the Technical Reviewer

David Storey heads up the Open the Web initiative at Opera. This global team is tasked with improving the compatibility of websites and applications across Opera's wide range of browsers, as well as promoting the Open Web, accessibility, and best practices so that the Web will work for all standards-aware browsers, platforms, devices, and users. He is the product manager of Opera Dragonfly and a member of the W3C SVG-IG Working Group. David previously worked for CERN, home of the World Wide Web, before taking up his post at Opera Software.

Acknowledgments

Writing this book was a long but exciting process; there were many long nights, many renounced weekends, and a lot of patience and perseverance, but it has ultimately made us grow as CSS authors. None of this would have been possible, though, without the help of some truly remarkable, patient, and (above all) inspiring people.

Thank you to everyone who supported us through this endeavor, who encouraged us to go ahead with an idea that came up after a night in the pub, and especially those who motivated us until the very end (even in those moments when we were *really* hard to be motivated).

Many thanks to our technical reviewer, David Storey, whose input has been invaluable and improved the content of this book manyfold. And to our foreword author, Bruce Lawson, whose opinion we both value greatly.

Special thanks to Adam Lang, André Luís, Andrew Fox, Andy Beeching, Anthony Killeen, Calum Land, Christian Heilmann, Dan Jeffrey, Darren Waddell, Edwina Arney, Felix Kennedy, Gavin Williams, Geoffrey Robichaux, Gernot Poetsch, Gonçalo Melo, Ian Pouncey, Isa Costa, Ivo Gomes, Jade Thomas, Jamie Newman, James Newbery, Janak Patel, Kushal Pisavadia, Leah Davenje, Marc Tobias Kunisch, Mark Stickley, Matt Gaddis, Nick Holmes, Nicklas Persson, Paddy Donnelly, Paul Stanton, Sijmen Mulder, Stephanie Hobson, Talia Kennedy, Than Khine, Velcro, everyone that goes to the MF Boat, everyone on The Mailing List™, and everyone who helped us on Twitter.

We would also like to thank those whose work inspires us and many other CSS authors, designers and developers everywhere every day: Andy Budd, Eric Meyer, Nicole Sullivan, Paul Irish, Steve Souders, Tantek Çelik, and all the others.

Of course, we could not have created this book without the support of Apress and everyone involved: our editors Ben Renow-Clarke and Mary Tobin in particular.

And finally, thank you to each other, Antony and Inayaili: writing a book was hard work, but fun nonetheless.

Preface

It is safe to assume—since you're holding this book—that you work for a company of a reasonable size. This means you have bureaucracy and red tape to deal with, and that you have to contend with many different levels of staff. Making changes to your software or websites is not immediate and is weighed down with legacy protocols and processes. If none of this describes your situation, then you are lucky because you are in the minority.

The items mentioned here all sound like negative attributes, but many of them are unavoidable outcomes—particularly in businesses that have undergone rapid growth. The larger a company is, the slower it is typically to respond to change. Antony recalls spending months working on a project for a large blue-chip company, only to find (during a tour of the offices upon project completion) that it had its own software department on the ground floor that was more than capable of undertaking the project he had just completed. This is common among large businesses; they become so large it is difficult for work to be effectively communicated across the entire staff. Often different teams find they have been working on the same thing, and they just had no way of knowing it.

Companies can be driven by many things. They can be finance-driven, reputation-driven, brand-driven, or design-driven, to mention but a few. The driver of the business defines the business practices and protocols. Aside from, perhaps, the brand or design-driven company, the visual backbone of the software we developers build is not considered from the outset.

The CSS developer is often overlooked in the teams developing websites for these companies. Considered by many to be an easy thing to learn, CSS is often handed to server-side developers rather than web development experts, and the frameworks and static files that sit around CSS are frequently considered at the last minute rather than as part of the infrastructure from the beginning. Although the syntax of CSS is simple, the implications of its implementation are not trivial. A good CSS developer has experience in cross-browser pitfalls and how to avoid them, semantics, accessibility, search engine optimization, and the problems that arise due to badly built and documented CSS. A well-built CSS framework can have dramatic implications for the performance of a website. Moreover, a well-documented CSS framework is easy for many developers to work on in a consistent fashion. Particularly at the beginning of a website's life, getting this done right from the outset can pay dividends in the end.

We do not profess to be able to make your business fast to respond, with great communications and happy staff. However, throughout this book we aim to give you a good grounding in some of the processes you can follow to ensure that CSS is not the bottleneck in the development or performance of your website. In the final chapter and appendices, we will give practical examples of everything we have covered, and you can see code examples at the book's website (http://www.procssforhightrafficwebsites.com).

Background Information

This book assumes certain pieces of knowledge on the reader's part. This section aims to ensure that you are aware of these pieces of information, and explain what you can get out of this book. Seasoned developers or anyone who has been working in the web industry for a reasonable amount of time should be able to safely skip to the first chapter.

Who Is This Book For?

Although we will be providing examples of CSS code to demonstrate techniques and subjects we are covering, these are not to demonstrate the latest selectors or properties, but instead to demonstrate how to format, comment, and model your code to keep it sane and follow best practices in your processes. To that end, this book is about the entire team as much as it is about the developer and should be of value to all of its members.

This book is for the following:

- Anyone working on a high-traffic website. This is any website expecting upward of 10,000 unique visitors per day, or with occasional spikes of traffic higher than this amount.

- Anyone working on a very large website one with perhaps upward of 2,000 individual pages or with more than 30 minisites.

- Anyone working on websites in companies with large amounts of staff modifying the same codebase, with upward of 30 developers working on the CSS.

- Anyone working for a company with the capacity to become a very large company and wanting to build a good basis for its web development processes.

- Developers without previous experience of working in large teams.

However, the practices involved are best practices for websites of any size.

What Will I Learn?

Throughout the course of this book, you will learn the following:

- The value of process

- How to share knowledge among staff and teams

- How to quickly get new CSS developers up and running

- How to incorporate CSS into builds and deployments

- How to write reusable and modular CSS

- How to maximize performance of your website(s)

- How to keep branding consistent

- Best practices for cross-browser and accessible CSS

- Dynamic CSS techniques

The final chapter provides a simple CSS framework we developed specifically for this book that demonstrates many of the things that we touch upon, as well as the process we have followed to build it. The four appendices provide concrete examples of guides and processes that you should find useful.

Why Is This Book Different From Others?

Before embarking on the writing of this book, we did much investigation into which alternative resources were available. A plethora of books on learning the basics of CSS, advanced CSS techniques, CSS3 selectors/properties, and different CSS design patterns are all easily obtainable.

This book does not compete with or replace these titles. This book instead explores the challenges of working in large teams or among large numbers of individual teams, on sites with many pages or subsites that receive considerable traffic. This book is not about using the latest and flashiest techniques for image replacement or cross-browser rounded corners; rather, it is focused on making it easy for newcomers to teams to easily comprehend and add to existing code, and for CSS within your infrastructure to be considered from the outset and built in a sane and performant manner.

Even though this book is aimed at both beginners and experts alike, we assume that you are comfortable using HTML and CSS, or are at least familiar with their syntax. We will be discussing the usage of modular, reusable code that is both robust and practical throughout the chapters in this book.

Separation of Concerns

Separation of concerns is an important concept to understand when writing CSS. Many different architectures for applications and systems exist. The justifications and benefits of them are far beyond the scope of this book; however, it is worth giving a very simple explanation of multitier architecture since the logic behind it is easily applicable to CSS and the browser application model.

A multitier architecture approach is a design that separates logic, data, and presentation.[1] This usually describes a client-server system, where there is a client application and a server application. The majority of the processing takes place on the server, and the client is concerned with displaying the information and giving the user an interface to manipulate it. The multitier approach applies as such:

- *Client application*: presentation

- *Application*: logic

---

[1] Model View Controller (MVC) is an example of this.

- *Server*: data

Separating the tiers in this way gives clear ownership of any particular piece of code, function, or task. It also keeps everything reusable and easily maintainable.

This is how more traditional client-server applications would typically behave. This approach obviously applies to a web browser, web server, and database, but the code that runs in the web browser can also be broken down this way. We typically write our front-end code in three "languages": HTML, CSS, and JavaScript. It is possible for our code to be all jumbled up together, much like the following example:

```
<a id="clickableAnchor" href="#" style="color:blue;" onclick="alert('clicked!');">Click
me</a>
```

Technically there is nothing wrong with this; the text will be blue, and the JavaScript will run when it is clicked. However, there are several reasons why this kind of code is bad practice:

- There is no clear separation of the different types of code. When CSS developers want to change the color of the text, they cannot do so without modifying that page. When JavaScript developers want to change the text in the alert box, they cannot do so without modifying that page.

- There is no way this code can be reused. If all our code was written like this, and it was decided that all anchor text should be red, we would have to modify the code in every single place where there was an anchor.

- The more code there is on the page, the larger the file to download. In a way, this is restating the previous point because reusable and external code need be downloaded only once. This, however, also has implications for search engine optimization (SEO).

- Fewer types of code in a document make it easier to read, parse, and edit.

A more appropriate solution would be the following:

In the head:

```
<style>
        #clickableAnchor {color:blue;}
</style>
<script>
        $('#clickableAnchor').click(function(){
                alert('clicked!');
        });
</script>
```

---

[2] We have used jQuery for this example to keep things simple. We are not advocating jQuery over any other JavaScript library or framework.

In the body:

```
<a href="#" id="clickableAnchor">Click me</a>
```

This method breaks our three languages apart; it is much tidier, but there's an even better solution:

In the head:

```
<link rel="stylesheet" href="/css/screen.css" />
<script src="/js/main.js"></script>
```

In the body:

```
<a href="#" id="clickableAnchor">Click me</a>
```

This solution finally separates our three tiers; it creates *separation of concerns*. Now these files can be easily shared across many pages and cached for better performance. Our tiers relate in the front-end realm like so:

- *HTML*: data
- *CSS*: presentation
- *JavaScript*: behavior

Let's touch on these in a little more detail.

Data

For the purposes of websites, we usually refer to this as *content* rather than *data*. You will often hear the phrase "Content is king," and this is good advice. Your markup should be semantic and well structured; on its own, it should read as a valid and sensibly ordered document. This ensures that machines as well as humans have a good chance of understanding both the intent of the content within the document and the words. If a piece of content is a heading, it should be marked up as such (instead of being marked up as, for example, a paragraph set in bold); if it is clearly a list of items, it should also be marked up as such (as opposed to a succession of divs or some other less relevant element), and so on. When machines understand our intent, they have the ability to do the following:

- Understand what a page is about and which parts are more/less important— this is especially important for search engines and assistive devices.

- Display the page in different ways without affecting legibility (for example, by using user style sheets). This also means that your website can degrade gracefully in older browsers and display your content in a way that does not impede comprehension.

- Allow access to the data in a nonlinear fashion, which is, again, particularly useful to assistive devices.

Presentation

This layer concerns itself only with how the page looks. Anything superficial or purely decorative goes here. If you are choosing the font, laying out a page, or changing colors, this is the appropriate layer. If your branding calls for text to be in lowercase or for very small headings, we can do that in CSS without ruining the semantics of the "true" content in our page.

Behavior

This is sometimes called the Logic, Business, or Business Logic layer. Where we are interacting with the page in nonstandard ways—for example, dragging and dropping, or making Asynchronous JavaScript Across XML (AJAX) requests (a method of fetching information from the server without requesting an entirely new page), the JavaScript is the part responsible for this.

Front-End Development Is Full of Exceptions

Although the resulting benefits of the tiered approach are clear, it is never as clear-cut as we have just made it seem. *Expressions* can reside in CSS files, making calculations (although we do not advocate it). JavaScript can be responsible for presentation (such as the appearance/animation of menus). Sometimes JavaScript is responsible for adding new content to the page. There are many other examples. However, intending and attempting to separate the layers in this manner gives us a good starting point, and approaching web development in this way can often result in new and clever ways to avoid duplication of content and maintain high performance.

With these basic pieces of information under our belt, we're ready to get started. The first chapter will introduce you to the importance of process. Although not strictly a CSS subject, it is an important base to build your projects upon.

CHAPTER 1

■ ■ ■

The Value of Process

In this chapter, we aim to focus on how processes in your team and company can help rather than hinder your productivity. Many of these topics are not specific to CSS (Cascading Style Sheets), but to write CSS that is scalable and shared among many teams or websites it is vital to have solid processes and consistency. We willtalk about development methodologies, how to ensure consistent code styles, source control, tools, and naming conventions. Because we aim to give you useful practical examples, we will present an example process at the end of this book.

In this chapter, we will look at:

- The team and its parts
- Scaling a business
- Dealing with loss of staff
- Consistency of code
- Tools
- Version control
- Backup
- Prototyping
- Development methodologies

The Team

Arguably, the most important element in CSS development is the team that supports the developer. Every team is different, not just the personalities of the members or the sizes of the teams but also the disciplines and skills within it. Some teams include a few server-side developers and a single front-end developer, some include the entire skillset required to build a web solution: designers, front-end developers, server-side developers, database specialists, testers, and so on.

A team this size has the benefit of rapid communication between its component parts but has the disadvantage of size; larger teams are slower to respond to requirements for various reasons. The primary reason for this is something researchers call "diffusion of responsibility." This means that in larger teams, members assume that someone else is doing any given task at any given point rather than taking it upon themselves to do it. Without clear guidelines in place, it can be difficult to be sure of who is or should be responsible for unexpected problems or tasks, so even though these issues are noticed, they are forgotten. In smaller teams, besides communications being more immediate and effective, more attention is on each individual, and members will assume responsibility and be more proactive.

This issue, however, can be overcome with good project management. If you have all your tasks mapped out with clear areas of responsibility, there is no room for confusion.

■ **NOTE:** There are many terms that describe people that write CSS: front-end developers, client-side developers, web developers, and web designers are just a few.

The processes within your company change dramatically depending on the type of team you have. For teams that do not include designers, if the requirements fed to your team already include complete designs and specifications, there is little room or time to feed back any issues to the designers or information architects and the development is more siloed away from the requirement creation process. If the teams do not include testers, and the user testing process is outside of your team, errors or problems they find are fed back to you after you have finished developing, which is the least efficient time to fix them.

It also makes a big difference who writes your CSS. If it is written by web designers (hopefully the same people who made the designs for what you are developing), then as long as they are good at what they do they will have taken into account things like accessibility, usability, and templating. If the designers are separate from your team, you may find the designs they provide do not intrinsically consider these things. The worst case is where the CSS is written by those who don't specialize in front-end code at all because they are not expert in what they are doing, and may do more harm than good. CSS is deceptively simple, and it is easy to write inefficient bloated code that quickly becomes legacy code. However, companies' processes are often based in legacy and not that easy to change.

The project manager is responsible for getting the most out of the team and dealing with these issues. One of the most important pieces of a process is defining areas of responsibility. These areas need to be mapped out clearly before a team is even put together, so you know who to include in the team. A simple example is as follows:

- *Project Manager.* The project manager is responsible for representing his team to the business (as well as the business to the team), ensuring that everything is recorded correctly, facilitating meetings, and making sure that the members of his team know what they should be doing and have everything they need to do it (including helping to remove any obstacles that prevent them from doing it). As far as the team goes, the buck stops here; if a project fails, it is likely to be the project manager that is held accountable.

- *Team Lead/Technical Lead:* Team leads are responsible for the technical delivery of the product. They need to ensure they understand the general direction the project is going in as well as the methods being used to address technical challenges, and to communicate with members of their team to find any potential risks or pitfalls, and suggest ways to resolve them.

- *Developer.* The term *developer* is a broad term. For the sake of this example, the developer is the person undertaking the actual tasks within the project (writing the CSS). He is responsible for giving estimates and details necessary to record the tasks, feeding back technical issues to the team lead and logistical issues to the project manager, and completing the tasks.

With these roles clearly defined, it becomes obvious who should be doing what. With regular meetings any problems should be located and dealt with quickly.

We have not mentioned designers or testers because they are not always within the team that develops the project, but if they are members of your team it is important to also list their responsibilities. If your team includes web designers who can write HTML and CSS, you can consider them developers for the sake of this nomenclature.

Once you have your team planned out, it is easy for your company to begin using that template for every team you have and for every project you have. We encourage you to continue to consider how your team is formed on a project-by-project basis. Although strict processes are a good thing, if you don't change them on occasion you may never discover better ways to run your development.

Figure 1-1 shows an example hierarchical diagram of a team setup.

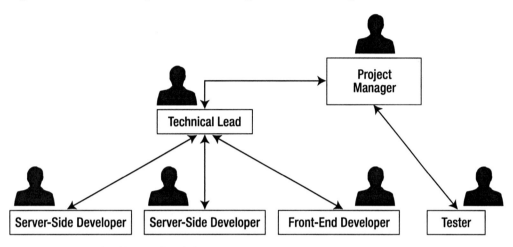

Figure 1-1. An example of hierarchical design

Getting Too Big for Your Boots

Once you have your process in place and all the members of the team know it inside out, there should be very few surprises. In smaller companies or teams, though, strict processes are thought to be less important. Assuming that everyone is a useful and hard-working contributor (in smaller companies they will be caught out quickly if this is not the case), communications can be facilitated with quick spontaneous meetings and face-to-face conversation. Because interaction between staff is more intimate, training new employees is a much more hands-on task. Policies can be changed day to day, and although processes are still useful for efficient performance, a little chaos can, in fact, help with creativity.

As companies and teams grow larger, this becomes less of a luxury and more of a cumbersome chore. Trying to train all your new staff as they are recruited becomes a mammoth task requiring dedicated space and further staff. Keeping communication open and flowing between teams becomes more difficult and more time-consuming. The carefully crafted CSS styles and verbally agreed-to methods of working and keeping your website consistent and clean start to get lost between the increasing number of teams. If your team grows larger, more and more time is taken up in the administration of the individuals, and even just waiting your turn to speak in meetings. If you have off-site resources, the meetings become even less productive as they morph from in-person conversations into conference calls and e-mail.

There are clear and obvious advantages to off-site resources, in that you only use (and pay!) them when you need them, and they are often dramatically cheaper—but this comes at a loss of personal communication.

The benefits of face-to-face communication are as follows:

- Gestures

- Facial expressions

- Body language

- Whiteboards

- Immediacy

- Clarity

The disadvantages of remote communication are the following:

- Technical difficulties

- Loss of meaning and intent

- Loss of focus

- Loss of priority

- Lesser comprehension

- Wasted time and resources

■ **NOTE:** Using video conferencing, screen-sharing and whiteboarding software can allay some of these concerns, but they introduce new technical difficulties and a loss of immediacy and instant gratification.

If you have members of teams that are in different countries, time zone differences and potential language barriers further compound these issues. However, the reduction of cost in using remote developers in countries like India or Estonia is often too attractive to the business to overlook and potentially for good reason.

It is clear that the previously acceptable methods when the company was small and growing of sticking hastily scribbled post-it notes to a big whiteboard and shouting important messages across the room are no longer effective means of management. A solid process that everyone in the team (and hopefully, the company) has bought into and agreed upon will help to alleviate many of these concerns. As mentioned before, if it is clear what tasks everyone should be performing and when, it becomes more difficult for misunderstandings to occur.

If what everyone is doing is recorded in a trackable and consistent manner, any remaining misunderstandings can be uncovered and addressed. More so, whereas in a smaller company it is difficult for neglectful, incompetent, or unproductive members of the team to go unnoticed—writing CSS inconsistent with legacy code, modifying code without due diligence or causing bugs and defects in dependent pieces of code—in larger companies these costly individuals can creep under the radar for months. The processes that we willcover in this chapter can surface and expose their activities (or lack of them) much more quickly.

In smaller companies, every individual has a voice. However, in larger companies this voice can get drowned out by the crowd or simply have no route to the ears of those who need to hear it. Great ideas and improvements can go unheard, and staff members are less invested in a company on which they can leave no impression or mark. Simple processes like feedback sessions, company meetings, available line managers, and fewer levels of hierarchy can help ensure that every staff member has an opportunity to participate and contribute.

If these processes can become ingrained in the company's way of thinking from the start, they will be much easier to implement and a good base for growth.

High Staff Churn Rate

Many larger companies tend to have a high rate of employee turnover—people come and go more frequently, taking their knowledge and the skills invested in them. This is especially true for front-end developers; they are very much in demand in today's markets and often work as contractors with short notice periods, and as such can jump from role to role with little warning. Although company founders want to think that their employees will stay loyal to them forever, the truth is that most people will at some point leave and move on. For smaller companies, a lot is invested into each employee financially and sometimes even emotionally. Every new employee taken on (whether replacing an employee that has left or filling roles that have become necessary due to growth) requires induction and training. These employees help shape the company, and choosing the right people is something that must be considered carefully. In a larger company this becomes even more important. Larger companies gain their own personalities and characteristics and there is more to learn to fit in. New employees must almost be assimilated into the company's behaviors. It can take quite a while to start being productive and longer still to reach the level of productivity that comes with being comfortable in your environment. More-complicated processes mean more user accounts and passwords to set up, documentation to read, policies to learn, and larger premises to find their way around. This means that inducting your staff and training them is paramount to efficiency—you are still paying staff during their unproductive periods, after all.

■ **TIP:** It is important to do whatever you can to get new staff up and running as quickly as possible.

Something else you should be exploring is how to retain these employees more effectively. Every staff member imposes costs on the business, but the knowledge they acquire over time builds exponentially, as does the value of a good team member. First, consider whether you are offering salary and benefit packages that stand up well against those of your competitors. Evidence has been found in many studies that indicate that the simple concept of increasing monetary reward to increase performance only holds true when considering manual labor. In the instance of more cerebral pursuits, it is more important that staff members feel challenged and valued. To this end, it is important to pay them enough that money is not the concern, but you don't have to pay above market rates to get good loyal people. Nonmonetary rewards to increase the individual's happiness in the workplace are valuable also. Things like flexible working hours, training, vacation time, and even just providing a bowl of fruit each morning all serve to add to an employee's level of satisfaction in the workplace. A good canteen doesn't just make your staff happy and well fed—it also keeps them closer to their desk and thus quicker to get back to work!

Another thing that will help retain staff is to demonstrate appreciation for their contributions. Awards ceremonies or other forms of recognition, parties, and nights out demonstrate an appreciation of their commitment to the company and further strengthen the team as a whole.

Although you want your staff to meet your deadlines and requirements and be as productive as possible, you also do not want them to suffer burnout. Ensuring that your deadlines are as realistic as possible (by involving staff in the estimation process and basing estimation accuracy on previous estimates) and that your employees are content in the workplace will help sustain a good work ethic and rate of achievement.

Finally, you want to ensure that your staff members are proud of what they do and feel invested in it. Doing your best to give everyone a voice will help with that. Some companies like Google give their employees opportunities to work on their own products, and support and recognize them if they develop something of value to the company as a whole. Every Friday at Google is "Google Friday," when developers are encouraged to play with new technologies. This playing has resulted in Gmail, Google News, Orkut, the Google logo becoming a fully functional Pacman game, and other internal innovations. At Atlassian, once every three months their employees are allowed to do whatever development they like for a day, as long as they present their results to the company afterward. Developers take pride in their work, and this is demonstrated in the items the developers choose to work on when given free reign. Bugs that are important to developers (but not the business) are fixed, spelling mistakes are rectified, vital refactoring takes place, issues with process are isolated, and solutions appear for existing business problems during this time. The result is that you have better software, but more than that, you have happier and prouder people.

All these suggestions apply just as well to CSS developers as other members of staff. However, the web development world progresses and changes rapidly, and it can be difficult to keep up. If staff members are passionate about what they do, they will want to keep their skills up to date, and if the company wants them to be happy, it will help them achieve this. Although newer CSS techniques might not be ready for prime time due to patchy browser support, time should be allocated for the CSS developers to read about and become familiar with these techniques. Allowing your web developers opportunities to attend conferences (and perhaps even speak at them to represent your company) demonstrates a commitment to the employee and to the technologies they care about. Keeping a good library of reference books (like this one!) and considering subscriptions to magazines helps, too, as does giving the developers time to read them as well as blogs and other articles online. Allowing them to present their own findings online via a company blog is often something they will appreciate, but this may depend upon your company's public stance and policies.

Keeping staff happy should be a primary concern and will help retain them longer, but employees resigning should be planned for, not a cause for panic.

Consistency Is More Important than Quality

When hiring new staff, you should always strive to hire high-caliber individuals. You want people who know their stuff, and have things to share with the rest of the team. However, particularly in the realms of programming and coding, different people have different styles of writing.

Inconsistency of code is a cost, both in terms of time and resources. Although writing CSS selectors in a particular way may be more efficient and clever, due to the potentially high churn of staff, if this code is unusual or more difficult to understand it becomes difficult to share among the team members. Writing your own CSS framework is a good thing, as long as it is not too complicated to pick up. You should also consider some of the already available CSS frameworks that we talk about in Chapter 4. If the process of implementing your own CSS framework requires complicated build scripts and makes debugging difficult, perhaps the solution is being over-engineered. We are not suggesting at all that build scripts (which you can read about in Chapter 9) should not be employed for reasons of performance and efficiency, but the process should be simple. CSS developers typically work very fast, often flicking between their text editor and a browser many times a minute. Any processes required to get your code to run should be implemented in an unobtrusive manner. A build process that hinders that has a much larger hit on the developer's efficiency than many might think. Entering a CSS debugging mode should be just as simple, so in the case of CSS being minified upon reaching production, the CSS developers can see their code as they wrote it instead of a CSS/DOM inspector reporting the selector as being on line 1, where there is only one line.

A single developer hoarding all the knowledge of how certain parts of your code work should be an obvious red flag. If this developer chooses to leave the company, or for some reason cannot work for them anymore, there is an immediate knowledge deficit. New developers may have trouble understanding the code, and a period of stagnation begins, while these developers struggle to come to grips with the complexity of the code. Without the previous CSS developer there to mentor them, huge areas of CSS may just be left in place for years because no other developer is brave enough to remove them for fear of causing issues elsewhere in the site. This kind of stagnation of legacy code is very common and is difficult and costly to resolve.

To that end, it must be preferable to have simpler and clearer code wherever possible so that knowledge hoarding remains at a minimum. Some companies choose to frequently rotate their developers onto different pieces of their projects at particular intervals to combat this. In fact, despite the obvious cost in time, this methodology has some considerable benefits, in that every team member has a good idea of how the project works as a whole and may consider factors that could otherwise have been overlooked without this holistic view. Problems found during development rather than during planning are always more costly to overcome. The main downside to this methodology is that developers are constantly moving from one piece of the puzzle to another and may find it difficult to "get into the zone," which can be frustrating and a further cost.

The value of consistency in these scenarios cannot be overstated. As a very basic example, one individual may compose their CSS code in this fashion:

```
/* Main Heading */
#mainHeading {
    font-size: 2em;
    font-weight: bold;
    color: red;
}
```

Another may write it like this:

```
/*=======================================================================
   Main Heading
=======================================================================*/
#main-heading {font-size:20px;font-weight:bold;color:#ff0000}
```

Both of these are completely valid and technically correct ways of writing CSS. However, if these two individuals both worked on the same CSS file at different times, you could end up with a mixture of these two very different coding styles in the same document. This leads to a document that is hard to scan and read. Many developers, upon finding the style of code that was different to their own, may reformat it in a way they find is preferable to them. The original developer may then format it back the same way. This is both inefficient and unnecessary.

CSS suffers from this problem more than most coding languages. It is so easy to just throw lines of code into a file until something renders correctly, and it is very difficult to isolate the pieces that you can safely remove or that are no longer in use. To that end, strictly formatting your CSS documents and keeping the selectors and rules in the right place is paramount to avoiding a big mess of code with legacy and leftover pieces that are difficult to locate. Code that is badly or hastily written is known as "technical debt", a term coined by Ward Cunningham in 1992. A little debt is okay as long as you pay it back (refactor and fix the code), but the longer you wait, the more the interest builds up (code built on top of and dependent upon the initial code) until you go bankrupt (have to start all over again).

To solve this problem, it is important to have standards predefined in a guide so everyone knows that CSS is written in a particular way in your organization. Most companies of any size have some kind of wiki (see following) or company handbook, which is an appropriate place to store a guide like this. Although outdated, the BBC makes its CSS Guide available online at `www.bbc.co.uk/guidelines/futuremedia/technical/css.shtml`.

We don't recommend having rigid guidelines that are enforced strictly (for example, you should not use `!important`,[1] but there may be situations where it is the most appropriate thing to do). However, we do recommend some form of guidelines exist. Here is an example of a section of a CSS formatting guide:

- All related blocks of CSS should be prefixed with a comment in this format to aid visual scanning and searchability of the CSS document:

```
/*=====================================================================
   Main Heading
=====================================================================*/
```

- All colors should be in hexadecimal format (#123456).

- All CSS selectors and rules should be on a single line to save space and to fit more selectors on a screen simultaneously.

These points serve as an example, not necessarily steps that we recommend you take. We will present you with an example CSS formatting guide at the end of this book. For this guide, it is useful to employ *MoSCoW* (a common method for prioritization). MoSCoW (in this context) means the following:

- **Must do this**
  - This rule must be followed at all times, with no exceptions.

- **Should do this**
  - This rule should be followed at all times, unless there is an acceptable reason not to that has been justified.

- **Could do this**
  - This is more of a tip than a rule that can be employed where appropriate.

- **Won't do this now but Would like to in the future**
  - This is something you can't do now (perhaps because of a lack of browser support), but might consider in the future.

Using this method is useful because it means all CSS topics are captured to demonstrate they have already been considered, and previous conclusions can be kept for future discussions.

It is also important wherever possible, and where it is not clear, to explain the reasons for the rules in our guide.

From the business perspective, creating clean and well-written CSS is very hard to justify. It's not that the business wants bad or messy code to be written, it is that our work is typically based upon business requirements. The business wants those requirements delivered and for the team to be ready to

---

[1] `!important` is mentioned in greater detail in Chapter 3.

move onto other pieces of work as soon as possible. To that end, you need a good compromise. You want good clean code—you know it makes life easier in the future and it allows you to take pride in your work. But perhaps complicated and terse code (which is not always the same as good code) is more of a hindrance than a benefit. If you have a solid and rigid structure and methodology that you stick to, our new staff can adjust to our in-house coding style with the minimum of fuss and get straight to being productive. If you know which styles go in which files and how to locate the blocks of CSS in those files, you can find the pieces you need to amend straight away, with no need for endless debates (with very little business value) about which location to use.

Of course—taking this to the extreme—excessively verbose and overly commented code is just as hard to work with. Selectors may become too specific, and comments may take up all our screen estate, making it difficult to scan the document. We willbe looking at comment usage in Chapter 2.

This does not mean using newer technologies is a bad thing or that you should not debate techniques. It does mean, however, that these debates should have an appropriate forum at set intervals as part of our process. You can amend documents as and when you need to, as long as you communicate the changes to everyone who needs to know. If you keep your CSS guide in a wiki (see the section on Wikis under the Tools heading below), they will typically support some kind of notification mechanism via "watched pages" or similar means. This means that upon any revision that is not specifically marked as minor, a list of subscribers will be alerted to the change. Anyone working on the CSS within the organization should be a member of this list. They should also have the ability to modify the guide themselves (and, in turn, notify the others). It is very important however, that someone owns this document—that is, that someone is responsible for the changes that occur within it—and makes sure the others are aware of any changes made to it.

Let's say that the *RGBA (Red Green Blue Alpha)* method of declaring colors has recently found favor among our CSS developers. In our imaginary organization, *Igloo Refrigerator Parts Inc*, we have a monthly meeting between all our front-end developers. It is proposed and agreed at this month's meeting that this method has value, and we want to start using it. Using *RGB (Red Green Blue)* as a flat-out replacement for hexadecimal code is found to have good support in the browsers in which we look to maintain adequate functionality (see "Graded Browser Support" in Chapter 6), and RGBA gives us a capability we did not have before (notably alpha transparency), so we want to add it to our CSS Formatting Guide and amend our previous recommendation. Again, this is an example, not our suggestion.

Before, we had this line:

- All colors should be in hexadecimal format: #123456.

We can now amend it like so:

- All colors should be in RGB format: rgb(100,100,100).

- Where colors need to support alpha transparency, we should use the RGBA format: rgba(100,100,100,0.5).

■ **TIP:** Always declare a non-alpha RGB color first and don't rely on the alpha transparency for older browsers.

At the meeting, someone is given the responsibility to make these amendments, and to make sure that everyone is notified about them. Note that this does not mean we should immediately revisit all our CSS code and convert all hexadecimal colors to RGB, but it does mean that any future colors should be in RGB. The next time we have an opportunity to refactor is an opportunity to convert the rest of the legacy code across to satisfy the new guidelines.

Often, in larger organizations, different departments will not communicate with each other, and the business may be so large that indeed they never even know the others exist. We would encourage you to reach out to everyone in your business that writes CSS, and try to get everyone speaking the same language and working together.

Tools

Many tools exist to help us develop our website and manage our processes. There are myriad pieces of software to manage our tasks, store our files, store documentation, create mock-ups, share files, develop our code, communicate with each other, and so on. This section discusses some of the types of software that are likely to be useful to your process and mentions a few examples of each type. It is impossible to mention (and have used) everything, so please consider these tools a list of potential candidates with notes on important features, and not a complete overview. Review the options available before deciding on particular choices.

Wikis

A *wiki* is a piece of software (almost always based in a web browser) that serves as a repository for documents, and allows particular groups of people to edit them. They often include features such as "watched" pages that allow users to be sent notifications when they change, and storing version information on previous revisions of documents. The most famous example of a wiki is, of course, the famous www.wikipedia.org. Having all of your documentation stored centrally in a well-organized fashion has many benefits:

- Easy to back up

- Obvious where to locate particular kinds of data

- Data does not go stale or get into conflict (everyone works on the same piece of information rather than having multiple versions in multiple places)

- Potentially available remotely

- Platform-independent

- Previous revisions of documents are not lost

It is very easy for a wiki to get out of control. Ensure someone is responsible for owning the wiki, enforcing a sensible, structured taxonomy, and performing housekeeping. Many examples of wiki software exist. Some hosted, some you can host yourself, many are free, many are paid for… They employ many different languages for formatting.[2]

Here are some of the most prolific and well known.

---

[2] A markup language known as Creole aims to standardize the languages used in wikis and has been adopted (though not necessarily as the default language) by many of the less well-known wikis. You can read about Creole at www.wikicreole.org/.

MediaWiki

Arguably the most famous wiki software—this is the wiki behind Wikipedia. MediaWiki (`www.mediawiki.org`) is open source, highly configurable, and simple to set up. It supports most databases and is written in PHP. Plugins are available. Some authentication features are built in, but they feel unfinished and untested. MediaWiki also has a reputation for being very slow. As is often the case, the benefit of using open source software (it is free!) is tempered by the downside, which is that it *feels* like open-source software.

Atlassian Confluence

Confluence (`www.atlassian.com/software/confluence`) is not free, but it is one of the more polished and full-featured wikis out there with a great WYSIWYG (What You See Is What You Get) interface. There is a hosted solution as well as one you can run internally. Confluence is written in Java and supports most common databases. Confluence can be neatly integrated with Atlassian's other products, and has some basic social networking capabilities. A large plugin library is available. You can (at the time of writing) purchase a license for up to 10 users for $10, but it quickly becomes more expensive when your needs exceed that (which they are likely to in large environments).

Mac OS X Server Wiki

If you are running OS X Server (from version 10.5 upward), you already have this wiki installed (`www.apple.com/server/macosx/`). Every user group gets its own wiki by default, but you can build more. The authentication features work well. Mac OS X Server Wiki uses HTML behind the user interface to format data, but has a very strict white list to control which tags and attributes are available, which can quickly become a hindrance. You can modify this list, but it's not much fun to do so. It is very attractive, polished, and simple to set up and use, but it is a bit limited on functionality.

Trac

Trac (`http://trac.edgewall.org/`) includes a bug/issue tracker and is a dedicated wiki specifically for software development projects. Trac combines a bug tracker and wiki into one, which might simplify your workflow. It is open source and free, but it does not feel as polished as some others on this list.

▦ **TIP:** A great resource for comparing different wikis is at `www.wikimatrix.org`.

Bug Reporting

Bug reporting software serves the purpose of giving us a centralized place to record any bugs or defects that are found in your software. As in the case of wikis, some are hosted, some can be self-hosted, some are expensive, and some are free. Bug trackers are used for testers to raise bugs with different priorities.[3]

Some examples of dedicated bug reporting software are discussed in the following sections.

Lighthouse

Lighthouse (http://lighthouseapp.com/) is *software as a service (SaaS)* that offers a clean and simple interface that runs in your browser. It is not free, but is reasonably priced.

BugZilla

Bugzilla (www.bugzilla.org/) is a free open-source bug tracker from Mozilla. It is full-featured, mature, and has great support for version control systems. It is written in Perl and supports user interfaces using Web, e-mail, RSS, web service, and command line. MySQL and PostgreSQL are both supported as databases.

Atlassian JIRA

JIRA (www.atlassian.com/software/jira/) is not free, but has a huge feature set. The administration of it may be a bit daunting, but it is flexible enough to handle pretty much any process or workflow. Installation and maintenance (particularly upgrades) are not as simple as they could be, but the caliber of plugins available goes a long way toward making up for this.

Trac

Trac (http://trac.edgewall.org/) gets a second mention due to its bug-tracking capabilities. You may find that having a wiki and bug tracker combined is useful in your company, and Trac is very capable in both respects. The previous critiques still apply.

Task Management

Task management software lets us record tasks we expect our team to undertake. It may include functionality like resource/time management and comprehensive reporting capabilities. The role of this kind of software is to present a simple and unintrusive interface for entering and reviewing tasks. Enterprise task management software (which can also be called project management software) is often built around agile processes.

Some examples are shown in the following sections.

---

[3] You can read about Antony's standardized method of recording and prioritizing bugs called SEERS (Screenshot, Environment, Expected/Actual Behaviour, Reproduction, Severity) on his blog at http://zeroedandnoughted.com/standardised-bug-reporting-with-seers/.

Things

A desktop application for OS X, Things (`http://culturedcode.com/things/`) is really for managing tasks at an individual level rather than sharing them between the team. Many people find this extra level of self-management useful. An iPhone app is also available that syncs with the desktop version over wifi (sadly, not via the cloud).

Rally

Rally (`www.rallydev.com/`) is a hosted and paid-for solution. Although unintuitive and lacking in some features, it deals very well with resource and time management when your staff may be working on several projects concurrently.

Mingle

Mingle (`www.thoughtworks-studios.com/mingle-agile-project-management`) is developed by ThoughtWorks, which is well known for its contributions to the agile movement within the IT industry. Mingle includes a polished web-based interface, with a built-in wiki. The user interface works solely on the metaphor of cards on a whiteboard, and the processes are very customizable. The pricing is on a per-user basis and unlikely to be cheap, although a free 1 year trial is available for up to five users.

Bug Tracking and Task Management

Rather than keeping these two systems disparate, some solutions exist that cover both of these requirements. This makes good sense—our bugs need to be fixed, and the fixing of them is of course a task. In a good process, these things can be managed together. The fewer pieces of software to maintain the better, and the training costs will decrease if there is only one application your developers need to learn.

Here are a few examples of pieces of software that combine task management with bug tracking:

Atlassian JIRA (with Green Hopper plugin)

Green Hopper (`www.atlassian.com/software/greenhopper`) turns JIRA into a full-featured agile task tracker. It is very configurable, and easy to make JIRA resemble the whiteboards and cards that many of us are used to. Kanban (a less common agile development methodology) is also supported well. It's hard to find a setup that improves upon this, but (for larger teams) it is not cheap, or easy to administer, install, and maintain.[4]

Agilo

Agilo (`www.agile42.com/cms/pages/agilo/`) is based upon and supports integration with Trac to provide a full-featured solution for SCRUM (an agile development methodology). A free alternative is available as well as a paid for version. Installers are provided, as well as a Python Egg if you are familiar with Python, which it is written in.

---

[4] We do not work for Atlassian. We just really like their stuff.

FogBugz

Originally an internal bug-tracking tool for Fog Creek Software, Fogbugz (`www.fogcreek.com/fogbugz/`) was first released in 2000. It has since expanded to include wikis, forums, and task management. It supports Evidence-Based Scheduling (EBS)[5] and has a built-in API for connecting to your own software. It is available as a hosted solution (with a 45-day free trial) or installable on your own servers, and is reasonably priced.

It is very easy to reach software overload. Many companies have three or four wikis running simultaneously as well as different versions of task- or bug-tracking software. This kind of situation is so inefficient and detrimental to processes that it must be avoided at all costs. Make a decision about which software to use in your business and then apply it. Try to use strict and enforceable rules how to organize your information without making it too complicated.

■ **TIP:** Where your tools send e-mail, if you are able to configure it as such, it is important to keep this e-mail to a minimum, relevant, and to the point. If your developers are overwhelmed, the e-mail will not be read.

Source Control

Source control comes in many flavors, but at the heart of every one is the concept of maintaining a history of every file in your project (stored in a *repository*) with the ability to roll back to previous versions of any file. There is also (typically) the concept that one file may have been worked on by many people, and thus needs to be "merged" to include everyone's changes.

The main copy of the files in our project is called the *trunk*. When a version of software is released (considered safe to put in a production environment), it is very common to *tag* the current state of the repository, or *branch* the repository (which means to create a duplicate version of the current state of the repository). We do this so that if problems are found with the version on production, we can make amendments to that code without worrying about more recent changes that might conflict or not be ready for release. Typically we should work in the trunk where possible because merging the changes between branches can be problematic.

Some examples of source control systems are shown in the following sections.

Visual SourceSafe (VSS)

VSS (`www.microsoft.com/visualstudio`) is now widely considered a legacy and outdated method of source control. When one user chooses to work on a file (by checking it out), that file is locked from being worked on by any other user until it is committed back into the repository (checked in).

There is a benefit of this methodology: files almost never need to be merged because they are always left in a state the developer is happy with. However, this means that developers can never simultaneously work on the same file and often forget to commit their files, thereby locking the file away from other users.

---

[5] A method of estimating tasks more accurately, created by Joel Spolsky. Read more about it at `www.joelonsoftware.com/items/2007/10/26.html`

Concurrent Versions System (CVS)

CVS (www.nongnu.org/cvs/) was developed by Dick Grune in July 1986. Although other versioning systems similar to CVS existed before (this was the first that allowed files to be modified by multiple people simultaneously) to gain widespread acceptance. The CVS model keeps all files in a centralized repository on a server, and clients check out and commit files from and to that repository.

Subversion (SVN)

CVS had many shortcomings, and although it is still in common use today, Subversion (http://subversion.apache.org/) was created by CollabNet in 2000 as an attempt to fix many of the bugs in CVS and to add many of the much requested "missing features." As such, it operates in a very similar manner to CVS. Due to its relative stability and maturity, it is one of the most common version control systems in companies today.

Git

Git[6] (http://git-scm.com/) is a form of *distributed version control*. This means that the developer has a repository on his own machine as well as one (or many) stored centrally. Rather than "hoarding changes" for fear of committing faulty code (and therefore increasing the potential for data loss due to crashes or hardware failure), users commit their code to their local repository and can manage revisions from there. Instead of being a single library, Git is actually formed from a series of individual tools with which it is possible to come up with pretty much any version control process you might like. Although the merging algorithm used in Git is well respected and has been proven by merging 12 Linux kernel patches simultaneously, Git is a complicated system to get your head around and may well be overkill for your projects.[7]

Mercurial

Another distributed version control system, Mercurial (http://mercurial.selenic.com/), is sometimes known by its command-line name: hg. It was developed by Matt Mackall and released in 2005. Git and Mercurial were developed concurrently because the free version of BitKeeper—the source control software used at that time by the Linux kernel project—was withdrawn by its developer, BitMover. Although Git was ultimately used by the Linux kernel project, Mercurial is still championed by many in the industry. Less full-featured than Git, Mercurial is still very functional and fast, and simpler to use— particularly for those migrating from Subversion.

▨ **NOTE:** BitBucket (http://bitbucket.org/) is a service similar to GitHub for Mercurial projects.

---

[6] *Git* is an unpleasant thing to call someone equally unpleasant in British English slang. Linus Torvalds, the creator of Git, said, "I'm an egotistical bastard, and I name all my projects after myself. First Linux, now git."

[7] GitHub (http://github.com/) provides free public repositories that might be appropriate for your projects.

Graphical User Interfaces

Almost all version control systems ship with command-line interfaces, but many graphical user interfaces (GUIs) exist as well as plugins to enable integrated development environments (IDEs) and other pieces of software to communicate with them. To mention them all would be beyond the scope of this book, but it is worth mentioning the Tortoise family of shell extensions for the Windows platform (TortoiseCVS, TortoiseSVN, TortoiseHG, and so on). They integrate tightly within Windows, adding functionality to the right-click menu within the file system explorer as well as icons signifying state, which is the most intuitive place for them to be. Copycat versions have been attempted for OS X and Linux, but none have (at time of writing) been integrated as tightly and intuitively as Tortoise.

Using Version Control Systems

When working with source control, when you are happy with what you have done, you *commit* the file to the repository. This updates the central code with the version you are working on. If you are using distributed version control, you should commit to the local repository often, and only commit to the central repository when you are confident your code is working correctly. You can see a visual comparison between version control and distributed version control in Figures 1-2 and 1-3.

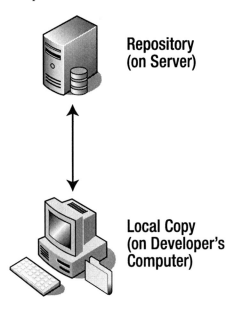

Repository (on Server)

Local Copy (on Developer's Computer)

Figure 1-2. Diagram of normal version control

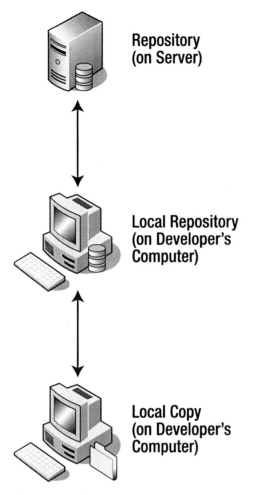

Figure 1-3. Diagram of distributed version control

Using version control systems is vital when you work on CSS in teams. It gives you the added confidence to work on files that other developers may be working on, as well as the reassurance of a restorable history for each change we commit. When we work with CSS, we often work in small chunks. We make small changes, switch to our browser, refresh the page, change, switch, F5, and so on. We should remember to commit our changes often, so that we have a good history of everything we have been doing.

When committing your changes, most version control systems will ask you for a *comment* describing what you have changed. When your version control system is further embedded in your processes, these comments become invaluable. It is therefore of utmost importance that your comments are relevant, descriptive and helpful.

A comment like this is of very little value:

```
Changed some bits and pieces.
```

But a comment like this describes exactly what happened within the file:

```
Changed hex colors to RGB colors.
```

When things go wrong (which they will), you will find yourself viewing the commit history of the files with the problem and useful comments will be very helpful in clarifying what changed in each revision.

Typically, you are encouraged to *update* a file by hand before beginning work on it. This means to fetch the latest version from the repository. If you fail to update and begin work on an outdated version of the file, or if another developer has committed changes after you began work, you are required to merge the files. Because two developers have been working on it simultaneously, the changes between your local copy and the version in the repository are non-linear. It is impossible to work out which pieces to keep and which to replace in an automatic fashion; this results in the files being *in conflict*. To resolve the conflict, it is necessary to locate the differences, edit the file appropriately, and then mark the conflict as *resolved* so that you can commit the amended version of the file.

Diff Tools

To deal with these conflicts, you will want to see exactly what the differences are between the two files. A special type of application exists that does just this: a *Diff* program. Again, lots of them exist, and we don't intend to promote one over the other. The purpose of these programs is to compare two similar files and show the differences between them.

The intention is to make it easy to recognize and resolve the conflicts between two versions of the same file. Because CSS is often less modular than we would like it to be (or can have effects in unexpected places), and although conflicts can be resolved, we should still avoid them wherever possible. The best way to do this is to communicate effectively with your team and let everyone know exactly which files you are working on at any one time.

Where these conflicts exist, we must merge and resolve them. Resolving conflicts and merging changes are some of the biggest headaches of having multiple individuals working on the same file. Older style command-line Diff programs show only the differences between the files, similar to the output shown in Figure 1-4.

Figure 1-4. An example output of a command-line Diff tool

More modern Diff programs ease this pain by letting you view two documents side by side. Differences between the two documents are highlighted, and any section that is different can be copied from either document to the other document (see Figure 1-5).

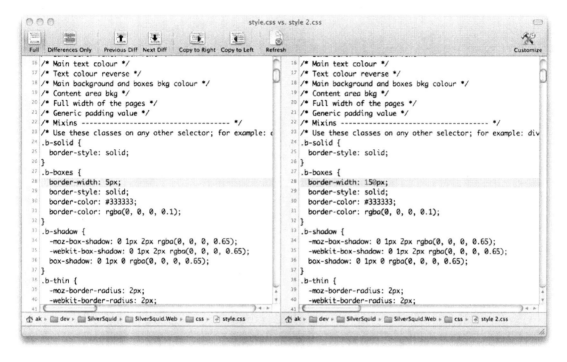

Figure 1-5. An example output of a GUI-based Diff tool

Often simple versions of Diff tools will be available within your IDE or version control system, but the following sections describe examples of other dedicated Diff programs.

Araxis Merge

The standard version of Araxis Merge (`www.araxis.com`) can compare two documents, but the professional version can compare and merge three separate documents simultaneously. It is reasonably priced, and available for both Windows and Mac platforms with great performance on both platforms.

WinDiff

WinDiff (`http://support.microsoft.com/kb/159214`) is included with Microsoft Visual Studio, so it is free if you already develop with that platform. You can also download it from `www.microsoft.com/downloads/details.aspx?familyid=49ae8576-9bb9-4126-9761-ba8011fabf38&displaylang=en` if you are running Windows XP, but it is included on the CD for versions of Windows including Windows 2000 and later.

WinMerge

WinMerge (`http://winmerge.org/`), as the name suggests, is a Windows application. It is open source, available for free, and performs well.

Beyond Compare

Beyond Compare (`www.scootersoftware.com/`) is developed by Scooter Software and on its third revision. It is available for Windows and Linux. It is reasonably priced, and has a great reputation and feature set.

Changes

Changes (`http://connectedflow.com/changes/`) is a Mac-based application that integrates well with other apps on OS X. Figure 1-5 shows Changes in action. It is inexpensive and can compare folders as well as files.

Kaleidoscope

Kaleidoscope (`http://kaleidoscopeapp.com/`) deserves a mention as a very attractive and intuitive Diff tool. It is made by Sofa (which also makes the Versions SVN client for OS X at `http://versionsapp.com`) and is a great example of beautiful and intuitive software at a low price. Unfortunately, as of version 1 (the current version at time of writing), it includes no merging capability, which may limit its usefulness to you.

A more complete list of Diff tools is available at `http://en.wikipedia.org/wiki/Comparison_of_file_comparison_tools`.

Resolving Conflicts

Let's demonstrate how to resolve an SVN conflict. We willuse the Versions SVN client and Changes Diff tool, both on OS X. For the sake of example, we are working on a file specifically for Internet Explorer 8 called ie8.css. We have updated our local repository and then worked on the file locally. The contents of the file initially were the following:

```
#imagePath {
    filter: alpha(opacity=0);
}
#tryit-form .input-file {
    height:18px;
    width:217px;
}
```

We have added an extra selector and changed the height and width for #triyit-form .input-file, so the file now looks like this:

```
#imagePath {
    filter: alpha(opacity=0);
}
img.example {
```

```
    float:left;
}
#tryit-form .input-file {
    height:22px;
    width:220px;
}
```

We tested these changes and they work fine, so we go to commit the file with an appropriate comment (see Figure 1-6).

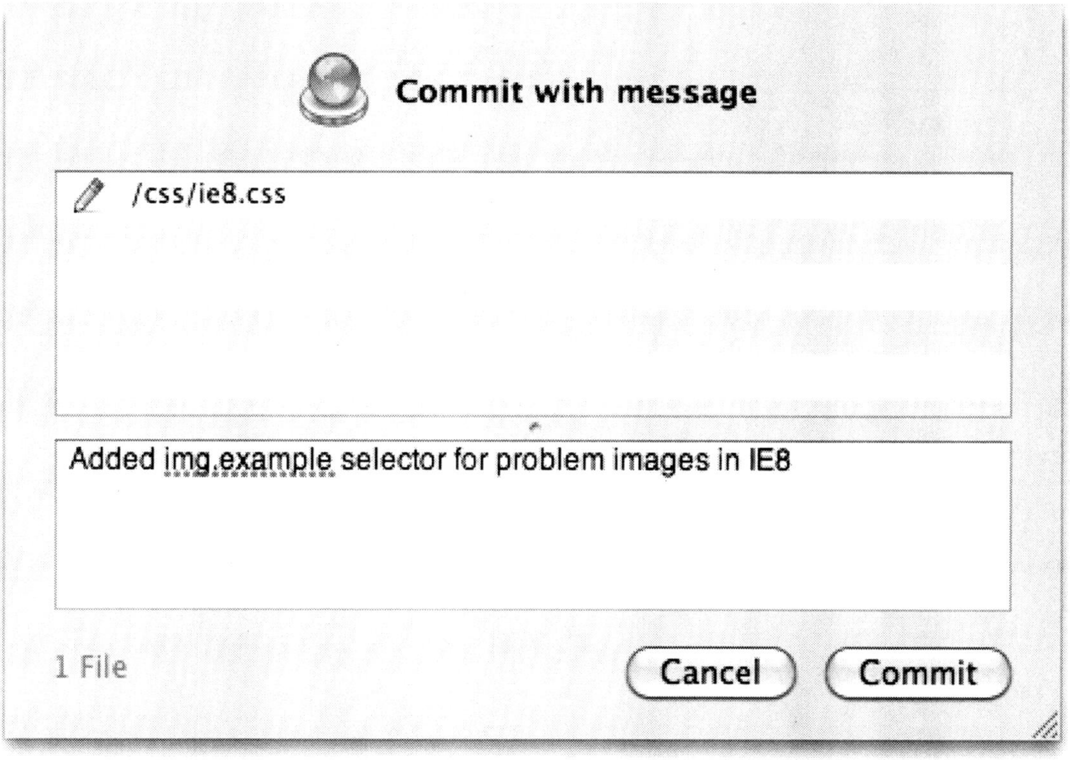

Figure 1-6. An example SVN commit dialog

The result is shown in Figure 1-7.

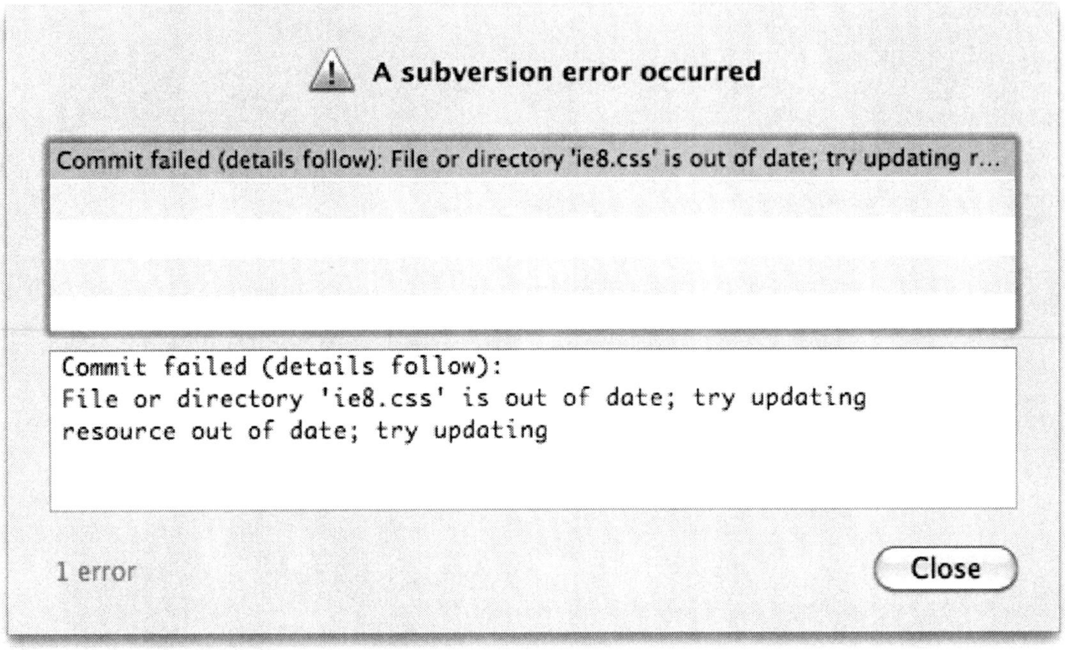

Figure 1-7. An example SVN conflict dialog

This figure tells us that this file has been modified and committed since we last updated it. As suggested, we will now perform another update of our local copy to pull down the latest changes (see Figure 1-8).

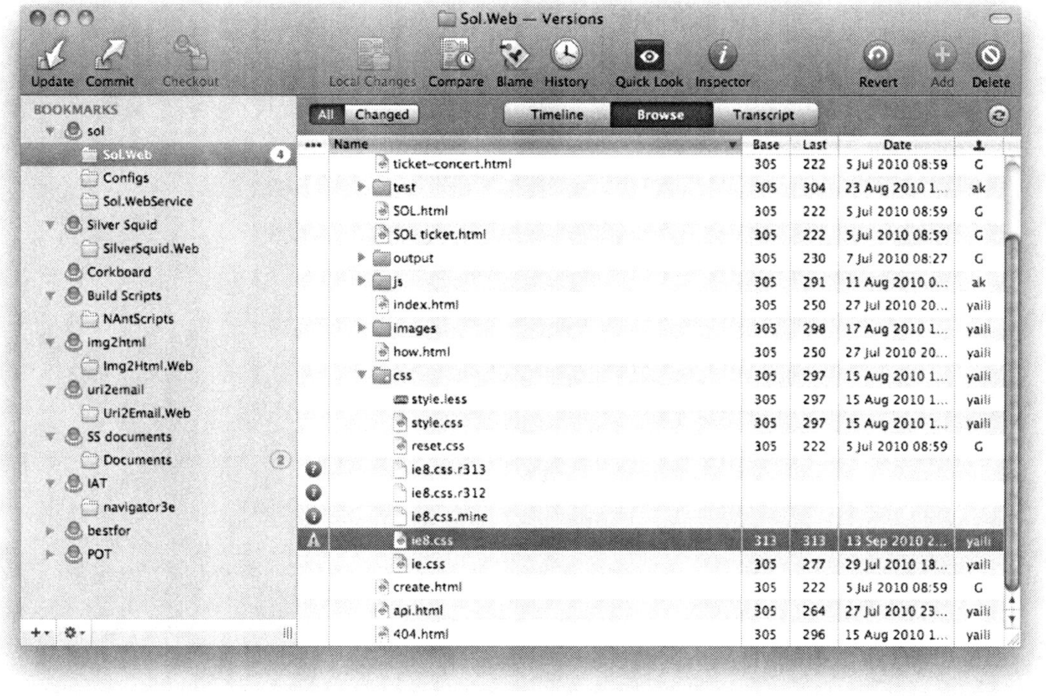

Figure 1-8. The SVN conflict in the file browser window

Versions now shows several new files and icons. ie8.css has an exclamation mark next to it, which indicates it is currently in conflict. But three brand-new files have appeared, too:

- ie8.css.r313
- ie8.css.r312
- ie8.css.mine

Each of these files has a purpose:

- ie8.css.r313 is the latest version of this file in the repository.
- ie8.css.r312 is the version of the file we downloaded from the repository when we last updated.
- ie8.css.mine is the version of the file we just tried to commit.
- ie8.css now contains markers, the version we created, and the changes in the repository.

The contents look like this:

```
#imagePath {
    filter: alpha(opacity=0);
}
img.example {
    float:left;
}
#tryit-form .input-file {
<<<<<<< .mine
    height: 22px;
    width: 220px;
=======
    height: 24px;
    width: 320px;
    float: left;
}
.clearfix {
    zoom: 1;
>>>>>>> .r313
}
```

The markers show what has changed. Everything between <<<<<<< .mine and ======= were changed since updating, and everything between ======= and >>>>>>> .r313 were changed by someone else. Notice that SVN is not suggesting that our img.example selector and rules are in conflict because it is clever enough to resolve and merge those changes itself.

To resolve this, let's compare our version and the latest version from the repository. First, we open both of those files in Changes (see Figure 1-9). We need to consider that one of these files as the master file, so we willuse the .mine file and make sure that file is selected first so it appears on the left.

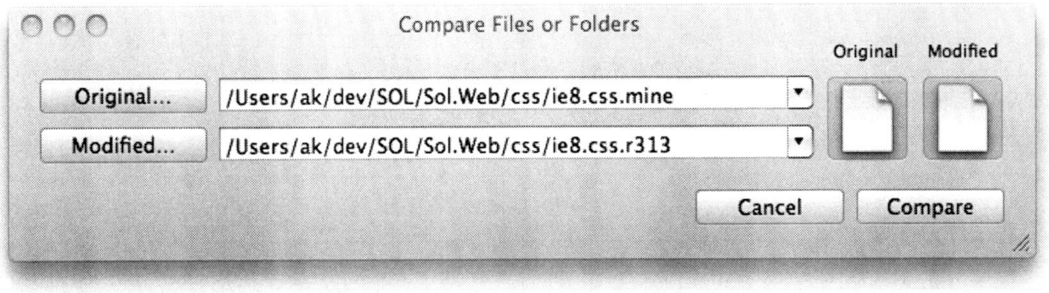

Figure 1-9. *The Changes app file selection dialog*

The result is shown in Figure 1-10.

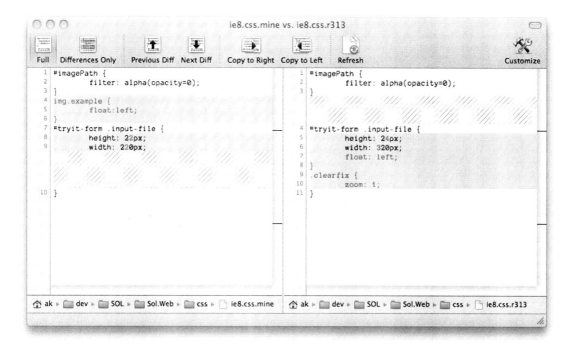

Figure 1-10. *A file comparison in the Changes app*

The differences in the files are now very obvious. We added a section for the selector `img.example`, someone else has added `.clearfix`, and the contents of the other selector have been modified. We check the logs quickly, and find out who has changed this file and read their commit comment. If necessary, we can then contact them to ask them about their changes. It turns out that a change in design required the change to height and width of a particular element, and that our changes to them are no longer necessary. Using the left file in Changes as our master, we now merge our changes. We just want the bottom part of the file, so we click anywhere in that section in the document on the right and click Copy to Left (see Figure 1-11).

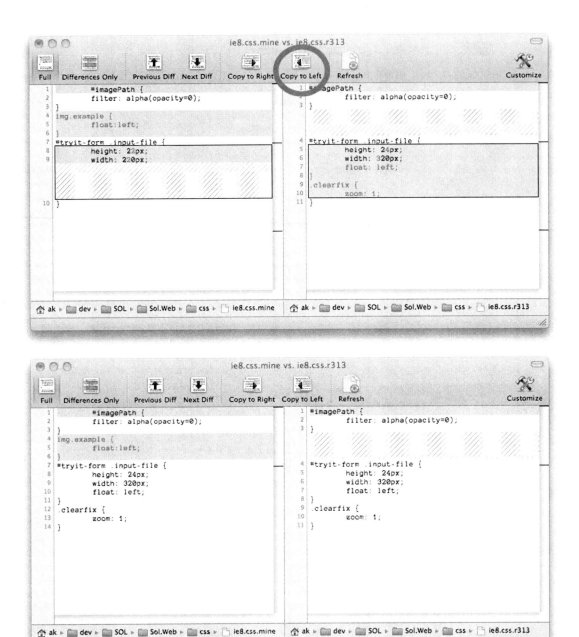

Figure 1-11. Merging files in the Changes app

The file on the left is now how we intend the file to be. We copy and paste the contents into ie8.css file, and in Versions mark it as "resolved" (see Figure 1-12).

Figure 1-12. Resolved conflict in the Changes app

Finally, we do another update from the repository, and test the file to ensure that it works correctly. It does (hopefully!), so we commit it to SVN.[8]

Backup

It goes without saying that backups are a vital element of any development process. It is of huge importance that you back up your repository and other important data. Where possible, versions of these backups should be stored in several discrete locations. Hardware failure, data corruption, and fire or flood damage can destroy months or even years of work in a moment.

A backup should be treated like insurance. You almost never need it, but if and when you do, it is potentially hugely more valuable than the cost to implement it. You should also have backups of different days—something like one backup a day for the last seven days at any point, and possibly even monthly backups going farther back. Sometimes we find we want to revert to a version that was lost a few days ago or look at a legacy version of a product, and not everything will be stored in source control.

---

[8] It was actually quite difficult to create a conflict for this example, which demonstrates that SVN does a pretty good job of merging files on its own, except when you want it to.

It is important to ensure that your backups actually work. It is all well and good to religiously remember to take different backup tapes home, but if you don't run a test restore, you could find out at the worst possible time that all that hard work has gone to waste.

Developers' machines are less vital than your repository and servers. A simple hard drive backup should be adequate; the goal is to be able to get a developer back up and running as fast as possible when the hard drive fails (which is inevitable).

▨ **CAUTION:** Hard drives *do* fail. It is not a matter of *if*, but *when*. Be prepared.

Online Backup

Several online backup examples are available, often with free and paid-for offerings. Some examples include the following:

- Dropbox (www.dropbox.com/)

- Live Mesh (www.mesh.com)

- iDisk (www.apple.com/mobileme/features/idisk.html)

- SpiderOak (https://spideroak.com/)

Each of them supports Windows and OS X (and Linux in many cases), and allows you to share your content with other users. Some kind of scripted action can copy to each of them from your local machine, and if you don't have much data (developers typically only need one or two folders on their machine backed up), they are usually free. Being able to share big files is often very useful if any of your staff are working from home or remotely, although many large companies don't like any of their files to be on other companies' servers.

Desktop Backup

If you want a more automated out-of-the-box solution, there are many of these available, too:

- Microsoft NTBackup/Windows Backup and Restore Center/Windows Server Backup (free with some Windows versions)
  - www.microsoft.com/athome/setup/backupdata.aspx

- Time Machine (free with recent versions of OS X)
  - www.apple.com/support/leopard/timemachine/

- Symantic Backup Exec
  - www.symantec.com/business/products/family.jsp?familyid=backupexec

- Roxio Retrospect
  - www.retrospect.com/

There are in fact more backup options than we can list here by a long margin. A more complete list and comparison of backup software can be found at http://en.wikipedia.org/wiki/List_of_backup_software.

Prototyping

As part of the scoping process, it often becomes necessary to create a basic version of what we are going to build to give a hands-on example of what may otherwise be a complicated concept to explain. The considerations we would give to production-quality code—things like accessibility, file size, browser support, and so on—are not important here. The code we are developing is to be seen in-house only, and we can specify browser requirements. Any frameworks (read more about frameworks in Chapter 4) and shortcuts to speed up development are completely acceptable when creating prototypes.

Often the completed prototype is considered good enough and becomes production code, despite not being written as well as other code. This should be avoided because it encourages code bloat and technical debt, as well as other CSS sins. To that end, it is often a good idea to cripple the prototype somehow, so that we will definitely be given an opportunity to refactor and rewrite it later on.

If it is something purely visual we want to prototype, like a layout or user journey through a site, many tools exist to help us with this. A great example is Balsamiq Mockups (www.balsamiq.com/products/mockups), which has the benefit of creating diagrams that can be functional, but still look like sketches (one of the only valid uses for Comic Sans!). They cannot be mistaken for production imagery, and the discussions focus on the content and layout rather than things like fonts and color.

Spikes are similar to prototypes. A *spike* is named as such because it is a visual description of a tangent from our current path. If during development we find something we need to develop, and we're unsure of the best path to follow, we can "spike" development at that point. We would create a very rough example to demonstrate our intended path and to prove that it works. This example wouldn't include anything but the pieces necessary to demonstrate that our approach will achieve what we want it to, and would by definition (unless it is something very visual we are spiking) be unattractive and limited. Although a prototype is something we would copy and paste and modify to our needs, a spike will pretty much always be discarded after it has been proven (or failed to be).

Development Methodologies

Many development methodologies and processes exist. Each of them warrants a book of its own, but we will touch quickly on the two most popular kinds (by a long way), Waterfall and Agile.

Waterfall Development

The waterfall model has its roots in manufacturing. Although the word *waterfall* was never used, the first official description of this model is commonly thought to have come from an article Winston W. Royce wrote in 1970. Royce was actually writing about the model in order to point out that it is, in his opinion, a flawed and problematic way of working.

Waterfall (in software) describes a legacy development methodology, although still in use in many organizations. In its most basic form, it is the process of producing a technical specification for what we intend to deliver, giving details of the levels of effort (time periods) required by our resource (staff) and very granular descriptions of the exact details of the solution we will be building. Once the specification is agreed upon, the developers work on delivering exactly what is in the specification until it is complete, at which point it is presented to the business or client. It is at this point either rejected and then amended, or signed off and marked as approved.

The phases can be described like so (see Figure 1-13):

- Requirement Gathering (or Scoping)

- Design

- Implementation (or Build)

- Verification (or Testing)

- Maintenance (or Support)

The term *waterfall* was coined because of the concept that once we have reached a phase, it is impossible to change the output of (or return to) the phase previous to that one. That is, we can only flow in one direction.

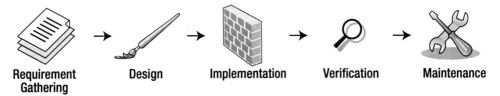

Requirement Gathering **Design** **Implementation** **Verification** **Maintenance**

Figure 1-13. An example waterfall process

As with all methodologies, there are pros and cons of waterfall development:

- Pros

  - The business/client has a clear indication of expected costs and timescales.

  - There is a definition of exactly what is being built.

- Cons

  - The specification is often incomplete or has errors that are too low level to isolate before the build commences. This results in the development team and client arguing over whether particular pieces of the solution were included in the original costings. Without making the specification ridiculously fine and detailed, items that may be obvious, implicit, and intuitive to the client/business could be misunderstood by the developers.

  - There is a paradox: to write a perfectly accurate specification requires the author to have already built the solution.

  - The specification leaves no allowance for change during the process; if the business/client finds another requirement that has to be included, it is necessary to wait until the "waterfall" runs dry before that requirement can even be considered.

Regardless of which development methodology you employ, it is rare to find a business or client that does not inherently work in a waterfall manner. When we as a business need something built, we need to know how much it will cost and how long it will take. To that end, it is common to treat the project from their perspective as a waterfall, but to use different methodologies internally during the project lifecycle.

Agile Development

Agile development has been gaining popularity for 10–15 years now. At the heart of agile development is the concept that the team should be agile, that is, that the team should be able to switch and change their processes, concepts and tasks with ease. Agile methods are based on iterative development, and allow teams to reflect on successes or failures within each block of time and modify their processes and respond quickly to changes in requirements. Many earlier agile workflows such as SCRUM and extreme programming are now referred to as agile methodologies, after the publication in 2001 of the Agile Manifesto.

The Agile Manifesto can be found at `http://agilemanifesto.org/`, but we include it here for clarity:

> *We are uncovering better ways of developing software by doing it and helping others do it. Through this work we have come to value*

- Individuals and interactions over processes and tools

- Working software over comprehensive documentation

- Customer collaboration over contract negotiation

- Responding to change over following a plan

That is, while there is value in the items on the right, we value the items on the left more.

Here are some pros and cons of agile development:

- Pros

    - The team is fast to change and react to new or changing requirements.

    - The process is always evolving, and every member of the team can have a voice and a part to play in that evolution.

- Cons

    - It is often difficult or impossible to commit to fixed deadlines.

    - The specification can be left too loose and missing features discovered too late.

Although many agile development methods exist, they all promote collaboration and easy-to-adapt processes. The following sections show examples of agile practices.

Test-Driven Development

Test-driven development (TDD) is the process of writing automatable tests (based on our requirements and acceptance criteria) before we write our code, and only writing code that helps us pass these tests. This helps minimize scope creep (the creation of new requirements) and unnecessary code. Whenever bugs in the software are found, we can immediately add a test to re-create these bugs. If this test remains within our test suite, we can be sure that we will not regress without knowing about it. You can read more about testing in Chapter 10.

Code Refactoring

Refactoring our code means to revisit it and ensure that it is as efficient, fast, and clean as possible, and no potential code smells are left behind.

▨ **NOTE:** *Code smell* is a term that resulted from a discussion between Martin Fowler and Kent Beck while Fowler was writing his book *Refactoring: Improving the Design of Existing Code*. A code smell is a piece of code that indicates a deeper problem.

Any notes of "To do: Fix this!" should be addressed during the refactoring of code. Code reviews can occur to help promote knowledge sharing among the team. Code refactoring is often a luxury; if you get the chance to do it, make sure you make the most of it. This could also be considered as paying off your technical debt. Try to get rid of any legacy code and consider whether there are other ways you can format your CSS in order to get the most out of a minimization algorithm or better rendering performance within the browser.

Continuous Integration

Continuous integration (CI) servers build and test our code, and perform other automated tasks in response to a commit into the version control repository or at predefined intervals. We cover this further in Chapter 9.

Pair Programming

Many companies now advocate the *pair programming* process: working beside another developer to avoid knowledge hoarding, mentor, and help other members of the team, as it reduces the chances of bugs in the finished product. Two heads are better than one. Some other companies believe having two developers work on the same piece of work simultaneously is inefficient. We suggest that where a piece of work is complex enough, pair programming can be invaluable, but usually code reviews are enough. Cycling developers between teams is an alternative effective method of avoiding knowledge hoarding.

Planning Poker

Planning poker (sometimes called the *planning game*) is a method of gathering resource estimates against tasks. It is called a game of poker because it uses cards or tokens to represent votes. After the task to be estimated for is described in reasonable detail, every person of a particular discipline (be it server-side development, client-side development, testers, designers, and so on) holds up a card showing the amount of time they would expect one person to take to complete the task. The person with the highest value justifies their choice, the person with the lowest value justifies their choice, and we repeat the process until we have a unanimous decision.

Planning poker can be a very time-consuming exercise and may not be right for all companies, but it has the benefit of ensuring that every member of the team has a good understanding of what we are delivering and may consider and think of bugs that might slip into the implementation phase otherwise.

Often the time estimate is represented by cards or tokens in different ways; for example, as story points or as numbers of days reflecting the Fibonacci sequence (1,2,3,5,8,13, and so on).

■ **NOTE:** The Fibonacci sequence actually begins with 0, 1, 1, but obviously that would be counterproductive in this instance.

Code Reviews

Code reviews are similar to pair programming in that they provide other developers a chance to comment on code that has already been written. Often the learning goes in both directions, with the reviewer asking why things were done in a particular way as well as providing feedback. It is less costly than pair programming in terms of time and is a more efficient way of assuring the quality of code in smaller teams.

Daily Standup Meetings

These meetings occur every day, as soon as the entire team is available. In these meetings we use the concept of chickens and pigs. This terminology comes from an old joke:

A pig and a chicken are chatting one day when the chicken says, "Hey, I was thinking we should start a restaurant together!"
"We should? What would we call it?" asks the pig.
"How about 'Ham and Eggs'?" the chicken suggests.
"No thanks!" exclaims the pig. "I'd be committed, but you'd only be involved!"

A *pig* is someone actually building the project. A *chicken* is someone involved in the project. A chicken (project manager, or scrum master) should facilitate the daily standup, but only the pigs should contribute. This helps because the chicken should be interested in the project being successful as a whole, whereas each pig may have his own bias or agenda. Typically the pigs are the developers, and the chickens are everyone else. During the daily standup, in turn, each pig should say the following:

- What they were doing yesterday

- What they are doing today

- If there are any issues affecting their ability to work

To avoid long conversations, there is a very useful question we can ask at any point: "Does everyone care?"

- If there are issues that affect everyone at the daily standup, they should explain them, and the facilitator should encourage discussions to resolve the issue.

- If there are issues that only affect certain people, the facilitator should ask those people to stay afterward to discuss them further. This is often called taking the conversation *offline*.

The daily standup should typically be very fast—no more than one or two minutes per person contributing.

Retrospectives

At specific points in our process, it is very useful to have a *retrospective*. This is a chance to review our processes up until this point, and improve or change them where necessary. There are many different formats for retrospectives, but each team can decide for itself. Any interested parties may attend the retrospective, but only pigs (see daily standup meetings previously) may contribute. The important components of a retrospective are as follows:

- The scrum master or project manager should facilitate the retrospective.

- Every pig should contribute to the retrospective.

- The team should recognize successful individuals and processes.

- The team should determine areas in the process that could be improved or problems that were encountered previously.

- For every negative point raised, the facilitator must define an *action* to resolve the problem and assign this *action* to an individual or themselves.

- There is no bad feedback! All of the team must feel able and welcome to participate.

An example of a typical process might be:

- Every pig has a pile of post-it notes.

- In one minute, every pig notes down a positive point about the previous iteration on a single note each.

- The facilitator arranges these notes on the wall, grouping similar items together. The more similar are the items, the more the team as a whole feel positive about something. Individuals should be recognized and commended if the team has said positive things about them.

- In one minute, every pig notes down a negative point about the previous iteration on a single note each.

- For every negative item, the facilitator discusses potential solutions (actions).

- When an action is found, the facilitator assigns it the relevant person.

The retrospective is one of the most important parts of any process. There needs to be a way for developers to feed back their thoughts. Often they will have very useful and intelligent suggestions; sometimes they might want to rant or vent about something (providing a forum for this is important). If possible, it's nice to arrange a retrospective to be in an outside environment and combined with a more social affair like a team lunch. Relaxed individuals will give more honest criticism and feedback.

Many, many books have been written on development methodologies, and we have really only skimmed the surface in this section.

Summary

This chapter focused on processes and tools that we can use to help us develop in the most efficient manner possible. Although processes change from company to company, and tools are often developed in-house, the basic tenets we have discussed still apply. Our processes must be strict to ensure that they are followed, and we must always ensure there is a "feedback loop" so our staff can highlight any failings in our processes and they can be changed to reflect this.

If possible, the team as a whole should pick and choose from all the styles and methodologies available and continue to perfect them over time. These processes apply to all kinds of development disciplines as well as to CSS development specifically, but they form the base of your working environment. To build a good team and write the best and most efficient CSS you can, you need a solid underpinning.

The next chapter will focus on CSS formatting guides and rules we can apply specifically to how we write and structure our style sheets. We willalso begin to look at best practices and discuss what you need to consider when working on high-traffic websites.

■ ■ ■

CHAPTER 2

CSS Style Guide

Every CSS author has his preferred way of writing code. For example, some people prefer to write each property and selector on a separate line, while others would rather have everything on one single line. Some authors never add a semicolon to the last property on a selector (because it isn't necessary); others prefer to remove the space between the colon and the value of a property. The list goes on.

These are just a few examples of how divergent CSS authoring can be from person to person—look into any CSS discussion forum and you will find endless ongoing debates on each of these topics, and many more. You will also probably come to the conclusion that no one is fully right or wrong—there are valid arguments on each side of the fence.

However, when dealing with large-scale style sheets—or style sheets that are to be applied to large-scale websites where performance and robustness are the most important factors—personal preferences usually have to be set aside to give way to a more flexible, coherent way of writing the code.

This approach will not be the most effective at the start (a newly hired developer will have to adapt to the conventions used in the organization, so he won't be able to immediately start coding without becoming familiar with them), but it will make it easier for staff to edit and update style sheets created by other developers without having to take the time to understand (sometimes the correct word would be "decipher") and become familiar with someone else's CSS writing style.

Having a set of conventions in place will also make it easier for authors to know which path to take. Even though there is always a degree of subjectivity when creating CSS solutions, if a CSS style guide is in place, many of the doubts will become non-existent since there are "rules" to be followed. It also becomes easier to detect errors, typos, and mistakes.

This chapter focuses on the most important points where CSS authoring can be made more consistent and efficient. You will learn the following:

- Why you should have a CSS style guide in place

- Effective ways of formatting CSS

- How to use CSS comments in a useful way

- Best practices on ID and class naming

- Namespacing

CSS Style Guides

If you are producing a CSS style guide (as we recommend) that will be known and used by all the members of the team, it can and should include a reference to how CSS is formatted. This will make reading style sheets created by others easier and it will remove part of the subjectivity that is common among CSS authors when creating or editing the files. It should also indicate how comments should be made and encourage the use of them.

Creating and implementing a CSS style guide will remove some of the inconsistency that is often related to coding CSS, where different developers have different coding styles that can sometimes be extremely difficult for other people to read and understand. This slows down the development process and promotes errors, redundancy, and code bloat. A style guide is an instrumental tool to avoid this, allowing for code reusability and efficiency through consistency, for a streamlined team environment for developing high-traffic sites.

Companies such as the BBC (see Figure 2-1) or Drupal (see Figure 2-2) have CSS style guides in place that are publicly available and act as good references for anyone who is creating one.

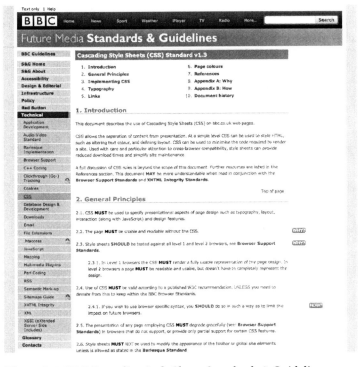

Figure 2-1. *BBC Cascading Style Sheets Standards & Guidelines*
(www.bbc.co.uk/guidelines/futuremedia/technical/css.shtml)

Figure 2-2. Drupal CSS coding standards page (`http://drupal.org/node/302199`)

One thing that is important to remember, however, is that a guide is exactly that, just a guide. The developers will always have to make most of the decisions for themselves, even with a guide in place. A style guide should not strive to remove subjectivity completely, as that will never happen, and should allow for a certain degree of flexibility and freedom.

In the following sections of this chapter, we will cover some of the aspects that a CSS style guide should refer to. You can find an example of a complete CSS style guide at the end of this book, in Appendix 1.

CSS Formatting

CSS is a language that (like HTML) is loosely formatted, in that whitespace is generally ignored when it is parsed so you can use as many spaces, tabs, or returns as you like in order to format it in the way you find easiest to read and write. Because of this, it lends itself to being formatted in multiple ways.

Even though there are similarities between writing styles, there are so many variations on the small details that it is hard to present a definitive solution that everyone will agree is the best.

What we can do is show you the most common options, and why some are better or more efficient than others. After all, efficiency is what we all want to achieve by reading this book, right?

Single- versus Multiline

If there is one CSS discussion that usually leads to no useful conclusion it is the one about different styles of CSS formatting. The fence tends to divide those who prefer to write their rules on one single line from those who prefer to declare each individual property on its own line.

This is an example of single-line CSS, where selector, properties, and values are on the same line:

```
div { width: 200px; height: 300px; padding: 20px; background: #efefef; }
```

And here is a multiline version:

```
div {
    width: 200px;
    height: 300px;
    padding: 20px;
    background: #efefef;
}
```

The main arguments for the multiline method are as follows:

- It is easier to read, especially if you're not familiar with the file.

- It is easier to make file comparisons (using Diff tools, mentioned in greater detail in Chapter 1).

- There is no horizontal scrolling.

Single-line CSS also has its advantages:

- Fewer lines in the document

- Selectors are easier to scan

- Reduced file size

For the sake of consistency, this book will use the multiline method. The reasoning behind this choice is the following:

- It is easier to annotate changes and comments.

- It is the easier format to read for smaller files.

- We assume that CSS files will end up being minified or compressed at a later stage of development (more on CSS minifying and compression in Chapter 8).

Even though this doesn't mean we believe this to be the absolute best CSS formatting style, we agree that it is the one that provides a clearer way to read the selectors and properties. It is also easier to comment on specific properties and values, which is an important factor when dealing with CSS files that are shared between many hands, and most developers are more comfortable with multiline CSS than with its single-line version.

One of the main arguments in favor of multiline CSS is that single-line CSS makes using Diff tools more difficult because in some cases these tools indicate differences between file versions per line (see Figure 2-3). Alternatively, if they locate the actual difference, it may be toward the end of a long line, requiring horizontal scrolling.

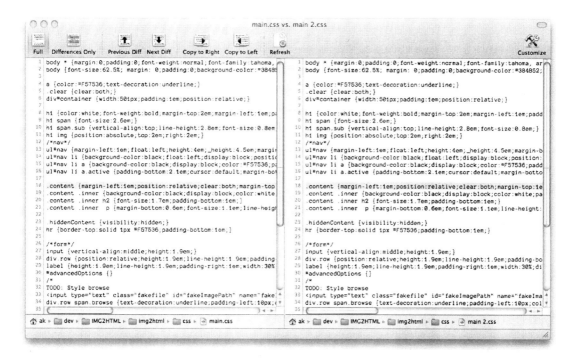

Figure 2-3. *In this example, in the Changes app, although the line is highlighted we cannot see the actual difference.*

Good Diff tools will highlight differences, no matter how the file is formatted (see Figure 2-4); the formatting debate should be virtually a non-issue when it comes to file comparison. It is true that at a glance, it may be more difficult to spot these differences if they are offscreen, but this issue is not so big that you should change your practices. If it is really causing you problems, you may find a different Diff tool may help.

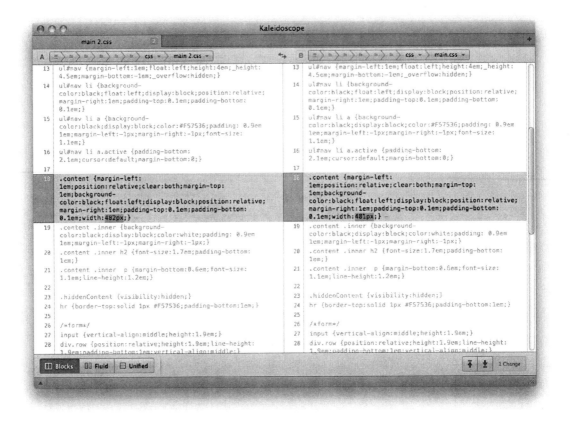

Figure 2-4. In the Kaleidoscope app, the various methods of viewing the differences negate the problem.

Indenting

Indentation in CSS files can improve their legibility and also aid understanding of the structure of the HTML documents being styled.

Properties can be indented within the selector itself, making it easier to scan only the selectors on the style sheet, as in the following example:

```
section {
    width: 400px;
    font-size: 14px;
    float: left;
}

footer {
    border-top: 1px solid #000000;
    font-size: 12px;
    clear: both;
}
```

Some authors choose to indent selectors according to the document tree of the HTML file the style sheet is being applied to:

```
section {
   width: 800px;
}

   section article {
      border-bottom: 1px solid #999999;
      padding-bottom: 10px;
   }

      section article footer {
         font-size: 11px;
         font-style: italic;
      }
```

Even though the structure of the document becomes a lot clearer using this formatting method, it can easily become too complicated or subjective, and where the markup is complex, your rules may begin disappearing off the right side of the page. We recommend that if you feel this would be a nice addition to your style sheets, use it within the section where you specify the main dividing blocks of your document tree, and don't try to replicate it in other sections such as links or typography.

Tabs versus Spaces

The tabs-versus-spaces argument is far older than CSS development, and not something likely to be resolved in this book. We can however, explain the advantages and disadvantages of each.

When indenting your code, you have the choice of using tabs or a predefined amount of spaces to act as a single level of indentation. Most text editors give you the choice of converting tabs to a certain amount of spaces when you save a document (soft tabs) or representing tabs with different widths. Some people like their indentation to be represented by two spaces, some like four, and some have even more complicated personal rules than these.

The benefits of using tabs are as follows:

- A single character takes up less file space than several spaces.

- It is usually possible to control the width of a single tab within your text editor (so developers can choose how it displays visually).

- If you are not using a monospaced font, your code will still be indented correctly.

The benefits of using spaces include the following:

- Your indentations will be the same width regardless of which editor you are using.

- Spaces can be relied upon to always appear in the same place, whereas tab stops may change from editor to editor.

- Spaces are consistent between environments.

The conclusions we will offer (which are highly subjective) are these:

- Use tabs for indentation.

- Use a monospaced font.

- Use spaces for alignment.

If you and your team disagree (it seems to be a one-in-two chance that you will), this is not a problem. The goal is that every member of your team does the same thing, whether it is spaces or tabs. Consistency is always our primary concern.

Colons and Semicolons

In the quest for smaller file sizes, some authors choose to omit the semicolon that follows the last property in a CSS rule. So instead of this:

```
img {
    border: 2px solid red;
    float: left;
}
```

We would have this:

```
img {
    border: 2px solid red;
    float: left
}
```

In fact, if file size is a major concern, we can also omit the spaces between the selector and the braces between the colons and the values of each property, as well as the final space, right after the last property value—it would still work, albeit rendering it a lot harder to read:

```
img{border:2px solid red;float:left}
```

When going to these extremes, however, we are approaching the effects of what minifying does to a CSS document.

When working on large-scale websites, performance is a constant concern; compressing and minifying your CSS so that it has the lowest file size possible should always be a step in the development process. (You can read more about minifying in Chapter 8.) What we are referring to in this section is how a CSS file is formatted while it is still being edited, when file size is not a concern, at least at the level of whether to add the last semicolon or whether to have a space after the colons.

As before, whatever you decide needs to be adhered to by your team. Assuming the files will be minified, when you are working on the files you should care primarily about their legibility and whatever works best for the team.

Commenting and CSS Metadata

CSS comments are often forgotten or overlooked by authors, but they can be very useful if they are consistent and kept up to date.

Here's a quick reminder of how a simple CSS comment looks:

```
/* This is a CSS comment */
```

> ▪ **NOTE:** You may notice this is the same as a block comment in JavaScript and many other languages. Unfortunately, CSS does not support single-line comments like the following:
>
> ```
> //This is a CSS comment
> ```
>
> But there are some options such as LESS (Leaner CSS) that can enable this for you (see Chapter 9).

A comment can be added inline to comment on a particular property for example:

```
.myClass {
    color: red; /* Same color as logo */
}
```

Or on a separate line, for example, to separate selectors into meaningful sections:

```
/* Table headings */

thead th {
        font-weight: bold;
}
tbody th {
        font-weight: normal;
}

/* Table rows */

.odd {
        color: red;
}
.even {
        color: blue;
}
```

CSS comments can span as many lines as you like. Comments tend to be the first thing to be stripped out of CSS files when they are minified (we talk about minifying in more detail in Chapter 8), but there are a number of different ways in which they can be useful during the development stage.

Existing Standards: CSSDOC

There have been some attempts to create CSS documenting standards. One example is CSSDOC, an adaptation of Javadoc (a documentation generator that extracts comments from Java source code into HTML).

CSSDOC uses *DocBlocks*, a term borrowed from the PHPDocumentor Project. A DocBlock is a human and machine readable block of data, and has the following structure:

```
/**
 * Short description
 *
 * Long description (this can have multiple lines and contain <p> tags
 *
 * @tags (optional)
 */
```

A DocBlock begins with /** and ends with a space followed by */ (like a normal CSS comment). Each line must start with a space followed by an asterisk (*), or else it will be ignored by the documentation generator. Tags start with an asterisk and then their name (with no spaces). The tags can contain information such as @author, @copyright, @todo, and so on. Their description or value should be preceded by a space, right after the tag name.

The CSSDOC standard suggests that a CSS file should include a *file comment* at the top of the file, which should contain metadata relevant to the whole file. This file comment should include information such as the title of the document; a description; and tags such as @project, @version, @author, @copyright, or even @colordef tags, indicating which colors are used within the file.

The file comment can be followed by zero or more *section comments* that divide the style sheet into relevant blocks. Hacks and bug fixes should be placed at the end of each section. Section comments include the tag @section, as such:

```
/**
 * Typography
 *
 * @section typography
 */
```

Some text editors, such as Textmate or CSSEdit, support the @group tag within normal CSS comments to divide the CSS files into sections. CSSEdit uses these groups to create the visual outline of the document; Textmate requires a bundle for this setting to work (there are a few available). The @group tag hasn't been incorporated into the CSSDOC specification, although the latest draft makes mention of it. It allows CSS authors to group selectors into meaningful sections that can be folded and expanded as needed, making it easier to scan and work with long CSS files. There are separate bundles available for Textmate to add CSSDOC functionality.[1]

There is a lot more to the CSSDOC standard (enough to fill an entire chapter), so we recommend taking a look at the official page, http://cssdoc.net, for more in-depth information.

Having a standard in place not only makes sharing code with other CSS authors simpler but also makes it easier to extract the comments from a CSS file in an automated fashion, for documentation purposes.

In this section, we will refer to and borrow some of the guidelines included in the CSSDOC documentation, mainly because they denote a view forward into the standardization of CSS comments, which would be beneficial to everyone writing CSS. We believe, however, that there are some instances where CSS metadata should live outside of the files themselves (such as versioning and authorship) and maintaining such comments can easily become a laborious task rather than an effective one. As soon as the comments become outdated, they quickly lose their value.

---

[1] The excellent GetBundles bundle (https://github.com/adamsalter/GetBundles.tmbundle) by Adam Salter makes it far easier to locate, update and install TextMate bundles.

File Info

The most common use of CSS comments is for author information and creation and last update dates. Frequently, CSS files have a comment like this one at the beginning:

```
/* CSS file, created by John Doe, http://domain.com, on 12.28.2009 */
```

Others go to the trouble of adding more information, such as who the last person to update the file was, and when:

```
/* CSS file, created by John Doe, http://domain.com, on 12.28.2009
Last update by: Jane Doe, on 5.19.2010 */
```

Although we believe that some of this data is better stored within a version control system which generates it automatically—CSS authors will frequently forget to update it, which renders the data pointless—there is some information pertinent to the style sheet that should probably live in it and be easily reachable.

This is a good time to mention any dependencies that the file may have—for example, whether it is using a master reset file (CSS reset files are mentioned in greater depth in Chapter 4) or any other imported style sheets. It can also state for which site, subsite, or page the file was created, and whether it is overriding other style sheets. If needed, there could also be a reference to namespacing implementations relevant to that particular file.

Here is an example that contains all of these:

```
/*

Style sheet for: Igloo Refrigerator Parts Inc Christmas website

Created by John Doe, http://domain.com, on 12.28.2009

Importing reset file: /css/resets/master.css

Overriding: /css/base.css

Namespacing: use the "xmas" prefix for all the classes and IDs referenced in this file. For
example: .xmasLatestNews or #xmasLatestNews

*/
```

If you were using CSSDOC type comments, the file info area (or *file comment*) would look something like the following (all the descriptions and tags are optional):

```
/**
 * Christmas theme
 *
 * CSS theme for the Christmas version of the Igloo Refrigerator Parts Inc website
 *
 * This theme has been developed by the Design Team at IRP Inc and should be used between
 * the dates of November 7th and January 7th
 *
```

```
 * @project    IRP Christmas Site
 * @author     Design Team at IRP Inc
 * @copyright  2010 Igloo Refrigerator Parts Inc
 * @cssdoc     version 1.0-pre
 */
```

These are examples of pieces of data that would be useful for a developer to have at hand to avoid having to delve into a version control system to access them. Depending on the type of content the style sheet is being applied to, many other details could be added.

The main concern here is that this information must stay relevant and up to date—it must not be easy to neglect because that would defeat the purpose of this comment block.

Table of Contents

Comments can be used to insert a table of contents at the beginning of a style sheet. This is useful since it will remove the need to scroll through a CSS file (which can easily have thousands of lines) to find out what it contains and where to find specific information.

A table of contents can be as simple as the following:

```
/* Table of contents:

1. Reusable classes
2. Structural elements
3. Colors and typography
4. Visual media
5. Widgets

*/
```

Or it can be as detailed as the following:

```
/* Table of contents:

Imports
Reusable classes
Structure
Navigation
Links
Typography
    Headings
    Body text
    Blockquotes
Lists
    Generic
    Definition lists
Forms
Images
Sidebars
Footers
Homepage
```

```
Widgets

*/
```

Whichever format you choose for the table of contents, it is important that it is constantly updated to always reflect the structure of the style sheet.

Some CSS editors create a visual table of contents automatically, like, for example, MacRabbit's popular CSSEdit (see Figure 2-5).

Figure 2-5. *CSSEdit creates an automatic outline of the CSS file on the left*
(http://macrabbit.com/cssedit/)

However, if the software isn't available or the developer prefers to use some other tool, it is always helpful to include a manually updated table of contents (even if succinct) at the top of the CSS file.

Sectioning

A table of contents only makes sense when the style sheet is actually divided into sections.

When creating sections in a CSS file, you will probably want to make them easily recognizable among the rest of the code. Something like the following division will not be very distinctive:

```
.myClassA {
    font-size: 14px;
}

.myClassB {
    font-size: 18px;
}

.myClassC {
    font-size: 24px;
}

/* Colors */

.error {
    color: red;
}

.success {
    color: green;
}
```

If you, instead, use something like this:

```
.myClassA {
    font-size: 14px;
}

.myClassB {
    font-size: 18px;
}

.myClassC {
    font-size: 24px;
}

/* Colors
-------------------------------------------------------- */

.error {
    color: red;
}

.success {
    color: green;
}
```

the division will be a lot easier to find.

In his excellent *CSS Mastery,*[2] Andy Budd proposes that sections should also be easily searchable. If we name a section *Headings* and, in the same file, we have classes named *sidebarHeadings* or *footerHeadings*, when using the built-in software search tools we may have to go through several nonrelevant results to get to the section title we want. If instead we add a character before the section title that will not be used in the rest of the style sheet, the search process will be easier. Andy suggests the equals sign:

```
/* =Headings */
```

If you search for "=Head", the software will probably only produce one result.

If you are using CSSDOC comments, a section division could be formatted as follows:

```
/**
 * Typography [optional]
 *
 * Description [optional]
 *
 * @section typography
 */
```

Regardless of the style you choose to go with, it is important that the section titles are distinctive and, most of all, that they divide the style sheet into logical blocks. They should make it easier, not harder, to navigate through a document; therefore, the sections created should be intuitive, even if they follow an established convention within the organization.

When separating a style sheet into sections, it is also a good idea to make sure that elements that are recurrent on every page are separated from those that are page-specific.

This will make it easier when looking for redundant or unnecessary selectors—by keeping them isolated, it is easier to comment them out when testing or removing them completely (perhaps moving them to a separate style sheet).

You might also consider separating sections of CSS that are always in use and those that are interaction-dependent. For example, the main heading will always show on the page, but an error message might show only in certain situations. Making this clear makes it easier to locate obsolete legacy code at a later date.

Color Palettes

Another useful piece of information to have at the top of a CSS document is a reference to the colors used throughout the site.

One common slip of CSS authors is to use colors that are only approximate to the ones that should be used. This might be because there isn't an established branding guide, or when there is it's not at hand, or there simply isn't enough time to consult one. Colors end up being selected using tools like Firebug, xScope, or Photoshop, which can result in mere approximations (especially if the CSS developers are provided jpegs at less than 100% quality, as often happens), leading to dozens of similar but different colors used throughout one single style sheet. Although the performance implications for getting the colors wrong are small, over time the colors can get farther and farther from their original values. Depending on the placement and use of colors, and the end user's monitor and display settings, these mistakes may become more obvious. Also, if you use consistent colors, the file size is likely to be smaller when compressed due to the repeating text patterns enabling more efficient compression.

---

[2] `www.cssmastery.com/`

If a color reference is added to the CSS file, these misinterpretations can be avoided. This can easily be done using a comment at the top of the style sheet:

```
/* Color reference:

Main text      #111111
Headings       #999999
:link          #9f0000
:visited       #720000
:hover,
:active,
:focus         #004899
...

*/
```

The color reference can, and should, be more detailed than the preceding example. It can contain background and border colors, more detailed typographic colors, different types of link colors, colors according to site sections, and so on.

One important thing to remember is that the description of each element or group of elements should be fundamentally immutable. If instead of "Main text" we had used "Dark grey text," the purpose of the reference table would have been lost.

This doesn't mean that such references shouldn't be specified—there is certainly a place for stating the appropriate red or pink that the website should use. But they may be seen more as a secondary element within the Color Reference rather than one of the main structural or typographical ones.

Using dynamic CSS (which is explained in greater detail in Chapter 9) can also reduce the need for constantly referring to a Color Reference table.

For example, when using LESS, you can declare variables at the top of the style sheet that can resemble something like this:

```
@mainText:    #111111;
@headings:    #999999;
@links:       #9f0000;
```

This will allow you to refer to the variable instead of the actual color value throughout the CSS file, making it also easier to change the color—you only need to do it once, where the variable is initially declared, and it will change all instances of the color like this one:

```
body {
    color: @mainText;
}
```

When using CSSDOC-type comments, the color information is added to the file comment at the top of the CSS file, using the @colordef tags:

```
/**
 * Christmas theme
 *
 * CSS theme for the Christmas version of the Igloo Refrigerator Parts Inc website
 *
 * This theme has been developed by the Design Team at IRP Inc and should be used between
```

```
* the dates of November 7th and January 7th
*
* @project     IRP Christmas Site
* @author      Design Team at IRP Inc
* @copyright   2010 Igloo Refrigerator Parts Inc
* @cssdoc      version 1.0-pre
*
* @colordef    #111111; main text
* @colordef    #999999; headings
* @colordef    #9f0000; links
*/
```

Folder Paths

Comments can be used to explain folder paths. What does this mean exactly?

Although we recommend having a clear and practical folder structure (this book goes into more detail about folder structures in Chapter 8), there is often the need to go several levels deep—for example, to keep images better organized. When this happens, it is useful to refer to these paths within the style sheets where these files will be referenced, mainly as a way to avoid mistakes from developers who haven't initially written that particular part of the CSS.

These comments at the top of the CSS document can be as simple as the following:

```
/* Branding elements are located in the Assets/Branding folder at the root of the main website
*/
```

Just remember to keep them concise and up to date; otherwise, they won't be useful.

Measurements

When creating complex CSS layouts, calculations are inevitable.

Let's picture a fluid layout with two columns (see Figure 2-6). The main content column should have a variable width, according to the size of the user's screen; the sidebar should be 200 pixels wide; we also want 20 pixels separating both columns vertically.

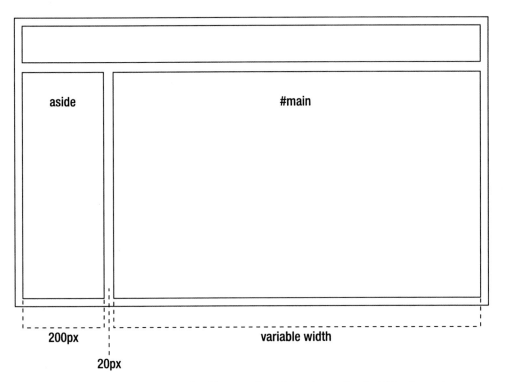

Figure 2-6. A simple two-column fluid layout: the sidebar has a fixed width; the main content area has a variable width.

Our CSS may look similar to the following:

```
#main {
    margin-left: 220px;
}

aside {
    width: 200px;
    float: left;
}
```

Someone who updates the CSS after the initial measurements have been calculated may find it hard to understand some of the values used.

Using comments, we can write a better, documented solution:

```
#main {
    margin-left: 220px; /* aside width + 20px of margin */
}
```

```
aside {
   width: 200px;
   float: left;
}
```

Measurement comments are also useful on typographic calculations.

Imagine that you have a page with the text set to 14 pixels, with a `line-height` of 1.5. This means each line on the page has a height of 21 pixels: 14 x 1.5.

If the headings on this page are set to 18 pixels, to keep the vertical rhythm of the page intact, we need to grab our calculators and do some math—we need to find the adjusted `line-height` for the headings. This thought process is a good candidate for a CSS comment:

```
h2 {
   font-size: 18px;
   line-height: 1.167; /* 21 (original line-height) / 18 (h2 font-size) */
}
```

Even though someone not familiar with typographical concepts might not fully understand the need for this calculation, showing the steps that were taken to reach this particular value is invaluable to avoid future mistakes.[3] Using a CSS pre-processor like those described in Chapter 9, you could use variables and equations to calculate this values on your behalf.

■ **NOTE:** This is not a typography book, so we are not going into too much detail about how vertical spacing works or should be calculated. For a great introduction to typography on the Web, read Richard Rutter's "Elements of Typographic Style Applied to the Web", Section 2.2.2

`http://webtypography.net/Rhythm_and_Proportion/Vertical_Motion/2.2.2/.`

Document Hacks and Bug Fixes

Hacks and bug fix documentation are some of the most important uses of CSS comments.

Often a CSS author will be working on a particular style sheet and come across a solution that either someone else created or wrote some time ago that doesn't seem clear or even right. Perhaps a simpler solution could have been used, a solution that wouldn't make the CSS file invalid, or maybe there wasn't a problem to begin with.

What usually happens is that even though the code is not the cleanest, it was probably the best solution that the previous developer could write, taking into account time and budget constraints, browser support, and other factors that may have influenced the decision process.

Comments come in handy in these situations. They can, for example, refer to a specific article on the Web that explains the solution taken or that documents the bug further:

```
aside section {
   float: left;
```

---

[3] There is no standard set for rounding up or down, so browsers do not consistently round values that include decimal places.

```
    width: 50%;
    display: inline; /* display: inline; fixes the Double Float Margin bug on IE5/6. More on
this bug/solution: http://www.positioniseverything.net/explorer/doubled-margin.html */
}
```

This type of documenting comment should explain briefly what the bug is (if it is a well-known and documented bug, using the most common name for it), the solution taken (providing a link where this is explained further, if one exists), and the consequences of editing or deleting that particular hack.

When using the CSSDOC convention, hacks and workarounds should be commented as such:

```
/**
 * Name of the bug
 *
 * @workaround [or @bugfix]
 * @affected   IE6
 * @valid      yes [or no]
 * @see        [include, for example, a link to an online article describing the bug]
 */
```

Documenting CSS hacks and bugs may seem cumbersome, especially when dealing with well-known and well-documented Internet Explorer bugs, but we must remember that even though some of us are familiar with them and their solutions, many developers are not. Taking the defensive approach toward our code is usually the best option.

Using a Template

Having a CSS style guide that developers can refer to is useful and advisable, but it is also recommended that they are provided with an actual bare-bones structure version of the CSS that will make it easier to understand how the file or files should be organized, and which comment conventions are being used within the organization or the team.

In this template, you should include the following:

- Document information section, including file dependencies, overrides, namespacing conventions, and so on

- Table of contents, containing the most common sections

- Color palette, which can be prefilled with the branding colors or just include an example of how it should be populated

- Sections such as "Reusable classes," "Structure," "Typography," and so on.

As mentioned previously, information such as the last person to edit the file and when should be relegated to more suitable and reliable methods, such as the version control system to automate the process and avoid duplication of effort. Developers should be encouraged to update any relevant sections as they edit these files.

Class and ID Naming

Without going into too much detail about what classes and IDs are (we assume you are at least familiar with the most basic concepts of CSS), we will briefly explain the difference between the two.

Classes and IDs are methods of providing hooks into your HTML—that is, ways to isolate and reference particular elements. Take the following HTML snippet as an example:

```
<ul>
<li>Home</li>
<li>Contact Us</li>
<li>Search</li>
</ul>
```

There is no simple way to reference the Contact Us list item. We could use an nth-child selector to target the second child of the unordered list element:

```
ul li:nth-child(2) {
    …
}
```

But that means that if we ever added any list items before that one our CSS would fail to reference it immediately (this is an example of fragile CSS, which is covered in chapter 4). This selector also has incomplete browser support in the browsers we are likely to intend to cater for. By adding an ID, like so:

```
<ul>
<li>Home</li>
<li id="contactLink">Contact Us</li>
<li>Search</li>
</ul>
```

We can now easily target this element via CSS like this:

```
#contactLink {
    …
}
```

An ID is a unique identifier. This means that in any one page, it can occur only once. Each page—from our HTML's perspective—is a distinct entity. So, we can reuse IDs throughout our site as much as we like. Using an ID more than once on the same page will cause unpredictable results: Only the first item may be targeted, or only the last, or all of them, or none at all. It will also render our HTML invalid (which can make debugging and parsing more difficult and affect our search engine ranking). An element can only ever have a maximum of one ID.

So what do we do if we want to target multiple items? This is exactly what classes are for. In the previous example, if we wanted to target all list items except the Home item, we could modify the HTML like so:

```
<ul>
<li>Home</li>
<li id="contactLink" class="nonHomeLink ">Contact Us</li>
<li class="nonHomeLink">Search</li>
</ul>
```

We can now easily target both of these list items:

```
.nonHomeLink {
    ...
}
```

Elements can have as many classes as you like, and if you use more than one, they should be separated with spaces. If we want to target elements with multiple classes and make each of those classes obligatory, we can chain classes together like this:

```
.warning.error {
    ...
}
```

This will target any element with a class of "warning" and a class of "error." Be aware, however, that Internet Explorer (IE) 6 and earlier versions don't understand selectors that use multiple classes. In the preceding example, IE 6 and 5 will only read the last class, "error", which is likely to cause many a headache. The easiest way to avoid problems is to steer clear from using chained classes in selectors but rather declare each class separately, making sure they complement each other. IE 6 will interpret HTML with multiple classes defined correctly, but not the multiple class selector.

Although the exact way in which you name the classes and IDs of your elements is not desperately important, there are several things that you should bear in mind:

- Semantics

- Accepted characters

- Convention

- Consistency

Semantics

The way in which you name the hooks for your CSS should be semantic and descriptive of the content, not descriptive of the presentation. Here are some examples of bad ID and class names:

- PurpleBold

- BigHeading

- top_left_box

- underlined-and-green

Much more appropriate are the following:

- mainNavigationItem

- errorMessage

- externalLink

- sideContent

The W3C website has a page on this subject, where it explains that "Often people use class names like bluetext, or redborder. A much better way to name your classes is with the role a certain HTML element of that class has." You can read more about this at www.w3.org/QA/Tips/goodclassnames.

Using nonpresentational class and ID names will make them reusable and adaptable to change. For example, if your footer has a purple background color, and the container has a class name of "purple," what happens when the branding is updated and the new company logo is orange? The class name "purple" becomes obsolete and incoherent—the logo is orange!

This is why it is important to choose class and ID names that tie in with the content, so, instead of naming the sidebar as "boxLeft," it should be named "sidebar"—you don't know if next week it will be moved to the right. Or instead of naming a red warning box "red," it is wiser to call it "warning," so the name still makes sense if someday it is changed to yellow.

However, there might be instances where using presentational class names is a more flexible option than using structural ones. For example, if in more than one instance on the website a certain type of container box is used (like a container with a border), using a presentational name such as "bordered" might be the most clever solution, making it reusable and not tying that particular container style to a certain content type (creating redundancy and making the file larger).

We are not encouraging the use of presentational class and ID names everywhere on your CSS files, though—sometimes the best solution is just not the cleanest or prettiest one, and we need to shift to a more versatile frame of mind.

Accepted Characters

The W3C specifies which characters and combinations are valid for classes and IDs at `www.w3.org/TR/CSS21/grammar.html#scanner`. In essence, a class name or ID must start with an underscore, hyphen, or letter. The second character can be an underscore or letter, and it can be followed by any number of underscores, hyphens, letters, or numbers. You are also able to include escaped Unicode characters.

However, certain characters and combinations should be avoided when using class and ID names. Some of these include:

- *Underscores*: At one point, underscores were legal in HTML attributes according to the HTML standards, but not according to the CSS standard. There were various methods implemented to escape underscores in some browsers with various levels of success. Some older browsers (including Netscape 4.x and Opera 3.5x) misunderstand underscores in class or ID names, so although it is very unlikely that you support these browsers, it seems good practice to avoid using these characters.

- *Forward or backward slashes*: These are not accepted characters.

- *Asterisks*: These are not accepted characters.

- *Beginning class or ID names with numeric characters*: some browsers will accept these, but many will not.

- *Beginning class names or IDs with hyphens*: some browsers will accept these, but many will not.

There are ways that these characters can be escaped; for example:

"To make ".55ft" a valid class, CSS2 requires the first digit to be escaped (".\35 5ft")"
`www.w3.org/TR/CSS2/grammar.html`

This is nontrivial and as an edge case is likely to be interpreted incorrectly by different browsers. It is best to simply avoid these characters instead. You should also remember that ID and class names are case-sensitive.

As you can see, the support for more obscure characters varies, and bugs in newer browsers may occur if you choose to use characters or naming conventions that fall outside of the simplest rules and are less likely to have been well tested. The best rule to obey is to always use only alphanumeric characters or hyphens, and to only begin the class or ID name with an alphabetic character. You should avoid any accented or Unicode characters. You can safely use hyphens, but these seem a waste of a single character, which is significant when you are considering large enough amounts of bandwidth—although they do make for more legible values.

Conventions

Even though there are no rules as to what we should name our classes and IDs, some conventions are now fairly established and it's common to find naming practices that are ubiquitous.

These are examples of some of the classes and IDs that you might see in most style sheets:

- .header/#header

- .footer/#footer

- .sidebar/#sidebar

- .nav/#nav

The ubiquity of these names made them the obvious choices (with some variations) when developing the new HTML 5 elements: `header`, `footer`, `aside`, `nav`. In fact, authors who decide not to jump onto HTML5 right now are encouraged to use the new element names as the class or ID name of more established elements instead, such as `div` or `ul`.

There are numerous class and ID names that are understood by anyone, even if not familiar with the specific style sheet at hand. Some examples are header, nav (or navigation), sidebar (or aside, secondaryContent), footer, main, wrapper, content (or main, mainContent), col (or column), submit, error, warning, post, and actions.

When possible, we recommend that these easily understandable names are used, instead of more obscure ones. This will make the code more predictable and therefore easier to understand for anyone who hasn't created the initial naming.

Within the organization, other naming conventions might be in place that aren't known outside of it. For example, when namespacing CSS selectors (more on namespacing later on in this chapter), there should be an internal convention in place, so that it doesn't fall into each CSS author's personal preference.

A combination of sensible naming and clearly defined internal guidelines should produce class and ID names that are consistent and intuitive.

Further than that, using predictable class names and IDs can aid some screen readers or parsers, and improve SEO. Microformats are a set of standardized specifications to describe things like people, calendars, product reviews and more. Using these will help search engines understand your content and present these in a more attractive fashion in search results as well as numerous other benefits. Read more about microformats at `http://microformats.org/`.

Case

The result of using semantic class names/IDs and adhering to our list of accepted characters still results in a large pool of potential acceptable classes and IDs that we can use for our elements. All the following are completely valid class names:

- MAIN-CONTENT

- heroimage

- PrimaryNavigation

The most important thing here is that we are consistent and record what we expect our developers to use as their ID or class names as reference. Where possible, it makes sense to try not to string words together for simplicity's sake. However, when this is not possible there are two popular schools of thought on which way you should name your classes and IDs.

Camel Case

A popular naming convention is called *camel case*. Camel case is the practice of always beginning a name with a lowercase character, removing all spaces and punctuation, and making every consecutive word begin with a capital letter. For example:

- mainContent

- heroImage

- primaryNavigation

When using acronyms, you should group them together in the same case. If at the beginning of the name, make them all lowercase; otherwise, make them all uppercase as in the following examples:

- pdfLink

- linkToPDF

■ **NOTE:** JavaScript is actually internally inconsistent in how it uses camel case. A commonly used method is getElementById(), and a commonly used property is innerHTML. We would suggest the method we have used is the more legible, but as always, choose your preferred method and be consistent.

Camel case is a well-understood term in the IT industry, adds no unnecessary characters, and doesn't interfere with semantics. Most importantly, new developers are likely to already know it, and it is easy to explain succinctly. By not using any other characters, we can use those characters as clear separators for namespaces (see later in this chapter) and save the amount of characters in use.

Hyphenated

There are pitfalls to using camel case. If the developers are not also JavaScript developers, they may not be used to this method and might find it hard to read or scan without some kind of delimiter. CSS is a hyphenated syntax (`background-color`, `border-radius`, and so on), and many feel more comfortable using just one syntax, although yet others find the visual distinction useful. Some also feel that HTML is typically a lowercase language and that in camel case it is easier to make mistakes by mismatching cases. Class and ID names are case-sensitive, so saying "mainContent" is not the same as "maincontent," and it is easier to always stick to lowercase. Hyphenated classes and IDs look like this:

- main-content

- hero-image

- primary-navigation

This convention is easier to read and has other performance benefits too. Sticking to lowercase characters reduces your character set and is likely to increase repetitive patterns, which will make your compression algorithms more effective. However, the hyphenation adds extra characters and leaves less horizontal space when viewing the files in an editor.

The important thing to have in mind when deciding which convention to adhere to is that the most valuable outcome of having one in place is that it ensures and promotes consistency, making it easier for developers to come up with new names that will be understood by everyone else. We will use camel case for our examples within this book, but you should use whichever you feel is more appropriate.

Namespacing

Namespacing is one of the techniques of defensive CSS. By isolating parts of the code, we are making best endeavors to be sure that they won't affect in any way existing and future code developed by ourselves or others, or be affected by code written in the future.

Let's look at an example. Imagine that there is a sidebar widget that lists recent posts from your company's blog. This widget can be inserted in any of the company's sites or minisites, or even in external sites (you may encourage company employees to add it to personal blogs or suppliers to add it to their corporate sites). When creating the CSS for this widget, and its classes and IDs, the final result could be something like this:

```
<section class="blog">

    <h1>Latest posts from the company blog</h1>

    <ul>
        <li><a href="/blog/post1.html">Great news for all the shareholders</a></li>
        <li><a href="/blog/post2.html">Christmas party venue confirmed</a></li>
    </ul>

    <p class="feedLink"><a href="/blog/feed.xml">Subscribe to the RSS feed</a></p>

</section>
```

This all looks well and good, but what happens if the code is injected in a page where there is another class named "blog" (which doesn't sound completely unlikely)? The code is asking for trouble.

The purpose of namespacing in CSS is to avoid these class and ID conflicts. By adding prefixes to the classes and IDs, we are separating them from the rest of the existing and coming ones that could otherwise interfere with our code (or be affected by it).

In the preceding case, we could instead have the following, where the prefix "irpb-" would stand for Igloo Refrigerator Parts Blog (the name of our fictitious organization):

```
<section class="irpb-blog">

  <h1>Latest posts from the company blog</h1>

  <ul>
    <li><a href="/blog/post1.html">Great news for all the shareholders</a></li>
    <li><a href="/blog/post2.html">Christmas party venue confirmed</a></li>
  </ul>

  <p class="irpb-feedLink"><a href="/blog/feed.xml">Subscribe to the RSS feed</a></p>

</section>
```

Now this code snippet has been isolated within its own (emulated) namespace. It is very unlikely that another website will be using the same class prefix, and, if all the team members are aware of the conventions within your organization to come up with new namespaces, there also shouldn't be any conflicts with internal sites. The hyphen as a delimiter acts as a clear visual indicator that "irpb" is a namespace.

Namespacing makes the CSS more modular; it allows us to have transferable code snippets that can be inserted into various places, whether inside or outside of the range of websites the team has to work with. If your website includes third-party content in the form of widgets or advertising, namespacing can be an extra reassurance that their code will play nicely with yours.

WordPress is a good example of a company that namespaces everything. The tables in the WordPress database are called wp_users, wp_options, wp_posts, and so on. Plugin developers are recommended to use the name of their plugin as the namespace for any classes within their plugin. Here is an example:

```
<div class="sociable">
<div class="sociable_tagline">
<strong>Share this Article:</strong>
</div>
<ul>
        <li class="sociablefirst"><a rel="nofollow"  href="…" title="Print"><img src="…"
title="Print" alt="Print" style="…" class="sociable-hovers" /></a></li>
…
</ul>
</div>
```

There are some pretty awful things wrong with this code (see the following note), but ignoring them, here are the classes we can see:

- sociable

- sociable_tagline

- sociableFirst

- sociable-hovers

The namespace is obviously "sociable," so as long as no other classes on our page begin with *sociable*, there will be no conflicts.

░ **NOTE:** Four different conventions for class names! Four! Obviously, four different developers have worked on this plugin (or one *very* inconsistent one).

Reusable Classes

As you've seen so far, one of the downsides of namespacing is the need for proper documentation. It usually uses class and ID prefixes that aren't immediately recognizable by someone not familiar with the code—often abbreviations or acronyms—so their meaning should be explained, either at the top of the actual CSS file or, better yet, in a company wiki.

Because namespacing is bound to be something that will be created repeatedly, it's also a good idea to define the appropriate conventions that CSS authors should follow when generating more cases.

Whereas we might have decided to use camel case for the naming of our IDs and classes, we might like to include a hyphen after the namespace we are prefixing with. This demonstrates visually that the prefix is a namespace, and makes it even less likely that these classes or IDs will conflict with anything else. Some examples are as follows:

- irpb-mainContent

- irpb-heroImage

- irpb-primaryNavigation

This is really being as defensive as we can. It might be that we just want to treat pages in different ways depending on the page or page type. To achieve that, another frequently used namespacing technique is to give the body (or html) element its own class or ID:

```
<body class="homepage">
```

This will make it easier to style elements differently according to the page they are in, and it is something that a lot of content management systems add to the body element by default.

In this case, if we want to style the footer on the homepage differently, maybe even hide it completely, we can use the class that was given to the body:

```
footer {
    display: block;
}

.homepage footer {
    display: none;
}
```

Where you have many rules though, this can make your CSS very verbose. Remember that giving the body an ID or class will make the selectors that use that ID or class more specific (more on specificity in Chapter 3).

CSS namespacing is not actually strict namespacing, as in other languages such as XML. It is instead an emulation of it. In XML we can define groups of tags in specific namespaces, and when we include those tags, we prefix them with the namespace and a colon, something like this:

```
<namespace:tagname />
```

In XML this naming convention is functional and required. In CSS, it is something we can choose to implement as a tool to help us protect and categorize our code.

CSS Namespaces Module

Although it applies primarily to XML and less so to HTML, it is worth mentioning that the CSS3 Namespacing module is in Candidate Recommendation phase at the W3C at the time of writing (www.w3.org/TR/css3-namespace/). The @namespace declaration is currently supported by all modern browsers, and the next version of Internet Explorer, IE 9, should support it, too.

Using the @namespace rule, you can declare the namespace prefix as the following example (the prefixes are case-sensitive):

```
@namespace irpb "http://example.com/irpb"
```

In the previous example, "irpb" is the prefix (alias) used to represent the namespace, and "http://example.com/irpb" is the full representation of the namespace, which should be unique on the page (which is why URLs are often used). To call the namespace in a CSS selector, you need to use the type selector with a vertical bar (|). The part of the selector that precedes the bar is the namespace prefix. If no namespace is declared in the type selector, the rule applies to elements with no namespace; if an asterisk is used, the rule applies to elements that belong to any namespace:

```
irpb|div {
    …
}
|div {
    …
}
*|div {
    …
}
```

The namespace rule must be declared after @charset and @import rules, and must precede all other at-rules and normal rules. It only applies to that specific style sheet (not to imported style sheets). We include it here for interest, and do not recommend that you use it in production code.

Summary

This chapter highlighted the importance of having a defined set of guidelines that CSS authors within a team or an organization can follow in order to create more standardized and better documented code. These guidelines should be helpful for creating a thorough CSS style guide that can be shared and updated by anyone who has any kind of input or influence in creating and using style sheets.

Although we are not claiming to have the definitive answers to CSS formatting and best practices, we believe that the recommendations laid out in this chapter are the most widely observed and accepted among both new and experienced developers, which, in turn, makes them easier to translate into a coding standard that can be welcomed and used to promote coherent and effective code within your team.

In the next chapter we will look at the fundamentals of CSS, how it works and its quirks. These will empower you and your team to use CSS in a more efficient way, by taking advantage of its features and avoiding common problems.

CHAPTER 3

■ ■ ■

Fundamentals

When working with CSS, there are fundamental concepts that the developers should be aware of and understand intimately, but that tend to be overlooked or even ignored. Knowing these concepts in depth will mean that the CSS created will be better planned, bugs will be easier to avoid, and style sheets will be, in general, simpler, cleaner, and easier to maintain.

CSS is usually regarded as a relatively simple language to understand (its syntax is intuitive and easy to follow, even for someone who has never written a single line of CSS). But CSS authors need some experience to code complex CSS layouts that won't break in less-compliant browsers and at the same time keep their style sheets clean and flexible.

In an ideal world, all the visitors to our websites would use the latest browser, and we wouldn't need to litter our CSS documents with hacks, conditional comments, and workarounds: everything would work everywhere. We don't live in an ideal world, and because we have to deal with all sorts of browser inconsistencies, our CSS documents end up looking far from how we would like them to. A result of dealing with high-traffic websites is that our visitors will be using a wide range of browsers, from the latest beta releases of obscure browsers to the older versions of IE.

■ **NOTE:** The more traffic you have, the greater the likelihood of visits from more obscure devices. Your company should discuss internally which you support and which you don't, but it is important to understand that (for example) if only 0.5 percent of your users use IE 5 and your site was receiving 20 million hits per day, your site would be receiving 100,000 hits per day from users using IE 5! This is not an insignificant figure and should be considered carefully.

It is important to put into practice guidelines that cover how to best deal with these situations and also make sure that the members of the team are familiar with how CSS works fundamentally. Taking this step may mean a longer adaptation period for new staff, but you should recognize that guidelines will never cover all possible situations or browser bugs, and coders will be faced daily with making decisions that will influence the effectiveness and performance of your website(s). This extra training and knowledge within your team can only be a positive thing that empowers the team to better understand CSS and write good code, and it will be shared outward in a halo effect.

In this chapter, you will:

- Learn about important CSS concepts such as the cascade, importance, inheritance, and specificity

- Understand the importance of encoding and how to implement localization

- Learn how to handle browser-specific CSS

- Learn about the best way of dealing with hacks

- Discover whether server-side user agent detection is a good idea

- Look at examples of browser inconsistencies and how to best deal with them

The Cascade: Origin, Importance, and Inheritance

Knowing how the cascade works is fundamental to building flexible and robust style sheets. By disregarding these basic notions or by just adding rules ad hoc as the need arises without considering how they will affect each other, you would complicate your websites' CSS exponentially with each addition. You would be producing larger files, increasing redundancy, and making them more difficult for developers to understand or to further augment. Having a solid understanding of the underlying theory of the workings of CSS will empower you and your team to make the best decisions possible in order to keep style sheets simpler to maintain.

The notion of "cascading" is at the very heart of CSS. It is the process that determines which CSS rules will affect which elements, giving each rule a specific weight and priority. When everything is taken into account, rules with more weight will take precedence over those with less weight in cases where more than one rule applies to a particular element.

In order to attribute a weight to the rules, the cascade relies on three aspects: importance, inheritance, and specificity. If two or more rules that target the same element end up having the same weight, the one that comes last will win out over those previous. The same applies to properties that are repeated within the same rule (the property value that is defined last is the one that is applied).

In this section, we will be covering origin, importance, and inheritance; whereas specificity is complex enough to have its own separate section afterward.

Origin and Importance

Style sheets from three different origins can affect a Web page:

- User agent style sheets

- User style sheets

- Author style sheets

User agent style sheets (see Figure 3-1) are those present by default in the user agent (the device the user is using to access our code, typically the web browser). Even though when we open an HTML file with no CSS files linked to it, it appears to be unstyled; in fact, it is styled by the user agent style sheet. This is the style sheet that adds the typical blue to unvisited links, purple to visited links, different font sizes for different types of headings, and so on.

Figure 3-1. The homepage of bbc.co.uk with only the user agent style sheet applied (that of Firefox, in this instance).

User style sheets (see Figure 3-2) can be, for example, style sheets applied to a page based on the user's browser preferences, such as a larger font or a specific font family, for easier reading.

Figure 3-2. The front page of Wikipedia with a user style sheet applied: in this case, the user style sheet ensures that the text on any website is never smaller than 18px.

User style sheets can also be CSS files created by the user that the browser will read in order to change the design or details of a specific site. In this case, the external files are usually stored on the user's machine and referenced by the browser.

By default, author style sheets override user style sheets, which in turn override user agent style sheets. There is a way, however, to make user style sheets have more weight and override author declarations. This can be achieved using the `!important` declaration, which ensures that, no matter what, the user will always have the final say on how the pages will be displayed.

The `!important` declaration is used on a property-by-property basis, and it can be applied to inline, embedded, or external style sheets:

```
p {
    color: black !important;
}
p {
    color: red;
}
```

In the preceding example, because we are using the `!important` declaration, the first rule will be the one applied to the p element, even though the second rule comes later and has the same specificity (see the next section for more details on how to calculate a selector's specificity).[1]

`!important` should be used with care in author style sheets and avoided if possible since it will interfere with the specificity of the rules and make way for overly specific and complicated CSS.

Let's look at the following example, where the user hides an advertisement bar on a website:

```
#myfavoritesite .advertbanner {
    display: none !important;
}
```

User style sheets with the `!important` declaration will always override style sheets from any other origin, so in this case the user can be sure that the advertisement bar won't be displayed.

In order to make it easier for users to inject their own CSS rules into specific websites, some developers add an ID to the body element of their pages, or even go further than that by adding both site-wide IDs and page-by-page classes, so that users can easily point to specific pages if needed.

Author style sheets are those created by CSS authors, provided in the actual page returned by the server. They can be inline within the markup (using the HTML style attribute), embedded on the page (using the HTML style tag), or linked externally (using the HTML link tag or @import rules).

After adding `!important` to the mix, we are left with the following different types of declarations, from most to least important:

- User declarations marked as important

- Author declarations marked as important

- Author declarations

- User declarations

- User agent declarations

Inheritance

The W3C definition of inheritance states that "Inheritance is a way of propagating property values from parent elements to their children" (www.w3.org/TR/css3-cascade/).

This means that some CSS properties are by default (or can be forced to be) inheritable by child elements.

---

[1] In this example, we included a space before `!important` to make it easier to read. The space is unnecessary, which is something you might need to know if minifying files or when writing your CSS formatting guide.

Let's take a look at a typical scenario:

```
body {
    color: #111111;
    padding: 20px;
}
```

In the preceding example, the color property will be inherited by the elements that are children of the body element, so headings, paragraphs, lists, and other pieces of text will be dark grey ("#111111"). The padding property, however, will not be inherited; if we place a div or a paragraph inside the body element, they will not inherit a padding of 20 pixels.

These are examples of how inheritance works. In the first case, color, it makes sense that it affects the parent element's children; besides producing much larger files, it would be tiresome and inefficient to have to declare the color of every single element inside the parent. On the other hand, it would also be tiresome to override the 20 pixels of padding were they inherited by its children.

The W3C has a list of all CSS2.1 properties on its website, www.w3.org/TR/CSS21/propidx.html, which states whether they are inherited by default or not, initial (default) and possible values, and other characteristics.

Inheritance makes sense for the elements that do inherit by default, but it can also be forced for elements that don't by using the "inherit" value.

Let's say you wanted the section elements inside the aside parent to inherit its margin value:

```
aside {
    margin: 10px;
}
aside section {
    margin: inherit;
}
```

Using this CSS, every section element inside the aside element will now have 10 pixels of margin.

The way the user agent processes inheritance is explained in the W3C specification:

"The final value of a property is the result of a four-step calculation: the value is determined through specification (the 'specified value'), then resolved into a value that is used for inheritance (the 'computed value'), then converted into an absolute value if necessary (the 'used value'), and finally transformed according to the limitations of the local environment (the 'actual value')" (www.w3.org/TR/CSS2/cascade.html#value-stages).

According to the specification, these are the four values that the cascade looks for, in this order, to determine the final value of a property:

1. *Specified value*: The user agent determines whether the value of the property comes from a style sheet, is inherited, or should take its initial value (which is the value stated in the property specification).

2. *Computed value*: The specified value is resolved into a computed value and exists even when a property doesn't apply. The document doesn't have to be outlined at this stage.

3. *Used value*: The used value takes the computed value and resolves any dependencies that can only be calculated after the document has been drawn (for example, percentages).

4. *Actual value.* This is the value used for the final rendering, after any approximations have been applied (for example, rounding a decimal value to an integer).

The value used when calculating inheritance is the computed value. This value exists even if the property hasn't been declared in the CSS, making it possible to force inheritance even if the parent element doesn't specify the property.

Let's take a look at the following example:

HTML:

```
<body>
    <p>To find what you are looking for visit <a href="http://google.com">Google</a>.</p>
</body>
```

CSS:

```
body {
    font-family: Arial, sans-serif;
    font-size: 12px;
}
a:link {
    color: inherit;
}
```

If we hadn't specified a color for our link element ("a"), we would have been presented with the default blue from the browser (user agent) style sheet. Although we haven't specified a text color for the body element, when using the "inherit" value for the color property of the unvisited link selector ("a:link"), it will use the parent's computed value. In this case that is the initial value, which for the color property depends on the user agent (as stated in the W3C's property specification), but tends to be #000000 (black).

The "inherit" value is not commonly used, but it can be helpful in situations like the example above, when the child's properties are dependent on the parent's in such a way that it is easier to create a dependency than explicitly stating a value.

One of the reasons that the "inherit" value is so rarely used in practice is that it is not supported by versions of IE prior to version 8, except for the "direction" and "visibility" properties. It should be employed when the advantages of using it (for example, when it adds greater flexibility, making updates to the CSS quicker to do and less prone to mistakes) supersede any rendering differences that may occur in using it.

The opposite of the "inherit" keyword is the "initial" keyword, introduced in CSS3. This value allows you to cancel inheritance by specifying the initial value of that property (as stated in the property's specification) instead of the inherited one. This property is only supported, however, by Firefox (using the -moz-initial keyword) and WebKit.

Inheritance and the Universal Selector

The universal selector ("*") matches any single element in the document tree (notice the use of the word *single* here, as it will not match a combination of two or more elements, or zero elements). When used imprudently, it can break inheritance and easily transform a style sheet into an inheritance and specificity nightmare.

Take the following example:

HTML:

```
<section>
    <header>
        <hgroup>
            <h1>Main title</h1>
            <h2>Secondary <i>title</i></h2>
        </hgroup>
    </header>
        …
</section>
```

CSS:

```
section header * {
    color: red;
}
section header h2 {
    color: black;
}
```

The first CSS rule, which includes the universal selector, targets any and every element inside the header element, be it a direct child, grandchild, or deeper. With the second CSS rule, the expected behavior would be that any element inside the h2 should be black. But what happens if we have another element within h2 is that, because the initial rule is targeting any element within header, it will be the same as stating the following:

```
section header h2 i {
    color: red;
}
```

Because this selector is more specific than "section header h2", the final result will render the word "Secondary" in black, but "title" in red (see Figure 3-3).

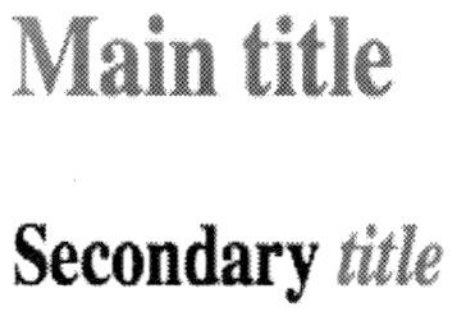

Main title

Secondary *title*

Figure 3-3. Inheritance is broken when using the universal selector

Although, at first, using the CSS universal selector in this scenario might have seemed like the safest option to make sure every element had the desired color, saving precious lines of code, this is not an example of robust CSS. It is instead an example of how breaking inheritance can lead to unnecessarily complicated, unpredictable, and verbose style sheets—exactly what we want to avoid in a high-traffic website where many individuals may be working on many files.

Specificity

Specificity needs to be carefully considered and planned for when working with CSS, and this is even truer when dealing with large CSS files that have frequently overridden and imported style sheets, as tends to happen in high-traffic websites.

It is a good rule of thumb to start developing a CSS file using more generic selectors, increasing specificity as you go where appropriate. Working the other way around is a lot harder and will invariably lead to overly specific selectors that cannot be reused and to unnecessarily long and inflexible style sheets.

Relying on the order of selectors makes the style sheets you create more fragile (this subject is further expanded upon in Chapter 4) and can lead to unnecessary redundancy. When you need to override a rule, you will create a new one later in the file, and this will happen several times until you've repeated the same thing over and over again. If for some reason the order is changed, the properties you wanted to be applied to the element (the ones that used to come last) won't be applied anymore because they were dependent on the order of the selectors. Relying on specificity rather than on the order of selectors will make style sheets easier to edit, maintain, and potentially refactor, as well as more robust.

Specificity of selectors can also have an impact on a website's performance, as parts of selectors are unintuitively evaluated from right-to-left and more specific/complex selectors incur greater hits when querying the DOM (Document Object Model). You can read more about this in Chapter 8.

It is ultimately your decision and a byproduct of how modular and flexible you need your CSS to be whether you need to, at a deeper level, use highly specific rules or not, but specificity should be a fundamental concern in the way your team plans its style sheets.

Calculating Specificity

When assigning a weight to a CSS rule, the cascade will first sort them according to their importance and origin (as seen in the previous section). If rules have the same importance and origin, they will then be prioritized by their specificity: a more specific selector will override a less specific selector. Finally, if two selectors have the same origin, importance, and specificity, the one that comes later in the style sheet will take priority over the preceding one. This also applies to single properties, so if in the same rule the same property is declared more than once, the last declaration will override those previous to it.

Because imported style sheets (using the @import declaration) have to be specified before the other rules, when there are other nonimported rules with the same weight in the rest of the CSS file, the imported ones will be overridden (their precedence is lesser because of the order of the selectors).

To calculate specificity, according to the W3C specification (www.w3.org/TR/css3-selectors/#specificity), we use four representations of numbers (a, b, c, and d) of descending importance, where

- a equals 1 if the declaration is within a style attribute; 0 if not

- b equals the number of ID selectors

- c equals the number of attribute selectors, classes, and pseudo-classes

- d equals the number of element names and pseudo-elements

Non-CSS presentational markup, such as the font attribute, will be attributed a specificity of 0. Based on this list, the following selector has a specificity of 1,0,0,0 (a=1, b=0, c=0, d=0):

```
<section style="padding-bottom: 10px;">
```

Because it is inline CSS, "a" equals 1, and the rest of the numbers equal 0. Bear in mind that even if a rule that was linked to rather than inline had 10 ID selectors within it (thus having a specificity of 0,10,0,0), it would still have less precedence than the selector above—specificity doesn't use a base ten (or decimal) system in its calculations, but rather base infinite: if "a" equals 1, the rule will always take precedence over those where it equals 0.

This more complicated selector will have a specificity of 0,0,1,3 (a=0, b=0, c=1, d=3):

```
article section h1.title {
    ….
}
```

Since it's not inline, "a" equals 0, "b" equals 0 because there are no IDs, "c" equals 1 because it has one class selector, and "d" equals 3 because it has three element selectors.

Calculating specificity based on the list provided may seem daunting, but the truth is that, with some experience, it is fairly easy to look at a selector and tell whether it is more or less specific than another one (perhaps it has one or two ID selectors or another obvious hint like that). While writing CSS, you should be careful not to create highly specific selectors where they aren't necessary and whenever a trickier situation arises, tools like Firebug or Safari Web Inspector will be there to help you understand how specificity is being applied by showing you the rules in order of specificity (with the more specific rules at the top) and striking through the properties that have been overridden by more specific rules. You can read more about these in Chapter 10. There are two important things to remember, though: inline CSS has higher priority than embedded or linked CSS, and one ID selector will win out over any number of class, attribute, or element selectors.

The !important Declaration

Using the !important declaration on shorthand properties is the same as redeclaring each subproperty as important (even if that means they are reverted to their initial (default) value).

For example, suppose that we have the following selector:

```
h1 {
    font-family: Georgia, serif;
    font-size: 18px;
    font-style: italic;
}
```

And later in the style sheet we declare the following:

```
h1 {
    font: 18px Arial, sans-serif !important;
}
```

The result will be the same as having the following:

```
h1 {
    font-style: normal !important;
    font-variant: normal !important;
    font-weight: normal !important;
    font-size: 18px !important;
```

```
    line-height: normal !important;
    font-family: Arial, sans-serif !important;
}
```

This happens because the properties that are not specifically defined within the !important declaration (in this case, font-style, font-variant, font-weight, and line-height) are reverted to their initial values (indicated in the property's specification), even if they had been declared in a less specific rule (like font-style: italic in this instance).

Namespacing and Specificity

There are situations where highly specific selectors are necessary. For example, when creating widgets or code snippets that are to be used across a wide range of pages, subsites, minisites, or even third-party sites, it is common practice to namespace that part of the code, which in CSS means basically to isolate it using a specific class, ID, or prefix to class or ID (we covered namespacing in more detail in Chapter 2). It is also common to namespace an entire page in order to style it differently; in this case, we would add an ID or a class to the body element, such as:

```
<body class="home">
```

It is important to acknowledge, though, that while this is a common and easy way of creating different styles for different pages or sections on a page, it will influence specificity. When targeting these pages or code snippets within our CSS, we will have to introduce a class or an ID to the rule, increasing its specificity and thus making it harder to be overridden. For example, to make the h2 headings in the page that we had attributed the class "home" bigger than in the rest of the site, we could have the following set of rules:

```
h2 {
    font-size: 24px;
}
.home h2 {
    font-size: 36px;
}
```

In the previous example, the rule would be applied even without the class since the rule would have the same specificity but would be declared later. This, however, would be relying on order, which is counterproductive since it will fail if the order of the rules is changed (you can read more about this in Chapter 4).

If for some reason we need to override this setting again, within the homepage, we will need to, for example, add a class to a specific heading and create a more specific rule:

```
.home h2.highlight {
    font-size: 30px;
}
```

This can create a snowball of overly specific rules that will invariably lead to unnecessarily complicated CSS. The trick here is to plan carefully for these situations, which happen more frequently as more variations of certain elements and designs are needed throughout the website(s) and can be aggravated when there isn't a design library in place, or there is one but it is not frequently updated (you can read more about design libraries and maintaining design consistency in Chapter 5). You should have an adaptable style sheet in place and a set of guidelines on how specific developers should be for particular cases—constant overriding of highly specific selectors is not conducive to creating flexible CSS, but avoiding classes and IDs when they are the more efficient and robust solution is also not an option for high-traffic websites.

Using Your Tools

Using tools such as Firebug (see Figure 3-4) or Safari's Web Inspector (see Figure 3-5) makes it easier to understand which properties are taking precedence and overriding others. These tools can also show user agent style sheets and computed values, even if they haven't been declared on the CSS.

Figure 3-4. Using Firefox's Firebug plugin to look deep into a website's markup and CSS

Figure 3-5. Safari's Web Inspector. These tools are helpful to see how the cascade works.

This doesn't mean it is not important to understand how the cascade works, but it makes the process of debugging less painful. You can read more about this in Chapter 10.

Encoding

Although rarely an issue with CSS, it is worth mentioning that character encoding can cause issues with CSS files (and others), and when the issues do occur they can be a very real problem and potentially difficult to isolate. Typically, files will be saved on your machine in the default locale encoding, which is ISO-8859-1 for Western countries using Latin character sets. This character set does not support many characters such as accented characters or unusual symbols. There are really only three places that this could cause a problem:

- Using pseudo-selectors that add content such as :after or :before

- Referencing images or files with unusual characters in their paths

- Comments that may include unusual characters

Although there are (very small) increased file size implications in using Unicode character sets, sticking to UTF-8 can avoid painful compatibility problems, help keep your documents more readable, and avoid issues with localization and escaping characters. If you are likely to be escaping many characters, this will actually save on characters and file size. Refer to www.w3.org/International/questions/qa-escapes for more information on why you should avoid escapes.

Consider this carefully, and include it in your CSS formatting guide. If there is any chance you will be using characters not included in your default character set, we recommend using UTF-8.

Localization

If your site needs to work within an array of different countries, localization is likely to become an issue. For dynamic content generated by a Content Management System (CMS) or other means, your text may be of an unpredictable size. German and Mandarin in particular are very verbose languages. There are two ways to deal with this.

Firstly, you can build every container to be fluid and change size dependant on its content. This may be achievable in some instances, but in many it can become impractical.

Secondly, you can give your CSS some kind of hook particular to certain country and language combinations. You could use server-side code to include an extra style sheet for those particular countries and languages after your primary style sheets so that you can implement overrides for them, something like this:

```
<link rel="stylesheet" href="css/en-gb/overrides.css" />
```

In this instance we have used a subfolder with a particular naming convention. We've used the ISO 639-1 standard for language codes—"en"—(http://en.wikipedia.org/wiki/ISO_639-1), which is simple and succinct; then a hyphen; and finally the ISO 3166-1 alpha-2 standard for country codes (http://en.wikipedia.org/wiki/ISO_3166-1_alpha-2)—"gb".[2]

This method incurs a performance hit, since there is an extra request, but it also ensures we do not try to cater for all countries and languages in a single file which would be inefficient. Another downside

---

[2] Although ISO 3166-1 has everything in upper case, we've put everything in lower case to aid compression and keep everything simple.

is that our rules are disparate, and we would have to maintain many files; when amending CSS for our primary language we might forget to amend the corresponding rule for the other countries and languages.

Another way to target these languages is to add classes to the html or body tags, like so:

```
<html class="en-gb">
```

This makes it easy to target pages in this language specifically, and keep all of our CSS in one place, but has the downside of making for very verbose and inefficient CSS, since we might be serving a great deal of code to users that will never use it. For this reason, we recommend the first method, and using comments in the primary style sheets to remind our developers that other files contain references to the same rules.

Another localization consideration is that some languages flow from right-to-left (RTL) rather than left-to-right (LTR). For these, you will almost certainly need to use a different template so that your markup is in the correct order, and then you can use the methods detailed above in tandem with this to ensure everything looks and reads as it should.

▨ **TIP:** Using the accept-language HTTP header, you can often detect the language of the user's device and return their content in the correct language, which is a nice touch that they will appreciate. You can also detect their location based on their IP address, but this is often inaccurate. The geolocation API in HTML5 (http://dev.w3.org/geo/api/spec-source.html) is much more accurate, but not yet well supported.

As mentioned before, sticking to UTF-8 for your CSS and markup files will save you many headaches, but you may need to implement other character sets for particular countries depending on your requirements.

Browser-Specific CSS

Working on large-scale and high-traffic websites is usually synonymous with having to cater for a wide array of browsers. Not everyone will be using the latest version of the most modern browsers, and it is often the decision that users should not be punished for a handicap that is probably not their fault.

Depending on which browsers the organization chooses to support (see more on graded browser support in Chapter 6), there will almost always be the need to target specific CSS at browsers that are not fully compliant, such as IE 7 or below.

There are various ways in which this can be implemented. Depending on the level of support that is necessary for such browsers and on the website design itself, the differences between the main CSS file and browser-specific ones may vary from a few adjustments on a couple of properties to many selectors that could deserve their own separate CSS file.

Opinions are divided. Advocates of separate style sheets present the argument that this will help keep the main file valid and free from hacks, making it also easier to later remove the browser-specific files. Others will say that it is not practical to update two or more different style sheets and that validation should only be a tool, not a goal. Some will even argue that because when we are dealing with browser specific CSS we are very often resorting to hacks—and hacks are "ugly"—these "stains" on our style sheets shouldn't be quarantined, but rather obvious and easy to spot. Having more CSS files has implications for performance that you can read about in Chapter 8. It is up to your company to decide which stance to take, as both have their own benefits.

Where you have a small amount of specific fixes for (for example) IE 6 and 7, it is typically most efficient to include hacks for these browsers alongside the default property declarations with comments explaining their use. Keeping the properties and their hack counterparts side by side makes it obvious that when updating one, you should update the other. Using external style sheets to apply small changes (even for a minority) incurs large performance hits for the users of those browsers and is rarely the most performant way to address this. However, if a large number of hacks need to be used, and the traffic to your site from the browsers you are targeting is minimal or unimportant to the purpose of your site, penalizing these users in order to give your main demographic a better experience may be preferable.

You should pay close attention to the reporting tools you have available for your site(s) and be very aware of the browsers and devices that are most relevant to you. With these figures in mind, you should measure HTTP performance with the hacks in your usual CSS as well as in separate style sheets to get a good idea of the pros and cons of each approach. Some people advocate placing very small hacks inline in the page within conditional comments, but we do not recommend this approach as it encourages disparate code (similar code in many different places) and removes the control over caching that you would have with individual files.

If the number of hacks in a CSS file accounts for more than 20 percent of the total code (after minification, concatenation, and so on) or greater than 50 KB, it would probably be practical to move the code into an external file, both for performance and considerations of bandwidth. If using separate style sheets it is very important that these be concatenated so that users are served as few extra files as possible.

As we have stated many times before, the most important thing is that a conversation takes place, a decision is made, and the decision is implemented consistently. There are other methods of targeting CSS at specific browsers and devices, though, as discussed in the following text.

Hacks and Filters

There are several ways to make CSS properties and selectors only visible to one (or more) browser(s) and also to hide them from certain browsers.

We will not list these techniques extensively, but we will mention some of the most commonly used ones so you can have an idea of what they look like and what they achieve. There are several resources online, starting with Wikipedia (`http://en.wikipedia.org/wiki/CSS_filter`), that feature complete catalogs of these hacks since they are now well known and thoroughly documented.

The Box Model Hack

Generally accepted as the first-ever CSS hack, the box model hack is used to serve different measures to IE 5 and 5.5, due to their broken box model (hence the name). We explain the IE box model further on in this chapter. Because of a browser parsing bug, only the first width (from the following example) is processed. Compliant browsers will understand both width values, overriding the first with the second one:

```
.box {
    width: 600px;
    voice-family: "\"}\"";
    voice-family: inherit;
    width: 560px;
}
```

```
html>body .box {
    width: 560px;
}
```

The voice-family property is used so it doesn't affect screen style sheets. A browser that doesn't have the parsing error will read the first `voice-family` value as "}", while one that has the parsing error will instead interpret that the whole rule ends with the closing brace that is included in the `voice-family` value, ignoring everything that follows. The second `voice-family` property is there so that in the unlikely event that a file named "}" actually exists, that value that can be overridden. The second rule exists for browsers that also experience the parsing bug, but that have a correct box model. IE 5 and 5.5 ignore it since these browsers don't understand the child selector (represented by ">").

The Underscore Hack

We can feed version 6 of IE and below with different property values by prepending an underscore to the property name, as such:

```
#logo {
    background-image: url(logo.png);
    _background-image: url(logo.gif);
}
```

Because beginning a property with an unescaped underscore is invalid CSS, other browsers will ignore the second property. IE 6 (and lower) on the other hand, deals with the underscore by ignoring it and parsing the property as normal, replacing the first value with the second.

The Star Hack

The star hack targets IE 7 and below. It turns out that IE 6 treats an asterisk in exactly the same way as it treats an underscore. Because the faulty treatment of the underscore gained so much attention, in IE 7 Microsoft made the browser treat the underscore correctly. However, it didn't fix the asterisk. By prefixing the property name with an asterisk, it will be ignored by all other browsers, working almost in the same way as the previous hack (the underscore hack):

```
section {
    width: 860px;
    *width: 960px;
}
```

This inconsistency makes it possible to target IE6 and IE7 separately like so:

```
section {
    width: 860px; /* all browsers */
    *width: 960px; / IE7 and below */
    _width: 1060px; / IE6 and below */
}
```

Because the last rule always takes precedence, for browsers that interpret properties beginning with an underscore (IE 6 and below) the previous property is overridden.

The Star Html Hack, IE4-6

Because IE 4 to 6 incorrectly include an invisible mystery element in the DOM before the root `html` element, by using the star html ("* html") hack, you can target these specific browsers in a rule:

```
* html h1 { background-image: url(logo.gif); }
```

Since no elements exist before the `html` element in any other browser, all other browsers will ignore this entire selector and all of its properties.

The Child Selector Hack

IE 6 and older versions do not understand the child selector (represented by ">"). We can therefore use it to hide rules from those browsers. For example, the second rule in the following block of code, where we apply a transparent PNG background to a `div` (unsupported by IE 6), will not be read by IE 6, making it use the plain background color stated previously:

```
div {
  background-color: #dd4814;
}
body > div {
  background-image: url(orange.png) no-repeat;
}
```

The Commented Backslash Hack

IE for Mac has its own idiosyncrasies (although it is no longer in common usage). This browser chose to (against the spec) let you escape asterisks within comments with a backslash. We can take advantage of this fact in that this browser doesn't understand that a comment is closed if written in a certain way, thus not reading the CSS that is placed between the escaped character and the normal comment:

```
/* IE for Mac doesn't understand this comment is closed \*/
(anything between the comments won't be read by IE for Mac)
/* IE for Mac will continue reading the CSS file after this comment */
```

The last IE for Mac's release dates back to 2003, and Microsoft dropped support for this browser in 2005, so traffic from this browser is unlikely to be a concern.

A Necessary Evil

Although we don't like to encourage the use of these so-called "filters," we understand that they may be useful in certain situations, and that using them instead of spending hours trying to work around the problem's origin may be a necessity due to time or budget constraints. Another way of separating browser-specific CSS is by using conditional comments, usually regarded as a cleaner solution. We cover conditional comments later in this chapter.

CSS Expressions

CSS expressions (or *dynamic properties*) were introduced in IE 5 and are supported up until version 7 (or 8 and 9, when rendering in compatibility mode). By placing JavaScript within an expression, we can return different results depending on environment or other factors.

A simple CSS expression (bear in mind that this is JavaScript, and as such the syntax is not in scope for this book) to concatenate two strings is as follows:

```
aside {
    width: expression("320"+ "px");
}
```

This is the same as having the following:

```
aside {
    width: 320px;
}
```

In the following example, the expression checks whether the body width is narrower than 1200 pixels; if that's true, the width is set to "1200px", if not, it is set to "auto":

```
#container{
    width: expression((document.body.clientWidth > 1200) ? "1200px" : "auto");
}
```

CSS expressions are resource-intensive and can seriously hamper the performance of a website. Yahoo!, on its High Performance Web Sites Rules series, lists rule 7 as "Avoid CSS Expressions," arguing that "Not only are they evaluated when the page is rendered and resized, but also when the page is scrolled and even when the user moves the mouse over the page." (http://developer.yahoo.net/blog/archives/2007/07/high_performanc_6.html).

Some expressions can have a stronger performance hit than others, so performance testing is always recommended (as with all JavaScript), as there may be a case where using one CSS expression is the fastest and most efficient solution for dealing with browser inconsistencies.

Another downside of CSS expressions is the fact that they are reliant on JavaScript to work, which is far from ideal since we are actually dealing with CSS, and the user may have JavaScript disabled. Seeing that we are creating a JavaScript dependency, our advice is to move these to JavaScript, keeping the CSS free from CSS expressions and avoiding the toll on performance that comes with them.

There are few cross-browser cases that actually require JavaScript to resolve, and an event-driven solution like CSS expressions is as subtle a solution as a brick wall on a motorway. Unless you have a really strong case for using them and it is a final resort, we would recommend against it.

Vendor-Specific Extensions

Browser-specific CSS doesn't just mean handling deficient IE renderings and working around its quirks. It may also include having vendor-specific properties to create more advanced effects that are in line with the latest CSS developments or not yet part of any specification.

For example, the syntax to create CSS border-radius needs to be written for browsers that have implemented the property in an experimental (and often incomplete) fashion, using its vendor-specific versions along with the official specification:

```
.box {
    -moz-border-radius:  4px
    -webkit-border-radius: 4px;
    border-radius: 4px;
}
```

In this example, we are basically stating the same thing three times in order to cater for the widest range of browsers possible. We have included the property as it is mentioned in the specification last, so when all browsers eventually implement it, it will still work, and the correct standards-compliant implementation will override the vendor-specific version.[3]

This results in a non-valid CSS file, since vendor-specific extensions are still parsed as errors by CSS validators (although some voices have risen to have this behavior changed). Bear in mind, though, that the use of these vendor-specific extensions by browser manufacturers is standard practice, anticipated in the W3C specification, where it is stated that "property names beginning with '-' or '_' are reserved for vendor-specific extensions" and that they are "guaranteed never to be used in a property or keyword by any current or future level of CSS" (www.w3.org/TR/CSS21/syndata.html#vendor-keywords). There should be no conflicts between vendors since it is very unlikely that two of them will choose the same prefix. It is possible (and not unlikely), however, that the implementation of these experimental properties may change while they're still in this "testing" phase—keeping up to date with the latest news from the W3C CSS Working Group is a good idea if you don't want to be caught by surprise.

Here is a list of the most commonly used vendor-specific prefixes:

- `-moz-`

    o   Gecko-based browsers

- `-webkit-`

    o   Webkit-based browsers

- `-apple-`

    o   Safari (in effect, the same as -webkit-)[4]

- `-ms-`

    o   IE

- `-o-`

    o   Opera

- `-khtml-`

    o   Konqueror

Notwithstanding that these properties are non-valid, vendor-specific CSS, they can't be qualified as hacks or workarounds, and they work as support for properties that are likely to be part of final

---

[3] The latest releases of browsers such as Safari or upcoming IE 9 support `border-radius` without the need for a vendor prefix, so including the default property is an important step that should never be forgotten.
[4] As WebKit was originally a forked version of KHTML, it used the `-khtml-` extension for CSS properties, while the `-apple-` extension was used for Apple-specific features. These were eventually merged into the `-webkit-` extension, although there are still some properties that are Safari-only and use the `-apple-` extension (for example, `-apple-line-clamp`). The Konqueror browser still uses the `-khtml-` extension.

specifications. Confining them to their own separate style sheet could prove a misstep in the search for efficiency: when one of the properties needs to be changed, all the others also need updating—the back and forth can be daunting. Also, again, the more individual CSS files there are (and therefore HTTP requests), the greater the performance hit.

Other solutions, such as relegating these vendor-specific properties to a separate section within the main CSS file, making them easier to find (and therefore, easier to delete if the need arises) might be a better labor-saving solution, although it results in duplicated selectors that are less efficient and can be more difficult to manage.

Media Queries

Rather than using hacks or other methods to only serve particular CSS to certain browsers, we are encouraged to use capability detection since this is a future-proof and sane method of targeting that is not dependent on bugs or easily overridden and spoofed properties. Media queries allow the creation of CSS that is dependent on the capabilities or features of the device that is being used to view the website. For example, you can write CSS that is only to be displayed on devices with monochrome screens, or a small viewport, printers, or even a combination of two or more features. Media queries don't target specific browsers, but rather the capabilities of the device that the website is being displayed on.

Media queries can be applied in three different ways:

- directly in the style sheet

- imported from within the style sheet

- using a link tag in the head of the HTML document

Here is an example of a media query embedded directly in the style sheet, alongside the rest of the CSS:

```
@media screen and (max-width: 320px) {
    aside {
        float: none;
    }
}
```

You can import a different file from the style sheet using the @import rule:

```
@import url(320.css) screen and (max-width: 320px);
```

And finally, a media query inserted in the link tag within the head of an HTML document:

```
<link rel="stylesheet" media="screen and (max-width: 320px)" href="320.css" />
```

Media queries are often cited when creating mobile versions of websites, but there are other factors apart from pure design that you should consider. Using media queries doesn't necessarily prevent images from being downloaded.[5] In fact, when using the link tag style sheets will be downloaded

---

[5] WebKit downloads images set to display:none; Firefox and Opera don't. This applies to desktop and mobile. It works better with media queries, in that background images aren't downloaded if the media query applies, but not if the media query is overriding another background image that has been applied in the generic style sheet—in this case both are downloaded. Basically, be aware that hiding things via CSS doesn't mean that the browser won't download them.

regardless of the media attribute, although they may not be applied. While media queries can be applied to create quick mobile versions of a website, when dealing with high-traffic websites, performance and accessibility considerations (a great deal of mobile devices still don't support media queries) will probably (and should) be at the top of the list and may invalidate the use of them for the most part. We talk about media queries in great detail in Chapter 7.

Conditional Comments

Conditional comments were introduced in IE 5 and are specially formatted HTML comments that allow targeting of specific versions of the Microsoft browser. They can be wrapped around another block of HTML and will effectively hide it from the browsers that are not being targeted.

A conditional comment can be used to target one specific version of IE:

```
<!--[if IE 8]>
        <link rel="stylesheet" href="ie8.css" />
<![endif]-->
```

In this case, the ie8.css file will only be requested by IE 8.

It can be used to target versions lower or greater than a particular version number:

```
<!--[if lt IE 7]>
        <link rel="stylesheet" href="ie6.css" />
<![endif]-->
```

```
<!--[if gt IE 7]>
        <link rel="stylesheet" href="ie8.css" />
<![endif]-->
```

In the first example, we are targeting IE versions from 5 to 6 (lt stands for "less than"). In the second example, we are targeting versions above but not including 7 (at the time of writing, that would include IE 8 and 9), using the gt operator ("greater than").

It can also be used to target versions lower or greater than a particular version, but including the one specified, like so:

```
<!--[if lte IE 6]>
        <link rel="stylesheet" href="ie6.css" />
<![endif]-->
```

```
<!--[if gte IE 7]>
        <link rel="stylesheet" href="ie7.css" />
<![endif]-->
```

The first example targets IE versions from 5 to 6, using the lte operator ("less than or equal to"). The second targets all versions above and including IE 7 (gte stands for "greater than or equal to").

It is also possible to use the NOT operator ("!", as used in many programming languages) in order to hide the comment from one or more browser versions. The following conditional comment will be ignored by IE 5, but not by other versions of IE:

```
<!--[if !(IE 5)]>
        <link rel="stylesheet" href="advanced.css" />
<![endif]-->
```

Although it is not common practice, conditional comments can become somewhat more complicated with the use of expressions, like the AND operator ("&"). Here is an example:

```
<!--[if (gte IE 5)&(lt IE 8)]>
        <link rel="stylesheet" href="hacks.css" />
<![endif]-->
```

Here we are targeting IE versions greater than and including IE 5 and lower than IE 8, so versions 5 through 7 inclusive. We can also use the OR operator ("|") in these expressions.

Conditional comments are sometimes listed among other hacks, but, unlike them, they do not rely on a browser bug to work, which makes them safer to use and more future-proof. They provide a cleaner way of separating browser-specific CSS from the base or more advanced style sheets, making it easier to remove these style sheets if and when support for older browsers is dropped.

In order to reduce HTTP requests, the CSS included in files that would be linked within conditional comments can be embedded directly on the head of the HTML document, as such:

```
<!--[if lte IE 6]>
        <style>
            li {
                display: inline;
                }
        </style>
<![endif]-->
```

This can be more advantageous than linking to external files for each browser that requires a separate style sheet, especially in situations when only a couple of rules are needed. This practice may hamper the maintainability of this snippet of code, but if the advantages in page performance are greater, it is a solution to consider and one that some high-traffic websites are employing already. Each request has a very real performance implication.

Conditional comments cannot be used within text nodes or attributes. For example, this won't work:

```
<style>
    li {
        display: block;
    }
        <!--[if IE 6]>
            li {
                display: inline;
                }
        <![endif]-->
</style>
```

And neither will this:

```
<div class="<!--[if IE 6]>ie6<![endif]-->">
    ...
</div>
```

To target browsers other than IE, i.e. hide contents from all IE browsers, it is necessary to use a "downlevel-revealed comment" so that the conditional comment is still read by IE, but does not comment content out in other browsers. This looks like this:

```
<!--[if !(IE)]><!-->
        <style>
            …
        </style>
<!--<![endif]-->
```

This includes complete comments around the entire of the two parts of the conditional comment. Using this methodology allows us to create markup that will still validate.

Conditional Comments in the html Element

Having separate style sheets for each browser can affect the maintainability of the CSS and also make debugging less straightforward (you may not immediately realize that a specific property or selector is affecting the buggy element if they are not in the main style sheet). Placing the CSS directly in a style tag in the page may save on HTTP requests, but it causes a problem with "separation of concerns" (http://en.wikipedia.org/wiki/Separation_of_concerns)—our presentational logic (CSS) should ideally not live within our content (HTML). With this in mind, front-end developer Paul Irish came up with a very simple but practical solution that uses conditional comments and the html (or body) element of the page.

Using this method, we conditionally add a class to the html tag, depending on which browser is being used to view the page:

```
<!--[if lt IE 7 ]><html class="ie6"><![endif]-->
<!--[if IE 7 ]><html class="ie7"><![endif]-->
<!--[if IE 8 ]><html class="ie8"><![endif]-->
<!--[if IE 9 ]><html class="ie9"><![endif]-->
<!--[if (gt IE 9)|!(IE)]><!--><html><!--<![endif]-->
```

With these conditional comments applied, we can then use the classes in our CSS to create selectors that will target that specific browser, as such:

```
#logo {
    background-image: url(logo.png);
}
.ie6 #logo {
    background-image: url(logo.gif);
}
```

Two (or more) style sheets will always be more difficult to manage than just one, and this simple technique can help minimize the need for various browser-specific CSS files (http://paulirish.com/2008/conditional-stylesheets-vs-css-hacks-answer-neither/).

When and How to Use Hacks

A CSS hack relies on browser bugs to address rendering issues. This means that it is basically relying on a bug to fix another bug, which is far from ideal.

Hacks are to be avoided. What happens when we use a hack to deal with a rendering problem is that we are not dealing with the fundamental issue in itself but rather applying a patch to cover up the damage.

Even though these patches feel like a good quick solution at first, what happens if the browser gets updated and the bugs fixed? (Remember, we are usually relying on two bugs when using a hack.) The consequences will be unpredictable.

"Safe" Hacks

The problem that may come with bugs being fixed in new browser releases doesn't relate to older browsers that are unlikely to see any kind of updates in the future. Browsers such as IE 5.5 or 6 have long lists of documented and well-known bugs. Some of these bugs can be avoided with careful CSS; other bugs will always be there, and yet other bugs are more temperamental and show up in an unpredictable and inconsistent fashion.

Because these older browsers aren't being actively developed any more (you should only expect any updates in the case of a very serious security issue needing to be fixed, and even then, CSS rendering probably will not be affected), using CSS hacks on them tends to be considered safe practice. Our opinion is that even in these cases, hacks have to be used in moderation. It is important to understand the risks involved in using them. Since they work due to inconsistencies or badly implemented CSS parsing and edge cases, it is possible that future browser versions may also be affected by them, although it is unlikely.

As an example of a safe hack to employ, let's take a look at the @import hack, commonly used to hide CSS files from versions 4 of browsers like IE or Netscape. Since these versions don't understand the @import directive, any style sheets referenced therein will not be requested. This hack (or filter) was publicized by Tantek Çelik. It can be used in the head of an HTML file, in conjunction with the style tag:

```
<style>
        @import "advanced.css";
</style>
```

It can also be located at the top of the actual CSS document:

```
@import "advanced.css";
```

In this particular case, though, be aware that using the @import declaration will result in extra HTTP requests and will affect the performance of the website. It is common practice to use no more than two @import declarations in a CSS file in order to avoid these issues. (We further discuss how the @import declaration can affect downloading speeds in Chapter 8.)

Modern browsers that conform to the latest web standards shouldn't have the need for any type of hack in order to render a CSS layout correctly. This, of course, will not produce a pixel-perfect copy of the original design across every available browser in the market, but that is something that is implied in the medium we are working with. If your company demands exactly identical rendering between every browser, it is worth demonstrating the costs in time versus lost features and even user testing to prove that users just don't notice that level of detail. If this is still unacceptable, you will just have to do the best you can with what you have. Choose your battles wisely.[6]

---

[6] Despite many who claim otherwise, it is a fact that due to font-rendering differences, browser chrome, implementation—and even color profile rendering in images—it is simply impossible for a website to look exactly the same in every browser.

The Real World

When faced with a situation where a hack is needed, the ideal scenario would be to revisit the markup and the CSS and see if there is a clean solution that is valid and not browser-specific, so that we can avoid the problem in the first place.

Another good option is to consider whether the bug is relevant enough to be fixed. For example, if the layout isn't broken, and we are dealing with almost unnoticeable pixel differences between browsers, is there really a need to waste time and man-hours fixing it? Weighing up the cost in time, and the lost potential features and development that could have occurred in that time, the answer is almost always no.

Although the best solution is always to write markup and CSS that avoid the need for hacks, issues are inevitable and employing hacks is necessary. Sometimes it is impossible to have access to the HTML, the existing CSS cannot be edited, or maybe the cost in time that it would take to deal with the problem in this manner is not acceptable.

In these situations, whenever possible, browser-specific hacks should be either relegated to a browser-specific style sheet or to a section in the CSS file where all the hacks are stored, making it easier to remove them when they are no longer necessary. As an alternative, specific comments could be used on the lines of the hacks, making them easy to locate later. The most common example is TODO, which is understood and implemented by many integrated development environments (IDEs) and could be employed like so:

```
/*
   TODO : Remove this when we drop support for IE6
*/ _float:left;
```

Labeling comments in this way makes it easy to search for and locate them later in the development process.[7] You could even use custom comments, with delimiters that are easy to locate and parse, such as the following:

```
/* HACK_IE7 */ *float:right;
/* HACK_IE6 */ _float:left;
```

If you are using CSSDOC-type comments, the @todo tag can be used within file and section comments. (CSSDOC is explained in more detail in Chapter 2.)

As with every aspect of CSS authoring within a team or organization, it is important that there is a set of guidelines in place as to which hacks are acceptable and which aren't. A safe approach to this matter is to allow CSS authors to freely apply only hacks from a predefined list of those that are well-known and documented and only for browsers that aren't being actively developed any more. Ideally, the developers would also know in which situations it is necessary that rendering is perfect or almost perfect and which situations browser inconsistencies can be overlooked. For example, the guidelines can mention that for measurements that break the layout of the page, hacks need to be employed for nonconforming browsers; for more decorative measurements, there is no need for hacks.

Server-Side User Agent Detection

We have other methods for serving specific content to different devices, other than in the browser or device itself. Sometimes we only want to present the necessary content, rather than all the files and logic

---

[7] You can read more about comment tags at
http://en.wikipedia.org/wiki/Comment_(computer_programming)#Tags.

necessary to differentiate between the devices. This saves on the amount the user has to download, but it impedes caching and can have server-side performance implications.

With every request to the server, various extra pieces of information are sent in *headers*: extra information associated with the request. Some examples are the *referrer* (the site the user came from to get to this address), the language the user's device is using, acceptable character sets, and so on.

▓ **NOTE:** In the initial proposal for the referrer to be added to the HTTP specification, Phillip Hallam-Baker misspelled it as *referer*. It has since then been spelled and implemented inconsistently, but the correct spelling is referrer.

One of these headers is called *user-agent*, which is a string of text representing various pieces of information about the user's device and environment. Here are some examples:

- `Mozilla/5.0 (Macintosh; U; Intel Mac OS X 10.6; en-US; rv:1.9.2.9) Gecko/20100824 Firefox/3.6.9`

- `Mozilla/5.0 (Windows; U; Windows NT 5.1; en-US) AppleWebKit/525.13 (KHTML, like Gecko) Chrome/0.2.149.29 Safari/525.13`

- `Mozilla/5.0 (Macintosh; U; PPC Mac OS X; en) AppleWebKit/125.2 (KHTML, like Gecko) Safari/125.8`

- `Mozilla/4.0 (compatible; MSIE 5.5; Windows 98; Win 9x 4.90)`

Using some simple string manipulation and conditional logic, it is pedestrian to use this data to infer and classify the browser that is being used to access a website. We are not encouraging you to use this methodology; but it is worth mentioning a few things here. The first is that it is very easy to replace request headers with anything you like, and it is therefore simple for users to impersonate devices other than those they are actually using.[8]

The second is that (as mentioned earlier) current thinking discourages us from detecting a browser and presenting to it in a particular way. We should be detecting capability, not device. However, this is not always an appropriate way to behave or the best solution, so it is good to understand the options we have.

Finally, you may be tempted to use these techniques to present different data to (for example) the spiders from Google or Yahoo! that are hopefully indexing your site. Although it is easy to do this, it is considered a black hat technique and if a search engine realizes that you are presenting different content for them than for your users, you may be penalized and your search result positioning negatively affected.

There *are* instances where detecting the user agent is the correct thing to do. If you are serving something to a specific device regardless of its capability, it is completely sensible to use the user agent. For example, "We've noticed you are using an iPhone! You can download our app here" is an appropriate scenario.

---

[8] This is not necessarily something for us to worry about. Particularly in the realm of CSS, there are no real security issues implied by this, but plugins, browser extensions, caching servers or even malware may modify this header, and it is important to know that it is possible.

Here are a few rough examples of code snippets that work with the user agent with some common server-side languages:

PHP[9]

```php
<?php
    function detectBrowser() {
        $ua = $_SERVER['HTTP_USER_AGENT'];
        if(strchr($ua,"MSIE")) return 'IE';
        if(strchr($ua,"Firefox")) return 'FIREFOX';
        if(strchr($ua,"Opera")) return 'Opera';
    }

    echo detectBrowser();
?>
```

ASP.NET (VB)

```vb
<script language="VB" runat="server">
  Sub Page_Load(sender as Object, e as EventArgs)
    dim browserType = Request.Browser.Type
    dim browserPlatform = Request.Browser.Platform
    dim browserVersion = Request.Browser.Version
    dim browserMajorVersion = Request.Browser.MajorVersion
    dim browserMinorVersion = Request.Browser.MinorVersion

    envDetails.Text = browserType & ", " & browserPlatform & ", Version: " & browserVersion &
", Major Version" & browserMajorVersion & ", Minor Version" & browserMinorVersion
  End Sub
</script>

Your environment: <asp:literal id="envDetails" runat="server" />
```

JSP

```jsp
<%
String ua = request.getHeader("user-agent");
out.print ("USER AGENT IS " +userAgent);
%>
```

Ruby

```ruby
user_agent = request.user_agent.downcase
```

As you can see, the method for accessing the user agent is very similar from language to language. Again, we would like to reiterate that we do not recommend this technique, but it is important to be pragmatic in your implementations and we mention it here since you may find that this method solves a particular problem you may be having, and we aim to be pragmatists over purists.

---

[9] Chris Chuld has a comprehensive PHP user agent detection library at
http://chrisschuld.com/projects/browser-php-detecting-a-users-browser-from-php/.

Some Examples of Browser Rendering Differences

We all know that different browsers render the same markup and CSS differently. Whether because of a bug or not, this is something CSS authors have to deal with every day. With experience, exposure to the most common differences is inevitable and this, ideally, will lead to a better knowledge of how to avoid or fix these problems.

While in smaller websites small percentages of visitors using older browsers mean only a few dozen people, the same does not apply to high-traffic websites, where even less than 1 percent of users can mean tens of thousands. This means that you should be familiar with at least the most common and destructive quirks that some browsers pose, in order to avoid any accessibility issues that might impede a considerable number of users to access content and navigate the pages of your website(s) or that might be diluting or even cramping the image of your organization.

In this section, we will list some of the most common browser differences, and give you some tips on how to plan for them or the most common ways on how to fix them. They are differences that can influence the design at different levels, from simple pixel variations to bugs that can break your layouts; while the larger problems will probably need to be fixed in most cases, whether or not you need to cater for the smaller ones should be defined on a team or organization level (preferably in a CSS style guide).

Quirks Mode

Older websites were developed relying on the deficient rendering of CSS by older browsers that were either following an unfinished or incomplete specification or simply chose not to implement some aspects of the documentation as stated by the W3C. With new browser releases that were more conformant with the standards, there was the problem of these older websites, developed around bugs and inconsistencies, being broken. In order to keep websites backward compatible (and not "break the Web"), modern browsers can often display pages in *quirks mode*, which mimics the behavior of older browsers.

A browser will decide which rendering mode to trigger usually based on the document type declaration of the page (this is called doctype switching). A complete doctype will trigger standards mode (without the need for the page to be actually valid), while an incomplete, invalid, or absent doctype will trigger quirks mode. IE 6 will also trigger quirks mode if the doctype is preceded by an XML prolog[10] while any IE version will trigger quirks mode when the doctype is preceded by a comment.[11]

Sooner or later, you will be faced with a browser rending difference that you can blame on the page being rendered in quirks mode. If editing the markup so that the correct doctype is applied or to remove any other portion of code that might be triggering quirks mode is not an option, the solution will have to rely on the CSS part of the equation.

Some Quirks

Different browsers implement different quirks, but here are some of the most common ones that might influence your layouts in a more evident way.

One of the main differences between standards and quirks mode rendering has to do with the box model, and IE's interpretation of it. Because this issue can have a bigger impact on the overall rendering of your websites, we've dedicated the following separate section to it.

---

[10] This is the correct spelling. The *XML Prolog* can state which version and encoding format is being used in the XML. Here is an example: `<?xml version="1.0" encoding="iso-8859-1"?>`.

[11] Wikipedia provides a comprehensive list of how different document types trigger different modes at `http://en.wikipedia.org/wiki/Quirks_mode#Comparison_of_document_types`.

margin: auto

One small but important difference that can influence the layout is the `margin: auto` property/value. If you apply `margin: auto` to an element with a set width it is possible to center it inside its parent unless the page is rendered in quirks mode on IE. However, by adding the property `text-align: center` to the parent, IE versions up to 7 will incorrectly center its block level children although achieving the desired effect, even in standards mode.

Font Properties Inheritance in Tables

Some older browsers broke the inheritance of font properties (`font-size`, `font-style`, `font-variant`, and `font-weight`) in tables, meaning that if, for example, you had set a `font-size` for the body element, it wouldn't be inherited by the text within the tables, showing the user agent's default instead. Quirks mode will emulate this behavior.

Overflow

If `overflow` is set to `visible`, rather than keeping the dimensions of the container intact and simply overflowing the content, the browser in quirks mode will stretch the size of the container to accommodate the content. IE 6 has this bug whether or not it is rendering in quirks mode.

Class Names are Case-Insensitive

There's not much to be added to the title of this particular section. In quirks mode, browsers will interpret *class="error"* the same way as *class="ERROR"* or *class="Error"*.

Color Values

Color values without the pound symbol (#) are accepted in quirks mode.

Almost Standards Mode

The *almost standards mode*, triggered by some DOCTYPES, is basically standards mode with a tweak that makes the rendering of images inside table cells behave differently. Firefox, Safari, IE 8, and Opera (7.5+) have this mode.

The difference between this mode and standards mode is the implementation of vertical sizing in table cells, which follows the CSS2 specification. The specification states that images are inline elements, which are aligned to the text baseline and should, therefore, reserve some space for descenders (lowercase characters such as *p* or *q* have descenders). We all know, however, that images do not have descenders. Almost standards mode (and quirks mode too, for that matter) will render images inside table cells without that gap, eliminating that inconvenient bottom space. This is especially useful on websites that have been created following the "slicing up images and placing them inside table cells" technique—if there is a white space below the images, the layout will be broken.

The recommendation here is that if you are using transitional markup, you should not use a doctype that triggers standards mode, but almost standard mode instead, avoiding any issues with decorative images.

The IE Box Model

When a document is laid out on visual media, CSS will represent each element as a rectangular box. These boxes can be placed after one another or nested. CSS3 defines three types of boxes:

- Block-level boxes; for example, a paragraph

- Line boxes: for example; a line of text

- Inline-level boxes; for example, words inside a line

Each box is composed of the actual content area and can optionally have a border, padding, and margins. The W3C defines that the border, padding,and margins should be added to the initial width and height of the element box, so if a div has the following CSS applied to it, according to the W3C specification, the div should have 124 pixels width and height (100px + 2*10px + 2*2px) with a 20-pixel margin on all sides:

```
div {
    width: 100px;
    height: 100px;
    padding: 10px;
    border: 2px solid #333333;
    margin: 20px;
}
```

However, IE 5 interprets things in a different way: For this browser, the padding and border of a box are to be subtracted from the specified width and height (in this case, 124px), as you can see in the bottom image in Figure 3-6.

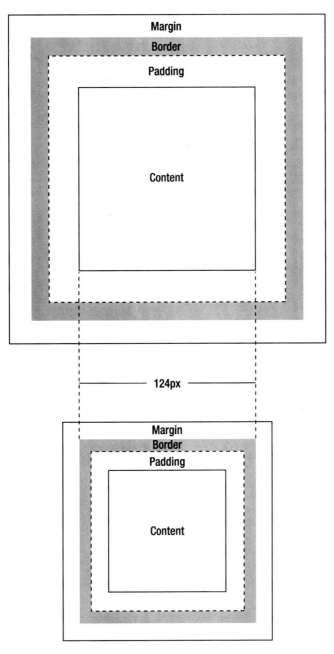

Figure 3-6. *The difference between the W3C box model (above) and IE's box model (below)*

Despite this interpretation being more logical, it is incorrect, and that is why this behavior was corrected with the release of IE 6. IE 6 and above will, however, render using its incorrect box model if quirks mode (explained previously) is triggered.

This bug can have disastrous implications if you don't plan for it and do the necessary testing since it will influence the dimensions of the boxes in your layouts and will render them with completely different sizes.

Imagine a simple scenario: an outer container that has 940px width and 10px padding with two inner boxes of 470px width, floated side by side. If IE renders in quirks mode, the actual available space inside the outer container will not be 940px but rather 920px (since the padding is subtracted from 940px, and not added, as it should be). This means that the boxes will not be placed side by side, but one above the other, since they don't fit on the same line. This is just a very simple example of how a layout can be broken by the wrong interpretation of the box model, which will lead to unnecessary time and resources spent debugging that could have been avoided.

There are three ways of dealing with this bug:

- Always use the correct document type so that quirks mode is not triggered.

- Do not specify both dimensions and padding/border on the same element (recommended).

- Rely on the IE box model and use CSS3 `box-sizing` for newer browsers.

By specifying only the dimensions on the parent element and then, separately, padding and borders on its child elements, you will be circumventing the problem without having to rely on whether or not the correct document type is being applied. This is one of the oldest tricks that CSS authors use to avoid broken layouts in IE 6. In the case that there is a child element to achieve this, this is a convenient and simple solution. However, if no child element exists, we recommend you use an alternative method to target IE6 specifically, rather than add unnecessary markup solely for one outdated browser.

Another option is to use the CSS3 property `box-sizing`, which is supported by all the modern browsers, including IE 8 (Firefox requires the `-moz-box-sizing` vendor-specific property, while Webkit-based browsers require the `-webkit-` prefix). The `box-sizing` property accepts one of two values: `content-box` or `border-box`. The `content-box` value will apply to that element the box model as specified by CSS2.1, where the padding and border are added to the given dimensions of the element. The `border-box` value will make the padding and border be subtracted from the specified width and height of the element, mimicking the IE box model.

One of the downsides of using this property is that it has to be added on an element-by-element basis. It can also be added to every element by using the universal selector (*) or by adding it to the elements that will most likely need it, like sectioning elements.

All in all, the box model issue is one that—although it may produce tragic outcomes when not catered for—can be easily avoided. The ideal solution would be to ensure that IE renders in standards-compliant mode; this solves many of the issues, and is really what we should be working toward as browsers modernize and move forward. We recommend that as part of your defensive CSS strategy (you can read more about this in Chapter 4) you avoid the problem altogether by not specifying dimensions and padding/border on the same element.

No matter which solution your team decides is best, it should be included in the internal CSS style guide.

hasLayout

The hasLayout concept is a Microsoft creation and applies only to IE; it "determines how elements draw and bound their content, interact with and relate to other elements, and react on and transmit application/user events" (www.satzansatz.de/cssd/onhavinglayout.html#def).

An element's hasLayout property can be either true or false. When it is true, the element "has layout." Some elements have layout by default, while you can trigger the property via CSS for others. This is not done via a specific hasLayout property but through other CSS properties.

According to Microsoft, the following elements have layout:

- html (in standards mode), body
- img
- table, tr, th, td
- hr
- input, button, select, textarea, fieldset, legend
- marquee
- frameset, frame
- iframe, embed, object, applet
- absolutely positioned elements
- floated elements
- inline-block elements
- filters (Microsoft proprietary; for example, rotations and drop shadows)

And the following property/value pairs will trigger hasLayout to be true for an element:

- position: absolute
- float: left/right
- display: inline-block
- width: a value other than auto
- zoom: a value other than normal
- writing-mode: tb-rl
- overflow: hidden/scroll/auto (IE 7)
- overflow-x/y: hidden/scroll/ auto (IE 7)

■ **TIP:** Since it is rare that CSS authors use the zoom property, often adding zoom:1; is an easy and safe way to quickly give an element layout and potentially fix numerous IE bugs. As mentioned earlier, it is important to separate or comment these specific fixes so they do not get mixed up with the rest of our CSS.

Many of IE's rendering bugs can be fixed by giving the concerned element layout. A few of the most exasperating rendering issues triggered by elements that have (or don't have) layout are:

- *Self-clearing floats*: Rather than sticking out of its parent container when its content is too long, a float will be self-cleared, so its parent will expand in order to fit. In a compliant browser, you would have to manually clear the float for this behavior to happen.

- *List elements*: A quick, frustrating example: when dealing with ordered lists in which one or more li elements have layout, those that do will have their counters reset to 1 (or the first representation of whichever style you have chosen to apply to the bullets).

- *Absolutely positioned elements*: The nearest positioned ancestor of absolutely positioned elements should be given layout; otherwise, they will end up in unexpected places.

There is a lot to be said about hasLayout that would be outside the scope of this book. Although not the most exciting subject in the world, it is easy to understand how important it is to be aware of it and know how best to handle it when faced with a problem. Problems triggered because of the hasLayout property are frequent and often affect the design of the pages in a way that can't just be ignored. We recommend that you read the comprehensive "On having layout" at www.satzansatz.de/cssd/onhavinglayout.html for more in-depth information.

▓ **NOTE:** Microsoft has fixed most of the problems that were caused by hasLayout in IE 8 and 9, but the property is still present.

Experimental CSS

CSS keeps evolving, the specification changes, and browser vendors experiment. And as with any other experiment, things keep changing as they are being perfected over time. What this means in practice for CSS authors is that, as much as we would like to be able to use properties such as border-radius or box-shadow comfortable in the knowledge that they will behave immutably and cross-browser, in reality browsers interpret them differently. The differences might not be great and will probably lead to its eventual homogenizing, but they exist.

This should not be a discouragement from using experimental CSS; quite the opposite. It is by wide implementation of new properties by CSS authors that browser vendors gather the knowledge of how they should operate in a way that is practical and in tune with the real necessities of developers, which will, in turn, reflect on the drafting of future specifications (since they are based on implementations and examples rather than on idealisms).

When working on high-traffic and high-profile websites, one will need to be more careful and mindful of which properties are safe to use and which not. Following the developments of the CSS working group and being up-to-date with new browser releases is fundamental. Participating in the working group, too, is a great way to keep on top of changes, making your voice heard and being a part of the movement. Although, ideally, every member of the team that has to deal with CSS would be interested in keeping abreast of the latest updates, it might be a good idea to appoint one member of the team to be responsible for following the latest news and keeping the rest of the team informed. Setting up an internal mailing list that could be subscribed to by all interested in the matter with links to relevant articles would benefit the front-end team immensely.

Summary

The main objective of this chapter was to introduce some of the fundamental concepts that are inherent to CSS but that many developers tend to overlook. There is no doubt that CSS is easy to grasp, but crafting well-coded style sheets that will not break when the website is rendered in IE (or that will only present minimal issues) while, at the same time, keeping them efficient and maintainable is something that requires years of experience and a deeper knowledge of the theories behind CSS.

While it is not necessary to know by heart the list of rendering differences between a browser in standards and quirks mode (and it's okay to search the Web for the best solution to our hasLayout problem) it makes a difference to understand why these problems arise and the terms to use when describing them and locating their fixes. By understanding, we can prevent, which will save precious resources for our company in terms of man-hours and money. By being aware, at the very least, you'll know what to search for on Google.

In the next chapter we will look at some of the most popular frameworks, how and why they can be useful (or not) and what we can learn from them. We will also look at some tips on how to make your CSS more robust.

CHAPTER 4

■ ■ ■

Frameworks and Integration

When working on high-traffic websites, we want to achieve the highest possible level of efficiency and maintainability. This, in terms of CSS, means our style sheets should be flexible, robust, and as small as possible.

There are tools that we can use and directives we can follow in working toward these goals. Any seasoned developer will know that starting from scratch any time he needs to build something is usually a waste of time and resources. This is truer when working in contained teams and organizations that tend to work on projects that already have (or should have) their foundations defined.

In previous chapters, we mentioned that it is important to have guidelines in place in order to homogenize your code and processes. In the next chapter, we will look at some tips to implement branding on your website(s) and what some design concepts mean when applied to CSS. We will also look at how to build a design library that you can translate into your CSS and use modularly. It all has to do with streamlining development, empowering developers to make their own choices by providing them with general rules that make sense and that they can follow. By having a defined set of guidelines, you will also be minimizing the margin for error and for personal preference (which are less important than consistency within your team and organization) to become involved.

Another step to achieve a high level of flexibility paired with efficiency and maintainable code is to have a framework in place designed for your needs. If such a framework is built properly, it should be modular and flexible enough that you can rely on it to start any project that follows the same design guidelines as other projects within your company. We look at creating a framework from scratch in the final chapter of the book, but in this chapter we will take a look at some of the existing and most popular CSS frameworks, how they work, and the pros and cons of using them.

The scale of the projects you work on will probably mean that frequently your code will not be forever isolated or only touched by responsible hands. You will eventually introduce a new hire to it, who will not be accustomed to your processes and may accidentally break something, or you may need to integrate third-party code, completely external to your team or company.

These are all eventualities and nuisances that come with working on high-traffic and high-performance websites, but are they not what makes your job fun, too? They are challenging, but there are things you can do to make your life easier.

In this chapter, you will do the following:

- Take a look at some of the most popular CSS frameworks, including reset style sheets

- Understand the principles behind Object Oriented CSS and how it works

- See how to deal with overriding CSS files

- Get some tips on how to handle third-party code

- Understand the principles of defensive CSS

- Learn how to avoid creating fragile CSS

- See how to work with metadata in CSS

Frameworks

Any CSS author with a little experience will know that creating flexible, robust, cross-browser CSS layouts is not an easy task. Nor is it a unique task—as much as we would like to deny it, only a certain number of grid layouts can be effective on the Web. We keep using the same elements over and over and the same number of columns—admittedly, with some variations.

This repetition isn't necessarily a bad thing; as much of a cliché as it is, there is no need to reinvent the wheel (or, for the sports enthusiasts, to change a winning team), and this is why CSS frameworks have become so popular among web designers and agencies. They provide a solid structure that we can build upon, taking away some of the repetitive and menial tasks that come with coding a CSS-based layout.

By doing this, though, frameworks have to be adaptable to any kind of layout variation that any designer chooses to go with. There is a trade-off between the flexibility necessary and keeping the code clean and simple.

Frameworks tend to suffer from divitis and classitis. While *divitis* is a term that qualifies layouts that overuse the div element, *classitis* (you guessed it) applies to style sheets that abuse the use of classes.

Not only do they suffer from these maladies but frameworks also tend to bring with them all sorts of unnecessary, verbose code—like any kind of framework. Because they cater for the highest possible number of variations, we may see things like the following snippet:

Listing 4-1. Code Extract from the Blueprint CSS Framework http://www.blueprintcss.org/

```
input.span-1, textarea.span-1 { width: 18px; }
input.span-2, textarea.span-2 { width: 58px; }
input.span-3, textarea.span-3 { width: 98px; }
input.span-4, textarea.span-4 { width: 138px; }
input.span-5, textarea.span-5 { width: 178px; }
input.span-6, textarea.span-6 { width: 218px; }
input.span-7, textarea.span-7 { width: 258px; }
input.span-8, textarea.span-8 { width: 298px; }
input.span-9, textarea.span-9 { width: 338px; }
```

In the preceding example, you can see a list of classes that CSS authors can use to determine the width of form inputs. This is just a short snippet, as the framework lists 24 possible widths within 48 different classes.

When using an off-the-shelf framework, you will be left with code that you do not need. There are tools you can use in order to scan the CSS files in relation to the HTML pages that will list any rules that aren't being used by the page.

An example of one of these tools is the Firefox add-on CSS Usage (https://addons.mozilla.org/en-US/firefox/addon/css-usage/), which is also an extension of Firebug (see Figure 4-1). This add-on will add a tab to Firebug, which you can click on a page-by-page basis and that will return a list of all the CSS rules linked or embedded in the page, highlighting the ones that are not in use in red. It also shows how many occurrences of the rules that are being used are in the page.

■ **NOTE:** CSS Usage will not pick up on rules that affect dynamically created elements via JavaScript however. Although it is not 100 percent effective, it is a very useful tool.

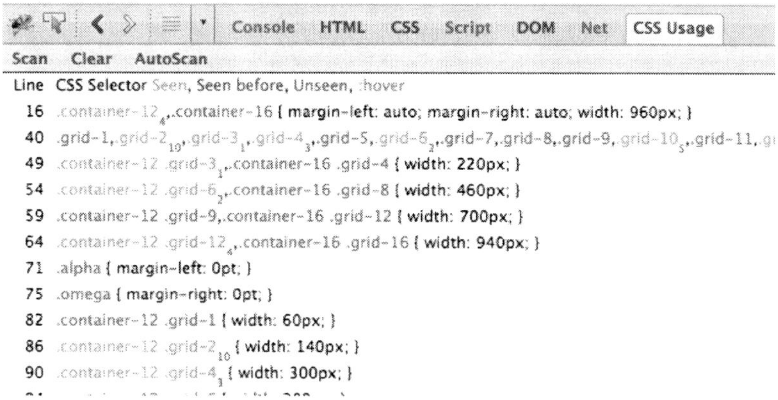

Figure 4-1. Firefox's add-on, CSS Usage, which is a Firebug extension that shows the unused selectors on a page.

These tools are not only useful for existing frameworks, but they can also be a helpful tool in determining whether your own style sheets are in need of spring cleaning.

Many CSS authors are opposed to the use of such frameworks. The main argument against them is that because of their need to be flexible, frameworks tend to use nonsemantic class naming and lend themselves to a very table-like layout approach. This happens because when coding a CSS layout using a framework, you have to visualize the layout as you would with a table, with all the nesting and spanning of cells. If you take a look at the example in Figure 4-2, which uses the same grid as in the code section in Listing 4-1, you can see an example of this table-like approach:

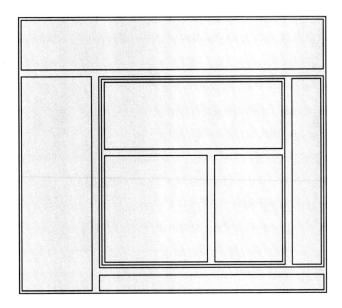

Figure 4-2. *Visualization of the necessary container elements to translate a layout into a CSS website, using a framework*

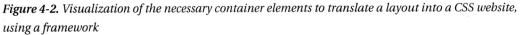

▓ **NOTE:** In the "Alternative Uses" section that follows we include a quick tutorial on how to create this layout using the Blueprint CSS framework.

One large advantage of using public frameworks is that new employees are much more likely to be familiar with and comfortable with them and therefore quicker to be productive with fewer problems and mistakes in their first projects and tasks. They are also already documented and may have a community mailing list, IRC channel, and so on.

There are a variety of CSS frameworks out there. The three better-known ones are

- Blueprint

- 960 Grid System

- YUI Grids

We will not recommend one framework over another—in fact, we think that for high-traffic websites, it is a better option to create a customized framework, even if it borrows from an existing one. We will, however, take a brief look at each of the most well-known ones.

Blueprint CSS

The Blueprint CSS framework was created by Olav Bjørkøy and released in August 2007 (see Figure 4-3). It is usually considered to be the most comprehensive CSS framework because it allows not only for the creation of grid-based layout but also provides a solid typographic foundation, considering aspects like vertical rhythm. It also provides a reset and print style sheet, and basic styling for forms.

Figure 4-3. Home page of the Blueprint CSS website (`http://www.blueprintcss.org/`)

The framework uses, by default, a 24-column layout (each column spans 30 pixels and has a right margin of 10 pixels), but you can create different layouts by using the compressor included in the files (you can find a tutorial for doing this in the official documentation `http://jdclayton.com/blueprints_compress_a_walkthrough.html`).

Using Blueprint is as easy as including a wrapper container with a class of "container", surrounding the blocks on the page. For example, depending on the width of each of the internal containers, you need to use a class of "span-24" for a div that spans across the entire width of the page or "span-8" for a block that spans across 8 columns. If the container is the last one within a particular container or column, it should also include a class of "last" (this will remove the right margin from that container because it's unnecessary). The HTML for a simple layout containing a header, sidebar, main content area, and footer would look like this:

```
<div class="container">
   <div class="span-24 last">
      Header
   </div>
   <div class="span-24 last">
```

```
    <div class="span-8">
        Sidebar
    </div>
    <div class="span-16">
        Main content
    </div>
</div>
<div class="span-24 last">
    Footer
</div>
</div>
```

One of the advantages of Blueprint is the community behind it, which is constantly creating and releasing new plugins, themes, and other tools that can be used in conjunction with the basic framework.

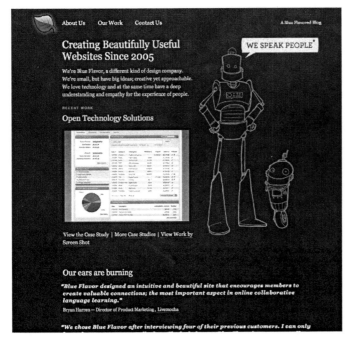

Figure 4-4. The Blue Favor website uses Blueprint (http://www.blueflavor.com/)

The core files of Blueprint (screen.css, ie.css, and print.css) add up to a total of 20 KB.

960 Grid System

The 960 Grid System CSS framework (see Figure 4-5) was developed by Nathan Smith and was released in March 2008. This framework was developed with a strong focus on the grid; even though it provides basic typographic styles, its main purpose is to deliver a cross-browser foundation (it has full A-Grade browser support.[1] You can read more about Graded Browser Support in Chapter 6) that allows for many variations on the most common grid-based layouts.

Figure 4-5. Home page of the 960 Grid System framework (`http://960.gs/`)

Following the same simple layout example that we've used to demonstrate Blueprint, we're going to create a version of it using 960 Grid System. The framework works, by default, on either a 12- or 16-column grid. We need to add a container surrounding our inner blocks with a class of "container_16" (or "container_12"); the inner containers should have classes of "grid_16", "grid_14", and so on, depending on how many columns they span. Here is the final HTML markup for our simple layout:

```
<body>
   <div class="container_16">
      <div class="grid_16">
         Header
      </div>
      <div class="grid_4">
         Sidebar
      </div>
      <div class"grid_12">
         Main content
      </div>
```

---

[1] Based on Yahoo!'s definition at `http://developer.yahoo.com/yui/articles/gbs/`.

```
        <div class="grid_16">
            Footer
        </div>
    </div>
</body>
```

As with Blueprint, there are several tools online that allow you to configure the framework to your needs (see Figure 4-6). Fluid 960 Grid System, created by Stephen Bau, is based on the original 960 Grid System, but allows for fluid and fixed layouts, and includes basic styling for elements such as navigation, tables, forms, articles, and typography.

Figure 4-6. *Home page of the Black Estate website, using the 960 Grid System framework*
(`http://blackestate.co.nz/`)

Minified, the main 960gs files (960.css and reset.css) take up 12 KB.

YUI 3 Grids

The YUI 3 Grids framework is part of the Yahoo! User Interface (YUI) Library (see Figure 4-7). The library includes JavaScript resources as well as CSS (YUI 3 CSS also incorporates reset and typography style sheets). It works in a similar way to the other frameworks presented in this chapter, with a difference: there is no predefined width for the main container; only predefined "units" in which a container can expand within another container.

Figure 4-7. *Home page of the YUI 3 Library, which includes the YUI 3 CSS (framework*
`http://developer.yahoo.com/yui/3/)`

To illustrate how YUI 3 Grids works, we will use the same example as previously. In this case, however, we need to add the desired width to the body element of our page, as such:

```
body {
    margin: auto;
    width: 960px;
}
```

The "margin: auto" property will center our content on the page. Next, as with the other frameworks, we need to include a wrapper container with the class "yui3-g." The containers within it will take class names based on the percentage of the width they should fill (or "units"). So, for example, if the sidebar takes up one-third of the total width, it should have a class of "yui3-u-1-3", and if the main content area takes up two-thirds of the total width, it should have a class of "yui3-u-2-3". YUI comes with a set of predefined unit classes (which are listed in the framework's website).

Our final example would have the following HTML:

109

```html
<body>
    <div class="yui3-g">
        <div class="yui3-u-1">
            Header
        </div>
        <div class="yui3-u-1-3">
            Sidebar
        </div>
        <div class="yui3-u-2-3">
            Main content
        </div>
        <div class="yui3-u-1">
            Footer
        </div>
    </div>
</body>
```

The minified YUI 3 Grids file takes up 4 KB. However, this includes only the grid, not text defaults or resets. The accompanying YUI Reset (mentioned in this chapter), YUI Base, and YUI Fonts are also 4 KB each (for a total of 12 KB).

Alternative Uses

One common use of CSS frameworks is in the prototyping phase, even by those who prefer not to use them in production. Because they provide a solid, cross-browser CSS solution, it's very easy to quickly create mock-ups, wireframes, and simplified versions of websites by using an existing framework.

Prototypes (which are covered in more detail in Chapter 1) by definition are made of code that we do not intend to put into production (at least, in its current state) and are written simply to create a proof of concept. With that in mind, semantics, accessibility, excessive markup, file size, and other usually vital considerations are unimportant compared with time of delivery and use of resources. It is sometimes in fact better to somehow cripple your prototype to avoid it becoming production code because it was "good enough."

Let's take the example of the basic wireframe from Figure 4-2 and translate it into HTML using the Blueprint CSS framework. The first step is to link the required CSS file in the head of the HTML document:

```html
<link rel="stylesheet" href="blueprint/screen.css" media="screen, projection" />
```

Next, we need to add a wrapper div with the class "container" in order for the container within to be targeted by the Blueprint files:

```html
<body>
        <div class="container">
        ...
        </div>
</body>
```

Our layout is composed of 8 columns; the Blueprint framework works with 24 columns by default, so we will count 3 columns for each of the ones in our wireframe. With this in mind, the top block spans across 24 columns, the left column spans 6 columns, the right side (including 5 containers) spans 18 columns, and so on.

If a container is the last one in a row, it should also have the class of "last", so the right margin is removed.

The basic structure of our wireframe should look like this:

```
<body>
    <div class="container">

        <div class="span-24">
          ...
        </div>
        <div class="span-6">
          ...
        </div>
        <div class="span-18 last">
           <div class="span-15">
              <div class="span-15 last">
                ...
              </div>
              <div class="span-9">
                ...
              </div>
              <div class="span-6 last">
                ...
              </div>
           </div>
           <div class="span-3 last">
             ...
           </div>
           <div class="span-18 last">
             ...
           </div>
        </div>
    </div>
</body>
```

The next steps are to add some simple text snippets to these containers, add a new class to the containers and reference that class in our CSS that we can use it to style the main containers further (remember, this is a simple wireframe, so for our example we have embedded this simple line of CSS directly in the HTML document::

```
<style>
        .b { background: #d4d4d4; margin-bottom: 10px; }
</style>
```

In Figure 4-8, you can see the completed wireframe.

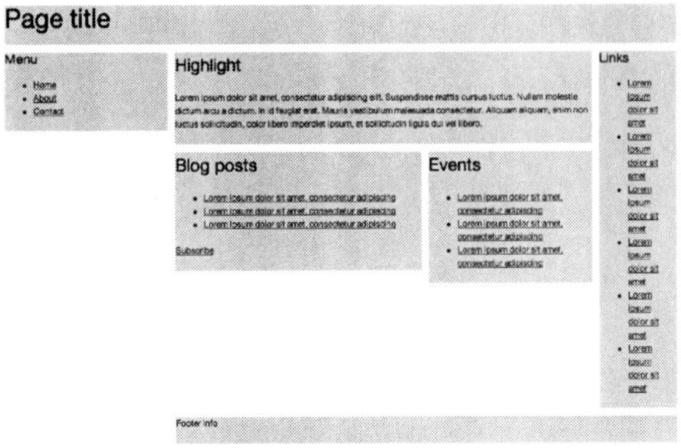

Figure 4-8. Simple wireframe created with the Blueprint CSS framework

As you can see from this simple example, existing frameworks are a useful tool to create quick wireframes and mockups (it took us less than 10 minutes from reading the Getting Started guide to creating the final product).

Reset Style Sheets

Despite the naysayers who speak against CSS frameworks, most CSS authors have always used one of its simplest forms: a reset style sheet. Each browser has a set of default styles that differs from the others in small details such as elements' margins and padding, vertical alignment, widths and heights, or font sizes (see Figure 4-9). Most recent browsers are fairly consistent in their user agent style sheets; even Internet Explorer in its latest versions (8 and 9) is quickly catching up and moving toward a similar approach.[2] To overcome the small inconsistencies that still exist though, especially in older browsers, and start from a common blank slate, authors resort to the so-called "reset style sheet."

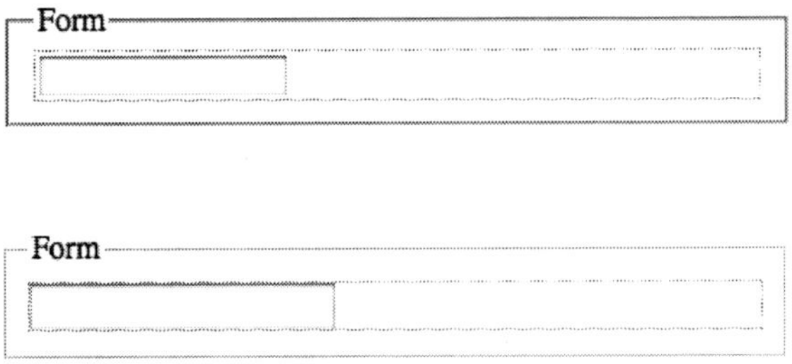

Figure 4-9. Comparison between rendering of an input element in Safari 5 (above) and Firefox 3.6 (below). Safari adds an extra margin around the element.

---

[2] You can see a comparison and evolution of the user agent style sheet in the different versions of Internet Explorer at http://www.iecss.com/.

There are advocates for and against reset style sheets. We are of the opinion that the cons listed by most can be overcome by planning and should not be a problem to an experienced and knowledgeable CSS author.

One of the drawbacks of using off-the-shelf reset style sheets is that we are not taking advantage of the browser's defaults, which we will promptly add back later in the CSS. People tend to use reset style sheets as is, without adapting them to their needs. This usually ends up with most of the rules being overwritten later in the CSS file, by ones that are more considerate to the design at hand. The lack of planning in these situations leaves us with unnecessary rules that will only make our files longer and harder to update and debug. If you want simple lists on your websites to have the default bullet, there is no reason to add a "li { list-style: none; }" rule to your reset (or base) style sheet; you should instead only style the lists that don't need bullets, like perhaps the navigation. And if the headings of your website are mainly bold, then there is also no reason to add a rule stating that they all should have a font-weight value of normal if you are going to have to override it.

Perhaps considering a reset style sheet more like a base style sheet (which many CSS authors propose) and embracing some of the browser's own defaults while creating them may be an easier way to understand the importance of having a common starting point, especially when working within a team.

The W3C has published a CSS2 default style sheet for HTML 4 which "developers are encouraged to use." It is now outdated and incomplete, but it can serve as a reference and starting point (http://www.w3.org/TR/CSS2/sample.html).

▦ **NOTE:** There is an unofficial (although based on the rendering section of the specification, which can be found at http://www.whatwg.org/specs/web-apps/current-work/multipage/rendering.html#the-css-user-agent-style-sheet-and-presentational-hints) HTML5 version of these defaults, created by Jonathan Neal (http://www.iecss.com/whatwg.css) and recommended by members of the W3C Working Group.

Let's look at a few of the more common reset methods and style sheets.

Universal Selector Reset

The universal selector reset is without a doubt the smallest of its kind. Even though it might feel like cutting off your nose to spite your face, its simplicity is irrefutable, and that benefit is paired with a saving in file size compared with other resets.

There is no simpler reset:

```
{
    margin: 0;
    padding: 0;
}
```

But can this really be considered a complete reset? After all, it only covers two properties, while there might be others that need resetting to define a consistent base cross-browser. As well as this, it will also remove margins and padding from elements that you may not want to be reset, such as form elements or tables, which you will have to override later. Consider also that the savings in file size will probably be outweighed by the fact that you will have to define margins and paddings for a lot of other elements used on your website(s) later in the file.

The universal selector is not known to impact negatively in your website's performance when used by itself (its nefarious effects occur when used in conjunction with other selectors), but it is not a refined or complete solution to overcoming browser inconsistencies.

▨ **NOTE:** Although the inefficiencies and performance implications of using the universal selector may seem obvious, performing a pure cross-browser study on this is not possible with current tools. We suggest avoiding the selector as a matter of course, but its use here is clear and pragmatic.

Eric Meyer's Reset

Eric Meyer's reset style sheet is the most popular and the one used by most CSS authors. This style sheet was originally inspired by an older version of the Yahoo! User Interface reset.css. Its main purpose is to explicitly state which elements should be reset, rather than using a catch-all selector, as the universal selector reset does.

The style sheet is carefully commented so that CSS authors do not forget that the styles should not be used right out of the box, but the truth is that many choose to ignore these comments and simply copy and paste the CSS as is. This has led to comments from people concerned that the reset (because it is so popular among developers) was hampering accessibility due to its most controversial rule: ":focus { outline: 0; }" that, in the original version, was preceded by a comment warning authors to define focus styles (which was often forgotten), but has been removed in the latest version.

Meyer has published a few versions of this reset, the latest one having been published in his blog on January 26th, 2011 (at the time of writing) at http://meyerweb.com/eric/tools/css/reset/.

```
/* http://meyerweb.com/eric/tools/css/reset/
   v2.0 | 20110126
   License: none (public domain) */
```

```css
html, body, div, span, applet, object, iframe,
h1, h2, h3, h4, h5, h6, p, blockquote, pre,
a, abbr, acronym, address, big, cite, code,
del, dfn, em, img, ins, kbd, q, s, samp,
small, strike, strong, sub, sup, tt, var,
b, u, i, center,
dl, dt, dd, ol, ul, li,
fieldset, form, label, legend,
table, caption, tbody, tfoot, thead, tr, th, td,
article, aside, canvas, details, embed,
figure, figcaption, footer, header, hgroup,
menu, nav, output, ruby, section, summary,
time, mark, audio, video {
    margin: 0;
    padding: 0;
    border: 0;
    font-size: 100%;
    font: inherit;
    vertical-align: baseline;
}
/* HTML5 display-role reset for older browsers */
article, aside, details, figcaption, figure,
footer, header, hgroup, menu, nav, section {
    display: block;
}
body {
    line-height: 1;
}
ol, ul {
    list-style: none;
}
blockquote, q {
    quotes: none;
}
blockquote:before, blockquote:after,
q:before, q:after {
    content: '';
    content: none;
}
table {
    border-collapse: collapse;
    border-spacing: 0;
}
```

This latest version of the reset, besides being more careful with the outline focus styles, also includes new HTML5 elements and removes deprecated HTML elements.

> ■ **NOTE:** In versions of Internet Explorer previous to 9 you cannot target the new HTML5 elements. To overcome this, it is necessary either to contain them within another element and target the containing element, or use a JavaScript trick known as the HTML5 Shiv to create a virtual element for each tag (without rendering it), which forces IE to notice that these tags exist. This technique was discovered by Sjoerd Visscher, made popular by John Resig and perfected by Remy Sharp at `http://remysharp.com/2009/01/07/html5-enabling-script/`. Both methods have disadvantages (the first creates superfluous markup, and the second creates a JavaScript dependency) so consider your audience before making a decision.

This is a fairly comprehensive reset style sheet, and one that we suggest you take inspiration from. We don't, however, recommend using it exactly as is (and neither does the author) because you may find yourself redefining some rules that you have previously reset—it will always depend on the needs of the design you are working on and which baseline styles you want your elements to have.

YUI 3 CSS Reset

The original YUI reset style sheet was released along with the full library in 2006. It is very precise in which elements it chooses to style and how. For example, it only removes margin and padding from block level elements and some form elements; it addresses font inheritance problems in form elements; and it adds browser-specific hacks to fix font resizing (`http://developer.yahoo.com/yui/3/cssreset/`).

Here is the commented version of the latest YUI reset (at the time of writing):

```
/*
Copyright (c) 2010, Yahoo! Inc. All rights reserved.
Code licensed under the BSD License:
http://developer.yahoo.com/yui/license.html
version: 3.3.0
build: 3167
*/
html{
    color:#000;
    background:#FFF;
}
body,div,dl,dt,dd,ul,ol,li,h1,h2,h3,h4,h5,h6,pre,code,form,fieldset,legend,input,textarea,p,bl
ockquote,th,td {
    margin:0;
    padding:0;
}
table {
    border-collapse:collapse;
    border-spacing:0;
}
fieldset,img {
    border:0;
}
address,caption,cite,code,dfn,em,strong,th,var {
```

```css
    font-style:normal;
    font-weight:normal;
}
li {
    list-style:none;
}
caption,th {
    text-align:left;
}
h1,h2,h3,h4,h5,h6 {
    font-size:100%;
    font-weight:normal;
}
q:before,q:after {
    content:'';
}
abbr,acronym {
    border:0;
    font-variant:normal;
}
/* to preserve line-height and selector appearance */
sup {
    vertical-align:text-top;
}
sub {
    vertical-align:text-bottom;
}
input,textarea,select {
    font-family:inherit;
    font-size:inherit;
    font-weight:inherit;
}
/*to enable resizing for IE*/
input,textarea,select {
    *font-size:100%;
}
/*because legend doesn't inherit in IE */
legend {
    color:#000;
}
```

Even though this reset has been refined over many years, it might not be the perfect solution for your specific problem. As mentioned earlier, you are dealing with a particular design style, and some of the rules declared in this style sheet might have to be overridden later in your code, which is not efficient.

Other Reset Examples

There are various other resets besides the ones mentioned previously, each slightly different from the other. However, they seem to have drawn inspiration from the same set of resets (mainly YUI's and Eric Meyer's) and share many of the rules and properties among them.

The Blueprint framework integrates its reset.css into the main screen.css file, but also provides a separate file in the source code folder. This is what the Blueprint reset.css looks like:

```
/* ----------------------------------------------------------------

    reset.css
    * Resets default browser CSS.

---------------------------------------------------------------- */

html {
    margin:0;
    padding:0;
    border:0;
}

body, div, span, object, iframe,
h1, h2, h3, h4, h5, h6, p, blockquote, pre,
a, abbr, acronym, address, code,
del, dfn, em, img, q, dl, dt, dd, ol, ul, li,
fieldset, form, label, legend,
table, caption, tbody, tfoot, thead, tr, th, td,
article, aside, dialog, figure, footer, header,
hgroup, nav, section {
  margin: 0;
  padding: 0;
  border: 0;
  font-weight: inherit;
  font-style: inherit;
  font-size: 100%;
  font-family: inherit;
  vertical-align: baseline;
}

/* This helps to make newer HTML5 elements behave like DIVs in older browers */
article, aside, dialog, figure, footer, header,
hgroup, nav, section {
    display:block;
}

/* Line-height should always be unitless! */
body {
  line-height: 1.5;
  background: white;
}

/* Tables still need 'cellspacing="0"' in the markup. */
table {
  border-collapse: separate;
  border-spacing: 0;
}
/* float:none prevents the span-x classes from breaking table-cell display */
```

```css
caption, th, td {
   text-align: left;
   font-weight: normal;
   float:none !important;
}
table, th, td {
   vertical-align: middle;
}

/* Remove possible quote marks (") from <q>, <blockquote>. */
blockquote:before, blockquote:after, q:before, q:after { content: ''; }
blockquote, q { quotes: "" ""; }

/* Remove annoying border on linked images. */
a img { border: none; }

/* Remember to define your own focus styles! */
:focus { outline: 0; }
```

960 Grid System's reset also draws inspiration from the same popular style sheets. Here is a formatted version of the 960.gs reset.css file (in its original version, the file is minified):

```css
html,body,div,span,applet,object,iframe,h1,h2,h3,h4,h5,h6,p,blockquote,pre,a,abbr,acronym,addr
ess,big,cite,code,del,dfn,em,font,img,ins,kbd,q,s,samp,small,strike,strong,sub,sup,tt,var,b,u,
i,center,dl,dt,dd,ol,ul,li,fieldset,form,label,legend,table,caption,tbody,tfoot,thead,tr,th,td
{
   margin:0;
   padding:0;
   border:0;
   outline:0;
   font-size:100%;
   vertical-align:baseline;
   background:transparent
}
body {
   line-height:1
}
ol,ul {
      list-style:none
}
blockquote,q {
   quotes:none
}
blockquote:before,blockquote:after,q:before,q:after {
   content:'';
   content:none
}
:focus {
   outline:0
}
ins {
   text-decoration:none
```

```
}
del {
    text-decoration:line-through
}
table {
    border-collapse:collapse;
    border-spacing:0
}
```

Starting From a Common Ground with Clever Defaults

There are dozens of different reset style sheets across the Web, some more exhaustive than others. The main idea behind a CSS reset is that it gives you a common ground across all browsers that you can build upon with confidence that inconsistencies will not come between your code and a cross-browser implementation of your designs.

When building websites that are to be visited by millions of users, it is a good idea to know that what you are creating has the right foundations and that the most unpleasant browser defaults will not creep into your less visible pages. This does not mean, however, that you should just use a reset style sheet off the shelf.

As an experienced CSS author, you should spend time thinking about which defaults you want to set for your pages; you should think about what you can use from existing style sheets and what you can learn from them, but do not forget that they exist and were created mainly for the needs of the developer who created them. Spend time customizing your base styles so that they are relevant to your websites: you want your CSS to be efficient and to avoid redundancy, so resetting everything to later add it back again is not a good idea.

Because you should always aim to minimize HTTP requests, our advice is that the reset part of your style sheets should not be treated as a separate file, but instead incorporated in your main CSS file.

Why Create Your Own Framework?

Modularity is a concept that is at the core of a flexible system of CSS files and is a goal that any team working on high-traffic websites should be aiming for.

The reason why modularity is important is that it allows for the code to be reused in different sections of the same website and in subsites from the same family. If your CSS is built with that in mind, it will be possible and easier to use snippets of code to style similar elements in different pages without breaking the existing code and without the need to embed or link to larger CSS files.

By creating your own framework, you are creating a library of code that can be reused, enhancing the efficiency of the team. A framework doesn't have to be extensive, but it should encompass elements such as basic typography and layout variations; form elements; modules that are used across a multitude of sites with small variations, such as navigation items; components such as slideshows, tooltips, or tabs; and every element that is prone to be used multiple times within one or more sites. It should also include separate style sheets for print and mobile versions of the website.

The reusability aspects that having a framework (or a CSS library) in place bring are invaluable to efficiency and file size, and allow for more coherent and robust code. Different authors have different ways of coding elements such as tabs or horizontal navigation; if there is a repository containing examples or modules that can be applied to existing style sheets that show how these elements should look and be coded, a large percentage of disparate coding styles will be eliminated.

Chapter 11 includes a step-by-step guide to creating your own CSS framework.

Object Oriented CSS

Object Oriented CSS (OOCSS) is a concept introduced by Nicole Sullivan, a front-end performance consultant. At the core of Nicole's project is the concept that CSS (especially for high-performance websites) should be approached in a modular, flexible way.

Object Oriented Programming

Object Oriented Programming (OOP) is a method of programming that breaks the code into discrete blocks (objects) and allows us to reuse them or build new blocks that inherit their properties.

As an example, we might have an object called *car*. This object has certain properties: it has doors, an engine, keys, windows, wheels, and so on. In many ways, we can consider this object similar to a template. We might use this template to create many cars. Although we are basing the cars on our basic template, they could have more specific properties; we might define the number of doors, engine size, color, make, model, and so on.

This methodology applies equally well to CSS, and it is very likely you have already used it without thinking. For example, we might have an object on our page that we think of as a *block*. For the sake of example, we'll say that a block has a green border, rounded corners, and gray background color.

```
<div class="block">I am a discrete block</div>
<div class="block">I am another discrete block</div>
```

But then, we might want some blocks to have more specific properties such as positions, widths, and so on:

```
<div class="block information">I am a discrete block</div>
<div class="block warning">I am another discrete block</div>
```

Using classes in this fashion allows us to have a base object and then make more specific objects that inherit the properties of the base object. We could even override properties of the base object by making our selectors more specific.

OOCSS

Although the term *object oriented* might be misleading—and is, in fact, the subject of many parallel discussions alongside the topic—OOCSS is a valid approach to coding our CSS.

One of the main objectives of OOCSS is to encourage the reuse of snippets of code independent of the location of the element we're trying to style—the CSS should work exactly the same anywhere: "An object should behave predictably no matter where you place it on the page, which is why Object Oriented CSS avoids location dependent styles." (http://www.stubbornella.org/content/2009/02/28/object-oriented-css-grids-on-github/).

This comes in opposition to the more sandboxed approach that teams generally have when developing their style sheets—for example, by namespacing CSS selectors, which is mentioned in more detail in Chapter 2.

The same location-agnostic principle applies in reverse: changing parts of the code shouldn't mean breaking the rest. If child elements do not need to be within a specific parent container to look right, in addition, a parent container should not be dependent on its children to render correctly on the page. Nicole sums this up as separating content from container—one of the principles of OOCSS.

In the following example, the styling rules for the container and for the heading within it are separated and reusable in other elements—the parent doesn't depend on its child to look correct and vice versa:

CSS:

```
.module {
    margin: 10px;
}
.hd {
    padding: 5px;
    color: #333333;
}
```

HTML:

```
<div class="module">
    <h1 class="hd">Title</h1>
</div>
```

The other principle recommends that the rules that control the structure of the elements (or objects) should be separated from the rules that control their skin (aesthetics). Let's look at an example:

CSS:

```
.module {
    margin: 10px;
}
.moduleSale {
    background: #efefef;
}
```

HTML:

```
<div class="module moduleSale">
    …
</div>
```

In the preceding example, we are extending a component with another class that controls its skin. Both the rule that controls the layout and the one that controls the skin can be reused independently for other components.

Abstracting repeating patterns to allow for reusability and overall modularity is a helpful approach in that you have to think about how you will structure your CSS before getting your hands dirty, based on a thorough analysis of all the elements in your designs. In OOCSS, you are encouraged to think about separate objects first and pages second; you should be able to construct any type of page using the existing modular CSS.

Not everything is an advantage when it comes to OOCSS, though. There is a compromise between having a smaller style sheet, in which redundancy is avoided at all costs, and having a bigger, class-cluttered HTML document.

Because OOCSS tries to steer clear of using element selectors—so that classes aren't limited to a particular element—it doesn't make the best use of the original markup's semantics. The cascade also isn't used to its full potential (you are, in fact, working against it) in an effort to keep away from specificity conflicts. Class-based selectors are created so that every rule has the same specificity in order to be capable of overriding (or better yet, extending) other classes.

Another weak spot of OOCSS, and the one that naysayers like to point out the most, is that its use of classes is nonsemantic.

Instead of having a class of "sidebar," taking an object-oriented approach to CSS, you would have a class of, for example, "module." This would happen because by naming it *sidebar* we are localizing it, and restricting it to a certain position on our pages—we may want to use the exact same styling for a `div` within the main content area of our site, so there needs to be flexibility in the naming. The problem is that by removing these more semantic and understandable class names, we seem to be approaching presentational classitis, which is a problem that frameworks also face, as we mentioned previously.

This problem can potentially be alleviated (to a degree) with the introduction of the new HTML5 elements, such as `header`, `footer`, and `aside`. By using these new elements, we are already indicating in the markup the basic semantic outline of the content we want to style. Of course, there will never be enough elements to indicate everything we could possibly want from a document. To be pragmatic, unless you are using class names that are very common or based on a standard (such as microformats), the semantics are more of a benefit to the developer than the user. We should strive for semantics where possible, but this is not the be-all and end-all of CSS.

OOCSS makes most sense when dealing with large websites that require flexible but robust code, and where coding practices consistency is a goal. Although we agree that it has valid strong arguments, and approve of many of the techniques that it recommends, we also feel that there should be a balance between having flexible CSS and flexible markup.

The balance between good semantics and reusable CSS is paramount to an efficient high-traffic website, and moving all the heavy lifting to the markup is not ideal. If your team is separate from the design team, you may find it very difficult to follow the processes implied by using this methodology. That said, there are many advocates of OOCSS, and you may find it appropriate for your needs.

If you're interested in reading more about OOCSS, head to `http://oocss.org/`.

Overriding CSS

The cascading nature of CSS allows us to override existing style sheets with more specific ones easily and without having to edit the original base file. This may be necessary for various reasons, such as a seasonal redesign, the need for a slightly different color scheme for each different company department, the existence of subsites that borrow from the main one, and special one-off pages that don't follow the same design patterns included in the main style sheet, to name but a few. These cases are bound to occur in large, high-traffic websites.

Usually this means that more specific CSS rules will be placed in a separate file, which will either be concatenated with the existing style sheet, placed in style tags in the head element of the particular page (causing a separation of concerns issue), or linked to the HTML document after the main style sheet, overriding it at some points (although in the last case you will be adding a costly HTTP request that will lower the performance of your website).

Overriding CSS as a complement to the main style sheet is generally the most efficient way of creating different themes and variations on a design. If your style sheets have been built in a modular and flexible fashion, they will lend themselves to being complemented by other more specific rules without the need for added redundancy to your code.

Creating new style sheets that will override the main one should, however, be avoided if the cause is a major redesign, since a big part of the CSS will be made out of excessively specific rules that are only specific because there is an older, dated style sheet that needs to be deprioritized.

When overriding CSS files, the main factor you will be dealing with is specificity. You want to be able to take advantage of what already exists, but add to it without the need for repetition. For that, it is sane to start building your main style sheets from the ground up, focusing on creating sensible defaults first, so that you don't have to repeat the same declarations for similar elements. For example, suppose that most of your unordered lists should have a particular style. The following CSS would be hard to override (we're overriding it in the final rule):

```
#homepage #highlights ul li {
    list-style-type: disc;
    margin: 0 0 1em;
}
#homepage #popular ul li {
    list-style-type:disc;
    margin: 0 0 1em;
}
#homepage #special ul li {
    list-style: none;
    margin: 0 0 1em;
    background: url(star.gif) no-repeat left center;
    padding-left: 24px;
}
```

It would be easier to do the following:

```
li {
    margin: 0 0 1em;
}
#special li {
    list-style: none;
    background: url(star.gif) no-repeat left center;
    padding-left: 24px;
}
```

If we have not changed the list-style-type value for unordered list items in our reset, now we are taking advantage of the browser defaults, which as a rule state that the list-style-type value for unordered list items is disc. We are therefore not adding that to our CSS, and since we are using the same spacing for all lists with some exceptions, it is simpler to add it as a default style for all list items and then override it as needed.

This kind of thinking and planning will produce smaller style sheets that are easier to update and to understand by developers who are not familiar with the code.

Many large websites opt for adding a class or ID to the body of the page(s) as a way of indicating which template it should be using. This is a simple and effective technique, but one that you should use carefully, since it can easily prevent you from reusing code (because you will be sandboxing parts of your code for each template, you need to make sure that what you are building for one template will not be useful for all). If taken to extremes, it can also put you on the path of repetition and of overly specific rules when a new special template or theme needs to be put in place.

For example, if your style sheet has redundant or overly specific rules, you might have to override something like this when you want to add a Christmas border to some elements of your website:

```
#home .template-12 #main .col-1 .post img.thumbnail {
    border: 1px dotted green;
}
…
```

```
#europe .template-8 aside#secondary ol li img {
    border: 1px dotted #333333;
}
```

If the IDs home and europe are added to the html or body element, there is probably not another way for a clean override from your embedded style sheets (let's avoid inline CSS). It would be a lot easier to override the following snippet:

```
img { /* You should make an effort to make this initial style as generic as possible. Maybe
you would need a class or an ID before the element selector in your case */
    border: 1px dotted black;
}
…
.post img {
    border-color: green;
}
…
#secondary img {
    border-color: #333333;
}

…


/* Christmas styles */
#christmas img,
#christmas #secondary img {
    border-color: red;
}
```

There will probably be overlaps and patterns on how the image borders work in your site, so what you are doing is making the most common scenario the default style and only adding more specificity when needed.

If taking an OOCSS approach (mentioned previously in this chapter), the modular nature of the CSS will mean that the new files and rules introduced to the cascade will tend to complement the existing ones rather than overriding them. This is basically very similar to what we have described so far in this section, with a difference that the OOCSS techniques take less advantage of the cascade, focusing mainly on classes, avoiding IDs and classes complementing each other. In this case, your CSS would probably look more like the following:

```
img {
    border: 1px dotted black;
}
…
.img-post{
    border-color: green;
}
…
.img-secondary {
    border-color: #333333;
}
…
```

```
/* Christmas styles */
#christmas img {
    border-color: red;
}
```

Because we are using classes, the `christmas` ID is powerful enough to override any number of classes.

Overriding your existing CSS rules is something that is unavoidable in large websites. This is not bad; it's just how things work. Why start from scratch when there are styles that you can use as a base, right?

Everything that we have been saying and recommending in this book (how to avoid redundancy, strive for a modular and more flexible style sheet, don't complicate things when there is no need for it, and so on) should give you good guidelines for how to avoid making your CSS more complex than necessary.

Playing Nicely with Third-Party Code

Often website developers find themselves incorporating code written by others that they have no control over. This code could be a widget, plugin, or other form of website block designed to be dropped straight into your pages. Since this code is intended for the lowest-common-denominator scenario, the author intends it to work regardless of the surrounding code—the code is often more verbose than it might be for any one particular situation. If the code includes JavaScript and CSS, there will frequently be duplication of code that already exists in the website in question. There are two primary ways to deal with this situation:

- Rewrite the CSS yourself, and opt to not include the third-party CSS.

  o This solution gives the developer the greatest control over the code served to the user. Although it may seem appealing, this method is usually not an efficient way to work. If the third-party code is updated somehow (perhaps it is being written to the page by external JavaScript) and the CSS is not, visual or functional problems may begin to occur in the website. Often the CSS will be included from a server other than your own, which means you will also somehow have to modify the code in play on your site with overrides. You should also be aware that branching from the original code leaves you unable to easily upgrade when the third party releases newer and better versions of its code. The pragmatic approach is often to accept the third-party's code and build around it. If the code is so problematic that this is not a valid approach, you should really be questioning whether this third party is a good partner for your business, and looking at alternatives or the possibility of writing your own equivalent in-house.

- Build your CSS to minimize the likelihood of conflicts in your code; then test thoroughly.

  o This is a more realistic approach, though it involves some thought ahead of time. If including third-party code is a choice that was not easily predictable, it is likely for you to be unprepared for this situation.

The first thing you can do is try to isolate the third-party code away from yours. If the third-party code is being dropped straight into your markup, you should locate it and figure out how you can target its container. If it is adding elements via JavaScript, you can watch the DOM in your web development tools (see Chapter 10) and take note of the container's details, too. If there is no container, consider adding your own. This will give you the ability to target and fix any problems if they do occur.

You could use the considerate approach where, if there are particular areas that are likely to include third-party code, you could apply a basic CSS reset to them, targeting just those blocks. Avoid using !important (which you should be doing anyway), and where using very simple element selectors, try not to namespace those so that you have the least likelihood of affecting the third-party code with higher specificity.

You could also use the suspicious approach, in which you try to have more specific selectors to avoid affording the opportunity to vague selectors on the third party's side to affect your page.

We recommend the considerate approach, although this won't be appropriate for everyone. If code external to yours is written so badly that it affects yours, it is reasonable to expect (and demand) of them that they fix the problem. If your scenario demands you use that code no matter what, and it is that bad, rewrite it yourself or test thoroughly and create more specific rules for your markup as is required.

Going to extremes, you can include another page as an iframe to completely sandbox their code from yours. We do not recommend this for any but the most dramatic and unavoidable scenarios.

Conversely, if you are writing code to be included in other people's pages, be considerate. As much as possible you should be namespacing the container (using some kind of prefix, to make your code obviously separate from the rest) so that you can select it with a specific selector and then use that as a prefix to any selectors that apply to elements within your block. Don't target elements with just the element name. You may need to apply your own reset to your block, using the namespace and the container.

Defensive CSS

When you think your code is susceptible to being broken by either internal or external developers, you want to make sure you take all measures possible to prevent it from happening. This is especially true in large websites and within large organizations with different implementations and web teams. Defensive CSS is a practice that we recommend and provide tips for throughout this book. In this section, we will recapitulate them.

There are several things that can be done to code defensively. Bear in mind that defensive CSS is not the same as creating robust CSS. Robust and efficient CSS is what we ultimately want to achieve, and defensive CSS is one of the ways of achieve it. For example, making sure our CSS does not rely entirely on the order of selectors is not necessarily defensive CSS, but it is a characteristic of a robust style sheet.

Making sure that your style sheets are properly commented and documented, especially in their more fragile spots—such as when you resort to hacks or awkward solutions to fix a problem that others might not understand and want to fix back—is a way of being a defensive CSS author. You should state the original problem, explain why you have opted for that particular solution, provide links for a website that documents the solution (if it exists), and explain what will happen in case someone edits that bit of code (we have come across several "if you edit this code, all hell will break loose" type of comments in our observations, but we recommend something more descriptive). You can read more about commenting in Chapter 2.

Another way of taking the defensive approach is to declare properties that you do not necessarily need for that particular selector, but that will prevent other selectors from overriding it. This works particularly well when used in conjunction with namespacing. In the following example, we are declaring a namespaced rule to style headings in a sidebar widget:

```
#sidebar #sb-widget h2 {
    border: 1px solid #efefef;
    font-weight: bold;
```

```
    padding: 5px 10px;
}
```

If the following less specific rule were in our style sheet, the font-color property of the sidebar widget would also be changed because it isn't stated in the initial example:

```
h2 {
    color: #dd4814;
}
```

In order to prevent this from happening, you can add the initial value of the property to the more specific rule so that it stays exactly the way you want it to:

```
#sidebar #sb-widget h2 {
    border: 1px solid #efefef;
    font-weight: bold;
    padding: 5px 10px;
    color: #1448dd;
}
...
h2 {
    color: #dd4814;
}
```

Remember that this will make this rule a lot harder to override, but it is a disadvantage that you must take into account every time you decide to namespace parts of your code.

As noted earlier in this chapter, OOCSS is another way of creating defensive CSS. To reiterate, its main principles state that parents and children elements shouldn't depend on each other to look the same wherever they are positioned on the page, and also that layout should be separate from skin. So if someone makes a change on how part of the code works (for example, the headings inside widgets), that will not mean children, parent, or surrounding elements will necessarily break.

The extreme case of defensive CSS is namespacing (covered in more detail in Chapter 2). When you namespace sections of your code, you are making sure it doesn't affect nor is affected by the rest of the code. You are isolating it by increasing its specificity so that only the exact portion of the markup that you wish to style is targeted. Nothing else is affected, so nothing else can get broken in the process. This does not mean, however, that you should use namespacing as the silver bullet to secure your code. Its disadvantages are too costly: you will be left with bloated code due to repetition and an extreme lack of reusability. This is not how a team working on high-performance websites should work.

One of the most common scenarios in which you will have to take the defensive CSS approach is when dealing with content management systems that are usually utilized by nondevelopers, where copying and pasting text from Word documents is a frequent occurrence. In these situations, our recommendation is that you should provide the content editors with classes and IDs they can hook in to, and give them example blocks of code from a design library (which we mention in more detail in Chapter 5) so that as much as possible, you have done the thinking for them and they have everything they could need.

Where their needs are not satisfied, there should be a feedback loop: a process to make them request a new design library element and any changes they make themselves (inline CSS in style attributes, style tags, and so on) must be logged and replaced by them when the element is ready. Note that we never should stop content publishers from publishing something—big companies often have time-critical announcements or changes to make—but we should always provide content editors with a way to do what they want the right way rather than letting all the rubbish CSS build up or (unrealistically) stopping them from doing their work.

Clever defaults and making sure all possible elements have at least a basic styling also help to overcome some unpredictable situations when content editors are not familiar with CSS.

There needs to be a degree of trust within your team, and you should make sure to hire the best developers possible. This is not news to anyone, but that doesn't mean that you should not try to prevent mistakes from happening. This is what defensive CSS is about. It is about taking the measures at your reach so that errors are minimized.

Fragile CSS

As opposed to *robust CSS* (which translates into flexible style sheets that can be safely handled by many hands), *fragile CSS* is CSS that breaks easily. This can happen for a variety of reasons.

One common occurrence of fragile CSS is when CSS selectors have dependencies on the content of the page. Considering that our CSS is a separate, aesthetic layer, this may sound like something that should not be a concern—after all, CSS is there to style the content no matter what it may be. What we mean by this, however, is that when building dynamic websites, where the content is in constant mutation and not necessarily (or rarely) controlled by the person who created the code, there are times when we should avoid tying in the CSS with content on the page that is more likely to be changed, or rely on the order of the DOM elements, which can also change.

For example, let's say you have a list of books; each book has a title and an image of its cover:

```
<dl id="books">
    <dt>CSS Mastery</dt>
    <dd>by Andy Budd</dd>
    <dd><img src="book-cssmastery.jpg" /></dd>

    <dt>Designing With Web Standards</dt>
    <dd>by Jeffrey Zeldman</dd>
    <dd><img src="book-webstandards.jpg" /></dd>
</dl>
```

You want to target the image for the first book so it floats to the left, and then the image for the second book so it floats to the right. You could write the following CSS:

```
#books img[src="book-cssmastery.jpg"] {
    float: left;
}
#books img[src="book-webstandards.jpg"] {
    float: right;
}
```

It will have the result you are looking for, but what happens if the file names of the images are changed? Or if you replace these books with other books? This is a good example of how tying the CSS too closely to the content of the page can produce fragile CSS.

Another solution in this case is to use an nth-of-type selector to target the specific img element:

```
#books img:nth-of-type(1) {
    float: left;
}
```

```
#books img:nth-of-type(2) {
    float: right;
}
```

Now we are only targeting the first and second image. This is a more robust solution than the first one, but it is still somewhat fragile: the CSS now is dependent on the order of the content and the amount of books in the list.

A more straightforward solution is to add a class to each img element, like so:

```
<dl id="books">
  <dt>CSS Mastery</dt>
  <dd>by Andy Budd</dd>
  <dd><img class="odd" src="book-cssmastery.jpg" /></dd>
  <dt>Designing With Web Standards</dt>
  <dd>by Jeffrey Zeldman</dd>
  <dd><img class="even" src="book-webstandards.jpg" /></dd>
</dl>
```

Now we can just use the classes in the CSS, making it a lot simpler:

```
#books img.odd {
    float: left;
}
#books img.even {
    float: right;
}
```

This solution makes it also easier to reuse these classes somewhere else or even add more books to the collection. In this particular case, we could have also resorted to using the nth-of-type selector in a different way:

```
#books img:nth-of-type(odd) {
    float: left;
}
#books img:nth-of-type(even) {
    float: right;
}
```

Now, instead of just styling the first and second instances, we are defining a style that can scale as the list grows, and that is not dependent on the any number of items or any file names. There is a downside to this technique: older browsers will not understand this CSS3 selector.

■ **NOTE:** This is an issue to which the response should be clear within your team: you should have defined whether lack of support on older browsers for more advanced CSS selectors means they are to be left alone and the rendering differences accepted, or if there should be some kind of JavaScript fallback that can replicate the effect.

It is also worth mentioning that CSS3 selectors are much more complicated to parse than their simpler counterparts, and, as such, incur more of a performance hit. Although CSS performance will rarely be the bottleneck in your website, it is best to avoid them unless they are necessary.

By not tying ourselves to the content and abstracting this bit of CSS, we can go even further into what we are continuously looking for in our style sheets and create a design pattern that can be repeatedly used throughout our pages. In this case, that would be a list in which its items show alternating styles. Rather than using an ID selector to define this list, we could have created a class with a more convenient name (that allows for repetition) that could be used multiple times within a page and within the website (if we had kept the ID of "books," and we needed to style a list called "boardGames", the name would stop being semantic):

HTML:

```
<dl id="books" class="alt">
    <dt>CSS Mastery</dt>
    <dd>by Andy Budd</dd>
    <dd><img src="book-cssmastery.jpg" /></dd>

    <dt>Designing With Web Standards</dt>
    <dd>by Jeffrey Zeldman</dd>
    <dd><img src="book-webstandards.jpg" /></dd>
</dl>
```

CSS:

```
.alt img:nth-of-type(odd) {
    float: left;
}
.alt img:nth-of-type(even) {
    float: right;
}
```

Still following on from our initial example, but now illustrating another case of non-fragile CSS, rather than relying on the full name of files, we can instead create CSS that will look for a particular portion of a file's name and style it accordingly. For example, you might want to style all links to PDF and text documents with a small icon, indicating to the user what they should expect from that link. Let's use an altered version of the example markup above:

```
<dl id="books">
    <dt>CSS Mastery</dt>
    <dd>by Andy Budd</dd>
    <dd><a href="css-mastery-sample.pdf">Download a sample of the book</a></dd>

    <dt>Designing With Web Standards</dt>
    <dd>by Jeffrey Zeldman</dd>
    <dd><a href="designing-web-standards-sample.doc">Download a sample of the book</a></dd>
</dl>
```

Using attribute selectors, you can now target links whose href attribute value ends ("$") in a particular sequence of characters, as follows:

```
a[href$=".pdf"] {
    padding-left: 20px;
    background: url(pdf-icon.gif) no-repeat left center;
}
a[href$=".doc"],
a[href$=".txt"] {
    padding-left: 20px;
    background: url(txt-icon.gif) no-repeat left center;
}
```

Once again, bear in mind that these more advanced selectors will not be understood by older browsers.

There are different levels of fragile CSS, as you saw in the preceding examples. Fragile CSS does not mean only CSS that is weakly tied in with the markup, though. It also means CSS that will break within itself, for example with selectors that are added later and that override the original ones because they are later in the file or more specific. Overlooking specificity and order, and continuously adding selectors that will override the previous ones because they come later and are more specific is doing CSS the easy way, with no respect for (or insight on) how the cascade works. It adds a layer of complexity each time the code needs to be updated and debugged, and makes the code susceptible to breaking if there are any changes in the order of selectors in the future by a developer who is distracted or simply not familiar with the house of cards that he has inherited.

The solution for this should not be to sandbox everything so that things don't break when edits occur. This will create another harmful effect for high-traffic websites: redundancy. So the solutions are manifold. As we have been recommending throughout the book, plan your style sheets so that the code can be reutilized effectively, define solid base styles for all the elements you will need, make sure there are guidelines in place for dealing with legacy elements, have a well-defined design library of reusable components, and add IDs and classes only when you have to (where the DOM is likely to change, use them).

Fragile CSS tends to be complicated CSS (although not always). One frequent behavior of experienced and knowledgeable CSS authors is to write overly complicated selectors in order to target elements without the need to touch the original markup, when adding a simple class or ID would actually provide a simpler, elegant, and more efficient solution.

Classes and IDs exist exactly for that purpose—so that we can reach elements easily—they are there to be used. As the simplest selectors they are also the fastest (IDs in particular), and when used semantically they give our markup context and intent. You should not be afraid to use them when there is a place for them. Instead of trying to be too clever, consider whether the simplest solution is not the best solution first, and avoid adding an unnecessary degree of complexity to your code that will make it less efficient and more fragile.

Metadata in CSS

Metadata can be described as data about data. The meta tags in HTML serve as great examples, providing extra information about the document such as author, description, the language the page it is in, and so on. Whereas comments are only for the developer's benefit, metadata can be parsed and used by JavaScript or search engines. The tags are agnostic to the type of data they provide in that the name and content of the data are stored within the structure itself, like so:

```
<meta name="author" content="Anna Sasin" />
```

Since you can have multiple `meta` tags, it is theoretically possible to include an infinite and unrestricted amount of information.

While HTML provides a wrapper for all of the content in the page, and our classes and IDs (hopefully) tell us something about the roles of the elements they are set against, the HTML Document Type Definition (DTD) only defines a limited number of tags and attributes. Where we have static content this is always enough information to convey everything we want to. However, where we are employing JavaScript to move things around the page or modify the Document Object Model (DOM), there is often not enough information to achieve what we need to.

For example, perhaps we have a form with a field that needs to be in a particular format. It might be an order reference code, which we know always has three alphabetical characters and then three numeric characters. Although we could use HTML5 or other methods to validate this field, we have decided (for the sake of example) that in this instance we want to use JavaScript to validate this field:

```
<input type="text" id="orderReference" />
```

With this structure, we have no understanding of how to validate this field. We need to locate this field in JavaScript and decide based upon its ID (or class) what format it should be in. What we need is the ability to add metadata to the HTML element itself. There are a few ways of achieving this. First, we can add a custom attribute to the field:

```
<input type="text" id="orderReference" datatype="orderReference" />
```

However, this immediately makes our HTML invalid because `datatype` is not a valid attribute for the `input` tag. We could use classes to hold this information:

```
<input type="text" id="orderReference" class="dataTypeOrderReference" />
```

This only gives us Boolean values (`true` if the class is present or `false` if not) though, and if we wanted more complex values they would be difficult to represent.[3]

JavaScript has a method of storing information known as JavaScript Object Notation (JSON), which makes it very easy to present lots of information in a concise and versatile fashion. For this example, it would look something like this:

```
{dataType:'orderCode'}
```

If we put this information in the class, our HTML will still validate, we have the ability to represent complex data, and unless we have very obscurely named classes defined in our CSS there should never be any conflicts:

```
<input type="text" id="orderCode" class="{dataType:'orderCode'}" />
```

Although it feels semantically incorrect, the benefits of this technique outweigh the downsides.

---

[3] You could also create a custom DTD yourself for HTML or use a specific namespace with XHTML, but both of these options are not for the faint of heart, and neither guarantees a validating document.

TIP: If you are using HTML5 as your doctype, you have a solution to this problem in the form of data- attributes. By prefixing an attribute with data- we can represent as many extra fields as we want, like so:

```
<input type="text" id="orderCode" data-datatype="orderCode" data-errortext="Please enter a
valid order code." />
```

However, this method considers all values to be strings (groups of characters) and would make it difficult to represent other data types, such as numbers or Boolean values.

Another issue we may have is the error we want to display. We can include this in the HTML, and use CSS to hide it:

```
<input type="text" id="orderCode" class="{dataType:'orderCode'}" />
<div class="error hidden">Please enter a  valid order code.</div>
```

Anyone with CSS disabled for some reason, or using a device that does not support CSS (text-only browsers such as Lynx (http://lynx.browser.org), older browsers, some screen readers, search engine spiders, and so on) will still see this text. It shouldn't really exist in our HTML until we want to display it. If we include this information within our JSON structure, though, the JavaScript has everything it needs to display the error:

```
<input type="text" id="orderCode" class="{dataType:'orderCode',errorText:'Please enter a valid
order code.'}" />
```

This is a powerful and genuinely extensible method of adding extra information to our tags without invalidating our code, although it creates a JavaScript dependency and you should still use server-side validation, too.

A plugin for the popular jQuery library exists to make it easier to get to the data at http://plugins.jquery.com/project/metadata. The syntax is easy. Once you have included the jQuery library and the metadata plugin—as well as the previous HTML snippet—this code will create an alert dialog box, with the text "Please enter a valid order code":

```
alert($("orderCode").metadata().errorText);
```

You can read about more accessible ways to achieve the same thing in Chapter 6. You could also write your own parser to get at these values. If the user has disabled JavaScript, we can degrade gracefully and handle the error server-side, reloading the page with a visible error message.

Summary

In this chapter, we looked at how existing frameworks work, what we can learn from them, and where they fail. The flexibility and efficiency that having a framework in place provides is invaluable to any team working on a high-traffic website and should not be underestimated.

Besides frameworks, there are also other principles and coding practices that you can put in place that will not only mean your code should be less prone to errors but also less susceptible of being broken by either internal or external developers or code.

CSS, when composed carefully, can be clean but also robust and adaptable. Because it is not going to be quarantined forever, you should plan for the fact that it will interact with other code, with other developers, and even within itself.

In the next chapter, we will look at the importance of brand guidelines and how to work with them.

CHAPTER 5

■ ■ ■

Brand Implementation

Everyone knows that, online, our competition is just one click away. The average user's attention span is getting shorter quickly.[1] It is easy then to come to the conclusion that even though the typical user of your website may be slightly more engaged, you should make sure that the website has an impact and that the brand experience is translated to the Web correctly.

The brand will always affect how the website is handled: how it is designed, the tone of voice it uses—basically, how it conveys the brand message across the online medium. Making sure this is done correctly tends to be a competence attributed to marketing and design teams.

Even though web design and development teams don't usually work directly on the building of the brand, they face the challenge of implementing it on the Web. They often also face the challenge of letting marketing teams know what is and isn't possible to do online, why there are some conventions (and when they should and shouldn't be broken), and why the Web should be regarded as something organically different from print, rather than a medium that merely follows whatever it is dictated should be done by the visual identity guide for print.

Since the subject of this book is CSS, we will be covering mainly the aesthetic aspects of brand implementation. Areas such as brand culture, dealing with customer feedback, handling forms and error messages, or developing and keeping the correct tone of voice are all issues that wouldn't fall within the CSS realm (but that we would hope you are considering).

This chapter does not go into detail on how to develop a visual brand. Rather, it assumes that there is an existing brand, and branding guidelines are already in place. It focuses on how to overcome some of the difficulties in implementing these guidelines in an efficient manner. It covers

- What a brand is

- Working with brand style guides and design libraries

- Dealing with typography on the Web

- Efficient ways of working with color

- Keeping layouts consistent

- Handling theme variations

- Brand evolution

---

[1] Ron Kohavi and Roger Longbotham's 2007 article "Online Experiments: Lessons Learned"—published by The IEEE Computer Society—stated that on Amazon.com every 10-millisecond increase in page load time resulted in a 1 percent decrease in sales, and a 500-millisecond increase in Google's search results display time caused a 20 percent revenue decrease.

What Is a Brand?

A brand is often regarded as the most important asset of a company, product, or service—it is what distinguishes it from its competitors. But we should not confuse brand with merely the logo that identifies it. The brand can encompass attributes such as the following:

- Name, logo, tagline

- Colors, typography, imagery

- Tone of voice

- Values and mission

- Customer and feedback handling

- In-store experience

- Etc.

Basically, it involves everything that can be related to the way that the company (be it a product, service, or organization) is perceived; the message that it conveys to the outside world and within itself, to its employees.

There are various types of brands, but the three main groups are as follows:

- *Umbrella brands*: These brands are used across various products and services within the organization, and are used both internally and externally. For example, Amazon is the umbrella brand for Amazon Marketplace, Amazon MP3, Amazon S3, Amazon Mechanical Turk, and so on.

- *Sub-brands*: These brands, even though promoted individually, are associated with an umbrella brand in order to inherit and build upon the umbrella brand's reputation. For example, Kit Kat, Aero, and Smarties are sub-brands of Nestlé.

- *Individual brands*: These brands are marketed completely separately from their umbrella brands. For example, the individual brands Schweppes, Sprite, and Dr Pepper are all made by Coca Cola, but they are marketed without mention of their umbrella brand.

The reason that it's a good idea to be familiar with these terms (that fall under the discipline of Brand Architecture) is that when working with corporate brands, this organization often reflects how sub- and minisites will be designed and developed, and how the branding will be implemented across them.

Brand Style Guides

There are different types of branding style guides. Some cover merely the visual aspects of the brand, like logo usage, typography, colors, etc., while others go deeper into the brand culture and talk about values, work processes, or how to handle customers in different situations, among a variety of different subjects.

Style guides are more often than would be desired developed with print media in mind. This happens mostly when the guide was not developed recently, although shockingly some guides that are produced now still fail to provide reference on how to handle the brand online.

What happens when the Web isn't catered for in a style guide is that marketing teams and managers try to enforce rules that have been developed for print media. This causes all sorts of problems.

One of the best examples is trying to force website pages to behave exactly like their print counterparts. Whereas pages designed for print are static and don't change after being printed, online pages can suffer from a variety of alterations applied either by content teams or the user. Long articles can influence the height of the page, smaller or larger screen sizes will introduce (or remove) the need for scrolling, just as user style sheets can make the text larger or smaller, also influencing the page layout and flow. Not to mention the fact that browsers render fonts differently and demonstrate different anti-aliasing behaviors. There is no way to be sure your users will see exactly what you intend them to.

This doesn't mean there isn't a degree of control when designing and coding online pages, but these are just a few examples of how visual guides that have been created exclusively for print formats will make it harder for the departments that don't deal directly with the Web (or not on a daily basis, at least) to understand how to adapt the brand to it in an organic and integrated way.

Besides having a single person in the organization whose job is to verify branding consistency (a role usually attributed to a Brand Manager), it is beneficial that all employees are educated about what the brand should convey. This shouldn't just be relegated to customer facing roles and marketing departments, since people within other areas of the organization are also faced with making daily decisions that will affect the brand recognition.

For example, if a website fails to accommodate font size changes, the whole experience will be spoiled for users who have visual impairments and need to be using larger fonts. Or if a new page needs to be added to the website and its design doesn't represent the brand properly, the visitor may feel he or she is not on the same website and become compelled to leave or lose trust and goodwill toward the site.

Developers may not always be comfortable dealing with design aspects that will influence the brand consistency. Often front-end developers and web designers are different elements on a team (or on completely separate teams—sometimes not even in the same building or country), and there are moments when the front-end developers are faced with having to make design decisions that they might not be comfortable with. Flexible and adaptable brand guidelines should be in place for situations like these, ensuring consistency across the websites and ensuring the brand is not diluted as more and more hands fiddle with the style sheets or add new elements.

A comprehensive brand guideline document for the Web should include the following:

- Information about the underlying grid, its variations and how to use it

- Typographical information: preferred fonts, fallbacks, and scaling information

- Color palettes (translated into Web formats such as hexadecimal or RGBA) and how they should be used

- Measurements in web-friendly units, such as pixels, ems, or percentages

- Specifications for common and reusable elements, such as navigation, buttons, widgets, forms, notifications, and so on.

It is also useful to mention in this document what is and is not acceptable to look different in different browsers. For example, it might state that the company's logo and main calls-to-action must always look the same, regardless of whether a PNG or other format is employed, so that the necessary measures are taken to ensure that this happens.

Even the most thorough branding style guide can't anticipate everything. It is inevitable that developers will make design decisions at some stages. Although front-end developers are not usually required to have a design background, understanding the fundamental principles of how design works will make moments where design decisions fall into their hands a lot easier and more clear. For the diligent ones, we recommend Mark Boulton's *A Practical Guide to Designing for the Web* (`http://fivesimplesteps.com/books/practical-guide-designing-for-the-web`), part of the Five Simple

Steps series. This book is great for those with no design background and who want practical examples and a good understanding of the basics.

Guidelines Evolve

Because large websites are in constant mutation and expansion, it isn't rare for new elements to be introduced, new widgets designed, new palettes created for new sections, and so on. As the design evolves and grows, the guidelines should follow in its footsteps. The main aim of a brand style guide in the first place is to ensure consistency; by adding more and more different elements to a central reference that designers and developers can refer to. In order to be sure that they are not reinventing what someone else has already defined, the guidelines need to be kept up-to-date.

If a new standard for creating tertiary navigation is implemented in one of the main websites, it should be used as a reference when the next website has it applied. The way to keep this document updated is probably more complex than actually coming up with more patterns. Even though an internal wiki is usually the simplest setup (especially for technical staff, who are familiar with using wikis), design and marketing teams might not be comfortable managing them.

Whichever the technology used for this purpose, the most important thing is to make sure that the guidelines are updated regularly (this may be weekly, monthly or even less frequent, depending on the speed with which new guidelines are being generated) and stored in a central location that can be easily accessed by everyone involved; the benefit of everyone using one system is immense. It is also important that someone (or a team) takes ownership and oversees this repository, so that there are no duplicates, and no new elements whose differences from existing ones are imperceptible—if every new element designed generates a new standard, there will be no standard.

Design Libraries

For large websites, the process of adding new standards to guidelines will most likely (and should) result in the creation of a design library, where all the patterns are stored as snippets (images, HTML, and CSS). Adding new patterns to the library shouldn't be easy, though—as mentioned previously, most of the time it's more sensible to reuse an existing element rather than add a new design to the library. If someone feels the need to do so, they should justify it and make sure nothing that has been created so far fits the requirements. This means there is visual control of the branding and design, and everything stays consistent. It also means the CSS doesn't get out of hand, which makes everyone's life easier: fewer lines of code, less redundancy, more flexibility, and easier to maintain. However, this also means the elements that are introduced to the library need to be flexible enough that they can be injected into a variety of places in the websites and work as expected.

Imagine that in your websites you use three different styles of list boxes: simple box, double box, and tabbed box (see Figure 5-1).

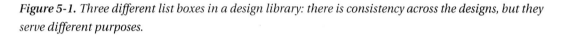

Figure 5-1. Three different list boxes in a design library: there is consistency across the designs, but they serve different purposes.

The design clearly follows a basic template, but there are three different variations depending on how prominent we need the box to be or the type of content it holds. For each of these boxes we provide the HTML, so different content or development teams can use the same code (this could even be supplied as a template file or a file that can be included so that changing the markup in one place changes it everywhere). The goal here is to make the HTML as similar as possible between the boxes (for example, clearly you will need different markup for the headings in the simple box and the tabbed box, but the double box doesn't need an extra element for the inner background color, you can use the list within the container).

The HTML for these boxes would look something like this:

```
<div class="box">
    <h2>Heading</h2>
    <ol>
        <li>
            <p class="content">Lorem ipsum…</p>
            <p class="info">13 January 2011</p>
        </li>
        <li>
            <p class="content">Curabitur…</p>
            <p class="info">28 December 2010</p>
        </li>
    </ol>
</div>
```

To switch between the styles of boxes, we would just add another class to the box container.[2]

The CSS for this HTML snippet does not need to be provided, since we can be sure it exists in the CSS for the site already, but image examples should show how the boxes cope with different types of

---

[2] For the tabbed boxes, we would add a class (e.g. "tab") to the box container and repeat it for each tab, wrapping all the divs in a container with a class (of "tabbed," for example), and use JavaScript to rewrite the DOM later. This way our code still makes semantic sense for users with JavaScript disabled.

content and how they behave in different positions in the pages. It would also be useful to provide Photoshop, Illustrator, or other layered artwork files that designers can copy and paste in their designs. This saves on the effort it takes to create new designs and ensures consistency between them.

It is clear that having a design library for this type of situation will save a lot of time that would be wasted in tasks such as going through existing pages of the website trying to find something that resembles the type of box we need, asking designers to come up with solutions that are already in place but aren't easily discoverable (resulting in many designs that are similar, but not exactly the same), or going through hundreds of lines of CSS to copy and adapt something that is only marginally different from another half a dozen solutions that already exist, adding redundancy and reducing flexibility.

These principles are very much in tune with what Object Oriented CSS (OOCSS) promotes: flexible CSS by the means of reusable classes, avoiding redundancy and reducing file size. This is a modular approach to CSS where each module can be placed anywhere in the markup and it will work correctly, adapting itself to its position with no dependencies on certain parents or children to obtain its characteristics. You can read more about OOCSS in Chapter 4.

■ **TIP:** *Modular Web Design*, by Nathan A. Curtis (`http://www.amazon.com/Modular-Web-Design-Components-Documentation/dp/0321601351`) is a great resource to draw upon when authoring your own design library.

Typography

Branding guidelines should provide CSS authors with the basics for consistent typography across the websites. Apart from the obvious type choice, they should state details such as `font-size` and `line-height`, `font-weight`, margins and padding, and color.

Without entering the domain of design, it is important that headings, body copy, lists, quotations, and so on have a clear hierarchy, and the brand guidelines should be created with this in mind.

There are legal implications in using fonts online. Fonts are licensed and not bought, and every font foundry has its own rules. The kind of license you have dictates where you can use them. Using Adobe as an example, it states that OpenType fonts can have four different categories for permission setting when embedding them in documents:

- *No Embedding*: These fonts cannot be shared with unlicensed users under any circumstances. This is the most restrictive form of licensing.

- *Preview & Print*: Fonts with this licensing scheme can be embedded in an electronic document in a read-only fashion, for example, in a PDF file.

- *Editable*: Fonts licensed in this fashion can be embedded in electronic documents for viewing, printing, or editing; and any changes can be saved in the initial document. The fonts cannot be exported from the document or installed on the (unlicensed) end user's machine.

- *Installable*: These fonts can be freely installed permanently upon users' computers.

Since using font files on the Web requires them to be (temporarily) installed on the user's computer via their local cache, the *Installable* type of license is the only one that is 100 percent safe to use. This precludes many fonts from being used in this fashion. Some font foundries offer fonts of this kind, but in a large organization it is likely the font used is licensed to the organization and therefore not suitable for distribution in this fashion.

Adobe provides more detail about its permissions at `http://www.adobe.com/type/browser/info/embedding.html` and provides a list of its fonts and licensing details at `http://www.adobe.com/type/browser/legal/embeddingeula.html`. If the font foundry that licenses your font does not have a similar list on its website, it is important to contact them to understand the licensing restrictions they impose. If you distribute fonts without the correct license, your company will be liable.

However, alternative methods of embedding fonts in web pages *can* use the *Preview & Print* license, as long as only a subset of the characters available is used. This is how sIFR (Scalable Inman Flash Replacement) can legally represent these images on web pages. As long as the entire character set of a font is unavailable, it's okay for fonts licensed in this way to be displayed on a web page.

Image Replacement versus Flexibility

On large websites that might have the need for internationalization and that suffer constant updates and additions, avoiding the use of images as a means to using custom fonts is paramount—today a lot is possible using just CSS (and we are not only referring to CSS3, but also to CSS2.1). More than that (particularly for links) text is seen by search engines to have greater value than `alt` attributes.

Although crucial elements like the logo, banners, or main headings may benefit from the use of the custom corporate font that your organization is using, you might want to think twice about using images for text on buttons, navigation, or normal headings.

This doesn't mean, however, that using fonts other than the typical web-safe ones (for example, Arial or Verdana) is out of the question. With the advent of `font-face` and the web services that it brings with it (explained further in the next section), serving custom typefaces to users across an assortment of platforms is an increasingly simple task.

The old way of replacing images is achieved with background images and a high negative `text-indent` value, to hide the original text off-screen. For example:

```
h2 {
    background: url(heading.png) no-repeat;
    text-indent: -1000px;
    height: 30px;
}
```

There are some disadvantages to using this method: users with CSS enabled but images disabled would see neither the text nor the background image replacement (leaving the text behind the image is not an option where the image is a transparent PNG), the image file slows the speed of the page, text is not selectable or scalable, and it is not easy to maintain.

Some variations of this technique include, for example, adding an extra element around the text, which is then hidden via CSS using `display: none` (or `visibility: hidden`). None of the techniques is perfect; each shows a combination of one or more problems such as the CSS on/images off scenario, making text invisible to screen readers or requiring superfluous HTML elements.

Another player in the image replacement field is Adobe's Scene7. It is typically used by large organizations as an automated way of creating headlines or images with custom text.

The other options for serving custom fonts are usually pared down to either Cufón or sIFR.

Cufón relies on JavaScript to work and even though it allows for text to be selected, there is no clear visual indication of it; sIFR relies on Flash to work, which makes it inappropriate for devices such as the iPhone or iPad, or in browsers that use Flash-blocking plugins. Both of these technologies also allow CSS authors to embed fonts whose distributing license doesn't permit them to be used online.

Cufón uses the HTML5 canvas tag (or VML in Internet Explorer). One of its main advantages over sIFR is its more straightforward implementation and font conversion process (you can do it directly on the project's website: http://cufon.shoqolate.com/generate/). After uploading the font to the generator and specifying the characters you require (which will result in a reduced character set), all you need to do is link to the Cufón script and to the generated JavaScript file that contains the font outline:

```
<script src="cufon-yui.js"></script>
<script src="LillyRegular.js"></script>
```

Then you need to call the JavaScript function for the bits of text you want to use Cufón on. For example:

```
<script>
        Cufon.replace('h1');
</script>
```

You can also lock your generated JavaScript representation of the font to particular domains, so that it can't be easily downloaded and used by third parties. There is an option to do this in the generator.

Both of these methods are accessible because they can be read by screen readers (which makes it at the same time SEO-friendly). However, Cufón wraps every word in a span that can cause some screen readers to announce each word as if it were an entire sentence, or worse, to only announce the first word in each instance.[3]

Unfortunately, Cufón will not resize the generated text when the user changes the font size in their browser; sIFR has been able to cope with this since version 3.

sIFR's biggest disadvantage is that it uses Flash (on top of JavaScript): as mentioned previously, Flash is blocked or unavailable on some devices, so people browsing your website with them will see the next available font in your font stack. Also CSS authors in your team may not necessarily have the tools to author Flash files at hand to create new text (even though there are plugins available to make this process automated, like the jQuery sIFR plugin). Both of these methods will introduce a Flash of Unstyled Text (FOUT) as they execute. We will describe this issue later in this chapter.

Scalable Vector Graphics (SVG) can also embed fonts and are scalable (unlike regular images).[4]

All these methods can be considered to be font embedding, but the legalities vary from font to font. If the End User Licensing Agreement (EULA) for the font you want to use is unclear, we strongly recommend you contact the font foundry directly to check and see what you are allowed to do with the font. Legally, sIFR is a safer option than Cufón, as Adobe Flash is allowed to embed fonts, and many type foundries cater for this scenario on their EULAs. Cufón embeds the fonts on the website, which is in violation of many font EULAs.

Both Cufón and sIFR are supported by Internet Explorer 6. Even though you can automate the way these two technologies work, they will invariably consume resources and add dependencies to your website. Cleaner methods such as font-face (mentioned in the next section) should always be considered first as the ideal solution. Image replacement is not recommended other than for small portions of text such as headings.

---

[3] If you set the "separate" option to "none" this problem is alleviated. However, the reason Cufón does this is so that it can wrap text onto the next line. Fixing the first problem reintroduces the second.

[4] We do not recommend SVG as a text replacement technique, since it is not supported by versions of Internet Explorer earlier than 9. You can fake it with SVGWeb (http://code.google.com/p/svgweb/), but that uses Flash, so you may as well be using sIFR.

When creating branding guidelines for the Web, it is important to take these factors into account. If these difficulties haven't been catered for, and the websites need to rely on image replacement for non–web-safe fonts, perhaps now is the right time to update the guidelines.

Font-face

The @font-face rule was introduced in CSS3 and allows CSS authors to link to fonts that they can then refer to within the style sheet. Internet Explorer was the first browser to add support for this rule from version 4 (supporting only its proprietary format, EOT, however).

■ **NOTE:** *Embedded OpenType (EOT)* is a proprietary font format created by Microsoft for embedding fonts on the Web. The process of converting fonts into the EOT format is notoriously painful, with Microsoft's Web Embedding Fonts Tool (WEFT) being commonly described as nothing far from torture by most web designers. Luckily, these days there are other tools to achieve similar results, such as Font Squirrel's @font-face Kit Generator (mentioned later in this chapter).

At the time of writing, Internet Explorer Platform Previews have shown support for the WOFF[5] format.

Inside an @font-face rule, various descriptors can provide information like the name that will be used to refer to the font later in the file (font-family; but be aware that IE does not support names that are longer than 31 characters), where the font file is located and its format (src), or the font's style and weight (font-style and font-weight). Here is an example of an @font-face rule:

```
@font-face {
    font-family: "Lilly";
    src: url("fonts/lilly.eot");
    src: local("LillyRegular"), url("fonts/lilly.woff") format ("woff"), url("fonts/lilly.ttf")
format("truetype"), url(" fonts/lilly.svg#LillyRegular") format("svg");
}
@font-face {
    font-family: "LillyItalic";
    src: url("fonts/lilly-italic.eot");
    src: local("LillyItalic"), url("fonts/lilly-italic.woff") format ("woff"),
url("fonts/lilly-italic.ttf") format("truetype"), url("fonts/lilly-italic.svg#LillyItalic")
format("svg");
}
```

---

[5] The WOFF font format was developed by the Mozilla Foundation alongside font designers Erik van Blokland and Tal Leming, and is in the process of becoming the standard recommendation by the W3C (after being submitted by Microsoft, Mozilla, and Opera). WOFF was developed with the Web in mind. It is a compressed font format that basically repackages font data; other formats like TrueType or OpenType can be converted to WOFF, and metadata such as font licensing information can be attached to the file. Many of the font foundries support WOFF, as they believe it to be more secure, so it is likely that more and more commercial fonts will be licensed to use via font-face with WOFF.

The @font-face rule links to five different file locations because different browsers support different font file formats. The "local" reference is to provide the ability for the style sheet to use the local version of the font if it is installed in the user's system. Notice also that we need to declare two different @font-face rules in order to have a regular and italic version of the same font. We could have instead used the font-style descriptor to declare the italic variation, maintaining the same font-family name, but Internet Explorer and Opera (prior to version 10.5) would fail to understand it properly.

Internet Explorer has a few problems understanding some of the @font-face rule syntax. It doesn't understand the format() hint or multiple locations, and it tries to download non-EOT files even though it cannot read them. That's why we link to the EOT format in a separate declaration (followed by a local() src descriptor, which it doesn't parse).

When adding local font names, make sure to state the Postscript version (if it differs from the full name), so that Safari on OS X can understand it.

Another important factor to take into consideration is that in Firefox (Gecko), font files have to be served from the same domain as the page using them. This can be circumvented by HTTP access controls allowing cross-site HTTP requests.[6]

Firefox supports TrueType and OpenType formats (from 3.5), while version 3.6 added support for WOFF; WebKit (since version 525) and Opera (since version 10.0) support TrueType and OpenType, as well as SVG fonts; Opera 11 and above support WOFF; Chrome also supports WOFF since version 5; Internet Explorer has supported the @font-face rule since version 4, although it only accepts EOT fonts.

■ **TIP:** Font Squirrel provides an automated "@font-face Kit Generator" that makes it easier to convert font files into different formats (`http://www.fontsquirrel.com/fontface/generator`).

There is a known problem with font permissions and having font managers installed in your system, which can cause unexpected characters to appear when the @font-face rule tries to use local fonts. To avoid this problem, Paul Irish has proposed a revised rule, one that makes the browser ignore the local() reference, forcing it to download the linked fonts:

```
@font-face {
    font-family: "Lilly";
    src: url("fonts/lilly.eot");
    src: local("☺"), url("fonts/lilly.woff ") format ("woff"), url("fonts/lilly.ttf")
format("truetype"), url("fonts/lilly.svg#LillyRegular") format("svg");
}
```

By using a character that is unlikely to be used as a real font name, this syntax avoids any issues that might arise from the user having software like FontExplorer X installed in their computer, but might force an unnecessary download.

---

[6] Read more about this at `http://openfontlibrary.org/wiki/Web_Font_linking_and_Cross-Origin_Resource_Sharing`.

■ **CAUTION:** Each browser has its own list of issues that need to be bypassed when working with font-face. Paul Irish has documented some of them in two posts that are frequently updated and that have had contributions from several developers at `http://paulirish.com/2009/bulletproof-font-face-implementation-syntax/` and `http://paulirish.com/2010/font-face-gotchas/`.

While `font-face` allows a lot of flexibility in designing websites, font licensing needs to be considered before using just any font at all. There are also bandwidth issues that should be taken into account, as font files tend to be quite large—although this can be combated by using reduced character sets and gzipping the font files (with the exception of WOFF, which is already a compressed format), as well as the fact that fonts are very cacheable.

■ **CAUTION:** If you need to support many languages, font files can get big very quickly. To support all known languages, the font needs to support glyphs numbering into the tens of thousands.

A number of online services now provide designers with large font libraries and make it easy to embed them in websites (see Figure 5-2). This may be an option, but you need to remember that these services need to be continually renewed and paid for as a subscription service, and you will be relying on someone else's servers and their uptime.

Figure 5-2. Typekit (above) and Fontdeck (below) are two online services that allow you to use font-face in your sites while providing the hosting and making sure all fonts are licensed to be used online.

■ **CAUTION:** To protect its fonts, TypeKit uses JavaScript, which creates a JavaScript dependency. Fontdeck uses a pure CSS solution to provide its fonts.

Free services like Font Squirrel have libraries of fonts that are free to use (see Figure 5-3). Usually you have to download the actual font files and host them yourself. Font Squirrel supplies an assortment of font formats to accommodate every browser (EOT, WOFF, SVG, and so on).

Figure 5-3. Font Squirrel has a large library of free fonts for commercial use.

Using custom embedded fonts is better than using images, but you need to be prepared for them to fail in some browsers, and you need to be aware that the legalities may not make this a feasible option for you or your organization. It also effectively makes the font publicly available, and it is pedestrian for third parties to download and use this font in any way they see fit, which many companies who are protective of their brand are uncomfortable with.

Fallback Fonts

CSS authors must anticipate that not every user will have the optimal font installed on their systems. This involves making sure that the style sheets include appropriate fallback fonts and also verifying if the layout of the website is flexible to accommodate variations in font sizes (some fonts may be larger than the optimal font and may break the layout if this isn't taken into account).

When choosing fallback fonts, one shouldn't simply pick fonts based on whether they are serif or sans serif. You should consider factors like whether or not the fallback font has an aspect ratio similar to the preferred font or not. An easy trick to determine whether a font is an appropriate substitute is to overlay words that use the different font options and check whether the height, width, and weight are similar enough to the optimal one. You can easily do this in a program like Photoshop or Fireworks (see Figure 5-4).

Figure 5-4. As you can see in the image, Chaparral Pro (dark gray) finds a better fallback in Times New Roman (right, light gray) than Georgia (left, light gray), although not perfect.

Making sure that the fallback fonts are similar to the preferred one is especially important when working with font-face related technologies, like Typekit or Fontdeck, mentioned previously. When using these, web pages will usually experience a delay in downloading and serving the correct font to the browser, showing, for a brief moment, the next available font. When this font is different in size and proportion from the one served by the font-face service, the contents on the page will jump, and the text flow will be rearranged, which can be disturbing for the users, particularly if they have a slow connection, or if they have reading and learning impairments, such as dyslexia. This is called a Flash of Unstyled Text (or FOUT), the font-specific version of the Flash of Unstyled Content (FOUC), which occurs when you can see the unstyled HTML of a website, before the CSS loads, or before JavaScript modifies the DOM.

The font-size-adjust property can minimize this, not only for when you are using font-face services and experience the jump but also when the user simply doesn't have the preferred font installed in the system or font-face is not in place. This property allows you to retain the aspect ratio of the preferred font if one of the fallback fonts is used. Let's take the following CSS:

```
p {
    font-family: Calibri, "Lucida Sans", Verdana, sans-serif;
    font-size-adjust: 0.47;
}
```

The `font-size-adjust` value will be divided by the original `font-size` value of the fallback fonts, preserving the x-height of the preferred font in the fallback ones. In the preceding example, if Lucida Sans, Verdana, or the default system sans serif font are used, in order for Calibri's aspect ratio to be preserved, their `font-size` will be divided by 0.47.

■ **TIP:** Some recommended font stacks can be found at `http://www.awayback.com/revised-font-stack/`.

Units

Text can be set in various different unit types on the Web, and much has been said on the old pixels versus ems[7] debate. The two main advantages of setting text in pixels meet the needs of designers and developers: we have more control over the design and we don't need to perform complicated calculations to determine font sizes. The disadvantage falls completely in the user's domain: some browsers don't support font resizing on text that has been set using pixels. From this, it should be easy to deduce which are the pros and cons of using more flexible units like ems or percentages. (We go deeper into the subject of units in Chapter 6.)

While most new browsers (even Internet Explorer 7) allow the user to zoom in to (and out of) the entire page, he or she might want to zoom the text only. Some browsers (like IE 6 to 9) will ignore this user setting if the text has been set in pixels. Zooming in on the entire page may also cause the browser to display horizontal bars on wider sites, which can be rather annoying since it restricts the user's viewport in ways website designers don't consider, and might make content nonsensical if it results in its being cropped. A surprising number of people choose to zoom or adjust their font size, be it because they have some kind of visual or cognitive impairment or unusual screen size or resolution.

Whether you decide to use pixels, ems, or other unit measures in your sites, the guidelines will need to reflect that. It is the job of the designer (or team of designers) that produces the guide to determine which are the best scales and proportions to use. Guidelines should use pixels for default scenarios, like, for example BBC's Global Experience Language (GEL), where the font scale and sizes are expressed in pixels but the actual CSS of the websites use ems, as they are a more accessible choice.

---

[7] An *em* is so called because it is thought to be the height of an upper case "M" character. In fact, according to typographer Robert Bringhurst, "The em is a sliding measure. One em is a distance equal to the type size. In 6 point type, an em is 6 points; in 12 point type an em is 12 points and in 60 point type an em is 60 points. Thus a one em space is proportionately the same in any size."

Figure 5-5. The BBC's Global Experience Language guidelines state the allowed type sizes in pixels, even though the BBC's websites use ems for font sizes.

On the BBC News home page, the h2 level heading of the top story has a font-size value of 2.461em. This number might seem odd, but if you look at the final computed value (you can use Firebug for this), you will see that it is in fact 32px (provided your browser is using the default type sizes). How have the developers come to this number? The font size of the body element is set to 62.5 percent. Since the default font size is usually 16px, this old trick makes it easier to do em calculations: 62.5 percent of 16 is 10. One em equals 10 pixels. Because the page wrapper and ancestor of the heading has "font-size: 1.3em" applied (making its computed value "13px"), we need to make the calculation of 32px/13px to know by how much we must increase the children's font-size so we get the desired 32px. Does it sound complicated? It is, and that is why, despite being a more accessible solution, so many CSS authors shy away from using ems as the type size unit in their style sheets. We recommend you take the time to do the work, and use ems where possible.

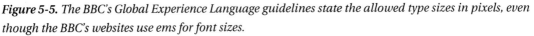

▓ **TIP:** A couple of good em calculators are available at http://topfunky.com/baseline-rhythm-calculator/ and http://jameswhittaker.com/journal/em-based-layouts-vertical-rhythm-calculator. There is also a handy reference chart at http://fordinteractive.com/tools/emchart/.

Color

Color is a fundamental factor in how a brand is perceived. Some brands are so connected to their colors that sometimes we don't even need to see their names and can recognize them from their colors and shapes (for example, the *National Geographic* golden rectangle or Coca-Cola's red script font).

Because of this, every brand style guide will almost certainly include a section related to color: what color palette can be used, what the appropriate combinations and ratios are, what each color represents in the branding color landscape, and so on.

With these guidelines in place, it is important that implementation teams are aware of them, and know how to use the colors and how they translate to the Web—it is not uncommon for front-end developers to not even be aware of the fact that there are predefined colors that they are supposed to be using on the websites they are building or augmenting, let alone understand the appropriate use for those colors. This then causes frustrations to both designers and developers and dilutes the brand to the users.

It is also important for designers to understand that colors work differently in print and on the Web, starting with the fact that whereas printed material will look the same for every person, every user browses the Web with a different monitor or device, with different capabilities, calibrations and configurations. When developing the style guides, web designers (as with print designers) should be considerate of people with visual impairment or color blindness, and make sure that the colors and color combinations included in the designs provide the right amount of contrast, but these are issues that fall into the accessibility spectrum rather than in the subject of this chapter and are therefore discussed further in Chapter 6.

Whether the brand guidelines were developed with web colors in mind first and followed by their print counterparts, or the other way around is a designer's choice; as long as there is a defined and agreed palette to be used on the Web.

Some visual branding guides, however, don't make any reference to screen colors. This can happen either because the guide was produced at a time when the Internet was not a medium taken into consideration, or simply because it's incomplete. In either case, the guide should be amended to include the appropriate color references to be used on the Web, avoiding time waste and imprecise usage of colors, since each CSS author will have to convert CMYK and Pantone colors to RGBA, hexadecimal, or the preferred color format for the website,[8] and this process should be signed off by a designer or design team.

Multiple Color Schemes

Color can be a powerful instrument in differentiating between subsites or sections of a website. For example, if you have a sub brand that is geared toward children, it will probably be designed with bolder and brighter colors, while if you have a premium brand within your organization, you might be using more classic and elegant colors.

When constructing sub-brands and their websites, rather than coming up with completely new layouts for the pages, it is easier from the point of view of both user and developer to maintain some consistency across the range of sites, while still keeping the differentiation clear—we want them to know they are still within our umbrella family of websites, but looking at a different product.

Fox is a great example of how, by using the same basic template you can have an almost unlimited range of different subsites, in this instance for each show. In Fox's case, the bold background images are relevant to the specific show, while the link color scheme follows the branding for that show. However,

---

[8] CMYK, RGB, and Pantone colors have different color gamut (subsets of colors), and some colors in one color model are "out of gamut" (cannot be accurately reproduced) in the others. Read more about color gamut here: `http://en.wikipedia.org/wiki/Gamut`.

the layout of the page and the navigational elements' design and behavior stays the same. This is a good demonstration of how to achieve the appearance of variation while in fact keeping the design templates consistent, resorting to color (and imagery) for differentiation and avoiding a jarring and inconsistent user experience.

Figure 5-6. Fox's American Dad and Master Chef websites: two examples of how by using the same template and employing different color schemes and images you can achieve differentiation.

One thing to bear in mind is that users rarely group sections of a website by color or understand its significance (even though people within the organization and developers might do) unless the color is already associated with a brand. The cases mentioned here are examples of that; color-coding the departments of your company is something completely different, as they aren't perceived to the outside as "brands."

Color Reference

As well as living within visual style guides, it is useful to have a color palette reference in the CSS files themselves. In Chapter 2, we show how these can be included within the CSS comments, so that there is always a handy reference for authors. Here is an example of how you can keep a color palette at the top of your CSS file:

```
/* Color reference:

Main text      #333333
Background     #f7f7f7
:link,
:visited       #dd4814
:hover,
:active,
:focus         #bc522d
…

*/
```

You may choose to use CSSDOC comments instead; you can see a more detailed explanation of how to do this in Chapter 2. This method does require you to maintain the information in two different places, and though keeping these references within your CSS files is convenient, you may prefer a single point of reference that is more likely to be accurate.

Dynamic Colors

Using dynamic CSS or compilers like LESS or Sass, colors and color updates on large websites can become more easily manageable. Using these technologies you can easily set up variables for the most commonly used colors like main text, links, backgrounds, or borders, taking out of the equation the need to constantly refer to a color guide to use the correct hexadecimal code or RGB reference. You can even generate entire color schemes based on three or four main colors, by basing other colors on these and using color calculations. We go into greater detail on this subject in Chapter 9.

Fallback Colors

Older browsers don't support the new CSS3 color formats, like RGBA or HSLA. For those browsers, you must always make sure to provide a fallback color. For example, if specifying a transparent background color on a div, you would supply older browsers with a declaration before the RGBA one (which will be ignored, as it is not supported):

```
div {
    background-color: #b9cf6a;
    background-color: rgba(255, 255, 255, 0.3);
}
```

In the previous example, we didn't specify the exact hexadecimal version of 255,255,255, as that would be solid white. Instead, using a color picker tool (like, for example, xScope `http://iconfactory.com/software/xscope`) you can select a color that is an approximation of the transparent color and the underlying color beneath it, to give older browsers a more accurate design. These fallback colors are unlikely to be specified in a branding guide, so it is the job of a diligent and thorough CSS author to make sure they are present and are accurately chosen. It is always better to be safe than sorry, so leaving a comment as a reminder to update the fallback color in case the original color changes is always a good idea.

When using CSS gradients, remember to always specify a fallback background color, making sure that, on browsers that don't support them, there is still enough contrast between background and foreground. The same applies to using images as background colors (to be exact, CSS gradients are in fact dynamically generated background images and *not* colors); always specify a background color for the container and always test the website with images turned off and CSS turned on—it can be extremely frustrating for users browsing with images disabled (on slower connections or on mobile devices) to not be able to access content because the developer forgot to define a background color and relied on the background image for contrast. Users on slow connections will also see your site with the images missing for a moment before they load anyway, and the less dramatically the screen changes, the less jarring it is for the user when it happens.

Layout

Defining the basic structure of the page is an important step when coding CSS websites and one that will influence the rest of the process. Rather than just throwing divs on to the page as the need arises, it is important that there is a solid foundation in place—a defined grid upon which each individual page can be built.

The use of grids and templates will also improve the flexibility (and adaptability) of your CSS files and designs, helping to maintain layout consistency.

Grids

Knowing how to best use grids is an essential skill for any designer, be it on the Web or outside of it.

Using grids doesn't mean creating rigid layouts, though—they are part of the foundation of the design, contributing to a solid, well-thought structure, and helping to make some of the decisions; but, as with any set of rules and constrains, they are also there to be broken.

Some of the most original layouts on the Web have been composed on top of properly defined grids. Let's look at an example (see Figure 5-7).

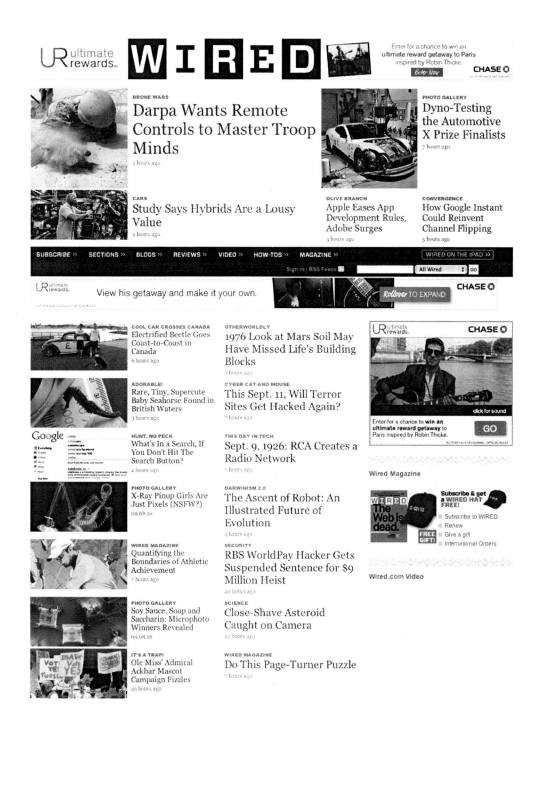

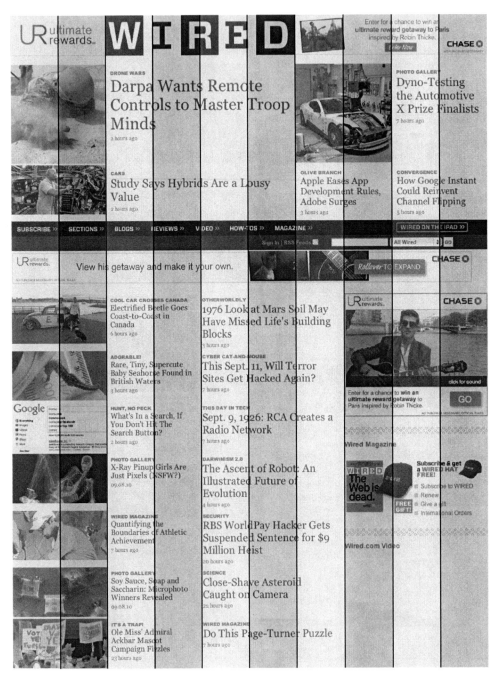

Figure 5-7. The Wired website (above) with a grid overlay (below) `http://www.wired.com/`

As you can see, even though it follows a grid, the design of Wired's website doesn't feel rigid. On the contrary, it feels expressive and dynamic.

A carefully considered grid is flexible, it lends itself to a multitude of layout designs, helping maintain uniformity between the different pages, and it should aid in keeping branding consistent. The designer's work is not complete when the grid is finalized, though; a good grid will be useless if its only purpose is to correctly align every element on the page.

Although correct alignment is a fundamental step in achieving balance and harmony, other aspects of the design will not be covered by it—the visual hierarchy of the elements, colors, typography and so on still need to be considered. Designing is not just positioning elements inside a grid.

One of the downsides of trying to translate a grid to HTML and CSS, is that the natural flow of the content (the outline of the document) may become neglected and be subsidiary to the grid. This happens when the layout starts to behave more like an old table-based layout.

Even though table-based sites were almost perfect when working with solid grids, one of their (many) downsides was the fact that form didn't follow content; content followed form. The visual position of the content on the page was more important than the meaning and flow of the content itself. If the HTML is basically creating boxes to be positioned, as a table would do, then we are not doing the content justice.

This is the approach that many CSS frameworks take, and it's one of the reasons why so many CSS authors prefer not to use them.

In Figure 5-8, we have a basic 8-column grid; each column is 100 pixels wide, with a right and left margin of 10 pixels each.

Figure 5-8. An example of a simple 8-column grid

The first instinct when coding this layout might be to focus on the columns and create eight containers that are floated to the left:

```
div {
    width: 100px;
    float: left;
    margin: 0 10px;
}
```

But more likely is a grid that will have elements within it that span across more than one column, as shown in Figure 5-9.

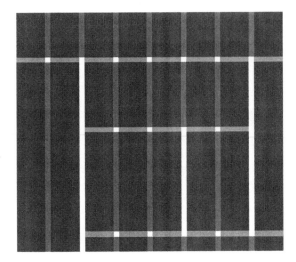

Figure 5-9. An 8-column grid with content blocks

This grid can be translated into HTML and CSS in many different ways, but the optimal way is always that one that takes the actual content and flow of the page into consideration and keeps the order intact. The grid is secondary, and the content shouldn't become its subordinate; it is merely an instrument to achieve layout consistency and harmony.

In our example, we could start by defining the most important content blocks and extract their widths from the underlying grid:

```
header {
    width: 940px; /* full width */
}
nav {
    width: 220px; /* 2*100px + 1x20px */
    float: left;
}
#highlight {
    width: 580px; /* 5*100px + 4x20px */
    float: left;
}

...

aside {
    width: 100px; /* single column = 100px */
    float: right;
}
```

The grid exists to provide the designer and CSS author with measurements in which he will base some of the design decisions and that will make the translation from the design phase into the coding phase less prone to subjectivity. If the person in charge of the CSS knows that an element that spans across two columns in the design is automatically 220 pixels wide, this will help the design maintain consistency and balance.

We will cover the process of working with a grid in more detail in Chapter 11, where we will create a framework from scratch.

Templates

HTML and CSS templates provide the authors with a solid base upon which they can build. Templates are a simple way of ensuring that key elements like headers, navigation, basic page structure, and typography are consistent across a range of sites and sub-sites.

There are a few differences between templates and CSS frameworks, even though their purposes intertwine. Existing CSS frameworks consist of libraries of prebuilt code that you can adapt to the project at hand. There are several existing CSS frameworks that are freely available and used by many developers and agencies (and which we cover in Chapter 4), such as 960gs or Blueprint. In some cases, teams create their own CSS framework (an approach that we highly recommend and cover in Chapter 11). Frameworks should be adaptable, flexible, and modular.

Templates can take a different approach. You may have an HTML and CSS template that includes the header, main navigation, content area, and footer of an example website, and that should be used across the family of websites within your organization. This doesn't imply, though, that this set of files permits for the modular and versatile approach that frameworks do.

Templates are basic examples of how the markup should be structured and how the CSS ties to it— they exist as a skeleton of what the page will be. The ideal scenario would be to build HTML and CSS templates based on the existing CSS framework, so that the developers can see living examples of how CSS files can be used, overridden, and adapted to the various page templates.

Themes

It is often customary for organizations to change the design and content of their websites according to relevant seasons, holidays and events, like the beginning of summer, Christmas, New Year's, or sales campaigns.

These updates are usually a good way of showing that the website isn't stagnant in time; that it is being constantly updated; and most importantly, that the company, product, or service behind it cares about the same things that their customers do—it increases engagement.

While sometimes rebranding may be related to a one time only occasion (for example, the 25th anniversary of the company), recurring events also instigate these updates (for example, yearly, like Christmas rebranding, or several times a year, like end of season sales campaigns).

One of the best examples of seasonal rebranding is Starbucks' Christmas website. Alongside the redecoration of their stores around the world to match the spirit of the season, Starbucks also presents their website visitors with a revamped design, in tune with the stores and ad campaigns, in perfect marketing choreography (see Figure 5-10).

Figure 5-10. Starbucks' Christmas themed website had a completely new design and layout.

It is the job of the designers to handle the creation of more involved re-theming of the sites in terms of design, but the changes will eventually fall into the hands of CSS authors and other developers, who will need to be able to override existing style sheets with the updates.

This can be seen as a trial of fire for CSS: the style sheets need to be flexible enough so that overriding some rules doesn't turn into a specificity nightmare.

■ **NOTE:** Notice how often the term *specificity nightmare* is mentioned in this book? This is due to the fact that we are sadly too familiar with it, as it is a frequent situation that CSS authors are faced with—the result of non-flexible and fragile style sheets.

If the CSS is using overly specific selectors, when creating a new theme you will have to create even more specific selectors. Ideally, you should be able to add a class or ID of, for example, "christmas" to the body element, and either link the seasonal style sheet after the default one in the header section of the HTML, or incorporate the new rules into the existing main file.

Threadless, for example, adds a class to the body tag so that certain elements of the site can be targeted and their CSS overridden with the changes (see Figure 5-11).

```
.holiday_week_2_3 .footer_wrap {
    background: url(/imgs/sale/black_friday/bg_footer.jpg) no-repeat scroll center 30px
#ffffff;
    clear: both;
    overflow: hidden;
    padding: 90px 0 0;
}
```

Figure 5-11. Threadless website featuring a saled-themed design.

You can read more about overriding CSS files in Chapter 4.

Flexible CSS and Brand Evolution

Brands don't stay unchanged forever. Even though the most established and recognizable brands tend to avoid radical rebrandings that could harm the way they are perceived by their customers and by the general public, it is not rare to see them make smaller updates, that are almost unnoticeable externally, but that still involve some amount of work to the web implementation teams.

These small changes can include typographical improvements, color changes, updates to the imagery used throughout the sites, minor layout and navigation adjustments, and logo replacement, among others.

It is also not uncommon to see large corporations refresh their websites once every two or three years. This may happen for a variety of reasons: an overall brand redesign needs to be reflected on the website, the website looks dated (this happens especially if it was designed to follow web design trends that have quickly gone out of fashion), the company has been restructured, or the content of the website itself has been restructured, to name but a few.

Even brands that tend to stay immutable through time make small alterations to their websites, mainly because of the fast-changing nature of the medium, and also because these changes are often less costly than, for example, redecorating an entire fleet or reprinting the stationary for thousands of employees.

Because there are usually costs associated with making these changes, and speed is always something that is sought after, it is important to prepare for them by creating flexible CSS documents that can be updated as easily as possible for small or large adjustments.

This is essentially what this book is about: making the CSS of your websites adaptable, easy to handle by a large number of people, and lend itself to being updated when the need arises without breaking everything else.

When a website faces a large update or a redesign, it is important to decide sooner rather than later whether it is better to start from scratch or whether the existing CSS is flexible and easy to adapt to the changes. Usually if the underlying markup is being redone, that will also mean that the CSS will need to be restructured, as the way the markup is built tends to be directly linked to how the CSS is organized.

The most common scenarios, though (and the ones that make it essential for large websites to have dedicated web teams), are related to less apparent, ongoing updates that, even though small, continually test the robustness of both markup and CSS. This could be something like adding a new link to the main navigation, updating the color of the text to make it more accessible, realigning the grid, creating a new sidebar widget, or preparing the site for a new version in a different language—common, day-to-day tasks in any web implementation team.

These are all great examples of why it is important to keep CSS consistent and flexible, and of how up-to-date and detailed CSS and design and brand style guides make it easier to implement new elements or expand existing ones.

Summary

A large part of CSS authors' and front-end developers' jobs is to make designs come to life on the Web. User experience designers, information architects, and visual and graphic designers put their knowledge and best efforts into creating distinctive brands and products. Making sure the implementation of their work is conducted seamlessly is vital, as it will influence how your organization is seen outside (and inside) and ultimately its success. There are various aspects that professionals working on the Web need to take into consideration, and we assume they know the medium's potentials but also its limitations. Establishing clear brand and design guidelines, making sure everyone knows and understands them, and having a process in place that sets up design rules but allows for flexibility and efficiency is what every team working on large-scale websites should strive for and what this chapter should help to achieve.

In the next chapter, we will discuss accessibility and how it impacts your CSS. We will look at the impairments that can affect our users and the steps you can go to ensure they have the best possible experience.

CHAPTER 6

■ ■ ■

CSS and Accessibility

In essence, making a website accessible means ensuring that everyone can get to everything. It does not mean everyone has to have the same experience, but it does mean there should be no piece of functionality or content that is unreachable (or inaccessible) by anyone, regardless of their individual ability, devices, browsers, or environment.

Accessibility is not checking off a list of requirements or using an automated tool to verify whether our code passes certain accessibility guidelines and validation. Although your organization might be required by law to pass certain accessibility levels (different countries have different laws governing accessibility), making sure your websites are accessible to the widest range of devices and users possible should be one of your main concerns when developing for high-traffic websites. It is something you should be doing for your users, your brand, and their goodwill toward it. Not breaking the law could be seen to be a serendipitous bonus.

A lot can be (and has been) said about online accessibility, enough to fill an entire book, or even a collection. Building accessible websites is to a great extent, but not only, a byproduct of building semantic websites. It is not something that falls only within the responsibilities of developers, though. Everyone involved with the website should be part of this effort: user experience designers should make sure the websites are easy to navigate and content is easy to find; designers should create layouts that take into consideration users with disabilities, such as colorblindness or poor motor skills; product managers and copywriters should create simple messages that are clear to everyone; and developers should write code that is semantic and accessible. There are several considerations, especially with high-traffic websites. Also, there are many HTML-related and content-related actions that you can take to make your content more accessible, but as a CSS-related book, they would be out of scope here. We will give you tips on how to open up your website and (most importantly) your content to the largest number of visitors and clients possible.[1]

In this chapter, we will look at

- An overview of some of the most common users' accessibility problems

- Existing accessibility guidelines and how to cater for them

- How to make things easier for visitors using assistive technologies

- Design and layout considerations for a more accessible site

- WAI-ARIA and how to use it in your projects

---

[1] It's not just a good, altruistic thing to do—it's also a profitable thing to do. The UK supermarket Tesco partnered with the Royal National Institute for the Blind (RNIB) to ensure that its website is accessible. This resulted in an extra £13 million a year in revenue that was simply not available before.

165

- CSS best practices for users with device or environmental impairments

- The difference between progressive enhancement and graceful degradation

- How to use Yahoo!'s Graded Browser Support

Impairment Problems Overview

What is and what is not considered *impairment* is a difficult thing to discuss in a politically correct manner. What some see as a disability, others see as just differences between people. When we talk about an impairment, we mean something that makes using a website potentially more difficult for that user. Some of the most common accessibility impairments are the following:

- Low vision, poor eyesight, or blindness

- Different kinds of colorblindness

- Motor disabilities or constricted motor skills

- Hearing impairments

- Cognitive and intellectual disabilities

- Young age, which can imply cognitive impairment

- Old age, which can imply many of the problems listed here

More often than you might expect, people will have more than one condition, which makes it even more difficult to cater for every combination possible.

Those who are deafblind, for example, communicate and absorb information via different means. Those who were initially deaf and then lost their vision later in life are likely to use a modified version of a sign language they already knew, in a tactile form. Whereas those who were born blind, and then became deaf are likely to use a tactile version of their written or spoken language. Even with a single impairment such as deafness there can be tens (or even hundreds) of solutions (for example, lip-reading, sign languages, advanced sign languages, hearing aids, and so on). There are many more combinations than we could possibly go into here. A vital thing to remember is that these users have already decided how they would and do like to use their devices and have applications in place to help them achieve this.

We are not experts in catering for those with impairments, nor could we realistically expect to be, but we can do our very best to not interfere with the chosen methodology of our users. The same applies for everyone—if one user has defined keyboard shortcuts, and we override them without permission, that is frustrating for the user and presumptuous of us. If another user tries to right-click on a page, and we cancel that behavior, again, it is rude of us to do so. Allowing the browser and the device the opportunity to act as they see fit, is often the most courteous and appropriate thing for us to do.

Let's take a look at some of the more common issues people with particular impairments are likely to face. This is, obviously, not an exhaustive list. We will go into more detail for each later in the chapter.

Partial Sightedness

Partially sighted (but not blind) users fall into one of two key groups. Those that find it hard to focus will benefit from clear, simple, medium-weighted fonts and large font sizes.[2] Allowing them the ability to

---

[2] Read what the RNIB has to say about fonts at
`http://www.rnib.org.uk/professionals/accessibleinformation/text/Pages/fonts.aspx`.

change font sizes and fonts within your website will make their lives easier. Ensuring you use relative values for font sizes will also let them use the built-in device methods for adjusting font size, and avoiding !important declarations will help ensure that you don't override any settings they may have made themselves.

Those that have a narrow field of vision (who can only focus on small areas of the screen at a time) will benefit from the ability to turn the font size down so that paragraphs take up less space onscreen. These users are more likely to zoom the entire website out, but everyone is different. You should always ensure that you have tested the site to be certain that you can turn the font size up and down by two steps within the browser without breaking the layout.

Blindness

Blind users are very likely to use screen readers (which we mention in a dedicated section later in this chapter). They also browse websites in a very different way from sighted users. They are likely to want to skip directly to sections of the website, access lists of all of the links in a page, or access an outline of the page built up out of the headings in the markup. Avoid language that points to specific physical positions on the page (for example, "click the link in the top-right corner") and use WAI-ARIA, semantics, and microformats. Newer technologies will be able to take advantage of these.

Colorblindness

Colorblind users may use their own style sheets or turn off CSS altogether. Offering them various alternative color schemes can be a great help to them and allows your organization to maintain control of its brand and ensure that your website remains attractive. We reference some tools to simulate colorblindness and check for problems with your color schemes later in this chapter.

Motor Impairment

Degrees of motor impairment can vary dramatically. In most cases, these users are already using their own assistive technologies to enable and empower them to use their devices, but there are small things we can do to help, like making clickable areas clear and as large as possible. Whenever possible, make sure the target areas of your links don't require a great deal of precision to be clicked on.[3] These considerations also apply to users with touch interfaces such as smartphones or tablets.

In many cases (such as tabs or buttons), not making the clickable area the size of the container is a confusing user experience, anyway.

Hearing Disabilities

Users with partial or complete deafness are generally less challenged with accessibility issues on the Internet, other than with specific audio or video content. Most websites don't (or definitely shouldn't!) play audio,[4] and as such will work for the hearing impaired just as well as for other users. You should avoid using sound alone to indicate any kind of state or information on your page. If your site presents audio or video as part of its primary purpose, you need to consider captioning for these pieces of media.

Open captioning is captioning that is "burned in" to the media it is associated with; for example, subtitles in a film that cannot be turned off. It is called "open" because it is shown by default. *Closed*

---

[3] Fitts' Law (http://en.wikipedia.org/wiki/Fitts's_law) predicts that the time it takes to rapidly move to a target area and click it depends upon the distance to travel and the size of the target. Bigger targets make everyone more efficient.
[4] Websites should certainly not auto-play audio because this can be jarring and confusing to users.

captioning is textual data associated with the media that is stored in text format and served alongside the video. Televisions, for example, have long been legally required to provide a closed captioning decoder. Closed captioning has the benefit of allowing several different "tracks" of text; for example, different languages or descriptions of sounds as well as conversation. It can be used with audio as lyrics for karaoke because it is time-coded. It also has the benefit of allowing us to potentially style the text with CSS (different positions to avoid important video elements, colors to represent different people, and so on).

Closed captioning sadly has poor support so far on the Web and many different solutions. HTML5 as yet does not have official support for closed captioning, but proven methods are already being implemented and standardization is sure to follow.[5]

For now, the CSS considerations for closed captioning depend very much upon your implementation, and a transcript is the only foolproof method for exposing this data. You can read more about captioning at `http://webaim.org/techniques/captions/`.

It is also important to be aware that those who were born deaf will likely have learned sign language as their first language. This means that English (or their local language) is akin to a second language for them, and therefore expressions, jargon, and colloquialisms may be harder for them to understand. For that reason, clear language is just as important as ever.

Cognitive Impairment

Cognitive impairments, such as dyslexia or autism, can make it difficult for users to process information. Typically, this kind of impairment is addressed with clear, unambiguous copy but there are other things you can do, too. Making layouts consistent and maintaining the positions of key elements like navigation will make life easier for all your users, but especially for those with cognitive impairments or learning disabilities. The same applies to not using too many different fonts (although the website should be flexible enough so that it is easy for users to specify their preferred font). Also, make sure there is enough space between lines, as this makes it easier for text to be read (a `line-height` value of 1.5 for normal text is a good default).

Dyslexia is a very common impairment, and although no accurate studies have been carried out, it is believed that dyslexia affects between 5 and 10 percent of the population. Dyslexics can suffer from a whole assortment of learning or cognitive impairments, which is why this particular problem is referred to so frequently when accessibility is mentioned. Some dyslexics prefer to print out pages rather than having to read the text on a screen. This is just one of various reasons why someone would print a page.

If you are not developing a website that is specifically targeted at dyslexics, it should not be necessary to proof every single detail of your website to be dyslexic-friendly, but you should remember that the most important factor in this situation is that users can customize the pages they visit to suit their very particular needs, making it easier to read and understand the content.

Young Age

Young users are as likely as anyone else to suffer many of the other impairments on this list, but they can also be considered to have a kind of cognitive impairment, in that you should use simple, clear language. Sites designed for children are also some of the only valid places to use the Comic Sans font, although some dyslexics may also find it easier to read.

---

[5] Web Video Text Tracks (WebVTT), previously known as WebSRT (based on the popular SRT (SubRip Text) format) is currently being implemented by several browsers, and so is currently the most likely proposal to be standardized. You can read about it at `http://www.whatwg.org/specs/web-apps/current-work/webvtt.html`.

Old Age

Older users can suffer any or many of the impairments on this list (apart from the one directly previous, of course). In particular, sight and hearing deteriorate with age. As such, if you are making sure that your websites are accessible, you have probably designed a website that is already accessible to older users. They may also be unfamiliar or unskilled with computers, so avoiding technical jargon and working with common visual associations works well.

Epilepsy

Epileptic users specifically may react badly to flickering or flashing pages, or elements within pages. It is law in many countries to provide a warning before presenting this kind of media. Avoid animations or Flashes of Unstyled Content (FOUC).

TIP: The BBC has a fantastic resource to help people with different accessibility issues learn what they need to know to make the Internet friendlier to them. Although it is still in beta at the time of writing, you can access it at `http://www.bbc.co.uk/accessibility/accessibility_beta/`.

Accessibility problems don't necessarily mean a physical or psychological problem with the user. It might mean simply that the device or environment they are using to visit your website has lower capabilities than expected.

Let's look at a list of common problems that might translate into accessibility impairments that are not physiological:

- Older browsers

- Dial-up or slow Internet connections

- Small or low-fidelity screens

- Touch screens

- No access to a mouse or keyboard

- Slow processors or older computers

- Environments where eyes, hands or ears may be occupied (for example, exercising or driving)

- JavaScript, CSS, images, or cookies intentionally disabled

There are no definitive numbers that can tell us how many users might fall into any of these categories. In many cases, they will probably be temporary impairments (they might be trying to verify some information while on the go, or using someone else's or their work's computer). But if we take the first issue alone and look at some statistics of how many users are still navigating the Web with older browsers, while not significant for many low-traffic websites, on high-traffic websites even small percentage numbers can translate into tens of thousands of visitors per day. Also, IE 6 usage may have dropped to around 4 or 5 percent of all Internet traffic worldwide, but it still makes up more than 12 percent of traffic for Africa. If your website gets worldwide traffic, looking at the statistics for the world rather than breaking them down by country can be misleading.[6]

You can read more about how to help users suffering from device and environmental impairments later in this chapter.

■ **TIP:** Being aware of all the accessibility issues that a user might be facing at a determinate time does not mean we should build our websites for the lowest common denominator. It means that we should be making sure that the content—the core of our website—is available to everyone.

Accessibility Guidelines

There are many accessibility guides and checklists. The Web Accessibility Initiative (WAI http://www.w3.org/WAI/about.html) is one of the domains of the W3C. They have several Working Groups, but the most commonly referenced and applied are the Web Content Accessibility Guidelines (WCAG http://www.w3.org/TR/WCAG10/full-checklist.html). This checklist—unlike many of the other documents to come out of the W3C—is relatively succinct and pretty easy to read. The page is designed to be printed and used as an actual checklist.

Items of consideration are grouped into *Priority 1*, *Priority 2*, or *Priority 3*. *Priority 1* items are considered essential to an accessible website. *Priority 2* items are strongly recommended, and *Priority 3* items are useful. You could consider these *musts*, *shoulds*, and *coulds*, respectively.

In essence, to comply with *Priority 1* items you must do the following:

- Provide textual equivalents for every graphical element on the page

- Clearly provide textual equivalents for information that is indicated via other means (for example, by color or positioning)

- Ensure that pages work well with CSS, JavaScript, or images disabled

- Use simple and clear language

- Avoid flickering

- If all else fails, link to an alternative version of the page that does follow the guidelines

There are many additional and finer points. We strongly recommend you read the page in detail and adhere to the suggestions as much as is reasonable. Some countries, such as Canada or Sweden, follow their own accessibility guidelines.[7]

---

[6] For more statistics on browser usage, visit http://gs.statcounter.com/ or http://www.w3counter.com/globalstats.php.

[7] Canada has the "Common Look and Feel Standards" (http://www.tbs-sct.gc.ca/clf2-nsi2/), which must be followed by government institutions and include standards on web addresses, accessibility and usability, web page formats, and e-mail. The now extinct Swedish Administrative Development Agency published the "Swedish National Guidelines for Public Sector Websites" in 2006; the guidelines have been maintained privately and were translated into English in 2008 (http://www.eutveckling.se/sidor/english/). They cover areas such as usability, privacy issues and information architecture, as well as web standards.

What's the Law?

Different countries have different sets of laws that regulate accessibility. Usually they tend to be not exclusively related to the Web, but acts against discrimination toward people with disabilities and promoting equality.

In the UK, there is the Disability Discrimination Act (DDA) of 1995, which also makes reference to websites. The vital text from the Code of Practice is this: "The Disability Discrimination Act makes it unlawful for a service provider to discriminate against a disabled person by refusing to provide any service which it provides to members of the public."

The Royal National Institute for the Blind (RNIB) and the Disability Rights Commission (DRC) have pushed for legal action with regard to the DDA. The RNIB has approached two large websites that made the demanded changes to avoid legal action and maintain their anonymity. The DRC investigated 1,000 sites, and found that more than 80 percent of them were in conflict with the DDA requirements. Those sites were threatened with unlimited compensation payments and legal action.

In the United States, the Americans with Disabilities Act (ADA) serves the same purpose. It applies not just to websites but also to any service—covering buildings, medical care, and telephones, to name but a few.

It is not uncommon for big organizations to be sued by consumer associations for their poor accessibility standards, which lock thousands of users with disabilities out of their websites and their content. There are precedents where the plaintiff has won large sums of money with these cases. For high-traffic and high-profile websites, this is a much more real threat and something that should not be taken lightly.

It is likely that the WCAG guidelines will be used in the case of legal action. The EU recommended level of compliance is *Priority 2*. We recommend trying to satisfy *Priority 2* as a minimum and striving to satisfy *Priority 3* where possible.[8]

Assistive Technologies

There are various types of assistive technologies for people with disabilities. The main objective of assistive technologies is to help people with disabilities be more autonomous in their day-to-day lives.

Some of the assistive technologies frequently applied to using computers (and consequently, the Internet) are screen readers, screen magnifiers, speech recognition software, and Braille displays and keyboards.

We will focus mainly on screen readers and keyboard-only users, as a lot of the guidelines for these cases also apply to other assistive technologies and they represent a large portion of assistive technologies used by people with disabilities.

Screen Readers

Screen readers are not a tool exclusive to users with visual impairments. Users with other types of disabilities find in screen readers an efficient and more tolerable way of browsing the Internet (for example, when tired, finding it hard to concentrate, or busy doing something else), something that presents content in a linear fashion, without imposing on them behaviors that might make them more

---

[8] In 2006, the National Federation of the Blind filed a lawsuit against Target, one of the largest retail companies in the United States, for having barriers on its website that made it difficult for blind customers to use it. Target settled, in 2008, for 6 million dollars. Other examples include a blind man successfully suing the Sydney Olympics Organizing Committee in 2000, and a New York case against Ramada.com and Priceline.com.

anxious, making it harder to understand the content. This brings the percentage of potential screen reader users up.

Like browsers, screen readers receive updates, and each update adds support for new functionalities. And, just like browsers, users don't necessarily update their screen reader software. One of the main reasons for this is cost. Screen readers are not trivial to build and are typically targeted at a niche market. As such, they are usually very expensive. The capabilities and behaviors of screen readers differ dramatically. VoiceOver (http://www.apple.com/accessibility/voiceover/) is an Apple screen reader that is free as part of OS X and is fully featured. If you are using a Mac, we recommend trying it out to introduce you to some of the issues your users will face. It is a genuinely enlightening experience. Press Command-F5 to turn VoiceOver on or off at any time. Windows has also included its basic screen reader, Windows Narrator, since Windows 2000.

Screen readers present methods of interacting with websites that are different from those used by sighted users. VoiceOver calls this the Web Item Rotor. This lets the user bring up lists of links, headings, and so on, and navigate straight to them instead of being forced to navigate through the website in a linear fashion until they find what they are looking for. This quickly surfaces many obvious accessibility problems. VoiceOver also presents visually what it speaks out loud. Figures 6-1, 6-2, and 6-3 show some examples.

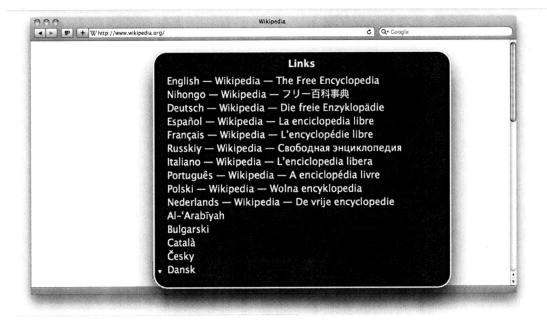

Figure 6-1. Wikipedia presents the user with sensible links, although there are 306 of them.

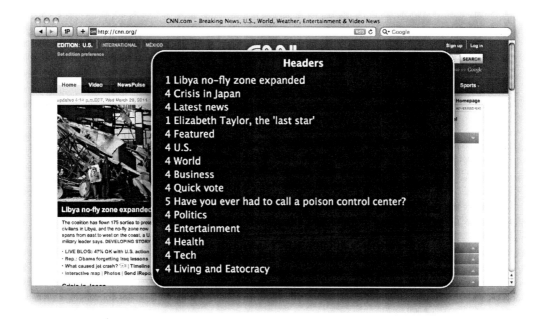

Figure 6-2. CNN has a reasonable list of headings, although the heading levels are confusing.

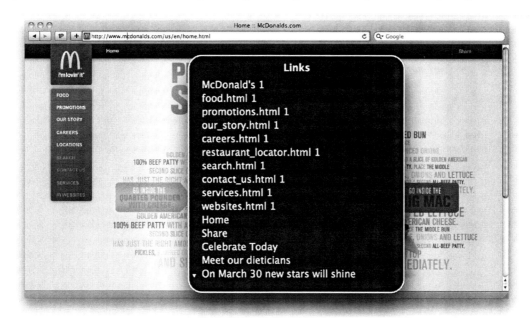

Figure 6-3. McDonald's only uses images for its links, with no title attributes. It gets worse, but let's move on.

Dealing with screen readers has a few considerations the CSS author should take into account.

- If your layout presents content in an order that might not make sense when read linearly, put it in the correct order in the markup and use CSS to rearrange the content as you like.

- If hiding content and using the :hover pseudo-class to show it, do the same with the :focus pseudo-class. These users are unlikely to use pointing devices such as trackpads or mice.

- Make a list of "skip links" right at the top of your page to link to primary sections of the page, such as navigation, content, and so on. Position these off the page, making them visible on focus. This ensures that your primary links are first in the page and that they are useful to all users.

- Give your publishers a means to hide content via CSS (see the next section) so that links that appear to say "Read more" can actually say "Read more about story XYZ" to screen reader users.

- When presenting text in unusual case (for example, all capitals), make this transformation via the text-transform CSS property, as screen readers might read uppercase HTML text in an unpredictable manner, like spelling them out or shouting them.

- Screen readers typically don't read out content inserted via CSS, so make sure that whatever content you add this way is purely decorative.

All these techniques will help your screen reader users, and also search engines and users of other unexpected devices in the future! To do a basic test, try turning your CSS off and verifying that the content still makes sense. However, we cannot understate the value of using your site with a screen reader yourself; some of the problems you will encounter are so easy to fix and so obvious that you will kick yourself, and your users will love you for fixing them.

The speech and (deprecated) aural media types are intended to help you target CSS at screen readers specifically. There are three reasons we suggest you avoid this technique.

- These media types are not widely supported by screen readers. There is no guarantee that they will be applied. Also, these style sheets will be downloaded by non–screen reader devices, resulting in a performance hit regardless.

- The extra CSS features they give us, such as changing the voice, volume, pauses, and mixing, all potentially override the user's settings. The user knows and has set exactly how they want their content to be read (the equivalent of a user style sheet). Not only do we not know this, we are certainly not qualified to make better decisions than them. The user is right, we are not; we simply shouldn't mess with it.

- Even if we were experts in these techniques, the changes we made would be specific to the content. Managing and maintaining this is an unrealistic and daunting prospect.

We are far better off dealing with as much as we can in a single style sheet, except in very specific and unlikely scenarios.

■ **TIP:** WebAIM did a survey of the preferences of screen reader users, which could prove invaluable when deciding on which defaults to test with. You can read it at `http://webaim.org/projects/screenreadersurvey/`.

Hiding Content with CSS

Often we will hide HTML elements from the visual representation of our page, using CSS properties such as `display`, `visibility`, or `text-indent`. For example, if we are replacing a heading with an image, we might use something similar to the following code:

```
h2 {
    background: url(img/heading.png) no-repeat;
    text-indent: -9999px;
}
```

By doing this, the original text is moved so far from the center of the page that it is now not visible, and instead we see the intended background, which usually contains text set in a custom non-web-safe font.[9]

Another common scenario is markup such as the following:

```
<a href="page.html">Read more</a>.
```

A screen reader being used to access lists of links will simply announce "Read more" with no context, often many times on a single page. This is very frustrating for the user.[10]

Providing a class for our publishers to hook into solves this issue gracefully. Here's another example of the markup:

```
<a href="page.html">Read more <span class="accessible">about the exploding lemming
epidemic</span></a>.
```

And here's the CSS we could use with it:

```
.accessible {
    position: absolute;
    text-indent: -9999px;
}
```

Now, although the page looks visually exactly as it did before, the screen reader will read out "Read more about the exploding lemming epidemic," which makes sense out of context.[11]

Even though `display:none` or `visibility:hidden` seem like valid solutions—and it is true of some screen readers that as long as the text is present in the markup, they will read it—this is not true for all

---

[9] Some CSS authors will use a value like -10000em. We recommend -9999px since the screen estate is unlikely to be wider than that; ems incur calculations by the browser and thus an (admittedly tiny) performance hit, and it saves one character.

[10] And again, wasted link equity search engines would love.

[11] Although tempting to write "click here to read more…", you should avoid this kind of language since it is mouse-specific, and the user may be using a keyboard, touch interface, or other input device.

screen readers. The `text-indent` we have suggested is currently the best solution we have for this problem. Users visiting the page with CSS disabled may see slightly more verbose text, but this is an acceptable compromise.

Keyboard-Only Users

Some users may not have the motor skills to use a mouse, or may just not have access to one. For these users, providing a focus state for links is vital, as a keyboard-only user can easily lose track of which link is selected if there isn't a visual indication of it. It may be tempting to hide the outline for links that are focused for aesthetic reasons, but if you do this make sure you provide some kind of visual alternative. Don't rely on hover for access to content or anything important, since you cannot guarantee that users will have a hover state (for example, when using a touch screen device).

Other Assistive Devices

There are many other devices users can use to make the Internet more accessible:

- Rollerball mice

- Adaptive keyboards

- Sticky keys

- Eye tracking

- Voice navigation

Again, these devices seek to solve problems on their own. If you follow the best practices outlined in this chapter, you will be doing the best you can to step out of their way and let them get on with it.

Design and Layout

A lot of the CSS recommendations for creating accessible websites are a byproduct of what has been decided in the information architecture, planning, content creation, and design phases. Aspects like color palettes and layout are usually not a developer's responsibility, but rather the designer's or design team's responsibility.

This means that everyone involved in the creation and maintenance of the website(s) should have some level of accessibility training. Even though there should ideally be a constant communication stream between all parties involved, developers will ultimately be implementing whatever design has been signed off on, or constructing pages based on guidelines created by other parts of the organization.

As a developer aware of accessibility best practices and web standards, you should always make an effort to point out what might be improved in the user experience, content, or design with the goal of making the content accessible to the largest number of people possible.

Color

Accessibility starts from the foundations that you are building upon (the HTML that marks up your content) but also goes farther up the ladder to the colors that you use on your website and even its behaviors.

Color impairments don't necessarily translate into a user with poor sight or colorblindness (to give only a couple of examples), it might be simply that the user is visiting your website using a screen that is not as well calibrated or expensive as the designer's that created the layout, the almost unnoticeably different shades of gray that you are using to convey the distinction between simple text and links might become imperceptible—for that user, your links are invisible.

As a basic guideline, you should always make sure there is enough contrast between background and foreground. Also remember that some users prefer low–contrast color schemes (and other very high–contrast color schemes such as lime or yellow text on black). While it may not be possible for you to provide all the alternatives, again, you should make it as easy as possible for your users to customize the colors of your website to the settings that are most comfortable to them.

As mentioned previously, this is a process that starts in the designer's hands, but can be checked during the implementation phase, too.

Besides differentiating links by color (with enough contrast), differentiating them from the rest of the text by shape (for example, making them bold, or underlined—which is universally recognized as the styling of a link) can help colorblind users to easily distinguish links from the rest of the text. To go a step farther, you can add bottom borders to links instead of the default text underline, which can make text harder to read since it runs across descenders (letters like *j* or *g* have descenders). You would also need a little padding to ensure that a gap exists between the text and the underline. For this, you would use the following CSS:

```
a {
 text-decoration: none;
 padding-bottom: 2px;
 border-bottom: 1px solid #333333;
}
```

In the preceding example, we only included the generic a element selector, but you should always make sure you have a different style for visited, hovered, active, and focused links.[12]

A complete default link style could be the following:

```
a, a:link {
 color: #333333;
 text-decoration: none;
 padding-bottom: 2px;
 border-bottom: 1px solid #333333;
}
a:visited {
 color: #6e5252;
border-bottom-color: #6e5252;
}
a:hover, a:active, a:focus {
 color: #e89121;
border-bottom-color: #e89121;
}
```

As we have already stressed, it is vital to ensure that your links have a visual indication of being focused, as keyboard users can easily lose track of where they are in the page.

It is also very important that the order of these selectors is correct. Let's see why. These are pseudo-class selectors; the :link (unvisited) and :visited pseudo-classes are mutually exclusive, while :hover, :active and :focus are not (they can be used with each other or even in conjunction with :link and :visited). All the selectors (bar the a selector, which has fewer) in the preceding code snippet have a specificity of 0,0,1,1 (one element selector and one pseudo-class selector—you can read Chapter 3 for

---

[12] Internet Explorer only supports the focus pseudo-class from version 8.

more detail on specificity), and that means that any of the selectors can override all the others by coming last in the code. Knowing this, we define the :link and :visited states before the other ones—if they were defined last, we would never see the other states, as they would be overridden by either the unvisited or visited states.

There are several tools online that can help you to see your websites through the eyes of someone with visual disabilities:

- *Colour Contrast Check*: One of the original tools, from Jonathan Snook (http://snook.ca/technical/colour_contrast/colour.html). It may not be the most beautiful of the bunch, but it is great for testing basic color schemes and contrast levels.

- *Color Scheme Designer*: This tool lets you verify color palettes against several levels of colorblindness (http://colorschemedesigner.com/). You can easily export the results into a variety of useful formats such as HTML and CSS or XML.

- *Color Oracle*: This colorblindness simulator works on Windows, Linux and Mac; it works by applying a filter to the screen (http://colororacle.cartography.ch/index.html).

- *Sim Daltonist* is a Mac-only colorblindness simulator (http://michelf.com/projects/sim-daltonism/). It works in a separate window that shows the area of the screen you are hovering over filtered by several different colorblindness types. You can have more than one window open with different filters at the same time.

- *Contrast-A*: This Flash tool checks a particular combination of background and foreground colors against the W3C's brightness and color and luminance guidelines (http://www.dasplankton.de/ContrastA/).

- *GrayBit*: GrayBit converts a full page into its grayscale version (http://graybit.com/).

- *Check My Colours*: This tool checks luminosity contrast ratio, brightness difference, and color difference of a website's elements' foreground and background color combinations against the W3C's guidelines (http://www.checkmycolours.com/). It also allows you to choose new colors that pass the validation directly on the website.

Don't panic when you see a long list of errors when you test your website's color contrast, though. This does not mean that all your content is inaccessible; you may choose to leave areas that don't have enough contrast, but also don't hold content, as they are.

When comparing color contrast, the specified thresholds may be too restrictive and unrealistic for your designers to work with. Instead, aim for at least 125 brightness difference and at least 400 color difference.

While not the same as testing the accessibility of your website with a real user, and experiencing his difficulties that you might have overseen, checking for cases where there is poor color contrast using these tools will put you one step closer to catering for the widest audience possible. Imagine the frustration that a user with colorblindness would feel were he faced with a poor contrasting navigation! If he can't read the text, how will he find anything on your website?

The BBC's accessibility site (see Figure 6-4) uses a system called Barlesque to deal with user problems with color.

Figure 6-4. *The BBC's accessibility site*

This page includes a small panel that allows users to change their font size (sadly, only two steps are available and both are higher than the default setting, but this can be easily set in the browser preferences) and color scheme. Aside from the default color scheme, there are options for an entirely blue color scheme (for colorblind users), a high–visibility color scheme (for users with poor eyesight), and a soft color scheme (for users with eye strain). These settings are saved and applied to the site via dynamic style sheets (read more about these in Chapter 9) and custom image paths. Although these settings once used to apply to all of the BBC's many sites using the "BBC Barlesque" template, it seems that this methodology has fallen from favor. This is a great shame since it presented a fantastic demonstration of the best way to cope with these color schemes, although managing them was difficult.

User style sheets and alternate style sheets (read about those later in this chapter) can still be used to achieve the same result.

Fonts and Units

Modern browsers have built-in page zooming, which enlarges the entire page, including fonts, images, layout elements, and so on. But this is not the silver bullet that saves us from having to deal with the eternal font zooming problem in older browsers, especially when dealing with high-traffic websites, where 5 percent of the visitors using Internet Explorer 6 might mean more than 50,000 visitors and potential clients. Zooming the page can also have negative side effects, like horizontal scrolling and less legible content (even though the opposite is the intent).

An alternative exists (and many use it): to zoom only the text. Let's look at a comparison. Figure 6-5 shows a news article on Yahoo!, which has been zoomed in by one step using the default full page zooming:

Figure 6-5. *A Yahoo! News article, zoomed in one step*

Figure 6-6 shows the same article, zoomed in one step with Zoom Text Only enabled:

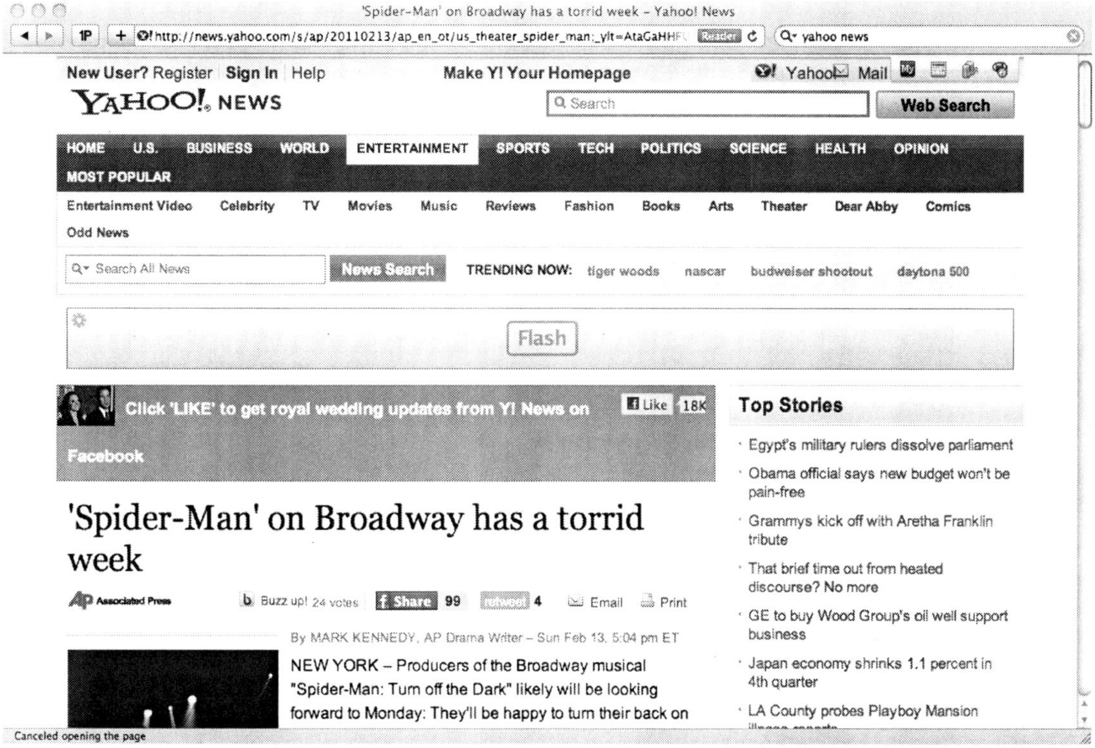

Figure 6-6. A Yahoo! News article zoomed in one step with Zoom Text Only enabled

As you can see, the first method immediately introduced horizontal scrolling and began to crop content on the right side of the screen. The second method zoomed text by the same level, but maintained the layout, while also avoiding the pixelation of images. There is no problem if your users prefer to use the default method: they are used to it, and your website will likely behave exactly as everyone else's. However, if they choose to only zoom the text (or have a browser that only supports this method), you should cater for them. You can do this by making an effort to use relative font sizes.

Because an em is a unit that is dependent on font size, changing the font size on the page with *Zoom Text Only* will affect all the elements that are sized using ems, not just the text. When developing for IE 6, it may be tempting to size everything in ems so that IE 6 exhibits the same zooming behavior as other browsers' defaults (zooming the entire page). However, this choice would preclude users from only zooming the text and as such is an inaccessible technique.

For fixed-sized elements such as images, pixels are the most sensible option. Older browsers will fail to zoom them, and newer browsers will zoom them in proportion with the rest of the page. Either way, the images will become pixelated, but the text is usually the most important part of the content.

For liquid widths, or dimensions that depend upon the size of the viewport or their container, percentages are the most appropriate unit to use. These sizes can change dynamically as you resize the window or by other means modify the dimensions of the window or parent elements.

Users with learning disabilities such as dyslexia may find it easier to read text set in particular fonts. There is not a rule that can be followed that caters for every scenario, as some people prefer to read sans-serif fonts, others find it easier to read serif fonts, and some will even prefer specific fonts like Comic

Sans. We do not recommend that you use Comic Sans across your websites, though, or even to restrict yourself to using just certain fonts that have been proved to be favored by many dyslexics. The important thing to retain here is that the more flexibly your websites are built, avoiding image replacement and trying to use plain text wherever possible (even if that sometimes means compromising the design at some levels) will make it a lot easier for users to browse your website the way they want to.

■ **TIP:** Remember that when users are visiting your website, on their computer, on their browser, on their time, your website is no longer for you—it is for them. It is running on their hardware, and they can do what they like with it.

Your website should pass the text increasing test. Increasing or reducing the text size by one or two sizes (or steps) should not be a problem for your layout.

Web-fonts and Dyslexia

A common issue with using font-face services (mentioned in greater detail in Chapter 5) is the Flash of Unstyled Text (FOUT) that the page suffers in some browsers from when the page hasn't yet loaded the embedded font to when it is fully loaded. For dyslexics, this behavior can render a page impossible to read as they favor consistency of layout, where the elements maintain the same position throughout all the pages of a website; sudden changes (like for example, a flashy hover behavior) make it hard for the user to follow and understand the content.

A simple way of trying to minimize this problem is to follow the recommendation mentioned in Chapter 5: make sure the fallback font that the browser will render before downloading the preferred font is as close in aspect ratio as possible to the embedded one. This will make the jump less obtrusive or (ideally) unnoticeable.

You can also use alternative style sheets (covered in the "Style Switchers" section later in this chapter) to disabled jarring animations or interaction behaviors.

User Customization

User style sheets (mentioned in Chapter 3) can play an important role in aiding users with disabilities to adapt websites to their needs. Making sure your (author) style sheets lend themselves to be easily overridden (mainly by not having complicated and overly specific selectors and avoiding the !important keyword) will make these users' lives a lot easier.

Another thing you can do to make it easier for users to customize your site is to provide hooks, in the shape of body classes or IDs, that they can use on their style sheets. For example, if you add two classes to the body element of your pages (one that is site-wide and another that is page-specific), it will be a lot easier for the user to create rules that affect only your site or a specific page (or section) that they have particular problems with (or visit often).

Having a user create a user style sheet for your site does not mean you failed in making sure your website is accessible. It is impossible to cater for every possible scenario. Just make sure to have flexible enough CSS so as not to make this task harder for the user.

■ **TIP:** If a user goes to the trouble of creating or installing a user style sheet for your site, this means they are a returning and loyal visitor and/or client who has put considerable effort into using your website. You want to make their experience as smooth and unimpeded as possible.

Style Switchers

Alternate style sheets can be put in place with simple link tags. Three different types of style sheet exist: persistent, preferred, and alternate. Persistent style sheets simply use the link tag with a rel attribute of "stylesheet" and no title, like so:

```
<link rel="stylesheet" href="persistent.css" />
```

Persistent style sheets will not be replaced if the user selects an alternate style sheet. Preferred style sheets look the same, but with a title tag:

```
<link rel="stylesheet" href="preferred.css" title="Basic" />
```

You can group several preferred style sheets together by giving them the same title:

```
<link rel="stylesheet" href="preferred1.css" title="Basic" />
<link rel="stylesheet" href="preferred2.css" title="Basic" />
<link rel="stylesheet" href="preferred3.css" title="Basic" />
```

Alternate style sheets will entirely replace the preferred style sheets. These are included in exactly the same way as preferred style sheets, but with a rel attribute of "alternate stylesheet". Again, you can group multiple files by duplicating the title:

```
<link rel="alternate stylesheet" href="alternate1.css" title="Alternate" />
<link rel="alternate stylesheet" href="alternate2.css" title="Alternate" />
<link rel="alternate stylesheet" href="alternate3.css" title="Alternate" />
```

The user can then switch between style sheets in the browser (see Figures 6-7 and 6-8).

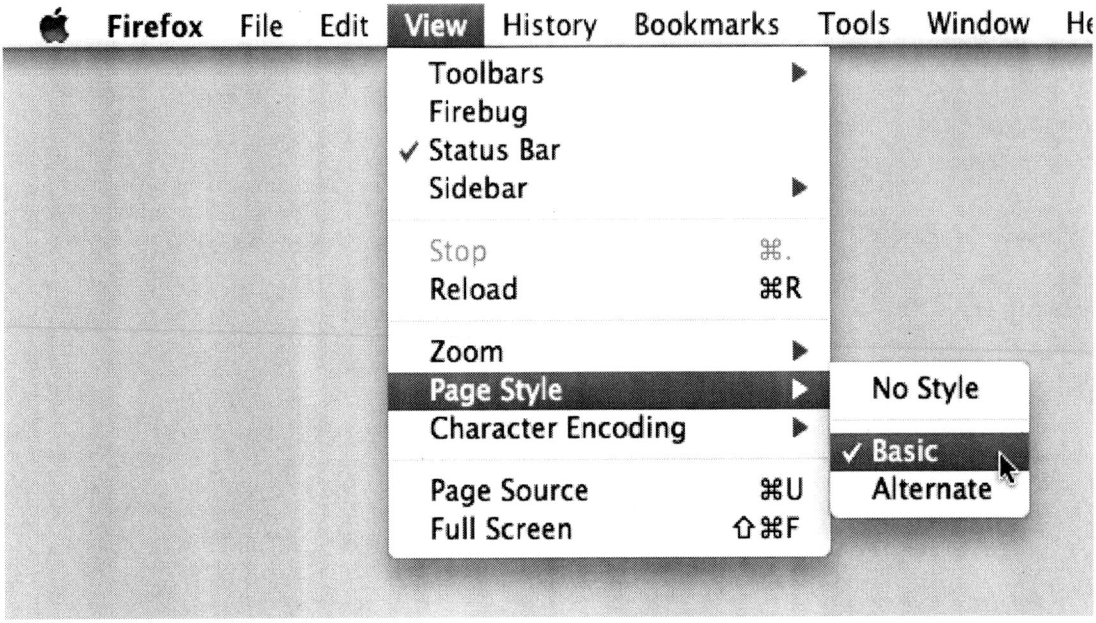

Figure 6-7. *The style switcher in Firefox*

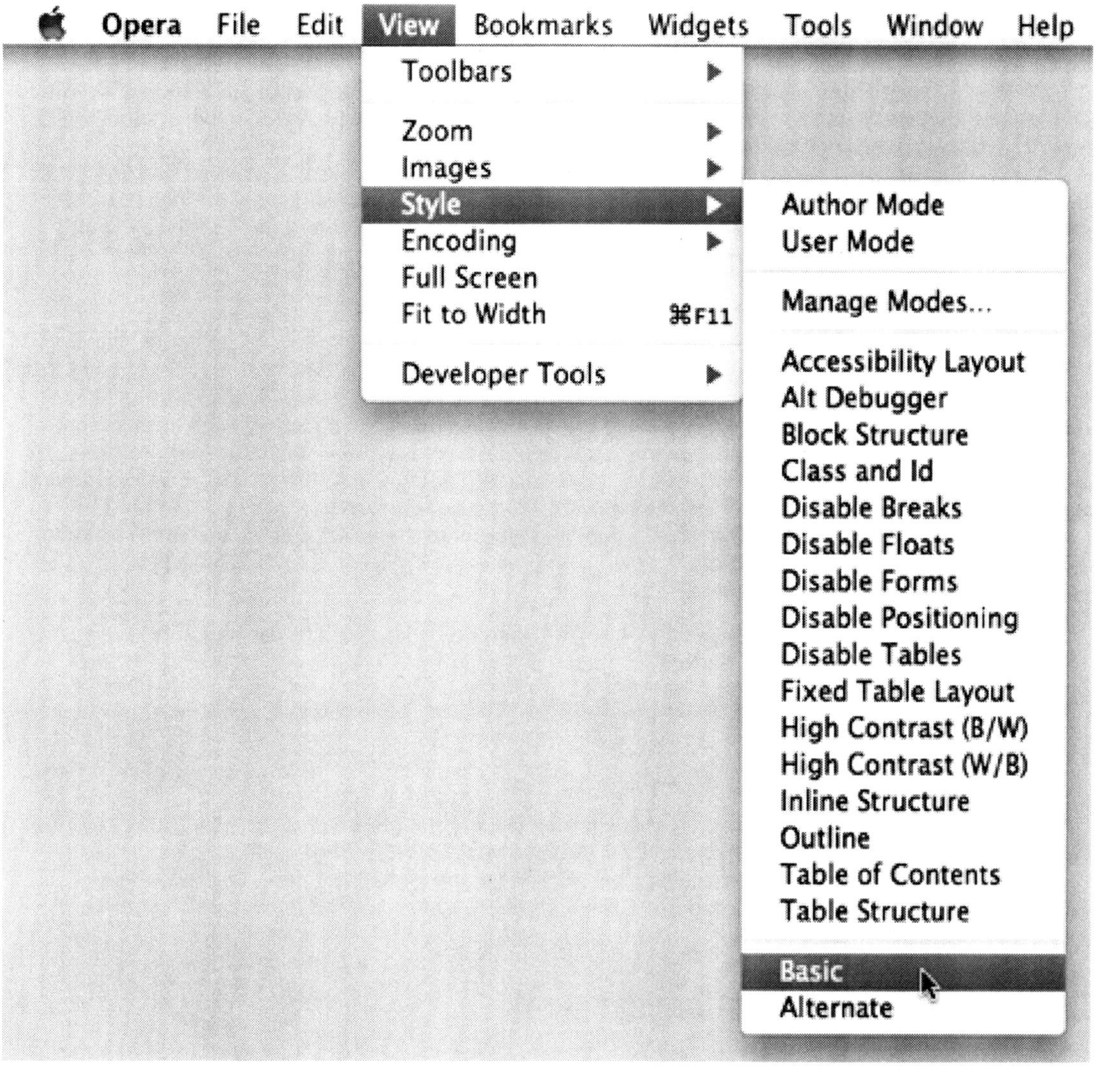

Figure 6-8. *The style switcher in Opera*

Unfortunately, there are two major caveats to this otherwise perfect technique:

- Despite being around for more than ten years, browser support is still lacking for this feature. At the time of writing, Opera and Firefox were the only major browser vendors to support alternate style sheets.

- Of these two browsers, neither saves the user's preference on a per-site basis; the user's choice does not persist.[13]

To offer genuine alternate style sheets' functionality and present it as part of your website's tools, allowing the user to choose, for example, a high–visibility color scheme, you need to write your own code. This entails JavaScript, but is fairly trivial to achieve.

Be aware, as always, that these style sheets will still download regardless of whether or not they are applied. As a result, apart from sites specifically targeted at users with impairments that alternate style sheets can help with, it is often better to simply ensure that it is easy for your users to override your styles via whatever means they think best.

WAI-ARIA

WAI-ARIA stands for Web Accessibility Initiative–Accessible Rich Internet Applications. The goal of this specification is to make Web content and applications more accessible to users with disabilities. According to the W3C website (`http://www.w3.org/WAI/intro/aria`), "It especially helps with dynamic content and advanced user interface controls" that would otherwise not be available to those users. For example, with simple HTML, there is currently no consistent, reliable way to warn a user using a screen reader that an area of the page has been refreshed and its content updated.

Using ARIA, you can also mark areas of a page as sections so that users can tab between sections rather than through each different link.

ARIA adds support for the following:

- Roles that describe the type of widget (for example, "`combobox`") or the structure of the page (for example, "`banner`")

- Properties that describe states (for example, "`checked`") or live regions that can suffer updates

- Keyboard navigation for the widgets and events

A large obstacle currently between a wider implementation of ARIA is the lack of feature detection: there is no way of detecting ARIA support in the browser or assistive technologies.

Since WAI-ARIA is an HTML technology, we will not go into detail on it here. The WAI-ARIA specification is, at the time of writing, in the Candidate Recommendation stage and can be found at `http://www.w3.org/TR/wai-aria/`[14].

Device and Environment Impairments

A type of impairment that is often overlooked is that of the device. The user may have a slow computer, no mouse, a slow Internet connection, a firewall that blocks certain types of content, and so on. A scenario that is more common than developers would like to assume is when users browse our websites with CSS on but images off. The main reason that this might happen is slow Internet connections. It might be a momentary problem, such as the connection being faulty before an external technician or the internal IT team resolves the problem, or the user might be accessing your website from a mobile device—a common scenario in developing countries, where Internet access tends to be slow and

---

[13] There are Firefox extensions to add this functionality.
[14] You could use the attributes in WAI-ARIA for semantic styling hooks with the attribute selector. Bear in mind, though, that this is a slower selector and is not supported in all browsers.

receiving data costly. Regardless of whether the situation is fleeting or more permanent, it happens, and visiting websites that are not ready for this, even at a basic level, is a frustrating experience.

Progressive enhancement (detailed in the next section) cures most of these problems, but is not a panacea. If you have built a website that looks good with just markup, you are most of the way there. If you then test with only CSS enabled, this will expose problems you might otherwise miss, like the lack of or inappropriate background colors under background images.[15]

In Chapter 8, we will demonstrate how you can intercept requests and modify them to, for example, emulate slow connections. Test everything as much as you can and aim for progressive enhancement, not graceful degradation. What are those? It's funny you should ask…

Progressive Enhancement or Graceful Degradation?

Progressive enhancement and graceful degradation are two ways of looking at the same problem: how to deal with browsers that don't support a feature we have made use of.

With *progressive enhancement*, you start from the lowest common denominator; you make the site work for everyone first. This means good semantics, sensible ordering of content, no CSS, no images, no JavaScript, and so on. Your markup should work well on its own. You then add the layers so that if for some reason one of the layers is to fail or be unsupported, the site content is still available in a sensible fashion. This is, obviously, an accessible approach—we are ensuring that we cater to the widest audience possible and leave no one out.

Graceful degradation is the opposite of this. We build all the layers at the same time, resulting in a great user experience for the majority, but not everyone. We then make sure that when it does fail, it does so in a reasonable fashion, and we still make our content accessible. This could mean building alternative versions of pages, or presenting warnings or guides on how to address any issues our users may come across. Some good examples of graceful degradation could be the `alt` attribute for images or `noscript` tags for browsers without JavaScript enabled. Graceful degradation is better than doing nothing, but implementing it means (in our opinion) that you have your priorities wrong. Often, the lower levels of potential failure are ignored, neglected, or forgotten about; and the costs of implementing them after the fact are greater. It also means we have already defined our top level—we started there and worked our way down, leaving ourselves little room to embrace newer technologies when they reach widespread acceptance.

Progressive enhancement, on the other hand, makes it impossible to leave our device-impaired users behind. Everything is built upon the lower levels, so they are key in reaching the full-featured website we hope most users will use. And since our top level is built upon a solid foundation, it is easy to bolt newer, cleverer things on at a later date and feel secure that we have not ostracized any of our existing user base.

The best example of progressive enhancement is CSS itself. It sits on top of our markup and improves upon it. We can further progressively enhance with CSS3 and experimental features, using media queries to ensure that we are not ruining the experience for everyone else. Then we can layer JavaScript on top of that, and so on.

Graceful degradation seems the fastest development option, and it is in the short term. We can quickly build the highest-level experience and work from there. However, it is adding the lower levels that soaks up time. Progressive enhancement takes more thought upfront, but makes for a more robust technical solution. However, exceptions exist. We understand that budgets are not infinite, and it may not always be in your organization's financial interests to try to serve everyone. In that instance, we suggest you do the best you can with the resources you have, using your reporting tools to target your most common user demographics. Furthermore, sites that are temporal (like a website for a short-lived promotion, or seasonal event) are unlikely to be online for long before being discarded forever. The

---

[15] A side benefit of this is that when the images do load, it will seem less jarring to the user.

return on investment (ROI) of progressive enhancement is likely to be low in this instance, and we do not recommend you invest too much time on something that will be thrown away. In that instance, graceful degradation (or, simply failing gracefully) might be a more viable option.

The Yahoo! Graded Browser Support (GBS) methodology (explained in more detailed in the next section of this chapter) favors progressive enhancement over graceful degradation because it "puts content at the center, and allows most browsers to receive more (and show more to the user)" as opposed to the latter, which "prioritizes presentation, and permits less widely-used browsers to receive less (and give less to the user)" (http://developer.yahoo.com/yui/articles/gbs/).

Can CSS3 Be Harmful?

CSS3 is one the latest buzzwords in the web industry, alongside HTML5. This means many developers jump in without thinking of the potential consequences of their actions. There are some very obvious ways using CSS3 can lead to inaccessible websites:

- Pseudo-elements such as ::before and ::after may not be visible to assistive devices. Use them for decoration, not for important content.[16]

- Gradients can compound color visibility issues more than flat colors.

- Using transitions, transformations, and animations for key features may make those features unavailable to users of browsers that don't support them.

The best way of dealing with these is to understand the potential issues that we have explained throughout this chapter. Remember to progressively enhance whenever possible and provide fallbacks for instances where these features may be unsupported. Be aware of the color accessibility issues some newer techniques might bring along with them, and try to provide alternate style sheets. Use transitions, transforms, and animations as decorative effects, not for vital features.

This is mainly common sense. Remember to test in older browsers, and pre-empt the problems users will have. Progressive enhancement is your friend.

Graded Browser Support (GBS)

In 2006, Yahoo! published its GBS methodology, developed by (at the time) Senior Front-end Engineer Nate Koechley. GBS divides browsers into three different levels (grades) of support: A-, C-, and X-grade. By *support* it is not meant that some browsers will be locked out of the content, but rather presented with a different experience of it, while still being able to access it fully. Let's look at what each of the different grades mean, in practical terms:

- *A-grade* is the highest support level. Browsers within this group will be presented with the full experience—visual and functional—and are whitelisted. All A-grade browsers should be tested and any bugs are labeled as high priority. Browsers in this list include (among others): Safari 5; Chrome's latest stable release; Firefox 3.6; and IE 6 to 8.

---

[16] Strictly speaking, these pseudo-elements were introduced in CSS2.1 as :before and :after.

- *C-grade* browsers are presented with only the HTML. These are older browsers (which represent a very small portion of the users) with lesser capabilities. Style and behavior should be omitted, and only a small sample of the browsers should be tested (or using a modern browser with both CSS and JavaScript disabled), but bugs also receive high priority status. The websites in this level of support are blacklisted. This list (in draft at the time of writing) includes Internet Explorer versions lower than 6 (including Mac OS versions); Safari and Firefox versions lower than 3; Opera versions lower than 9.5; Netscape versions lower than 8. It is expected that in the first quarter of 2011, IE 6 will be downgraded to C-grade support level.

- *X-grade* includes marginal browsers. These are rare or obscure browsers, browsers that are no longer being developed, or brand new (untested) browsers; they are to be as capable as A-grade browsers. As opposed to A-grade browsers, though, X-grade ones are not tested and bugs are not filed against them.

All browsers belong to one of the three levels of support, so there are no browsers that are "not supported" because content is available for all. The Yahoo! GBS page says that "in modern web development we must support all browsers. Choosing to exclude a segment of users is inappropriate, and, with a 'Graded Browser Support' strategy, unnecessary" (`http://developer.yahoo.com/yui/articles/gbs/`). It also says (and we agree) that "expecting two users using different browser software to have an identical experience fails to embrace or acknowledge the heterogeneous essence of the Web."

TIP: jQuery Mobile has its own GBS (`http://jquerymobile.com/gbs/`), which is a useful guide to the mobile browsers and their respective likely capabilities.

Although adopting the Yahoo! GBS verbatim is an easy and reasonable tactic for choosing which browsers you should support, it makes a lot more sense to use it as a base and refer to your reporting tools to ensure that the GBS matches well with your actual traffic. If it doesn't, amend it. When raising bugs within your organization, you should use your GBS chart to decide on the severity of your issues and thus how important it is that these bugs are fixed. Using a consistent method of raising bugs and measuring their severity will result in the most important bugs being fixed first, and each tester raising bugs in a more accurate and predictable fashion.

TIP: As mentioned before, SEERS (`http://zeroedandnoughted.com/standardised-bug-reporting-with-seers/`) is a methodology created and championed by Antony to try to create a standard for browser-based bug-testing. Using GBS is key to this process.

Summary

It is impossible to consider every single accessibility issue that your visitors might be suffering from, be it a temporary or permanent one. Because of this, you need to make your website flexible and prone to being adjusted and read by everyone—it is your website, but it is your visitor's browser, and he should have the final word.

It is important to not see this as a burden to your team. Also, you should not see this as a step in the development. Accessibility considerations should be present in your team's mind constantly and should always be a concern. By making your websites more accessible, you will be making sure that the largest number possible of people have access to your content and/or can buy your products without getting frustrated and moving on to your competitors.

These are simple techniques that will also make your website more flexible and easier to maintain (think of all the headaches using image replacement can bring, for example). As a result, you will also have websites that are more search engine–friendly.

The most vital thing to impart here is that every user, browser, or device should have access to your content and services, regardless of capability or environment.

In the next chapter, we will discuss the many devices available that can parse and render CSS. We will look at some of the restrictions and performance implications of coding for these, as well as how to target them with media types and media queries.

CHAPTER 7

■ ■ ■

Devices

With high-traffic websites, unusual devices make up a much higher number of visitors than they would otherwise. Depending upon the demographics that your site is targeting, and the results of your reporting tools, you may need to consider these devices seriously. When we discuss devices from a CSS perspective, really we are just talking about browsers with different capabilities. Whether our CSS is being served to a mobile phone, a laptop, or a search engine spider, in essence it's just another web browser, with a different resolution and different abilities to process our CSS.

With each of these devices come different considerations; when using a printer we need to care about page breaks and clarity in grayscale, as well as avoiding printing unnecessary content. For mobile devices, we need to be concerned with unusual screen sizes and resolutions, as well as slow processors or poor CSS support. Screen readers, too, can be considered devices, but we have discussed these in some detail in the previous chapter.

In this chapter, you will learn about

- Media types
- Media queries
- Media features
- Printing in detail
- Specific SEO considerations
- Mobile devices
- Other devices

Media Types

The more traffic your website receives, the higher the likelihood of it being accessed by unlikely or unusual devices. Whereas smaller websites can afford to ignore or neglect particular devices and/or web browsers, for larger websites they may make up a large enough number to require consideration as an important user group. Larger companies take great care of their brand and their customer experience, and at the very least you should be showing anyone interested enough to visit your website a reasonable experience regardless of what they are using to view it. To that end, you need to implement various methods to detect their platform and serve the most appropriate content.

The media attribute in the link tag we use to reference external style sheets is intended to identify the kind of device the style sheet is aimed at. Where devices/browsers support this, they will ignore irrelevant or unknown style sheet media types, and not include the contents of the file. It is worth noting that most modern browsers will still download the file, even where they do not intend to parse the contents.[1] This means this method is not of use from a performance perspective—it actually incurs more HTTP requests than not using it—but is only of use for targeting specific browsers or devices.

You can actually target media via three methods. The first is within the link tags, like so:

```
<link rel="stylesheet" href="style.css" media="screen" />
```

The second is via the @import directive:

```
@import url(style.css) screen;
```

@import commands must always precede any other rules in a style sheet (except for other @import commands). Again, most modern browsers download the file, even though they will not parse the contents of the file. Regardless, we don't recommend you use @import rules because they block the parsing of the rest of the file.

The final method is the @media directive, which allows us to use only certain parts of files with certain media types. Here's an example:

```
@media screen {
    body {
        font-family: arial;
    }
}
```

This would only target browsers and devices that report support for the screen media type.

For all three of these methods, you can comma-separate the media value to target multiple types, like so:

```
<link rel="stylesheet" href="style.css" media="screen, print" />
```

```
@import url(style.css) screen, print;
```

```
@media screen, print {
    body {
        font-family: arial;
    }
}
```

In these instances, if the browser or device supports only one of the media types, the file/rules will still be parsed.

For each media type, there are certain factors it is important to take into account. These are referred to as *media groups*.

Paged media (media that consists of pages—like a printed document—rather than one long document like a web page presented on a screen) supports some extra properties that continuous media does not.[2] Grid media (as opposed to bitmap media) considers fixed-width characters to be of importance. For example, braille media needs characters to be of a predictable and consistent width for

---

[1] This is so that their contents can still be accessed via the CSS Object Model (CSSOM), as well as being listed in document.styleSheets, which can be accessed via JavaScript to give details of all the style sheets attached to the document.

[2] We will mention them later in this chapter.

users to be able to understand it. We can group by static, interactive, or both, indicating whether the target is read-only or can be interacted with. Media can also be grouped as visual, audio, speech (for screen readers) or tactile (for devices that communicate with touch; braille, for example).

Let's take a look at the media types defined in the CSS2 specification.

all

Although not really a media type as such, *all* applies to all of the below media types and therefore all media groups. If you don't specify the media type, this is the default behavior.

braille

Braille is a tactile method of conveying characters, used primarily by the blind. Braille tactile feedback devices vary in their capability. The specification describes this media type as continuous rather than paged (a braille printer that can output paged media is considered within the embossed media type), tactile, grid, and both interactive and static.

embossed

The *embossed* media type is similar to the braille type, but is intended for output via a braille printer. For that reason it is considered paged (rather than continuous) and static. Other than that, it is exactly the same as the braille type.

handheld

The *handheld* type is intended for targeting handheld devices such as mobile phones. These devices will normally have slower connections and smaller screens, so need to be treated differently from others. Since handheld devices vary so much in capability, they are considered to be a part of every media group except tactile.[3]

Handheld devices vary from poor to powerful performance, and everything in between, and offer many different browsers. Since they change so quickly, we would suggest using media queries (described later in this chapter) to target them, rather than relying on just the media type. Remember though, that you cannot rely on media types or media queries to control what is downloaded; the browser or device may choose to download everything regardless so there is no performance benefit.

Since current handheld devices, such as smartphones and tablets, do their best to present the Web, and not a cut-down version of it, most of them would actually be targeted with the "screen" media type. WebKit (Mobile Safari and Android) and Firefox Mobile ignore this media type completely. Opera Mini and Opera Mobile will respect it if the user switches to "handheld mode" in the settings, or the document has a known mobile doctype.

print

The *print* media type applies specifically to printed media output, and as such is considered to be paged, visual, grid, and static. We will discuss print and paged media in detail later in this chapter.

---

[3] Actually, Nokia has been making inroads toward an experimental braille reader on its handsets since September 2009.

projection

The *projection* media type is intended for projected output, typically projectors. Since this kind of output would usually be from an unmanned terminal, it is considered to be paged, visual, and bitmap. The specification lists it as interactive only, which we assume to be a mistake. Opera respects this media type in full-screen presentation mode (Opera Show). We do not know of any other browser or device that implements this.

screen

The *screen* media type is undoubtedly the most common type. Primarily intended for computer screens (both desktop and laptop), this is the media type you are most likely to use, alongside *all*. Almost all devices use this media type, regardless of whether it is intended for them or not, because most of these devices intend to represent the Internet as it is in a web browser, rather than a cut-down version. Screen is considered to be continuous, bitmap, both interactive and static, and both visual and audio.

speech

The *speech* media type is intended for any device or application that will audibly read the contents of the page, such as a screen reader or other assistive technology. In older specs, it was referred to as *aural* (which is now deprecated), so it is safest to target both media types simultaneously, like so:

```
<link rel="stylesheet" href="style.css" media="speech, aural" />
```

This media type is considered to be continuous, speech, and both interactive and static. Grid or bitmap media groups are inapplicable in this instance. You can read more about this specific type of style sheet at http://www.w3.org/TR/CSS2/aural.html.

tty

This media type (which is short for "teletype") is intended for media that uses a "fixed-pitch character grid" (meaning a grid of characters that are all identical in width). Since there is no concept of pixel sizes for characters for this media type, authors should not supply them. There are very few devices currently available of this type, and fewer still that support the Internet, so support for—and use of—this media type is very rare. This media type is considered to be continuous, visual, grid, and both interactive and static.

tv

This media type is intended for television sets. Although the specification lists these devices as "low resolution, color, limited-scrollability screens, sound available", television sets vary greatly in their capability and this description will often be incorrect. Current large televisions often provide a higher resolution screen than their monitor counterparts, and sometimes even include web browsing software and the ability to scroll. Due to these inconsistencies in their capability, the tv media type is considered to be both continuous and paged, visual, audio, bitmap, and both interactive and static.

> **NOTE:** Although screen and print are by far the most commonly used media types in the wild, we are aware of devices that use all of the media types except tty. Media types were added to the spec, but not necessarily implemented by device manufacturers, often because of the sparse developer implementation.

Other devices may support media types not defined in this list, but we would advise against using them. You can read more about media types at http://www.w3.org/TR/CSS2/media.html. Since the media type is now rarely adequate to describe the capability of a device or browser, CSS3 introduced *media queries*, which provide us with the tools necessary to target a device by its features and capability instead of (or in tandem with) its media type. Most current mobile devices (including tablets) support media queries, and we recommend using them if you intend to target these devices.

Media Queries

Media types can give us the ability to target some of the devices we might expect to be browsing our sites, but their implementation in the devices is patchy. New devices are more predictable in their support, particularly those that your high-traffic websites are likely to see considerable visitors from. Again, these devices are likely to form a small fraction of your total traffic, but a large amount of people nonetheless. Media queries give us much better control over the devices and browsers we're targeting.

A media query is made up of two parts: a media type and zero or more queries that will be checked against the media features. When the media type matches the one of the device and all the queries are true, the media query is applied. If more than one media query is listed (using a comma-separated list), only one of the media queries needs to be true.

Here's a quick example:

```
<link rel="stylesheet" href="style.css" media="screen and (min-width:800px) and (max-
width:1500px)" />
```

As well as targeting browsers and devices that support the "screen" media type, we are also stating that the width of the viewport of the device must be at least 800 and at most 1,500 pixels. The features we are naming in the brackets above are known as "media features". You can comma separate media queries (exactly as with media types) as shorthand, like so:

```
<link rel="stylesheet" href="style.css" media="tv, projection, screen and (min-width:800px)
and (max-width:1500px)" />
```

In this instance, each comma-separated valued is evaluated in its entirety, (the parts following the "and" only apply to the media type immediately preceding them). The preceding media query is the same as the following:

```
<link rel="stylesheet" href="style.css" media="tv" />
<link rel="stylesheet" href="style.css" media="projection" />
<link rel="stylesheet" href="style.css" media="screen and (min-width:800px) and (max-
width:1500px)" />
```

You can use multiple "and" clauses in each list. You can also use "not" to negate an entire media query. However, you cannot negate individual parts of the query. The following will work:

```
<link rel="stylesheet" href="style.css" media="not screen and (min-width:800px) and (max-width:1500px)" />
```

This will parse style.css for only any browser or device that would fail the query without the "not" keyword applied (the media type screen is unsupported, or the width of the viewport is less than 800 pixels, or the width of the viewport is greater than 1500 pixels). The following (and other variants to attempt the same) does not work:

```
<link rel="stylesheet" href="style.css" media="screen and (min-width:800px) and not (max-width:1500px)" />
```

This lack of granularity can be frustrating for any developer used to basic conditional logic. To target multiple feature sets in this manner, it is necessary to first apply the default behavior to all devices then override this behavior for each device, like this:

```
/* Applied to every device and browser */
body {
    color: black;
}

@media screen and (min-width:800px) {
    /* Only applied to screen devices with a viewport width of at least 800 pixels */
body {
    color: red;
    }
}
```

Whenever a media query is not understood by the user agent (browser or device), it is considered to be "not all"—that is, it will not apply the contents of the linked style sheet or query.

The "only" keyword can be used to ensure that only CSS3-compliant browsers will apply the style sheet.

```
<link rel="stylesheet" href="style.css" media="only screen" />
```

Using the "only" keyword in the beginning of a media query will hide the media query from older browsers that don't support them (since they will think "only" is the name of a media type), while conforming browsers will ignore the "only" keyword and check for the media query that follows it.

As well as in the link tag, media queries can be used in the other two ways in your CSS files, exactly as media types alone can be used:

```
@import url(style.css) screen and (min-width:800px) and (max-width:1500px);

@media screen and (min-width:800px) and (max-width:1500px) {
    body {
        font-family: arial;
    }
}
```

■ **CAUTION:** Browsers will download linked files, even if they will not be applied to the document in question.

When a media feature will evaluate to a value other than zero (regardless of unit), you do not need to provide a value. For example:

```
<link rel="stylesheet" href="style.css" media="all and (width)" />
```

This style sheet would always be applied because the width of the viewport will always be greater than zero (except perhaps for primarily audible devices). You wouldn't use this method; we just include it as an example.

Before we get too deep into the media features available, it's worth spending a moment discussing the viewport itself. The viewport is the available rendering size on the device, not including any browser chrome.

With the introduction of Mobile Safari, Apple also introduced the *viewport meta tag*[4].

The viewport meta tag gives you some control over the size and behavior of the viewport. Although this is HTML, it is important to cover to understand some of the concepts we will deal with in this chapter. Here's a simple example:

```
<meta name="viewport" content="width=device-width" />
```

The name "viewport" identifies this meta tag. The content attribute contains the values we want to pass. The properties are key/value pairs divided with an equals sign; you can comma-separate them to have as many as you like. There are two important constants we can use:

- *device-width*: The actual pixel width (in landscape) of the device

- *device-height*: The actual pixel height (in landscape) of the device

There are also six important properties we can use:

- *width*: The initial width of the viewport (in landscape) in pixels. This value can also be either of the two constants. The default (on Mobile Safari) is 980 pixels.

- *height*: The initial height of the viewport (in landscape) in pixels. This value can also be either of the two constants. The default is set automatically depending on the width and the aspect ratio of the device.

- *initial-scale*: The scale is a multiplier used to calculate the size of the viewport. For example, if we set the viewport width to 400px and the scale to 1.5, the viewport would actually be 600px and extend 200px horizontally outside of the visible area. This property sets the initial scale value. By default, it would typically be automatically set to a value that fits the entire web page in the visible area. The user can zoom the device to adjust this value.

---

[4] You can read about the viewport meta tag at
http://developer.apple.com/library/safari/#documentation/AppleApplications/Reference/SafariHTMLRef/Articles/MetaTags.html and the viewport specifically at
http://developer.apple.com/library/safari/#documentation/AppleApplications/Reference/SafariWebContent/UsingtheViewport/UsingtheViewport.html.

- *minimum-scale*: This sets the minimum scale the user can zoom to.

- *maximum-scale*: This sets the maximum scale the user can zoom to.

- *user-scalable*: This sets whether users can adjust the size of the viewport whether they can zoom. Potential values are *yes* or *no*. The default is yes.

■ **TIP:** Opera has proposed a method for achieving the same thing in CSS, rather than in HTML, which is more appropriate. Sadly, there is no real support for this yet, but you can read the specification at
`http://dev.w3.org/csswg/css-device-adapt/`.

The vital thing to take away from this is that the viewport may exceed the visible area, but will never be less than the visible area. This is important because we use `viewport` in media features. There are many media features defined in the CSS3 specifications. We'll list these in the following sections.

width

The *width* media feature applies to the width of the viewport (for continuous media) or of the "page box" (for paged media).[5] Where there is a virtual viewport (i.e. the scale is greater than one) this applies to the width of the entire viewport, not just the renderable screen space.

It accepts numbers greater than zero (any less than that will render the query invalid). You can (as with many media features) prefix width with `min-` and `max-` as in our examples above. These effectively act the same as greater than or equal to, and less than or equal to respectively.[6]

Any units can be used, but where relative sized units are used those will be relative to the root element of the document (i.e. the `html` tag).

height

The *height* media feature behaves exactly as its "width" counterpart, but applies to the height of the viewport instead.

device-width

The *device-width* media feature describes the width of the entire rendering surface (i.e. displayable area) of the device. For screens, this is the width of the screen. For paged media this is the width of the page. Again, you can use `max-` and `min-` as prefixes, and any value less than zero will result in an invalid media query. This uses the actual screen width, and not the virtual viewport you may have set with the viewport `meta` tag, or the virtual viewport the user may have amended by zooming the page on his device.

device-height

The *device-height* media feature behaves exactly as `device-width`, but for height.

---

[5] As defined in the CSS 2.1 specification at `www.w3.org/TR/2009/CR-CSS2-20090908/page.html#page-box`.
[6] It was decided to avoid the < and > characters, since those could conflict with the characters in HTML.

orientation

The *orientation* media feature has two possible values: `landscape` and `portrait`. If the width viewport is greater than the height, the orientation is landscape. Otherwise it is portrait. If using this media feature in a query, you should always pass it a value. Using orientation without a value results in the browser or device not applying the CSS.

■ **NOTE:** There is no "square" value for orientation. If the width and height values are exactly equal, the orientation is considered to be portrait.

---

aspect-ratio

The *aspect-ratio* media feature is the ratio of the width of the viewport to the height, separated with a forward slash. Here's a quick example of it in use:

```
@media screen and (aspect-ratio: 4/3) {
   ...
}
```

device-aspect-ratio

The *device-aspect-ratio* media feature describes the ratio of the width of the entire renderable area of the device to the height, separated with a forward slash.

color

The *color* media feature describes the amount of bits per color component of the device. If, for example, the device used four bits each for red, green, and blue, this value would be four. If, for some reason, a different number of bits were used for each component, the smallest number would be the value. If the device is not color, or is not visual, this number will be zero. You can use `min-` and `max-` with the color media feature.

color-index

The *color-index* feature is used to query the amount of colors a device can display at once. This is often more intuitive to use than the color media feature. Devices typically support 16; 256; 65,536; or 16,777,215 colors. You can use `min-` and `max-` with `color-index`, and devices that are not color or not visual will present this value as zero.

■ **NOTE:** You can use commas in numerical values in media queries, which helps legibility a great deal. The following example would work fine:

```
<link rel="stylesheet" href="style.css" media="screen and (min-color-index:1,001)" />
```

---

monochrome

The *monochrome* media feature describes the amount of bits the device supports for the display of monochromatic colors (in effect, the higher the number, the more grays between white and black can be displayed). You can use min- and max- with this media feature, and if a device is color or has no display, the value would be zero.

resolution

The *resolution* media feature describes the density of the pixels on the device in dots per inch (DPI) or dots per centimeter (DPCM); you should use these units (DPI and DPCM, respectively) in your media query. This media feature supports the min- and max- prefixes. If using a device with non-square pixels and min-resolution, the least dense dimension (the one with the lesser DPI) will be used. When using max-resolution, the densest dimension will be compared. If using "resolution" (for an exact match) with non-square pixels, the style sheet will never be applied. This media feature applies only to bitmap-based media—applying it to grid media will result in the entire media query being treated as "not all."

scan

The *scan* media feature applies specifically to televisions (and thus the tv media type). The applicable values are "progressive" and "scan". If the device is not a television, this value will evaluate to zero.

grid

The *grid* media feature describes whether a device is grid- or bitmap-based. For grid output devices, this value is 1; otherwise, it is 0.

■ **TIP:** Media queries will be evaluated on the fly. That is, if you have set a media query to apply to devices with a viewport of less than 900 pixels and you are using a device with a resizable viewport, then resizing the window will cause the query to be applied or unapplied immediately.

You can read more about media queries at http://www.w3.org/TR/css3-mediaqueries/.

Since the introduction of CSS transformations, transitions, and animations in WebKit, the basic media features defined in the specification have clearly been inadequate to target just the browsers that support them. To that end, WebKit has defined four proprietary media features, discussed in the following sections:

transform-2d

The *transform-2d* media feature describes the availability of CSS transforms across two dimensions. This value will evaluate to 1 if available and 0 if not.

transform-3d

This media feature describes the availability of CSS transforms across three dimensions. This value will evaluate to 1 if available and 0 if not. Since support for CSS transforms across two dimensions is necessary for this feature to be available, you can safely infer from this feature's value being 1 that transform-2d also evaluates to 1.

transition

The *transition* media feature describes the availability of CSS transitions. This value will evaluate to 1 if available and 0 if not.

animation

The *animation* media feature describes the availability of CSS transitions. This value will evaluate to 1 if available and 0 if not.

CAUTION: Sadly, you cannot target devices that do not support these media features with something like "not (-webkit-animation)." Any unknown feature in a media query will immediately make the media query equivalent to "not all". For these devices, you will need to set default behavior and then override it, as we demonstrated previously.

Although all four of these media features are described and documented at http://webkit.org/specs/MediaQueriesExtensions.html and at http://developer.apple.com/library/safari/#documentation/appleapplications/reference/SafariCSS Ref/Articles/OtherStandardCSS3Features.html, in truth they cannot (at the time of writing) be used in practice. They all require the vendor-specific WebKit prefix in order for them to work properly. Here is a complete list of the working media features:

- -webkit-transform-2d
- -webkit-transform-3d
- -webkit-transition
- -webkit-animation

Using media queries can be frustrating, but it is important to remember that the specification is always evolving. For now, here are four points that might save you confusion when developing and using media queries:

- The "not" keyword negates the entire query. You cannot negate individual elements of the media query.

- There is no "or" operator to use within media queries (although you can comma-separate entire media queries).

- Externally referenced files will be downloaded regardless of the media query. Do not assume that applying media types to separate files will give you any kind of HTTP performance benefit. On the contrary, it will in fact result in more file requests.

- WebKit-specific media features require the vendor prefix.

Modernizr

Modernizr (http://www.modernizr.com/), created by developers Faruk Ateş, Paul Irish, and Alex Sexton, is a JavaScript library that detects and exposes browser functionality. It works by adding classes to the html element of a page; these classes indicate whether or not a particular feature (HTML5 and CSS3 features, to be exact) is present in the browser. Modernizr does not enable the functionality in the browser; it merely states whether it is available or not. It also adds support for styling the new HTML5 elements in less-capable browsers like Internet Explorer.

To use Modernizr, you just need to link to it in the head of your HTML document, like so:

```
<script src="js/modernizr-1.6.min.js"></script>
```

Second, you need to add a class of "no-js" to your html tag. This will be the default state of the page. If JavaScript is off, Modernizr will not work, and you will be able to detect this and provide a non-JavaScript version of the page to your users:

```
<html class="no-js">
```

If JavaScript is enabled, various classes, similar to the following, will replace this class:

```
<html class="js canvas canvastext geolocation rgba hsla multiplebgs borderimage borderradius
boxshadow opacity no-cssanimations csscolumns no-cssgradients no-cssreflections csstransforms
no-csstransforms3d no-csstransitions  video audio cufon-active fontface cufon-ready">
```

In the preceding example, we can see that the browser in question (Firefox 3.6, in this case) does not support CSS animations, CSS gradients, CSS reflections, CSS transforms in 3D, or CSS transitions (from the classes "no-cssanimations," "no-cssgradients," "no-cssreflections," "no-csstransform3d," and "no-csstransitions," respectively). It does support the other features, like canvas and geolocation.

With this knowledge, we can now write CSS accordingly. Let's imagine we want to add multiple backgrounds to the body element of a page. We can first specify the default style for all browsers and then override that style with a more specific one that will only target browsers that support the feature, as such:

```
body {
        background: url(simple.png) top left repeat-x;
```

```
}
.multiplebgs body {
        background: url(multiple-top.png) top left repeat-x,
        url(multiple-bottom.png) bottom left repeat-x;
}
```

In the case of the `html` element shown previously, Firefox 3.6 would understand and show the multiple backgrounds. Internet Explorer 8, for example, would only display the "simple.png" background image, as the class it would use would be "no-multiplebgs" instead.

It is also important to notice that in the preceding example, Firefox 3.6 would actually download both images because both rules could be applied (even though the less specific rule is overridden), so even though we are making sure to cater for users that can and can't see the features, we're penalizing those who can by making them download a completely unnecessary file. We could have avoided this by using ".no-multiplebgs body" in our first rule, rather than just "body."

Although a simple and useful solution, before you consider using it, remember that Modernizr will make for very verbose CSS that is downloaded by all users and not necessarily applied, and add a JavaScript dependency to your CSS, which is far from ideal.

Print Style Sheets

Print style sheets need to be considered as a special case. Users will often want to print pages from your site, and you can cater to their needs in a way that's different from how you would cater to typical users. Users printing your content are engaged users, and frustrating them with unnecessary content or pages that won't fit well on their media will reduce their goodwill toward your site and your company. On the other hand, providing them with just the information they need in a legible and friendly format shows attention to detail and consideration to their needs. Making a basic print style sheet is very easy, and if your markup and CSS is well thought out, often it will be very concise and work well across your entire site.

Including a print style sheet is easy. We'll reiterate how best to achieve that here:

```
<link rel="stylesheet" href="print.css" media="print" />
```

You could use the @import command to achieve the same thing, but this would not work for very old browsers. You could also use the @media command to target print devices specifically, but again this would exclude older browsers. There are several things you need to consider including in this style sheet for users who are printing your content.

- The user wants the content in the page, not the navigation or other superfluous elements (such as forms and other interactive elements that are useless in a static medium, as well as advertising unless you are specifically contracted to display them when printed which is unlikely). Consider a class like "noprint" on these elements so that it is easy to hide them with `display:none;`. Alternatively, you could use a class such as "print" for just those elements you want outputted to the printer.

- Think about whether you want to extend your screen style sheet (by using a media type of `all` for that style sheet) to maintain existing branding or replace it entirely (by using a media type of `screen` for that style sheet). Replacing it entirely often gives good results, and avoids unpredictable pitfalls, which are common when you have a great number of pages to consider.

- Serif fonts are easier to read on printed media (the converse is true of information presented on screen mediums). Consider an alternative serif font-stack.

- Avoid changing the font size in the print style sheet. The browser default is usually appropriate.

- If you do change the font size, set it in points (pt). 12 points is usually fine.

- Make any containers the width of the page (100%) and remove their margins. This will ensure they fill the space of the removed elements, as well as the printable area. This also helps make sure that they don't spill onto a second horizontal page, which makes for a poor printing experience. You should also add a small margin to the printed page with the @page rule, which we'll discuss later in this section. This will make for comfortable reading, particularly on printers that are capable of borderless printing.

- Don't float your containers. This can have unpredictable results.

- Background images and colors are usually disabled for printing by default, so ensure you specify dark (or black) font colors that are legible with a white background.

- In case background images or colors are printed, set the background to white. This avoids blurry or unclear content, can save on ink and will make pages print faster.

- Remove backgrounds (set them to transparent) on elements that don't need them for the same reasons stated previously.

- Links are not obvious on printed media, and there is no hover state. Underline your links so it is clear that they are links. We'll talk about other clever ways you can deal with links later in this section.

- Use units that are appropriate for the medium, such as points (pt), inches (in), and centimeters (cm).

■ **CAUTION:** Print style sheets block rendering in Internet Explorer. Because of this, you might like to consider deferring loading of these with JavaScript.

In his excellent article on A List Apart (http://www.alistapart.com/articles/goingtoprint/), Eric Meyer suggests using the :after pseudo-element to append the URLs linked to after their link text. This makes perfect sense; without the URL, the link text is effectively useless when printed. Here is a simplified version of the code he uses to achieve this:

```
a:after {
        content: " (" attr(href) ") ";
}
```

He goes on to say that this method will not work well with links relative to the root of the site, and offers a solution for this:

```
a[href^="/"]:after {
        content: " (http://www.alistapart.com" attr(href) ") ";
}
```

These solutions are not perfect. URLs that are relative to the current document will still not display their full path, and links at the end of a sentence will display a space after the closing bracket and before the period, but it is a great improvement on the alternative.

Here's an example of a printed A List Apart page:

A List Apart: Articles: The Accessibility of WAI-ARIA 16/02/2011 20:04

NOVEMBER 30, 2010 No. 319

The Accessibility of WAI-ARIA

by **DETLEV FISCHER**

Published in: Accessibility

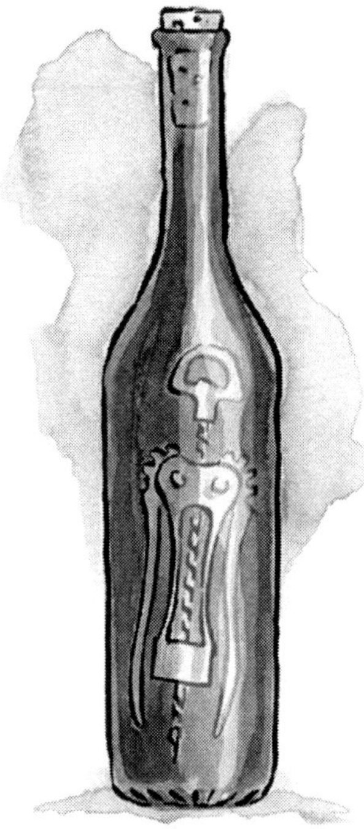

Web developers interested in accessibility issues often discuss WAI-ARIA (http://www.w3.org/TR/wai-aria/) , an upcoming W3C candidate recommendation aimed at making web applications more accessible to blind and visually impaired users. But, can we recommend WAI-ARIA without reservation?

The accessibility community has welcomed the development of WAI-ARIA. Clearly, there are many benefits for screen reader users. Previously, when webpages were dynamically updated, screen reader users were unaware that something had changed, or else were thrown back to the top of the page. Now, WAI-ARIA can inform the screen reader about dynamic changes. We can make complex custom widgets—such as pulldown menus, tabpanels, hierarchical trees, or sliders—accessible by mapping their elements to the roles, properties, and states defined in the standard and supported by the system's accessibility API—provided that users have recent versions of browsers and screen readers that support the standard.

Many users, however, have no access to the latest and greatest technology. Therefore, accessibility testing is typically based on software that "users out there" are likely to encounter at the workplace.

A benchmark for accessibility testing

This is why the German BITV-Test (http://www.bitvtest.eu) (BITV is the German federal regulation mandating accessible information technology) prescribes using a dated browser (currently Internet Explorer 7) that would typically be used in combination with a dated screen reader like JAWS 8 that does not yet support WAI-ARIA.

For practical reasons the BITV-Test does not involve tests with screen readers. However, its checkpoints consider the limitations of older assistive technologies. The test will lower the score for sites where authors *rely* on WAI-ARIA—for example, by implementing widgets in a way that makes them inaccessible for users of older screen readers such as JAWS 8.

The question remains: Should accessibility testing settle for an outdated combination of browser and assistive technology that does not yet support WAI-ARIA? Doesn't this create a disincentive for web developers who embrace WAI-ARIA to turn the dynamic web applications that clients demand into something that may be equally usable by blind users?

We have to step back a little to answer this question. First, what do the Web Content Accessibility Guidelines (WCAG) 2.0

http://www.alistapart.com/articles/the-accessibility-of-wai-aria/ Page 1 of 8

Figure 7-1. *An example printout from A List Apart*

Print and other paged media support several extra rules and properties to continuous media. The page itself can be targeted with @page for applying margins at the global level, like so:

```
@page {
    margin: 2cm 3cm;
}
```

You could apply the margin to the *body* element instead, but then you wouldn't get the margin at the bottom of each page.

There are also pseudo-classes for left and right pages. When printing double-sided documents, the second page is a "left" page, the third a "right" page, the fourth a "left," and so on. It is common to consider a larger gutter area between the pages in case the user staples or binds these pages together. This is easy to achieve:

```
@page:left {
    margin-right: 4cm;
}

@page:right {
    margin-left: 4cm;
}
```

You can also target the first page specifically, with the :first pseudo-class. The first page is neither considered left nor right:

```
@page:first{
    margin: 10cm;
}
```

Controlling Page Breaks

Several properties exist with the intent of giving us more control over where our pages are broken. The first three are page-break specific:

- page-break-before
- page-break-after
- page-break-inside

page-break-before and page-break-after accept five possible values (six if you include "inherit", which is their default):

- auto
  - This will have no effect on the printed output. Pages will be split wherever the printer (or paged device) runs out of space.
- always
  - A page break will always be forced before (or after, as appropriate) the element.

- avoid
  - The device will attempt to avoid page breaks before (or after, as appropriate) the element.
- left
  - The device will insert page breaks before (or after, as appropriate) so that the next page will be a "left" page (and can therefore be targeted with the :left pseudo-class).
- right
  - The device will insert page breaks before (or after, as appropriate) so that the next page will be a "right" page (and can therefore be targeted with the :right pseudo-class).

`page-break-inside` only supports "auto" and "avoid" from this list.

▨ **TIP:** If you use thead, tbody, and tfoot tags within your tables, the header and footers will repeat on every page making the tables easier to read. Table rows may still be split, which can be avoided with the following CSS in your print style sheet:

```
tr {
  page-break-inside: avoid;
}
```

You can read more about print behavior for tables at `http://www.w3.org/TR/CSS2/tables.html`.

Building print style sheets is an easy and worthwhile thing to do, from an accessibility and a usability point of view. Big websites don't always cater for printers, and as such give their users a poor experience; taking this step can help separate your site from the rest. Again, for a high-traffic website, more and more of your users are going to want to print your pages, perhaps because they don't have mobile Internet–enabled devices. There are examples of real-life print style sheets in Figures 7-2, 7-3 and 7-4.

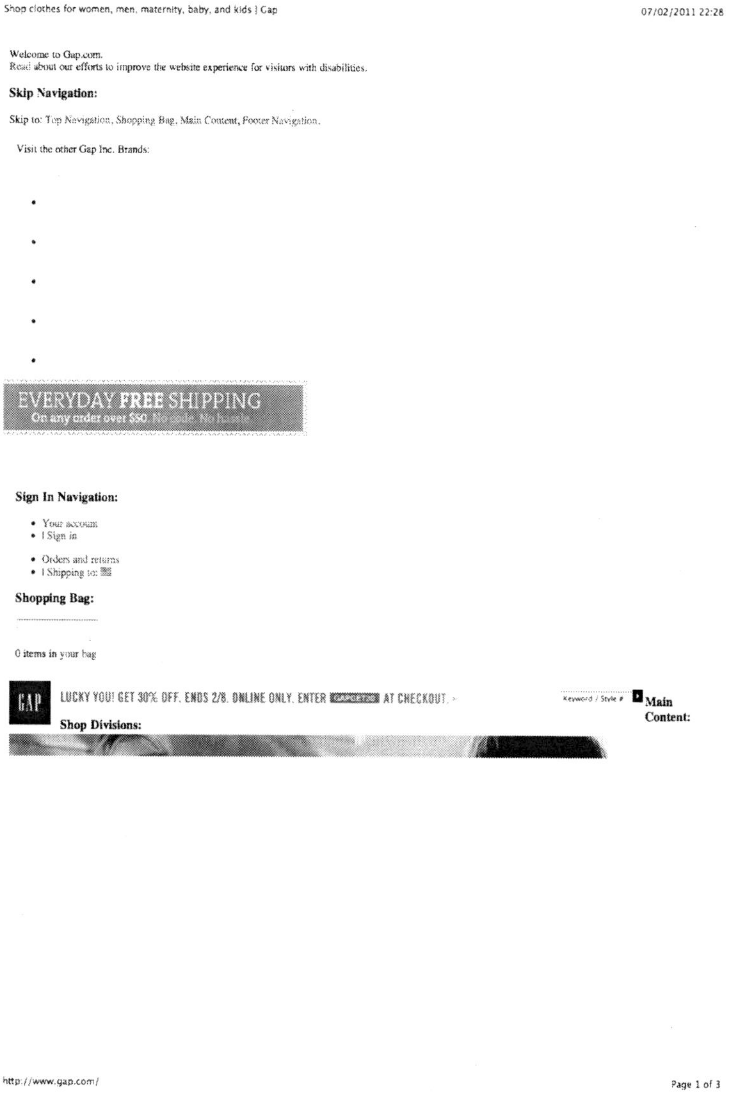

Shop clothes for women, men, maternity, baby, and kids | Gap   07/02/2011 22:28

Welcome to Gap.com.
Read about our efforts to improve the website experience for visitors with disabilities.

Skip Navigation:

Skip to: Top Navigation, Shopping Bag, Main Content, Footer Navigation.

Visit the other Gap Inc. Brands:

-
-
-
-
-

EVERYDAY **FREE** SHIPPING
On any order over $50. No code. No hassle.

Sign In Navigation:

- Your account
- | Sign in

- Orders and returns
- | Shipping to:

Shopping Bag:

0 items in your bag

GAP   LUCKY YOU! GET 30% OFF. ENDS 2/8. ONLINE ONLY. ENTER GAPCE230 AT CHECKOUT.   Keyword / Style # ▶ **Main**
          Shop Divisions: **Content:**

http://www.gap.com/   Page 1 of 3

Figure 7-2. Gap doesn't hide unnecessary elements or set its text to a dark color—as a result, much of the text is invisible, and the first printed page has no useful content.

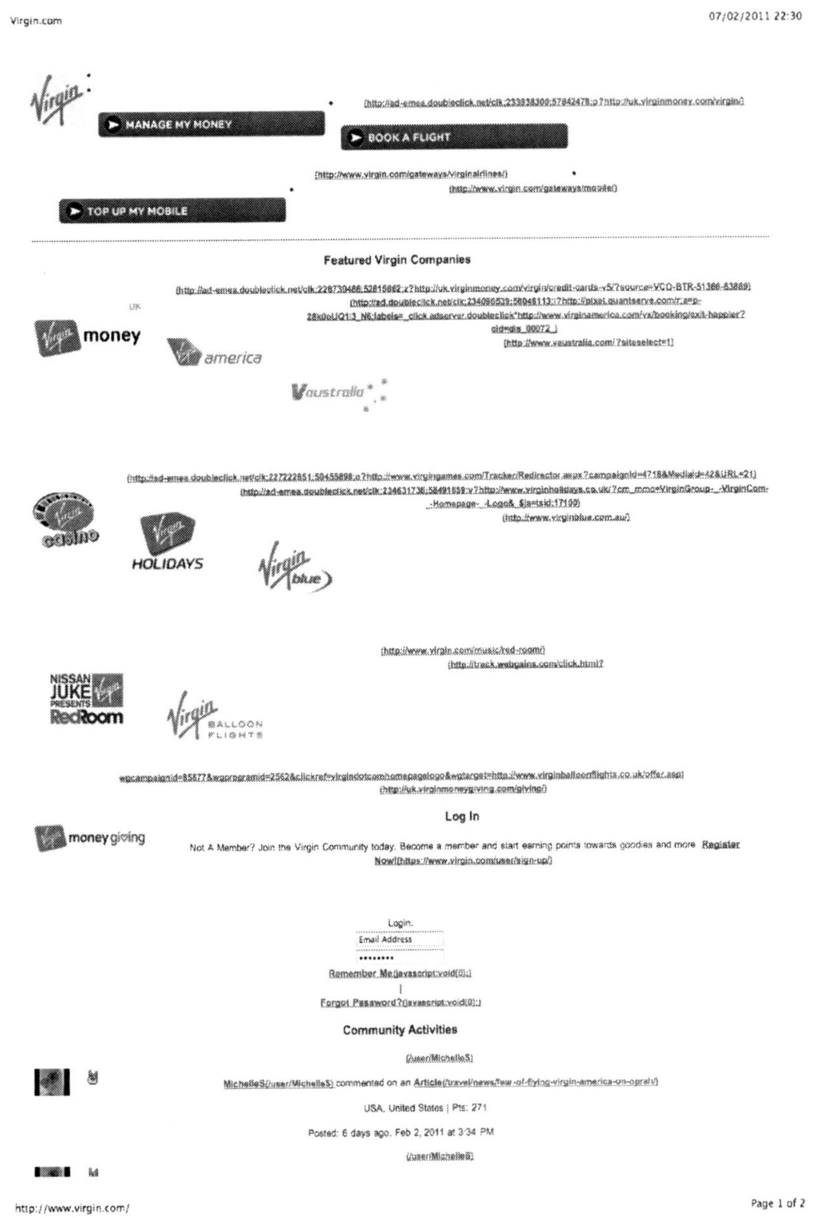

Figure 7-3. Virgin's website prints a huge mess before it gets to any content.

Figure 7-4. *The Onion lets its advertising get in the way of its content.*

As always, the browser implementation is inconsistent, and you still need to test your code. You can check the results of your work quickly in print previews rather than killing trees. You can also quickly switch the media type of your link tag (or @import or @media rules) to "all", but be aware that browsers may apply different styles by default to print style sheets than they do to screen ones. You can read the CSS 2.1 specification for paged media at http://www.w3.org/TR/2009/CR-CSS2-20090908/page.html#page-box. CSS3 adds more features to allow you to control page number counters, widowed lines (lines left at the top of the page) and orphaned lines (lines left at the bottom of the page). Although support is patchy now, it doesn't hurt to implement these. Read more about them at http://dev.w3.org/csswg/css3-page/.

Mobile Devices

The methods your users have of accessing your website are growing dramatically all the time. Many of your typical users are likely to now have several means of reaching the Internet: home computer, work computer, perhaps a set-top box of some kind, and cellular telephone. The cell phone has come a long way from the brick-shaped kilo of the 1980s, and many are now capable computers in their own right. They can access your data via many different technologies including WiFi, GPRS, 2G, and 3G, and faster standards are emerging all the time. For high-traffic websites, the likelihood of serving your data to mobile devices is very high, and your users will expect a lot from you. In fact, users in developing countries may bypass computers altogether and only own a mobile device. Tablets are also rapidly gaining in popularity and can be considered mobile devices.

There are some things in particular you need to consider when serving websites to mobile devices:

- *Latency.* The primary thorn in the side of the mobile web developer, latency is an unavoidable and inevitable concern. No matter how fast mobile Internet connections get, latency is likely to always be a problem. This means having fewer HTTP requests is more important than ever.

- *Small screen sizes.* Mobile devices are likely to have much smaller screens than those you are used to developing for.

- *Pixel density.* Some screens on mobile devices now have high enough pixel density (or are big enough, in the case of tablets) for your media queries to easily mistake them for desktop screens.

- *Orientation.* Many mobile devices now support switching from landscape to portrait, and vice versa. Your media queries should take advantage of this.[7]

- *Lesser processing power.* Your clever methods of offloading rendering to the GPU, and all of the transitions and transforms you've implemented aren't going to impress anyone at three frames per second.

- *Battery life.* Hitting the network and doing anything CPU-intensive will drain the user's battery at a higher rate than normal.

- *Cost.* Some users may be paying for their bandwidth. They won't appreciate unnecessary network access or unoptimized images.

---

[7] A specification for Geolocation 2 also introduces DeviceOrientation Events that you can hook into with JavaScript when browsers start supporting them. Read more about this at http://dev.w3.org/geo/api/spec-source-orientation.html.

- *Features*: Some features (notably `:focus`, `:hover` and `position:fixed`) may not be available on these devices.

You have several solutions for catering to your mobile users.

Another Website

The optimum solution is to provide different sites to mobile users. Redirecting your users based on server-side user agent detection (for example, to `http://m.facebook.com` or `http://touch.facebook.com`) allows you to build a complete experience for them based upon their likely resolutions and their latent and slow network speeds. Unfortunately, for all but the most popular devices, this is a hard thing to achieve. For one thing, the manufacturers of the browsers on that device (be it something proprietary, Opera Mini, Mobile Safari, Firefox Mobile, or otherwise) have gone to a lot of effort to ensure that users of those browsers can enjoy a decent experience, even on a small screen. Secondly, the user agents available are changing all the time with new ones crawling out of the woodwork every day.[8]

Facebook redirects you to a touch version of the full site when accessed via an iPhone (see Figure 7-5). It is also clever enough to use the `accept-language` HTTP header to present the correct language (the language the device is using) to the user.

---

[8] Opera actually masqueraded as IE for many years to avoid server-side user agent detection blocking the browser from content. Version 8.02 changed this behavior.

Figure 7-5. Facebook on the iPhone (above, portrait mode; below, landscape mode).

You can only realistically target the most common of these. You can use media queries to provide a link to the mobile site in a prominent position for devices with small heights and widths, but then remember that some of the newest devices have very high pixel densities and can easily have a higher resolution screen than a desktop machine. If you do provide a separate website, there are a few things you should do:

- Provide a link to the mobile website, in case you fail to detect and redirect the user correctly.

- Provide a link to the regular website, too. If the user follows it, remember his preference.

- Provide your images as CSS sprites as much as possible. Those HTTP requests are going to really hurt for mobile browsers.

- Consider text links instead of images.

- Consider a single column layout.

- Aim toward vertical scrolling rather than horizontal.

- Increase the font-size value.

- Avoid relying on any interactions that depend upon a mouse, such as `:hover`.

- Avoid relying on any interactions that depend upon a keyboard, such as `:focus`.

- Use `:active` states for touch screen devices and `:focus` states for devices with buttons.

- Avoid floated elements.

- Remember that users may change orientation, and cater for both landscape and portrait. Using percentages and a fluid layout rather than fixed pixel sizes will help you with this.

- Use HTML5 input types like "tel" and "email" to give the device hints on how to help the user enter information. Devices that don't support these types will gracefully degrade to text.

- Avoid CPU-intensive operations such as offloading to the GPU (read about this in Chapter 8), transforms, transitions, and animations.

- Although using the `accept-language` header to detect language is clever—and the geolocation API to detect location—avoid trying to detect location with IP addresses. This is notoriously unreliable.

The downside of this technique is it requires you to maintain two websites. If you can use the same content and a templating system to do this, it may make it less painful to achieve. This will give your users the best experience.

Pizza Express delivers a cut-down version of its website to mobile devices, with extra functionality such as detecting your location, and allowing you to dial that restaurant from within the browser. This is a good example of how you should be thinking about the mobile devices: not just ticking a box, but giving the best solution you can to everyone regardless of device.

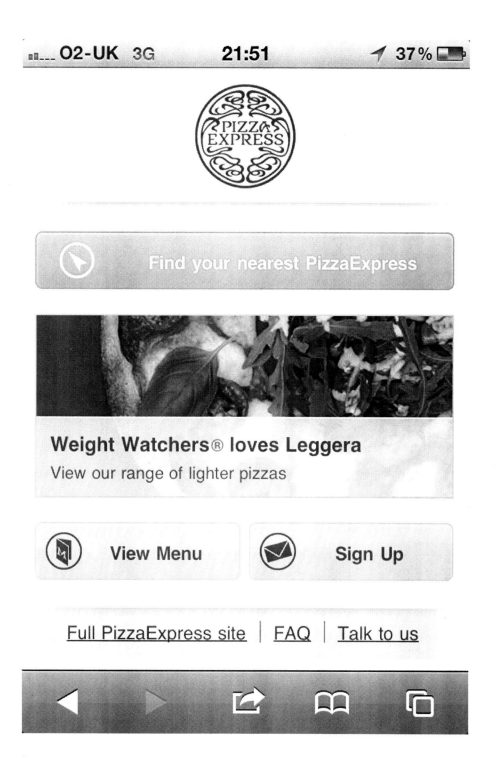

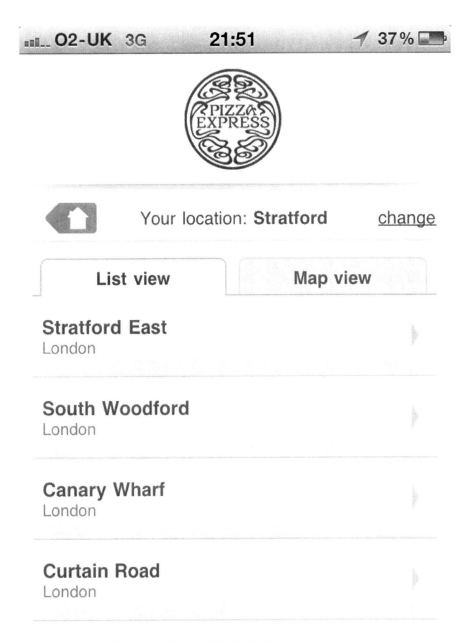

Figure 7-6. Pizza Express' website on Mobile Safari

Use Media Queries to Target Mobile Devices

You could also choose to use media queries to target these devices. Be aware though, that the performance implications of this method are considerable. Not only will your mobile users be penalized by downloading all the style sheets you link to, regardless of the ones that are applied (and often, many of the images you override, too), but your existing user base will also be forced to download the style sheets intended for mobile devices. This has the added cost of bandwidth from your company's side, with many files being served for no purpose.

Older devices that don't support media queries will ignore them or fail to parse the files. This leaves them to use their default behavior, which is often adequate (or has, at least, been designed to be).

Andy Clarke provides a series of media queries to target various mobile devices at `http://www.stuffandnonsense.co.uk/blog/about/hardboiled_css3_media_queries/`, which you may find useful. However, don't rely on them to target only the devices listed. New devices exist and are appearing every day, which may or may not meet the requirements for those queries. Also, don't use all these queries at the same time; that will result in a large amount of extra HTTP requests, which is even more damaging to the mobile device experience. If you have a genuine reason to target a single specific device rather than all devices of particular capabilities—for example, to point iOS users at an app you have developed for their platform—consider this one of the only valid uses to use server-side user agent detection. You should avoid UA detection wherever there is an alternative.

▦ **NOTE:** You can make telephone numbers clickable from within your websites with the tel: protocol, like so:

```
<a href="tel:12345678901">(123) 456-7890</a>
```

This is a genuinely useful piece of functionality for someone who is already using a cellular phone to browse your site. Remember to use an international number and start the number in the href with the country code.

Build an App Instead

You can also opt to build an app directly for the device you intend to support. While, again, this limits your audience somewhat, you can take advantage of device-specific capabilities and APIs that you could not otherwise. You can also test your website in a very locked-down environment and be a lot more confident in your results. Another option would be to display your website in a browser within the app, potentially tying it into more features as well as keeping it available as a website directly and only maintaining it in one place.

An equivalent of this is native web apps, which are gathering momentum as a plausible method of making cross-platform apps, with potentially the same codebase as the website but access to native APIs. PhoneGap (`http://www.phonegap.com/`) wraps your code and makes it into a native app for all the major mobile device manufacturers. Wholesale Applications Community (WAC `http://www.wacapps.net`) and the Device APIs and Policy Working Group (DAP `http://www.w3.org/2009/dap/`) are both immature, but worth keeping an eye on.

Other Devices

There are other devices you should consider, which you may or may not be able to target. Set-top boxes with built-in web browsers, games consoles, native browsers in Smart TVs, Google TV, and so on. Each of these will have its own capabilities and features. We recommend testing on everything you can.

Search Engine Optimization (SEO)

Search engine spiders (programs that scan your website by "crawling" all of the links they can find and sending the results back to the search engine) can be considered devices in their own right. They have their own unique user agents, and their own unique capabilities. *Search engine optimization* (SEO) is the practice of ensuring that these spiders have the best chance of reaching all your content and that it is as appropriate as possible when they do reach it. SEO is of huge importance to big companies since it can be a driver of vast amounts of traffic, and thus vast amounts of sales (or whatever the goal of your website is). SEO, like accessibility, needs to be considered from the outset, and implemented in a consistent and sane manner.

To discuss SEO techniques in any great detail would warrant its own book, but we will mention some high-level points here. First we'll talk about the differences between white, gray, and black hat techniques:

- *White hat:* These techniques are done with good and altruistic intent. With SEO in mind, this typically just means writing good content and linking to it as appropriate. Search engines love this kind of content; it helps them ensure that the search results are appropriate to the search terms, which is exactly what their users want too.

- *Gray hat:* These techniques could be considered attempts to cheat the system, but again are employed with good intent when no other good option is available. An example is using `text-indent:-9999px;` to hide text from browsers but not screen readers (as discussed in the previous chapter). This technique could also easily be used to stuff the page with keywords to the author of the site wants to rank for, but hide them from the user. Search engines typically accept this method without penalizing the site in question (since, at the moment, it is one of the best methods we have for maintaining accessibility), but do not give extra weight to words affected by it.

- *Black hat:* These techniques are out and out attempts to cheat the system. Examples are loading a page stuffed with the keywords you want to rank and then redirecting with JavaScript (doorway pages), using server-side user agent detection to present a completely different page to the search engine than to your users (cloaking), placing keywords in white text on a white background (invisible text), and so on. Using these techniques will result in your site being penalized and showing up later in the search engine results than it might do otherwise. In extreme examples, it could result in your site being banned from the results altogether.

Many people think they have found new and clever ways to cheat the search engines. In reality, all they are doing is wasting their time, giving their users a worse experience, wasting time that would be better spent improving their website, and delaying the inevitable. The search engines will figure out what you are doing in the long run, and they will penalize you for it. The truth is that the only one who knows exactly what will rank well against the search engine's algorithms is the search engine. Even then, your request could get directed to one of many servers with different versions of the algorithm, and the algorithm is likely to change often. Some general guidelines exist, however. To get good search engine ranking, it is important to

- Have good quality content.

- Ensure that your content is semantic and valid.

- Ensure that you have good site performance.

Really, this is just in line with making good quality websites, which we hope you are aiming to do anyway. Having good content is what the search engines appreciate the most. Making your content semantic and valid (including using microformats, and common class names and IDs) helps the search engines understand the content and your intent, and present it in a more comprehensive and attractive fashion on their search results page.

Depending on the search engine, the spiders have different capabilities as devices. Some parse JavaScript, some don't; some parse CSS, some don't. On the whole, search engines do now understand and apply CSS to the page. Typically, if they understand text to be invisible for whatever (gray hat) reason, they will not rank your page for this content or the words within it. If you are using JavaScript to show and hide pieces of information (for example, in a tabbed box), this means the tabs that are not active at page load will not have their content indexed. If the search engine supports JavaScript, then when crawling the links on the page, if a particular link makes content visible the search engine may choose to spider that content, although it is likely to consider it less important than text that showed initially.

For (at least) this reason, you should aim for your website to display in a sensible manner with JavaScript disabled. For a tabbed box, it would make sense to show each tab in the markup as a heading with the contents of the tab directly beneath. When the page loads,[9] your JavaScript can rearrange the page as need be, and attach the classes necessary to set up the tabs properly. As we mentioned before, this is a good approach for accessibility, too; if you make your site semantic and accessible, you get some SEO thrown in for free.

■ **NOTE:** Search engines will (almost) never submit forms.

Another thing search engines are valuing more and more is the performance of your website. If your site downloads fast and validates, you can get an easy boost in your rankings. If you have been following the guidelines laid out in this book, hopefully your CSS is small and fast and you don't have too many HTTP requests on the page. Using a content delivery network (CDN—see Chapter 8) can also give you a speed improvement, which the search engines will appreciate.

---

[9] JavaScript can hook into a "DOM-ready" event, which fires before the images load but after the DOM has loaded. Making changes to the document at this point (rather than at the "load" event, which fires after everything on the document has been downloaded) will avoid a Flash of Unstyled Content (FOUC), which can be very unsettling.

Summary

This chapter aimed to teach you about some of the devices you can expect your users to be using, and how best to target them. Media types and media queries are often useful, but they are not the panacea some of us might wish they were. Trying to keep your site easy to read and browse from the word go will pay dividends in these scenarios.

The next chapter is concerned with the performance of your CSS, and intends to teach you about how HTTP requests and responses work, caching strategies, and how to get the best out of both.

CHAPTER 8

■ ■ ■

Performance

CSS files are (typically) small files with (typically) simple syntax. It might seem that where performance is concerned there is little to be done to make a difference, and that improvements will be slight. In many cases, this may be true. However, when we are dealing with CSS at a grander scale, where our files may be reaching larger sizes and we expect them to be served millions or tens of millions of times a day, small improvements make big differences—both to the user and the developer. One kilobyte may seem a tiny amount of data by today's standards, but do the math—those kilobytes soon add up to gigabytes of data that the business needs to pay for in bandwidth. And when we are considering the payload the user downloads and the speed of the page rendering, it is a truism to say that every little bit counts.

There are several angles we must look at when concentrating on performance. From the user's perspective, it is important that the files are small, can be well cached (and hence loaded more quickly) and that the files are up to date. From the browser's perspective, we want our CSS to be as efficient as possible and for the content to be rendered (and re-rendered in response to interaction or animation, if necessary) as fast as possible. From the businesses' perspective, we want to serve from the user's cache (primarily, and our server cache secondarily) as much as possible and keep the amount we are sending to (and receiving from) the user to a minimum, while still being sure the user has the latest version of our code.

In this chapter, we will concentrate on how to improve performance from these three distinct angles, and you will learn several important things about each. You will learn about the following:

- File size concerns and best practices

- Having fewer HTTP requests is more important than file size

- Caching strategies

- Browser rendering and blocking

The Payload—Worry About File Size

Best practices in CSS require us to consider the number of characters we enter and the implications of them. Every character counts. Although high speed Internet is more widespread these days, as an author of CSS on a high-traffic website, you have many more demographics to worry about than most other companies. As such, your users may be on dial-up Internet access (out of choice or because of their location), using mobile devices in areas with poor reception, in countries far from the point of origin of your site (your servers), or any combination of these. Preprocessing may be taking place at many levels such as their ISP, firewalls and routers at their location, or firewalls and routers at levels even higher up the pathway of data. One of our primary concerns with our data reaching these machines as quickly as possible is the amount of data that we are sending. When we send data via TCP/IP (Transmission Control Protocol and Internet Protocol), the networking protocol typically used by the Internet, our information is grouped into bundles called *packets*. On networks there is a concept of maximum packet size, or maximum transmission unit (MTU), typically 1500 bytes on an Ethernet network. Having a packet that exceeds this size incurs a performance penalty (how big a penalty is dependent on many factors: MTU, packet size, network speed, and so on). Since we cannot be certain what the MTU of any particular network is—and even if we did, knowing which packet will exceed the limit is very difficult—to avoid this packet boundary all we can do is our very best to provide the smallest amount possible.

Users of the Internet are more fickle than, say, users in a shopping center. Deciding that a website is too slow and browsing to another affords instant gratification, whereas finding another store that sells saucepans requires a commitment from the user to leave the current store, locate another store, locate the product, and so on. The goodwill the user has toward our website is finite, and we must do whatever we can to keep the user happy and moving toward whatever our business goal is—be it buying products or services, viewing pages, or consuming content.

Keeping file size down and speed up isn't just good for our visitors. It's good for our business too—the less data we serve, the fewer bandwidth costs we incur. And furthermore, Google and other search engines care about how quickly our pages load. Performance of websites is fast becoming an important factor for effective SEO strategies. Additionally, Internet Explorer (IE) versions 7 and below cannot cope with CSS files above 288 KB.

▨ **NOTE:** With CSS files exceeding 288 KB, IE 7 and below will only parse the first 288 KB of the file. Although it is possible to break files larger than this into multiple files (with the performance implications of more requests), it is obviously preferable to keep our CSS smaller in the first place.

So what can we do to keep our file sizes down?[1]

Naming Conventions

As we have said before, it's important to come up with rules on how classes and IDs are named, and to adhere strictly to them. Unless there are good reasons not to do this in your organization or your developers are particularly opposed to it, we recommend naming your classes and IDs in camel case, as follows:

- mainContent

- heroImage

- emailAddress

Using camel case should help keep our code easy to read while avoiding the extra characters that hyphens, underscores, or other delimiters incur. If namespacing your code via prefixes, try to avoid verbose prefixes like these:

- ourCompanyHeroImage

- ourCompanyEmailAddress

---

[1] Google provides a guide to minimizing your payload at `http://code.google.com/speed/page-speed/docs/payload.html`. Yahoo! provides its own guide to maximizing performance of your website at `http://developer.yahoo.com/performance/rules.html`.

Instead, consider abbreviations or acronyms; for example:

- ocHeroImage

- ocEmailAddress

If these names are hard to read, we can now consider using a delimiter, safe in the knowledge that our prefix is still smaller than the alternative.

- oc-HeroImage

- oc-EmailAddress

Although we want our naming system to be semantic, we could also consider abbreviating it, as long as it is still easy for the developers to read:

- heroImg

- emailAddr

The downside of this approach is that there are many acceptable abbreviations for words, and developers may find the naming less intuitive, resulting in much flicking back and forward through the code, or inconsistent naming techniques. We recommend (as always) discussing what is acceptable within your organization for the best results, adding the technique to your CSS Coding Standards Guide and implementing it strictly.

File Names

File names are used throughout our code to link files together and reference them. To keep our file sizes really small, it is tempting to name our files a.css, b.css, and so on. In fact, as long as the files are being served with the correct mime type,[2] we could even name them **a.c** or just **a**. In practice, though, we would suggest that this creates too much of a cost in legibility and makes code difficult to write and files difficult to locate. Although file names should not be verbose, they should be long enough to be clear and easy to understand. Here is an example of a file being referenced in CSS:

```
input {background: url("/images/shadow background.gif");}
```

The double quotes in the URL are not usually required. They are included in this instance because of the space in the file name, which means quotes are required so that the browser understands the space is part of the file name. However, when naming files, we recommend you always use hyphens instead of spaces. We recommend this for a few reasons:

- Google will treat a hyphen in a URL path as if it were a space, but not other characters. If we name our file "shadow background.gif," Google comprehends this as being "shadow background.gif". Good SEO on images used for presentation rather than content (like background) may seem unnecessary, but Google image searches account for a surprising amount of traffic, and anything that might bring users to our site is a positive thing.

- Not using spaces means we don't need the quotes in the URL value, saving us two characters.

---

[2] A *mime type* is a response header identifying the type of file that is being served. The mime type for CSS files is "text/css".

- Using spaces means the browser needs to intelligently process them and change them to %20 in the URL (a space, URL encoded) and older browsers may not support this. You could, of course, place the encoded space directly in the URL, but this would result in two extra characters in every instance.

We also recommend you always name your files in lowercase, even if using a web server/operating system that is not case-sensitive. It is an easy rule to follow and will make your files more portable should you decide to switch web servers at a later date. Avoiding symbols and unusual characters will also ease transitions from one server to another and avoid unexpected issues. Although using dots in the file name has become common practice for versioning (as in jquery-1.4.4.min.js), you should avoid placing them at the beginning of the file name since Linux-based operating systems will interpret that as a hidden file. As a matter of best practice, it is best to stick to Latin alphanumeric characters, hyphens, and dots.

Folder Structure

At first glance, folder structure may seem to have little impact on file size. This, however, is untrue. Folders are referenced often throughout CSS code, be it pointing to background images, fonts, behaviors, or importing other stylesheets.[3]

The simplest way to minimize the characters used up by referencing folders is to keep all your files in the same directory as your CSS. This technique will quickly become unusable in a website of any size, however, and as always, we should aim for a good balance between what is a good practice and what will make a developer's life a nightmare.

Here is an example of a file being referenced in CSS:

```
input {background: url("/images/shadow background.gif");}
```

The first character in our URL is a forward slash, which means begin at the root of the URL. So, for a CSS file located at www.thedomain.com/css/style.css, this URL will point to www.thedomain.com/images/shadow%20background.gif. All URLs in CSS are relative to where the file containing the CSS is located, so suppose we changed the CSS to the following (with the slash omitted):

```
input {background: url("images/shadow background.gif");}
```

The URL would then point to www.thedomain.com/css/images/shadow%20background.gif.

Since any files we reference with CSS are for use primarily by CSS, it makes sense to keep them in a subfolder inside the same folder our CSS is residing in. This makes our CSS more portable since we can copy or move the CSS folder, and all the file paths and references will be intact. It also saves us the forward slash in the URL, or ../, to jump up a folder and locate the files we are looking for.

Often, folders are named as the plural of what they represent, such as these:

- images

- assets

- fonts

---

[3] Behaviors are implemented via HTML Component (HTC) files, and supported by IE versions 5 and above. They allow you to assign particular behaviors to elements via JavaScript. Since they introduce a dependency on JavaScript and are isolated to only the IE browsers, we do not recommend you use them.

By always using the singular instead, it is easy to save characters and to enforce this naming technique across our business. In folder names, abbreviations are much safer to use since our entire folder structure (at least at the high level) is likely to be very predictable, and exactly the same from project to project. This is yet another thing that you would do well to add to your CSS Coding Standards Guide:

- img

- asset

- font

Our line was originally 58 bytes, as follows:

```
input {background: url("/images/shadow background.gif");}
```

It is now 52 bytes, as follows:

```
input {background: url(img/shadow-background.gif);}
```

This is a 10 percent reduction. This might seem a small change, but if there were 100 lines similar to this in our document, we would now have saved 60 bytes, which translates into many more when we consider the amount of requests we are responding to.

You should also feel free to use common and well-understood abbreviations in your filenames, which can further reduce our CSS:

```
input {background: url(img/shadow-bg.gif);}
```

Our asset folder is simply a catchall folder for any files we want to reference that don't fall easily into another grouping, such as Shockwave Flash (SWF), multimedia Adobe Flash files. With all this in mind, let's take a look at an example folder-naming strategy:

```
/
    css
        img
        font
        asset
    img
    js
    asset
```

If you think about all the places where we are referencing these files, this all translates into smaller files, faster downloads, and less bandwidth.

Syntax

There are many parts to CSS syntax that we include for legibility that are simply not necessary. Since these can often be minimized via minification tools (read more about these later in this chapter), it is safe to keep these in your CSS whilst writing it if you are using them. However, it is important to know about these and the implications of them.

Whitespace

There are very few whitespace characters that are actually required by CSS. The spacing between parts of our selectors is necessary, as is the spacing between items referenced in shorthand CSS, or properties that take multiple parts as their values. Everything else exists purely to make it easier for us as developers to read and scan our code.

Note the following code:

```
body
{
        font-family: arial, sans-serif;
        font-size: 16px;
        background-color: #f4f4f4;
}

.clear
{
        clear: both;
}
```

From a browser's perspective, the preceding code is exactly the same as this:[4]

```
body{font-family:arial,sans-serif;font-size:16px;background-color:#f4f4f4;}.clear{clear:both;}
```

Although the second example is harder to read, it is a significant saving in file size. Some of this is worth explaining succinctly:

- The space between the selector and the opening brace is unnecessary.

- The space between the colon following the property name and the value is unnecessary.

- The space between comma-separated values is unnecessary.

- The carriage return after the closing brace is unnecessary.

- Spaces before !important are unnecessary (and any between ! and important).

In all of these instances, you could use other whitespace instead of space, such as tabs. As you can see, there are many savings to be had here. We do not recommend you write your CSS in this fashion as it would be impossible to manage (see the section on minifying your code later in this chapter).

■ **NOTE:** When using fonts with spaces in their names, you should surround them in quotes (either double or single) according to the CSS specifications. Although many browsers will have no problem with the quotes being omitted, others will not read the value properly.

---

[4] Although most browsers do not treat font names as case-sensitive, some older ones do. Notably, Adobe Flex (www.adobe.com/products/flex/—a framework for developing Adobe Flash and Adobe AIR applications) is known to have issues with incorrectly cased font names.

The Last Semicolon

The final semicolon after the last property and before the closing brace is unnecessary and easy to omit without affecting legibility.

Note the following:

```
.clear {clear:both;}
```

And the following:

```
.clear {clear:both}
```

Both of these lines are exactly the same as far as the browser is concerned, and save a single character for every rule.

Background Colors

When specifying a background color, rather than stating it (in perhaps a more correct fashion) as follows:

```
background-color: blue;
```

it is safe to instead use the following:

```
background: blue;
```

This saves six characters in every instance. Be aware, though, that this technique overrides the other properties set in this shorthand property and may have unintended effects.

Zeroes and Units

Since a zero is nothing regardless of the unit you are using, it is unnecessary to use a unit in this instance. Note these two properties:

```
border-width: 0px;
margin-top: 0em;
```

They can safely be written as follows:

```
border-width: 0;
margin-top: 0;
```

This would have no effect on the rendering of the page whatsoever.

Cancelling Borders

When removing borders, instead of stating the following:

```
border-width: 0;
```

Or the following:

```
border: none;
```

You can instead safely put the following:

```
border: 0;
```

Again, from the browser's perspective, this results in no border and fewer characters.

Zeros and Decimal Places

When using decimal places beginning with zero, the zero can be safely omitted. In other words, instead of stating the following:

```
font-size: 0.12em;
```

It is safe to instead put the following:

```
font-size: .12em;
```

These two statements are exactly equivalent and save a character in each instance, though they may be harder to read for some developers. This action is taken on your behalf by most CSS minification tools, so if you find legibility is affected and you are using these tools, it is safe to keep the zero in.

Margin/Padding Shorthand

Note the following CSS:

```
margin-left: 10px;
margin-right: 10px;
margin-top: 10px;
margin-bottom: 10px;
```

This can also be represented as this (in the order top, right, bottom, and left):

```
margin: 10px 10px 10px 10px;
```

It can also (since all four values are the same) be represented as this:

```
margin: 10px;
```

If you provide three values, the first represents the top, the second both horizontal values, and the third the bottom. Note the following CSS:

```
padding-left: 5px;
padding-right: 5px;
padding-top: 20px;
padding-bottom: 10px;
```

It is the same as this:

```
padding: 20px 5px 10px;
```

Additionally, if you only provide two values to the margin or padding properties they represent the vertical and horizontal value, respectively. Note the following CSS:

```
padding-left: 10px;
padding-right: 10px;
padding-top: 20px;
padding-bottom: 20px;
```

Which is exactly equivalent to this:

```
padding: 20px 10px;
```

Which is also exactly equivalent to this:

```
padding: 20px 10px 20px;
```

And this:

```
padding: 20px 10px 20px 10px;
```

Many other shorthand properties exist that are outside the scope of this book for border, border-radius, list-style, font, and many others. It is worth spending some time researching and documenting them, and ensuring that the rest of your team members are proficient in using them. As well as making your CSS files smaller, they can also make your CSS easier to read and scan. However, you need to be aware of caveats to this approach since a shorthand property overrides all the subproperties that make it up and may have unexpected consequences.

Colors

Every browser has a series of named colors (defined in the spec for HTML 3.0) that it understands and will render appropriately. These include the following:[5]

- aqua
- black

---

[5] The color "orange" is also included in the CSS2.1 spec, defined as #ffa500. The color "transparent" is included in the CSS1 spec for background colors, which has no hex color equivalent. CSS2 made this property applicable to border colors, and CSS3 defines it as applicable to any property that accepts a color value.

- blue

- fuchsia

- gray

- green

- lime

- maroon

- navy

- olive

- purple

- red

- silver

- teal

- white

- yellow

There are many more colors that browsers support, but which are not part of the W3C standard (`www.w3.org/TR/css3-color/#html4`). However, only eight of these colors are "absolute" colors, meaning they include a value of zero or 255 for each of their red, green, and blue values. These are the following:[6]

- aqua (#00ffff)

- black (#000000)

- blue (#0000ff)

- fuchsia (#ff00ff)

- lime (#00ff00)

- red (#ff0000)

- white (#ffffff)

- yellow (#ffff00)

Out of these colors, only the following are not open to interpretation:

- black (#000000)

- blue (#0000ff)

---

[6] Interestingly, the color "green" as an absolute is deemed too bright to be described as green, and is instead named "lime"; "green" as a keyword represents #008000, which is much darker than the absolute green.

- red (#ff0000)

- white (#ffffff)

- yellow (#ffff00)

We therefore recommend that these are the only ones to be used in your CSS. They are easier to read and comprehend, and in many cases shorter in characters than their hex counterparts (unless you use shorthand colors (mentioned below); in all cases, they are shorter than their RGB counterparts).

However, there are further savings that can be achieved. Colors represented as hexadecimal (referred to as "hex colors") are specified as a triplet (meaning they are made of three parts). Each part of the triplet is a hexadecimal byte: a value with 256 variations, in this case from 0 (00) to 255 (ff). The triplet itself has 16,777,216 variations. If each part of the triplet is formed of two identical characters, we can shorten these into one. For example:

- #112233 can be represented as #123

- #00aaff can be represented as #0af

- #99aa00 can be represented as #9a0

The decision to use named colors or hex colors is to be made within your organization. Where using hex colors it is safe to use the shorthand versions. You may decide to use named colors in the instances that they are appropriate, since they are easier to read, but any seasoned CSS developer will be so used to seeing #000 and #fff that there is no problem sticking specifically to hex colors in that instance. Although RGB colors are defined in the CSS2.1 specification, CSS3 extends this to support RGBA as well as HSL (Hue, Saturation, Lightness) and HSLA (Hue, Saturation, Lightness, Alpha). These accept non-hex values—the RGB values are integers between 0 and 255, and Alpha is a number between 0 (transparent) and 1 (opaque). Hue is in degrees (0 to 360), while Saturation and Lightness are percentages. Although all these values are more verbose (and add more file size) than hex colors, you may find them more useful to implement.

NOTE: If using RGBA, HSL, or HSLA color definitions in your CSS, make sure to provide an RGB or hex color fallback for browsers that do not support them. Also, if you are using the `filter` attribute in IE (possibly for cross-browser support with things like gradients, opacity, and so on), be aware that this attribute does not support shorthand colors, RGB, RGBA, HSL, or HSLA. Some older mobile browsers had issues with shorthand colors such as these. However, these browsers have all but disappeared, and even for sites with the highest traffic, we do not recommend being concerned with this demographic.

As a final example that uses many of these syntactical methods to save on file size, see the following CSS, weighing in at 146 bytes:

```
.our-company-main-content
{
    background-image: url("../../images/shadow background.gif");
    border: none;
    margin-top: 0px;
```

```
    color: #aabbcc;
}
```

This can easily be shortened to 110 bytes:

```
.oc-mainContent {
    background-image: url(img/shadow-background.gif);
    border: 0;
    margin-top: 0;
    color: #abc
}
```

There is no sacrifice in legibility, and yet we have saved 36 bytes, which is a 25 percent decrease—even before minifying the file.

Minimizing Image Sizes

It is vital to understand what image types are appropriate in which instance and how to keep their sizes down. In the following sections, we will discuss the three primary types of images you will use.

GIF (Graphics Interchange Format)

GIFs are limited to a maximum of 256 colors and support transparency, but not alpha transparency. This means that by using up one of our available 256 colors, we can set pixels to be completely transparent or completely opaque (nontransparent), but nothing in between (semitransparent). They are typically appropriate for button images, items with hard edges and images where color accuracy is important. GIFs are a lossless compression format, which means that as long as you are using 256 colors or fewer (including transparency) there should be no degradation of image quality. When saving GIFs, use your image editor to ensure you minimize the amount of colors in use and turn off transparency if you don't need it. GIFs can contain multiple frames and information to animate between and loop these frames for simple animations (which increase file size dramatically and should be used sparingly).

JPEG (Joint Photographic Experts Group)

JPEG compression is lossy, which means information is lost the more the image is compressed. Your image editor should include a slider or similar means of adjusting the amount of compression when you come to export your image. As you decrease the quality (increase the compression), the file size will decrease, but artifacts will become visible in the image. It is up to the designer to decide on an appropriate and visually acceptable level of compression, typically 80 percent to 90 percent is the best compromise and should result in artifacts that are not obviously detectable. JPEGs support 16 million colors and are best suited to photographs or complex images with many colors. JPEGs do not support transparency at all.

PNG (Portable Network Graphics)

PNG is a lossless format, typically with a better compression rate than GIF files. They can be saved with different color depths, meaning they can support as many colors as is appropriate for the current image. They also support alpha transparency, meaning pixels can be made semi-transparent. PNGs are generally appropriate as a replacement for GIFs, although animated PNGs do not have widespread support yet. When saving PNGs it is important to set the color depth to something appropriate for the image.

■ **NOTE:** Although IE 6 does not support alpha transparency, there are many hacks available to fix this using JavaScript, behavior files, filters, and mixtures of these. Our recommended approach is the Fireworks hack, or 8-bit PNG hack. If you save a PNG with alpha transparency in Adobe Fireworks as 8-bit (which is effectively a bug in the software), the result is that it displays properly in all browsers, except for IE 6, which makes any semi-transparent pixel completely transparent. This is often an acceptable compromise as long as your designers work with this constraint in mind.

Your image editor should have tools to help you minimize the file size of any of these files, and see the difference that various file formats, compression rates and color depths will have. However, even after this, there is likely to be extraneous information in your image files. Comments, metadata, and unnecessary color profiles may be left in your files. There are many individual tools for addressing these concerns, but ImageOptim (available at `http://imageoptim.pornel.net/`) is a free, open-source app for OS X that combines all of these. It often causes savings in file size of 30 percent to 35 percent. Implementing a tool like this in your build process is a worthwhile thing to do and should be seriously considered. Various Windows and Linux alternatives are available (albeit less fully featured) but you should be able to achieve the same result using multiple command-line utilities in your build process.

Minifying

Using the techniques outlined so far in this chapter, it would not be difficult to write your own CSS minification script, which automates all of them on your behalf. However, there are many things that would catch you out in that process. Fortunately, methods already exist to achieve this for you. The most common of these is YUI Compressor.

YUI Compressor is a Java-based tool for minifying JavaScript and CSS files that can be downloaded at `http://github.com/yui/yuicompressor/`. It automates tasks on our behalf, taking care of many of the methods of minimizing file size we have already discussed in this chapter, meaning that we can ignore them in our development code, but still reap the benefits in our production code. Once it is installed, the syntax is very easy to use. From the command prompt, the syntax is the following (where x.y.z. is the version number):

```
java -jar yuicompressor-x.y.z.jar [options] [input file]
```

Potential options that apply to CSS are:

```
--line-break
```

This option allows us to break our CSS into lines after a particular column (a *column* in this instance meaning a particular character on a line). For example, setting this to 1000 will insert a line break at the first opportunity after the one-thousandth character of every line. There are many cases where you might need this option, particularly for debugging (you can read more about debugging in Chapter 10). Set this to 0 to insert a line break after every rule.

`--type`

This option allows us to specify the format of the input file. This option should only be set if our file suffix is not .css (or .js), in which case we should always set this to css for our CSS files.

`--charset`

This option allows us to specify the character set of our input file. If you do not supply it, the default character set encoding of the system that the YUI Compressor is being run on is used. Although unnecessary in most cases, if you are using UTF-8 characters (for example, in the content property), this option should be set.

`-o`

This option specifies the name of the file we want to output to.
Here is an example command:

```
java -jar yuicompressor-x.y.z.jar style.css -o style.min.css
```

YUI Compressor performs the following functions on CSS files:

- Strips all comments[7]
- Removes unnecessary whitespace
- Removes the last semicolon from each rule
- Removes any extraneous semicolons
- Removes any rules with no properties
- Removes units on any values of zero
- Removes the leading zero on any values with decimal places that begin with zero
- Consolidates like properties into one, in margin, padding, and background position
- Converts any RGB colors into hex colors[8]

---

[7] If for some reason, you want particular comments to remain (perhaps for copyright or licensing purposes) you can use an exclamation mark at the beginning of the comment, like so:

```
/*!   This comment is far too important to be removed:    */
```

[8] As mentioned later in this chapter, when using CSS transitions there is a performance penalty in some browsers for using hex colors rather than RGB colors, so it is particularly important to be aware of this.

- Removes extraneous character sets[9]

- Shortens alpha opacity statements using the filter property to the IE4 style[10]

If you are using YUI Compressor, you can rest safe in the knowledge that all these actions will be performed, and, if you wish, not worry about them in your unminified code.

If you have used any hacks (many of which are detailed in Chapter 3), it is useful to be aware that YUI Compressor is tolerant of many of them and will not attempt to minify or otherwise break them. Accepted hacks include the following:

- The underscore hack

- The star hack

- The child selector hack

- The commented backslash hack

- The box model hack

If you do not wish to use the Java implementation of YUI Compressor, a JavaScript port is available at www.phpied.com/cssmin-js/. Many other options for minifying CSS exist, including the following:

- www.csscompressor.com/

- www.cleancss.com/

- www.cssdrive.com/index.php/main/csscompressor/

---

[9] It is possible to define the character set within CSS with a command like:

```
@charset "utf-8";
```

any CSS file can only contain one @charset statement.

[10] The filter property (proprietary to Internet Explorer) allows you to set various visual effects. To set opacity, the recommended syntax is:

```
selector {
-ms-filter: "progid:DXImageTransform.Microsoft.Alpha(Opacity=65)";
filter: progid:DXImageTransform.Microsoft.Alpha(Opacity=65);
}
```

The filter property is for versions of IE 8 and lower. The –ms-filter property is for IE 9 and above. YUI Compressor minifies these to their shorthand equivalents, like so:

```
selector {
-ms-filter:"alpha(opacity=65)";
filter:alpha(opacity=65);
}
```

Because of the widespread use of YUI Compressor, it is the one we recommend. The sheer amount of developers using it and contributing to the community mean it is a very robust and well-tested solution. Whatever you decide, we definitely recommend using a minification tool with your CSS code despite the implications for debugging (you can read more about debugging in Chapter 10) which can be overcome.

Compression

After we've got our files as small as we can get them, there are still some tricks we can employ to get the data transferred from the server to the user even smaller. One of these is compression. Compression of files involves using algorithms for storage of repetitive data, and representing that data just once instead of many times. There are two main kinds of compression: lossless and lossy. Lossy compression means some information is lost in the compression process—JPEG is an example of a lossy compression format. The more we compress a JPEG image, the more artifacts show up and the further we are from the original image. This is acceptable for an image format since what we are trying to convey is not completely lost. However, for CSS files, any artifacts introduced into the data would break our syntax, and render our files unpredictable and useless. Lossless formats, such as zip, tar, and rar files are what we need for data where every character is important.

HTTP 1.1—the protocol used to deliver web pages—supports three compression methods in its specification: gzip (GNU zip), deflate, and compress. The uptake for deflate and compress by browsers and servers has been slower than for gzip. All modern browsers and servers support gzip compression for data and as such, it has become the industry standard technique to compress data over the Internet.[11]

An example process of a request from the browser to the server and the response from the server is shown here:

- The browser makes a request to the server, and includes headers similar to these:

```
GET /index.html HTTP/1.1
Host: www.domain.com
Accept-Encoding: gzip
User-Agent: Firefox/3.6
```

These lines in turn, mean the following:

  - The browser is requesting the file /index.html using the HTTP 1.1 protocol.

  - The browser specifies the domain it wants the file from.

  - The browser indicates that it supports gzip encoding.

  - The browser identifies itself as Firefox 3.6.

- The server locates the file and reads it into memory.

- If the browser indicated that it supports gzip compression (which it did in this instance) the server compresses the file.

---

[11] You should be aware that when using gzip, the compression rates achieved are greater for smaller character sets since there are individual characters for the compression algorithm to be concerned with. An easy way to improve performance is to aim to use lowercase characters wherever possible, although this is less important than having fewer characters.

- The server returns the data, with headers similar to the following:

```
HTTP/1.1 200 OK
Server: Apache
Content-Type: text/html
Content-Encoding: gzip
Content-Length: 12345
```

These lines in turn mean the following:

- The server confirms it is using HTTP 1.1 as the protocol, and sends a 200 status code to indicate everything is okay.

- The server identifies itself as Apache.

- The server identifies the contents of the response as HTML.

- The server informs the browser that the data is compressed using gzip.

- The server specifies the size of the data it is returning, so that the browser can show a progress bar, and be sure of when it has received all the data.

- The browser decompresses the data, and reads it.

Implementing gzip compress on the server is easy with the latest web servers, as you'll see in the next few sections.

Apache

mod_deflate is the module Apache uses to compress files. It is included in the Apache 2.0.x source package. With Apache installed, edit the appropriate .conf file and make sure the following line exists:

```
LoadModule deflate_module modules/mod_deflate.so
```

Some older browsers have issues with particular types of data being compressed. It is easy to target them, and there are no performance implications in doing so. Netscape 4.x has issues with anything other than HTML files being compressed, so we should add the following:

```
BrowserMatch ^Mozilla/4 gzip-only-text/html
```

Specific versions of Netscape 4 have worse problems even than that, so we can disable gzip compression for those entirely:

```
BrowserMatch ^Mozilla/4\.0[678] no-gzip
```

Although IE has a user-agent that also begins with "Mozilla/4" it has no issues with gzip compression, so we can cancel those commands for that browser:[12]

```
BrowserMatch \bMSI[E] !no-gzip !gzip-only-text/html
```

---

[12] Apache 2.0.48 has a bug in mod_setenvif, which is why the regular expression looks a bit weird in this example.

We don't want to compress images since they have their own compression already. Compressing those files only inflicts greater processing loads on the server and browser needlessly, with no file size advantage. We can stop that with this line:

```
SetEnvIfNoCase Request_URI \
\.(?:gif|jpe?g|png)$ no-gzip dont-vary
```

Some versions of Adobe Flash have issues with being compressed via gzip, so if you find you are having problems with SWF files, you can amend the line to be as follows:

```
SetEnvIfNoCase Request_URI \
\.(?:gif|jpe?g|png|swf)$ no-gzip dont-vary
```

Finally, some proxies and caching servers make their own decisions about what to compress and what not to, and may deliver the wrong content with this configuration. The following line tells those servers to enforce the rules we have set:

```
Header append Vary User-Agent env=!dont-vary
```

Now any requests for CSS files (as well as other files) will be gzipped for browsers that support it.

Microsoft IIS (Internet Information Services)

Enabling gzip in IIE is even easier.

For IIS 6 (see Figure 8-1), right-click Websites (or just the website you want to enable compression on) and choose Properties. Click the Service tab. You can choose to enable compression for all static files (images, CSS, fonts, JavaScript, SWFs, and so on), all application (dynamic) files, or both.

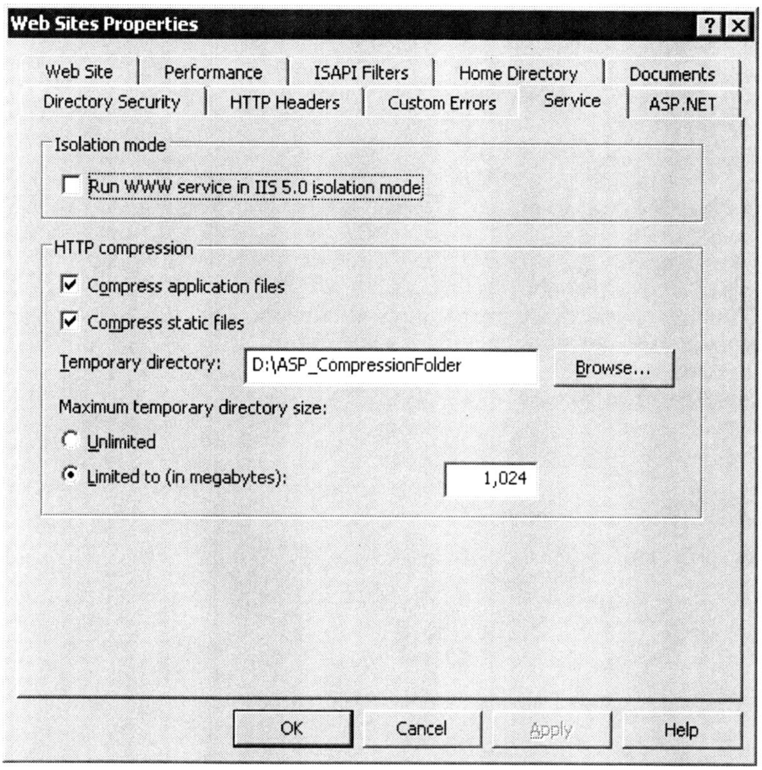

Figure 8-1. Enabling HTTP compression in IIS 6

For IIS 7, gzip compression is enabled by default for static files. For dynamic (application) files, you can enable it with the following command:

```
appcmd set config -section:urlCompression /doDynamicCompression:true
```

For versions of IIS previous to 6, file compression was unreliable, and we do not recommend it be enabled in a production environment. For version 6, you can specify the static file types to compress with the two following commands:

```
cscript adsutil.vbs SET W3SVC/Filters/Compression/Deflate/HcFileExtensions "htm html txt css"
cscript adsutil.vbs SET W3SVC/Filters/Compression/gzip/HcFileExtensions "htm html txt css"
```

The final argument (in quotes) lists the static files to be compressed in a space-delimited list.

For IIS 7, there is a file called applicationHost.config that uses XML syntax, which typically lives at C:\Windows\System32\inetsrv\config\applicationHost.config. This file lists the mime types for dynamic and static files that should be compressed. The static files are in a tag called `<staticTypes>`. Here's some example content for this tag:

```
<staticTypes>
    <add mimeType="text/*" enabled="true" />
    <add mimeType="message/*" enabled="true" />
    <add mimeType="application/javascript" enabled="true" />
    <add mimeType="*/*" enabled="false" />
</staticTypes>
```

This tag supports wildcards in the mime type, so the entry "text/*" will tell IIS 7 to compress CSS (for which the mime type is "text/css").

Almost all modern web servers will support gzip compression. Check the documentation for your web server to find out how to enable it, if it is not enabled by default.

Using an inspection tool like Firebug (or one of many other tools, see Chapter 10), you can inspect the responses and requests taking place, to ensure gzip compression is occurring, and to get an idea of how well your files are being compressed.

Here is an example of the request/response process taking place for a particular site, in this instance: http://stackoverflow.com.

First the request (see Figure 8-2).

Request Headers   view source

```
         Host  sstatic.net
   User-Agent  Mozilla/5.0 (Macintosh; U; Intel Mac OS X 10.6; en-US; rv:1.9.2.10) Gecko/20100914 Firefox/3.6.10
       Accept  text/css,*/*;q=0.1
Accept-Language  en-us,en;q=0.5
Accept-Encoding  gzip,deflate
 Accept-Charset  ISO-8859-1,utf-8;q=0.7,*;q=0.7
   Keep-Alive  115
   Connection  keep-alive
      Referer  http://stackoverflow.com/
```

Figure 8-2. Request headers

Then the response (see Figure 8-3).

Response Headers   view source

```
    Cache-Control  max-age=604800
     Content-Type  text/css
 Content-Encoding  gzip
    Last-Modified  Sat, 16 Oct 2010 06:25:39 GMT
    Accept-Ranges  bytes
             Etag  "803351f3fa6ccb1:0"
             Vary  Accept-Encoding
      X-Powered-By  ASP.NET
             Date  Sun, 17 Oct 2010 16:16:29 GMT
   Content-Length  7823
```

Figure 8-3. Response headers

You can see from these that our initial Accept-Encoding header stated that we support gzip (as well as deflate). You can then see that the response was encoded with gzip (by examining the Content-Encoding header). This proves that gzip is working on the server. You can also look at the line above this section to see the overall result of the request at a glance (see Figure 8-4).

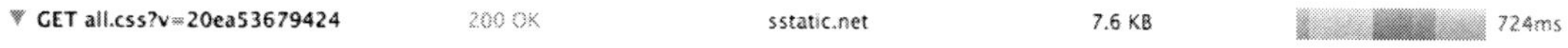

▼ GET all.css?v=20ea53679424   200 OK   sstatic.net   7.6 KB   724ms

Figure 8-4. Basic HTTP request details

We can see from this the exact file that was requested, the HTTP status code returned from the server, the domain the file was requested from, the size of the file, and the amount of time it took to load the file (broken down into smaller parts). We will look at Firebug in a lot more detail in Chapter 10.

Using another add-on for Firefox from Yahoo! called YSlow, you can also see the size of the file before being gzipped (see Figure 8-5):[13]

CSS   31.7K   7.8K

Figure 8-5. YSlow showing file size before and after compression

This shows us that the file was 31.7 KB before being gzipped, and 7.8 KB after. That's a saving of approximately 75 percent! As is clear, this technique is an essential and easy thing to implement to keep our file sizes down.

A more fully featured alternative to YSlow is Web Page Test (`www.webpagetest.org/`), which was developed by AOL before being open sourced in 2008. It allows you to run tests specifically against all versions of IE, and even run them multiple times and show averages, for more accurate results.

Content Distribution Networks (CDNs) and Domains

Browsers impose a limit for the number of connections they can have simultaneously (usually around 35). This is a sensible thing; if we tried to concurrently request 200 files at exactly the same time, the speed of each connection would drop dramatically. But more than that, they impose a limit on the amount of simultaneous connections they can have to a particular domain. This restriction has loosened recently, and some browsers let you modify this value, but by default:[14]

- IE 6 and 7 support 2 simultaneous connections per domain.

- IE 8 supports 6 simultaneous connections per domain.

- IE 9 supports 2 simultaneous connections per domain (at the time of writing— presumably this limit will increase when IE 9 leaves beta).

- Firefox 2 supports 2 simultaneous connections per domain.

- Firefox 3 supports 6 simultaneous connections per domain.

- Firefox 4 supports 6 simultaneous connections per domain.

- Safari 3, 4, and 5 support 4 simultaneous connections per domain.

- Chrome 6, 7, 8 and 9 support 6 simultaneous connections per domain.

---

[13] YSlow is a very useful tool for locating exactly what is slowing down your website, and more than that, gives great indications of things you can do to fix them. You can download it at `http://developer.yahoo.com/yslow/`.

[14] Interestingly, the connections are not just increasing but going up and down through browser revisions.

- Opera 9 supports 4 simultaneous connections per domain.

- Opera 10 supports 8 simultaneous connections per domain.

Most current browsers support at least 4 simultaneous connections per domain. What this means is that if we have an HTML file, a CSS file, a JavaScript file, 4 background images, and 4 inline images, we already have 11 individual items we need to connect to, and at most 9 of them could be queuing behind other connections.

TIP: Browserscope (`www.browserscope.org/`) is a fantastic resource for comparing browser capabilities such as these.

Also, when sending requests for files, the headers we've shown so far are not the only ones that get sent with our request. Another header that deserves careful attention is the "Cookie" header. Cookies are pieces of information used to store persistent data and session information on the user's machine, so that when browsing from page to page, data can be kept locally and referenced by the server. Expiration dates can be set on a cookie, so they can even persist when the browser is closed and reopened at a later date. Cookies are associated with a domain, and any request for resources from that domain includes the cookie in the request. Read that again—"any request." Where we are requesting dynamic content from the server, the cookies can be vital to the correct functioning of these pages, but cookies also get sent with requests to static files like images or CSS files.

On some sites, these cookies can be of a not insignificant size. The maximum size for an individual cookie is 4096 bytes (4 KB), and a maximum of 20 can be set against a particular domain, resulting in a total cookie size of potentially 80 KB for a given domain, excluding the delimiters required to send them. Although this is an extreme case, if we sent 80 KB of data with every image request for a page, the time to download all those images would increase a great deal.

The solution to these issues is simple. If we break our main/dynamic content and our static content domains apart, two big things happen:

- Our cookies are no longer sent to our static content. This results in a smaller request, which is great news and has no impact since that data was worthless, anyway.

- Our connection limit applies to the individual domains instead of just one, doubling our connection limit.

Achieving this does not mean a huge rethinking of our architecture. If we have an initial domain of `http://somedomain.com`, we can continue to serve our home page and dynamic content from `http://somedomain.com` and `http://www.somedomain.com`. We can then create `http://assets.somedomain.com` and point that to the same location with domain name server (DNS) entries. Nothing needs to change in our folder structure and already we have improvements to our performance. This doubles our connection limit, but we can take it even further than that. A simple rule we can follow lets us be consistent in these subdomains, and yet have lots of them. If we consider the file suffix of the types of files we are referencing, we can use those in our domain names. For example:

- `http://www.somedomain.com` and `http://somedomain.com` for our primary and dynamic content

- `http://gif.somedomain.com` for gif images

- `http://jpg.somedomain.com` for jpeg images

- `http://png.somedomain.com` for png images

- `http://swf.somedomain.com` for swf files

- `http://css.somedomain.com` for css files

- `http://js.somedomain.com` for js files

If we implemented this consistently, our CSS would end up with rules such as:

```
input {background: url(http://css.somedomain.com/css/img/shadow-background.gif);}
```

This completely goes against our attempts to minimize file size. Instead, we should point the domain `http://css.somedomain.com` directly to our CSS folder, and continue to reference files within this folder relatively. This is a good compromise between minimizing the file size of our CSS files, and having multiple domains. We can reference our CSS with:

```
<link rel="stylesheet" href="http://css.somedomain.com/style.css" type="text/css" />
```

and continue to reference our images like so:

```
input {background: url(img/shadow-background.gif);}
```

Although the example above may be overkill, and it may not be feasible to implement quite so many subdomains, just one will give worthwhile performance and bandwidth cost improvements. In fact, there is an impact in performance of having multiple domains. Each extra DNS lookup incurs a performance hit, and so the benefits of these must be weighed up against the DNS lookup cost. Up to four extra domains can be considered a reasonable amount.

An alternative to using subdomains is to use a content distribution network (CDN).

As you will see later in this chapter, there are many points between a user's computer and the server they are connecting to; each one having performance implications.

CDNs distribute your static content over many servers and always attempt to respond to the user from the CDN closest to the user's location. This can result in great performance improvements. The difficulties in implementing a CDN vary vastly between the options available, but the benefits of using them are undeniable. Although there are several free CDNs available, for high-traffic websites you need to use a commercial offering to deal with the kind of bandwidth you are concerned with. Some of the better-known commercial CDN offerings are the following:

- *Akamai*—`www.akamai.com/`

- *Amazon CloudFront*—`http://aws.amazon.com/cloudfront/`

- *Microsoft Windows Azure*—`www.microsoft.com/windowsazure/`

Whether you choose to serve your static CSS files locally with subdomains or via a CDN, for a high-performance website, these are things that must be considered.

Having Fewer Requests Is More Important than File Size

With a website of a reasonable size, there will not be just one CSS file that you are working on. Working in that manner would be ridiculous, for several reasons:

- Multiple developers would probably be working on the same file simultaneously, with all the negative issues that accompany this methodology such as conflicts and merging problems.

- Scanning and reading files of this size is difficult, when you are only concerned with a small portion of them.

- Serving just one file for a website penalizes users. Downloading one large file on the home page makes that page very slow to render, when many rules or selectors may not be needed except for specific areas of the site.

It makes a lot more sense to section off the CSS and work on little pieces individually. For the sake of example, let's list a few files we might be using:

- reset.css

- global.css

- home.css

- login.css

The reset.css and global.css files are ones we expect to use on every page, whereas home.css is just for the home page, and login.css is just for the login page. If we left the files like this, our home page code to link to our CSS files would look like this:

```
<link rel="stylesheet" href="http://css.somedomain.com/reset.css" type="text/css" />
<link rel="stylesheet" href="http://css.somedomain.com/global.css" type="text/css" />
<link rel="stylesheet" href="http://css.somedomain.com/home.css" type="text/css" />
```

This has a few implications. The most obvious is that our home page HTML is a bit bigger than it needs to be. Next, we have to create three separate connections to fetch each of these files. Quite aside from the maximum connection limits, this has another more extreme impact on performance.

It turns out that file size and connection limits are not the only things that make files slow to load. Let's look again at the section of Firebug that shows us how long the file took to download (see Figure 8-6).

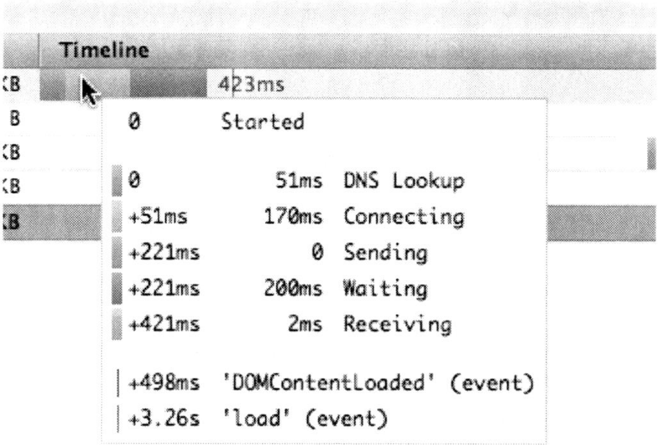

Figure 8-6. *The stages of an HTTP request/response*

You can see here that the receiving of data is not the biggest culprit in this particular item's load time. Let's break this into pieces as if we were dealing with `http://css.somedomain.com/home.css`.

Domain Name Server (DNS) Lookup

DNS is a kind of directory to map domain names to IP addresses. At this point the browser is first trying to find out where `css.somedomain.com` points, so it contacts a DNS server (which one is specific to the user's network setup), asks that server for the IP address for that domain and receives a message back with the answer. If the server already knows the result, it returns it immediately from its cache; otherwise, it asks other DNS servers further upstream. The nslookup tool (see Figure 8-7) makes it easy for us to see the results of this process.[15]

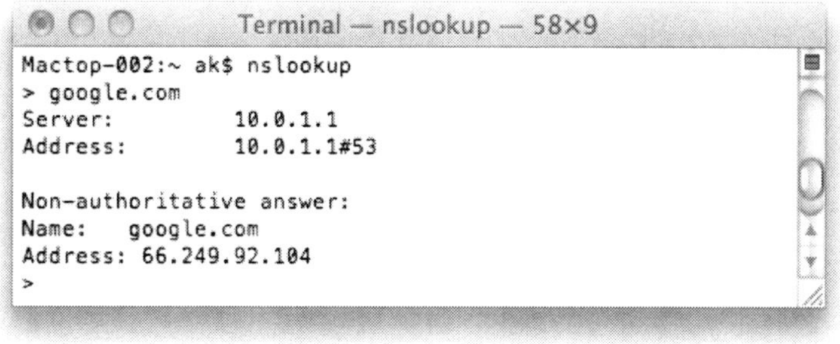

Figure 8-7. *The nslookup tool*

---

[15] Every DNS entry has a Time To Live (TTL). This is how long DNS servers should cache the result for. It is often set to a day or more and is why changes to DNS entries can take a while to propagate to all the servers.

Fortunately, DNS is very cacheable and typically very fast. Once the user's browser knows the IP address for a particular domain, it (typically) won't ask again in the short term. However, getting the response back from the server the first time does incur a performance hit.[16]

Connecting

At this point, the browser is actually establishing a connection with the server. Since it has the direct IP address, it is reasonable to assume that this process should be very fast, and the browser can connect directly to the remote machine. Unfortunately, this is not the case. In between the user's machine and the server are several routers the packets need to pass through to establish the connection. The traceroute command lets us see evidence of this (see Figure 8-8).

```
Terminal — bash — 105×15
Mactop-002:~ ak$ traceroute google.com
traceroute to google.com (66.249.92.104), 64 hops max, 52 byte packets
 1  10.0.1.1 (10.0.1.1)  3.002 ms  0.875 ms  1.066 ms
 2  10.58.92.1 (10.58.92.1)  73.024 ms  16.321 ms  26.637 ms
 3  popl-core-1b-ge-500-669.network.virginmedia.net (62.255.161.117)  37.838 ms  32.597 ms  8.313 ms
 4  popl-bb-1b-as2-0.network.virginmedia.net (213.105.174.238)  34.267 ms  12.316 ms  91.823 ms
 5  popl-bb-1a-ae0-0.network.virginmedia.net (213.105.174.229)  11.641 ms  15.483 ms  22.287 ms
 6  manc-bb-1b-as1-0.network.virginmedia.net (212.43.162.86)  80.743 ms  20.289 ms  57.275 ms
 7  tele-ic-3-ae0-0.network.virginmedia.net (212.43.163.70)  70.682 ms  21.596 ms  22.649 ms
 8  138-14-250-212.static.virginmedia.com (212.250.14.138)  41.025 ms  67.651 ms  48.278 ms
 9  209.85.252.76 (209.85.252.76)  29.407 ms  35.539 ms  37.666 ms
10  72.14.232.95 (72.14.232.95)  42.133 ms *  44.452 ms
11  64.233.175.115 (64.233.175.115)  31.658 ms  59.514 ms  31.100 ms
12  par03s01-in-f104.1e100.net (66.249.92.104)  43.685 ms  28.941 ms  65.599 ms
Mactop-002:~ ak$ 
```

Figure 8-8. The traceroute command

As you can see, in this particular example there are 11 separate routers between the user's computer and the server. This incurs a significant performance hit and happens for every request to the server.

Sending

At this point the connection is established, and the user's browser is sending data to the server. This data includes the request headers and any cookies stored locally for that particular domain. For CSS files, we have already discussed how best to minimize this delay. In the example shown previously, there is very little data to send, and this incurs virtually no delay.

Waiting

The server has now received the user's request and is processing it. A certain amount of processing will always take place, even if it just involves the remote server reading a file and returning it, or a caching server reading the data from memory. If the file requested is dynamic and requires processing particular to the user (that cannot be cached remotely), the performance hit will be larger.

---

[16] Some browsers, such as Firefox, have an internal DNS cache that they refer to. Getting past this cache requires the user to restart the browser or use an extension.

Receiving

Finally, the data is returned from the server, and the browser receives it. In this instance, the data returned is very small and the network speed very fast, so the delay is negligible.

What we can see from this process is that even when we minimize the data sent and received, there are still other factors that impact performance to a large degree. Every connection to the server incurs an overhead, and often this overhead is greater than the impact of increasing file size by a large amount. The lesson to be learned from this is that even though minimizing file sizes is best practices, and certainly something to strive for, having fewer requests has an even greater effect on performance.[17]

Concatenation

Our initial example shown following is now obviously not the optimal way to form our CSS files:

```
<link rel="stylesheet" href="http://css.somedomain.com/reset.css" type="text/css" />
<link rel="stylesheet" href="http://css.somedomain.com/global.css" type="text/css" />
<link rel="stylesheet" href="http://css.somedomain.com/home.css" type="text/css" />
```

Let's assume in this instance that our reset.css file is 2 KB in size, our global.css file is 4 KB in size, and our home.css file is 6 KB in size. Concatenating (joining together) some of these files into one is an obvious way to reduce the amount of connections to the server. Since reset.css and global.css are required on every page, it seems logical that we should join them together into one, and keep home.css separate to stop the user unnecessarily downloading duplicate content. Actually, for these kinds of small sizes, this is not the truth. If we concatenate all three of these files into one, we will achieve the greatest performance for this page. However, when the user browses to our login page, we want to include these files:

```
<link rel="stylesheet" href="http://css.somedomain.com/reset.css" type="text/css" />
<link rel="stylesheet" href="http://css.somedomain.com/global.css" type="text/css" />
<link rel="stylesheet" href="http://css.somedomain.com/login.css" type="text/css" />
```

It would seem counterintuitive to concatenate these three files into one—the user would be downloading the exact same 6 KB (reset.css and global.css) as before. This seems like a duplication of effort. But actually, the extra 6 KB download is unlikely to be as big a hit (for most users) as the cost of an extra HTTP request.

How this works on your high-traffic site is dependent on how big the global and specific files are and requires testing to ensure that you get the best results.

We could also consider concatenating all four files together. This is a larger initial hit, but will be cached after the first page, and not requested by the server for other pages that use the same CSS.

To join these files together is a simple process, but is best dealt with in your build process (as described in Chapter 9). This allows us to work with our uncompressed individual files for maximum legibility, while still ensuring that the code that goes into production is as small and efficient as possible.

---

[17] This is a good reason why the @import directive should be used sparingly; every extra request hampers our performance. Media selectors can be used with the `link` tag to reference individual files or inline in a CSS file to make our selectors more specific. Which ones you should use depends on how many rules you have that need to be this specific. HTTPS connections incur even greater overheads.

CSS Sprites

CSS sprites are a great way to improve performance, and to make pages feel snappier and more responsive. Often in our pages, a graphical button may have several states:[18]

- *Normal*—The regular state of the button

- *Hover*—An image displayed to indicate to users that their mouse is currently over something clickable

- *Clicked*—An image displayed to indicate to users that they have successfully interacted with the button

- *Disabled*—An image displayed to indicate to users that this button will not react to interaction

To achieve this effect, typically four separate images are used. For the sake of demonstration, let's look at the hover state:

```
a {
        background: transparent url(img/button.gif) no-repeat 0 0;
        height:40px;
        width:120px;
        display:block;
}

a:hover {
        background: transparent url(img/button-hover.gif) no-repeat 0 0;
}
```

How browsers choose to deal with the hover image varies from browser to browser. Some may load it immediately into a cache, so that there is no delay to load the image when the user hovers over the anchor. Others may choose to wait until the user hovers over the element before requesting the image from the server. The first example incurs the performance cost of an extra request to the server. The second incurs this cost, but only after load time when the impact is smaller. There is, however, a delay in showing this image to the user giving a worse experience.

There is a solution to this issue. CSS sprites allow us to stack multiple images into one (see Figure 8-9).

---

[18] Don't rely on hover states for anything functional on your pages. To do so is to create a device dependency; the user may have a disability that precludes him from using a mouse, or could be using a touchscreen interface that has no concept of a hover state.

Figure 8-9. An example sprite image

This image includes our regular button, and right beneath it our hover state for the same button. By using background positions, we can reference the same image in two places in our CSS, but effectively crop parts of it out to only display the parts we want. Using this technique, we can amend our CSS like so:

```
a {
        background: transparent url(img/button.gif) no-repeat 0 0;
        height:40px;
        width:120px;
        display:block;
}

a:hover {
        background-position: 0 40px;
}
```

Now there is only one HTTP request, and our button reacts instantly to the mouse hovering over it. It is easy to get enthusiastic about this technique and think "Hey! Let's put every single image on our entire site into one huge CSS sprite!" but before you get too excited, close Photoshop and read about why this is a bad idea:

- CSS sprites are not appropriate for everything. For elements where the size can be unpredictable (that may resize to their content or scale with font-size changes in the browser), the results may be unpredictable too.

- A large file full of images quickly becomes very difficult to manage, both for designers and your CSS developers.

- Deciding that a sprite in the middle of your image needs to change size has huge knock-on effects for the rest of the image.

Instead, we recommend that you use CSS sprites anywhere an image may have multiple states, such as the button demonstrated earlier. Try to avoid allowing elements that use sprites to change dimensions in such a way as to show other sprites or crop them in undesirable ways. If this is not possible, make sure to add enough space between each other, so the adjacent images aren't shown if the visible area changes (like when you increase font size or zoom in a page). As always, find the balance between what is good for your users and good for your developers, and make a decision within your organization on how to approach this. An exception to this would be for mobile sites, where the latency can be so large that every extra HTTP request makes a significant difference to page rendering speed.

Data URIs (Uniform Resource Indicators)

Instead of representing an image as an individual file, it is possible to encode images into a big string of data that we can insert straight into our files, like so:

```
<img src="data:image/png;base64,ABCDEFHIJKLMNOPQRSTUVWXYA" />
```

...or:

```
background-image: url("data:image/png;base64,ABCDEFHIJKLMNOPQRSTUVWXYA");
```

This method has one obvious massive benefit: It saves us that extra HTTP request for each image we include in this way. Where CSS sprites are not appropriate (for example, for elements with unpredictable sizes) they also give you immediately responsive hover states. Unfortunately, it has a lot more disadvantages:

- Control is lost for the caching of these images at a more granular level than that of the file they are included in

- The representation of the file actually ends up about a third bigger than the regular image file

- IE 7 and below do not support data URIs at all

- IE 8 limits data URIs to 32 KB or less

Due to these restrictions, we cannot recommend data URIs unless they are for use in an environment in which you can accurately predict or control the browsers in use.[19]

Caching

Caching is the act of storing commonly accessed data so that it can be more quickly retrieved to improve performance. Caches potentially exist at several different points:

- *Browser cache*—On the client (the browser) and specific to a single user of a machine (although multiple users may use this account)

---

[19] Sveinbjorn Thordarson provides more details about data URIs, as well as tools to generate them, at www.sveinbjorn.org/dataurls_css.

- *Proxy cache (or Shared Cache)*—Cache provided by the Internet service provider (ISP) or third party between the client and the server and shared between many users

- *Gateway cache*—Cache implemented by the owner of the web server such as caching servers or CDNs and shared between many users

Caches primarily serve two purposes: to reduce latency and reduce network traffic. Typically these two goals are in line with everyone's best interests. Everyone wants the user to receive timely information and data as quickly as possible. Everyone wants the least data transferred as possible to further decrease latency and save money. As the owner of a high-traffic website, the only caches we have full control over are the gateway caches that we have implemented. However, there are commands and hints we can give to the other caches and have a reasonable expectation that they will be followed. These commands are implemented via the response headers from the server, indicating to the browser and proxy caches in between whether (and for how long) a particular item should be stored locally before being requested again.

How the browser/proxy cache chooses to interpret this information is initially its choice, and there is no guarantee that the headers we use will be implemented properly, or read at all, although most browsers/proxies have now standardized and are fairly consistent in how they deal with this. Additionally, user settings in the browser may override this behavior and it is not uncommon for the cache to be disabled entirely on the client side. Caches may be implemented in the short term much more vigorously, so that the same image appearing in multiple places requires no further requests to the server, and that clicking the Back button gives an immediate response.[20]

When serving content, it is up to the web server to provide appropriate cache control headers. The first method for controlling cache historically was the Expires HTTP header, which can be set to a date, after which the browser re-requests the data from the server. This method has been deprecated for a few reasons: the time may be out of sync between the resources that are serving the data (such as the gateway cache and proxy caches) and it is necessary to update this value automatically at certain intervals. The HTTP 1.1 specification instead has defined a new header called Cache-Control, which stores a series of individual values that let the different caching layers make intelligent decisions about whether to serve the local copy of a file or fetch a new one. This decision is based upon two factors:[21]

- *Freshness*—A file can be marked as *fresh* for a certain period of time, after which it is *stale* and must be re-requested from the server.

- *Validation*—A request can be made that lets the caching mechanism know whether the local stored copy is the most recent without having to request the entire file.

Let's have a quick look at how the caching mechanism typically decides whether or not to fetch a new copy of the file.

- If there is a header specifying not to cache the file or it is served over a secure (HTTPS) connection, it will not be cached.

---

[20] Content served over HTTPS (secure HTTP connections) should not (and typically will not) be cached locally or at proxies due to security concerns.

[21] It is possible to attempt to control browser caching through `meta` tags in HTML, but few browsers honor them because the browser's caching mechanism inspects the data and makes caching decisions before the HTML is parsed. We do not recommend this technique.

- If the item is considered fresh, it will be cached until a request is made after this ceases to be the case.

- If an item is not considered fresh, an attempt will be made to validate it. If it is found to still be valid, the cached item will continue to be served. If it is not, a new copy will be requested from the server.

The Cache-Control header is made up of several comma-separated values. Here are some of the more important values, the implications of which should be well understood:

- *max-age*—Defines (in seconds) the period of time since the request that the file should be considered fresh.

- *must-revalidate*—Under special conditions, HTTP allows caches to serve stale caches of files. This header tells the caching mechanism not to follow that behavior.

- *no-cache*—Instructs the caching mechanism never to cache this file.

- *no-store*—Instructs the caching mechanism never to keep a copy of this file; a cache can be stored and served from memory, but never written to disk.

- *public*—Indicates specifically that an item is cacheable by shared caches, even if there is a secure connection in place.

- *private*—Indicates specifically that an item is cacheable, even if there is a secure connection in place—*but only in the client-side cache.*

- *proxy-revalidate*—Under special conditions, HTTP allows caches to serve stale caches of files. This header specifically tells *shared caches* not to follow that behavior.

- *s-maxage*—Defines (in seconds) the period of time since the request that the file should be considered fresh (but only for shared caches).

Here is an example header that tells all agents never to cache an item:

```
Cache-Control: no-cache, must-revalidate
```

Here is an example header that tells all agents to cache an item for a year, regardless of whether it is accessed through a secure connection:

```
Cache-Control: max-age=31536000, public
```

Validators are what the agent uses to detect whether an item has changed. In our first example, the caching mechanism will check for a new version on every request. In the second, it will wait a year before checking. *Validation* is the act of making a special request to the server, including validation information, where the server will not return the file if the cached copy is still valid. There are two main validators the caching mechanism will use.

The first validator is the time since the file was last modified, which is returned as a date in a response header called Last-Modified. Rather than making two requests (one to check the validity and another if the local copy is found to be invalid), the agent can make a specific type of request called If-Modified-Since and include the appropriate date with this request.

The second validator was introduced in HTTP 1.1 and is called the ETag. The ETag is built based upon the contents of the file, and is a kind of fingerprint of the file. When making requests to the server based upon stale caches, the agent will send a request header called If-None-Match and include the stored ETag.[22]

In both of these instances, if the content has not changed, a 304 HTTP status code is returned that means Not Modified and instructs the caching mechanism to use the stored representation of the file. If it has changed, the normal full response including the file contents is returned and should replace the cached copy.

Modern web servers return the Last-Modified and ETag headers automatically, and should require no further configuration.

⬛ **NOTE:** ETags are generated to be unique to the file they are generated for, but also for the server they are served from. Gateway caches or load balancing servers could make this header unpredictable. For this reason, they are often inappropriate for high-traffic websites, and Last-Modified tags should be used instead.

When using a browser, there are methods to force a full refresh and bypass the cache. For example, in Firefox hold down shift and F5 in Windows, or shift-command-R in OS X. This sends an extra request header called *pragma* with a value of no-cache, telling the server and any shared caches to ignore any caching commands in the request or caching data stored locally, and return up-to-date versions from the server.

What Should We Cache?

CSS files are typically very static and thus very cacheable. What this means is that their content does not change dependent on other factors, such as cookies or user-supplied content. What one person receives as the content of a CSS file is exactly the same as what another receives.[23]

Where this is true, caches are our friend and dramatically improve performance at every level. We should therefore set caches for images, CSS files, and other static files to be very long-lived. Also (typically) there are no security considerations for these kinds of files. This means that regardless of whether these files are being accessed over a secure connection, we should still cache them and serve the same copies to all users.

Our previous example of a long-lived cache is still appropriate in this instance:

```
Cache-Control: max-age=31536000, public
```

We could set a longer max-age than a year, but it is unlikely that someone would still be working from this cache in a year's time.

Edge Side caching is often a useful and effective technique, particularly for dynamic CSS. We will mention Edge Side caching in the next chapter.

---

[22] A fingerprint (or hash) of a file (commonly an MD5 hash) uses an algorithm to present a string. Checking the string against the original file lets us know if the contents of the file have changed. This is commonly used to be sure that a file you download is the intended file and has not become corrupt, but it also works perfectly in this instance to check to see whether a file has changed.

[23] This is not necessarily true of dynamically created CSS files. Read more about this in Chapter 9.

Best endeavors should be made to keep all CSS and JavaScript in external files, not inline in the page because HTML should have a short cache life, and CSS and JavaScript should have longer-lived caches.

Versioning

When working with cached files with long max-ages, versioning becomes a real problem. As we modify our CSS files, the caching mechanism behaves exactly as we asked it to, meaning that when we want to stop caching files we need a new tactic. The only real solution is to change the name of the file. Consider the following scenario.

Our file home.html has been modified, with substantial changes to the markup. Our main stylesheet style.css has also been modified to accommodate these changes. We have given our stylesheet a long cache expiration to ensure it is not requested when it is not necessary. Suddenly, all our users are complaining that home.html looks broken! What has happened is that the changes to home.html have reached our users, but the changes to style.css have not because that file is still available in their local cache.

The best way to fix this is to *version* our CSS. Versioning CSS files is much simpler than it sounds. We do this by simply manually modifying the name of the file to include a version number or date.

For example, style.css becomes style.1.0.css. The numbers 1 and 0 represent "major" and "minor" revisions, respectively. We increment the minor number whenever we make a small modification. If it is a dramatic modification, we increment the major number and reset the minor number to 0. So, in this instance we have only made a small change to the CSS, and the file name becomes style.1.1.css. Our new markup references this file. We have a very long cache expiration on the CSS files, but not on the HTML. If the user is fetching the latest version of our markup, they get style.1.1.css, which is not yet cached in their browser because it is a new file. If the user has an older version of our markup, they get style.1.0.css from their cache or as a new request if for some reason that piece of their cache is cleared or corrupted. We could just as easily have named the file style-2010-12-31.css or style-strawberries.css; the important thing is that the file name be unique. We could also have broken out of the cache by including a querystring in the URL, such as style.css?v=1.1, which would force the refresh of the file, but would preclude us from keeping the previous versions and thus our backwards-compatibility.

The benefit of multiple files existing simultaneously is that it ensures the integrity of our system, regardless of which version of home.html is running on the browser of our site visitors. If they have the old version for some reason (it is possible that there could be a problem with a shared cache or that a version is still cached) the appropriate version of CSS will still be requested. If they have the newer, the same is still true.

As part of our build process (see Chapter 9), we could make this automatic.

What About Offline Storage?

HTML5 gives us an offline storage mechanism so that we can serve pages and web applications without any requests to the server. This can be achieved via the `manifest` attribute in the `html` tag:

```
<!DOCTYPE html>
<html manifest="/cache.manifest">
...
```

The manifest file (which should be returned with the mimetype `text/cache-manifest`) that we specify contains information about which files should be automatically cached. These files will only be updated when the cache manifest file changes according to our normal caching rules (i.e. via ETags or Last-Modified). An example manifest file is as follows:

```
CACHE MANIFEST
/css/style.css
/css/img/background.png
/js/main.js
```

Since this file in effect overrides all of your existing caching mechanisms, when your files change this file also needs to change. Any line in a cache manifest beginning with the hash symbol is treated as a comment, and this is the easiest way to register changes to your files, without having to modify the manifest itself:

```
CACHE MANIFEST
# Updated 2010/04/01
/css/style.css
/css/img/background.png
/js/main.js
```

Any time this file is changed, *all* the files stated will be redownloaded and your existing cache strategies will not take effect. If only one file has changed (as will often be the case), this is a very inefficient manner of managing caching and performance. Because of this and the poor browser support at time of writing, we do not recommend it as a strategy for caching regular content, although it is still a great technique for its originally intended use.

Cache manifests are useful in all kinds of scenarios and have more complex syntax than that listed here, although they are beyond the scope of this book.

Rendering and Parsing

Comprehending how the browser renders our page is vital for understanding how to get the best performance from your pages. The browser reads the HTML first and then requests the items in the HTML from the top first to the bottom last. If the browser finds CSS files linked at the bottom of the page, many browsers will render nothing until everything in the page is loaded and then the CSS files last. Locating all your link tags in the head tag will ensure that those are loaded first, and the browser can then render the page progressively.

Whenever the browser finds an @import rule, it imports the file referenced, and includes the contents before anything following that directive. In some browsers (notably IE) this blocks the rest of the file from being read and from any other CSS files being downloaded. This means the browser has to wait for that file before continuing to download the rest of the assets for the page. This is just one of many reasons to avoid @import rules.

Because JavaScript files are read in a linear fashion, they block further parts of the page from loading until they have been executed. For this reason, placing them as close to the bottom of the page as possible ensures they will not block any of our other files from being downloaded and read in parallel.

When the browser parses our CSS, it reads our selectors from right-to-left, which can be very unintuitive. Although IDs are very efficient, if we follow them with other less specific selectors, like tag names, these selectors will be read first. As soon as the browser fails to find a match for one of its queries, it ignores the rest of the selector and moves on to the next rule. The fastest and most efficient selectors are those with IDs toward the right of the selector, and IDs are so specific that it often means the rest of the selector is unnecessary. This would indicate that the most efficient CSS possible, is based purely on IDs, but to fill our markup with IDs would be (probably) unsemantic and very difficult to manage. As always, a balance must be found between manageable and efficient code.

Suppose that an ID or class also includes a tag name, as in the following:

```
div#mainContent {…}
img.heroImg {…}
```

The browser first queries the document for all elements with those IDs or classes and then attempts to further query the tags within that result set. This is rarely necessary and should be avoided if possible.

The universal selector (*) is the least efficient selector you can use:

```
body * {…}
```

Although the selector seems it should be a simple query, it returns all the elements first, then checks the next part of the rule (in this instance, that the elements should be inside the body tag) and is a very inefficient method of locating nodes. You should avoid it as much as possible. You can use the universal selector on its own, like this:

```
* {…}
```

Some have noted that the performance implications are reduced in this scenario, but there is no way to do a pure test. It would be a "quantum test," i.e., the act of observing would impact the results. We recommend simply avoiding the universal selector unless it is necessary.

CSS3 selectors are more complex and use more resources to query for. As such, you should avoid them if they are unnecessary. IDs are always the fastest way for CSS to locate elements, with the next fastest being class names.

The loading of CSS files itself causes blocking in some browsers, notably Internet Explorer. As we have mentioned before, you might like to consider "lazy loading" print stylesheets after the page has loaded with JavaScript.

Being pragmatic, however, CSS performance is rarely the bottleneck in the performance of your website. You should always strive to follow best practices and keep CSS performance high, but not if it is at a cost of legibility or file size, as those are more important.

Changing Properties via JavaScript

It is often a requirement to modify styles upon interactions with the page, whether that be a simple visibility toggle for menus or something more elaborate. Lines like the following are very common:

```
$("#elementID").css({
    "height": "40px",
    "width": "40px",
});
```

In this example, we have located the element with the ID "elementID" and set its height and width to 40 pixels each. Because there is no way to set individual properties simultaneously, this is the same as the following code:

```
$("#elementID").css("height", "40px");
$("#elementID").css("width", "40px");
```

What is important to note is that setting properties in this way forces a redraw of the page in the browser, which is expensive in terms of performance. The positioning of everything must be recalculated twice. If we were setting even more properties, it would happen even more times. Instead, we should have added this to our CSS:

```
#elementID.modified {
    height: 40px;
    width: 40px;
}
```

And then changed our JavaScript to the following:

```
$("#elementID").addClass("modified");
```

Now the browser adds the class and is able to modify the two properties simultaneously and only forces one refresh. Although it feels as if we are maintaining this information in multiple places, actually the JavaScript is now responsible for the control of classes associated with an element, and all the presentational code is kept in the CSS files, as it should be. If we have to make this change in more than one place in our JavaScript, abstracting it to a simple class is obviously good practice.

Animation

Animation is one of the most resource intensive things our pages will do, and can be achieved in many ways (including via CSS). Although we will not go into the minutiae of CSS transforms and transitions, or exactly how to animate elements on your pages, we will point out some things that will have implications for performance. How the browser renders your pages is vital to understand how to get the best performance out of them.

When animating via JavaScript we want our code to be as efficient as possible. Unless we have a class for every step between the beginning and end of the animation, we cannot easily change multiple properties at a time. To animate with JavaScript, we change a CSS property by a certain amount at particular intervals until we have reached the goal value. If we wanted to animate a box from the left to the right, for example, we might modify the "left" property from 10px to 100px, in 10-pixel increments, every 40 milliseconds. Here's a series of good rules to follow:

- Animate as few properties as possible.

- Do as little work per iteration as possible.

- Set the interval period to the highest value that gives a good result. Setting it too low will result in poor performance; setting it too high will result in jerky animations.

Although animating via CSS is only really supported in WebKit at the time of writing, animating in this fashion brings great advantages—the biggest being that these animations are hardware-accelerated. It is possible to write code that feature detects for WebKit animation events and uses them if they are available, falling back to JavaScript if they are not. When animating via CSS, if animating colors, be aware that the browser converts everything to RGBA during the animation. You will see better performance if you provide the colors in this format in the first place.

Hardware Acceleration

Using CSS transitions and transforms will use hardware acceleration in browsers that support them. You can trick the browser into forcing hardware acceleration on an element (and its children) by moving an element into 3D space like so:

```
… {
    -webkit-transform-style: preserve-3d;
}
```

Although this does—in certain scenarios—result in increased performance, even on a 2D plane, in other scenarios this can cause problems. Mobile devices simply don't have the processing power of their laptop and desktop counterparts and do not cope well with this technique. Also, elements in 3D planes are processed through a different pipeline to others, and you may see different text rendering or anti-aliasing results. If you have control of your users' environments, this can be a useful thing to do, but it is not a technique we recommend for typical websites.

Summary

This chapter aims to teach you the many factors that affect your pages' performance, and show you some best practices that you can apply to your own CSS for significant performance gains. In many instances one size does not fit all, and testing will be necessary to understand the balance you need to find between these different techniques. This outlay will pay dividends, both in terms of your site visitors' experience (and therefore their goodwill toward your site and your organization) and in terms of your bandwidth costs.

The next chapter concerns itself with dynamic CSS, and will teach you how you can serve different CSS to different users, as well as using preprocessors such as LESS and Sass to make writing CSS quicker, more functional, and more fun.

CHAPTER 9

■ ■ ■

Dynamic CSS

Up until now, this book has considered CSS files to be static assets. That is, what is requested from the server and delivered to visitors of your site is exactly the same in every instance. Although this is almost always the expected behavior and most performant way to implement CSS, it is possible to tailor the output of our CSS dependent on other factors and deliver different CSS to different users.

There are several reasons you might like to do this, some for the benefit of developers and some for the benefit of users. From the developer's perspective, it can be useful to use variables[1] or to dynamically populate CSS. For any repetitive code, such as colors or particular blocks of CSS, storing this once and maintaining it in one place makes for stricter and more rigid code that is easier and safer to modify. Where a CMS is driving your CSS for whatever reason, connecting to server-side components or databases may be necessary to populate the CSS or to build/output selectors. And some tools exist that use dynamic behavior to improve upon the language, and make development more productive.

From the user's perspective, some sites choose to offer the user the ability to customize the CSS presented to them, such as multiple color schemes or typography. This may be for purely aesthetic reasons or to address accessibility concerns such as poor eyesight or color blindness.

In this chapter you will learn about the following:

- CSS extensions and preprocessors

- Evaluating third-party preprocessors

- Serving CSS with server-side technologies

- Continuous integration

- Caching considerations

CSS Extensions and Preprocessors

Several projects exist that intend to build upon CSS, and provide some of the features that many developers feel are missing. Variables, commenting styles, and shortcuts are common candidates for these to address. To use these features, the developer usually creates a file with a different file suffix and works within this file in the new syntax; then a compiler is employed to read this file and output a regular CSS file that may be parsed as normal. There are two big contenders in this space, LESS and Sass, and although they deal with many of the same issues there are important differences between them.

---

[1] Discussions on including CSS variables in the specifications are underway, and have been for some time. The latest (personal) draft from Tab Atkins Jr can be read at http://www.xanthir.com/blog/b4AD0.

LESS

LESS is a preprocessor created by Alexis Sellie. It uses CSS-like syntax and offers many improvements upon CSS. We performed our tests on version 1.0.41. It is built-in JavaScript, so you can include a LESS file as if it were regular CSS (albeit with a different rel attribute), and less.js (from http://lesscss.org), and it will be compiled at page load.

```
<link rel="stylesheet/less" href="styles.less">
<script src="less.js"></script>
```

Using less.js, however, introduces a JavaScript dependency to CSS, so we recommend instead using the command-line compiler. The latest version of LESS is available for node.js (a server-side JavaScript framework for creating network applications). Get node.js from http://nodejs.org. Once you have that installed, the easiest way to get the LESS package, is with the Node Package Manager. Instructions on installing this are available at http://howtonode.org/introduction-to-npm. Finally, you can run this command to install the LESS package:

```
npm install less
```

The result is shown in Figure 9-1.

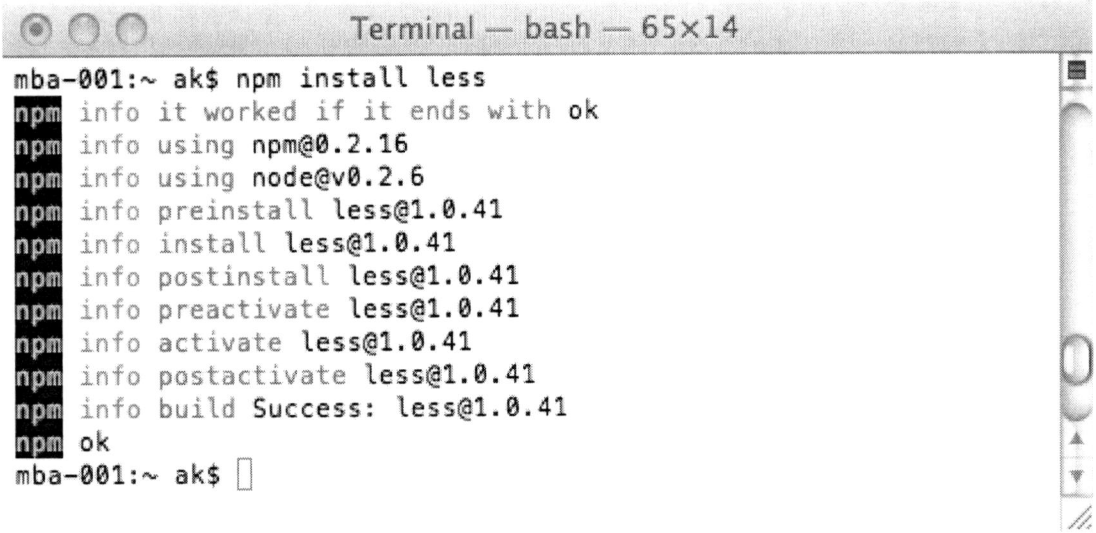

Figure 9-1. Installing the LESS node package

That's the end of the hard work.[2] It's installed. This installation gives you one primary tool: `lessc`—the LESS compiler. Using this is simple. You just run this file, pass it the path to the LESS file you want it to compile, and LESS will create a CSS file with the same name as the source file, but with a suffix of "css". By default, lessc will output to the stdout—directly outputted to the terminal (see Figure 9-2).

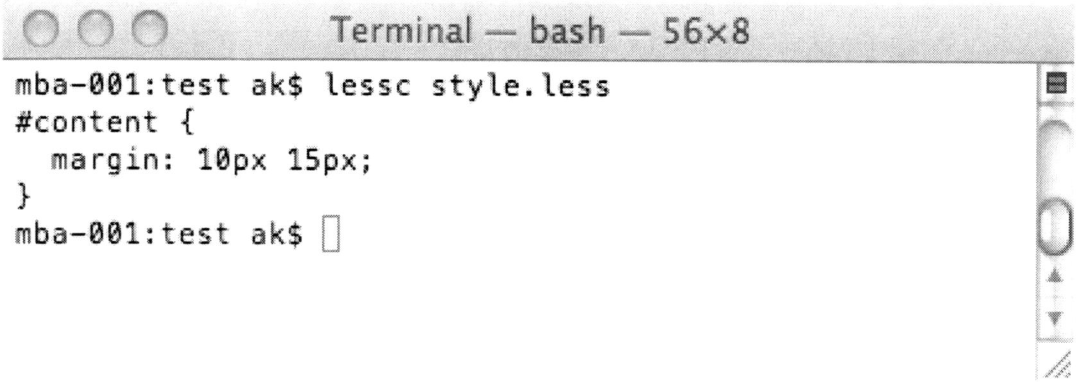

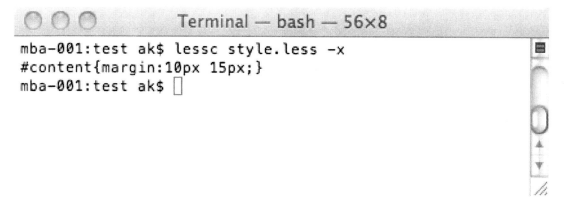

Figure 9-2. lessc output to stdout

To output to a file, direct lessc to that file.

```
lessc style.less > compiled/style.css
```

You can also use the built-in minification by passing –x as an argument (see Figure 9-3).

Figure 9-3. lessc minification

---

[2] The original version of LESS was built in Ruby and was far simpler to install—especially on OS X, which already includes Ruby. In fact, LESS switched to node.js officially after the first draft of this chapter was finished! This demonstrates that LESS is still under active development.

This minification is not as effective as YUI Compressor—it's leaving the trailing semicolon for a start—so we recommend using another compressor in conjunction with this.

The command-line tool is one way to get started, but there are other friendlier ways we will look at in a moment. For now, let's look at the extra functionality LESS gives us in detail.

Variables

Often cited as one of the biggest missing features of CSS, variables can be very powerful and very useful. You can use variables to store any piece of information you expect to use multiple times and define it in one place. This means that changing this definition once will affect every instance in which we have used the variable. This is a very efficient and robust way of working. Any variable in LESS is prefixed with the @ symbol. Declaring variables in LESS is as simple as stating the name, a colon, the value, and a semicolon to end the line. Since the variables will never reach the final parsed CSS, the rules about which characters you can use are much simpler; you are building for one parser instead of many browsers.

Variables cannot be set again and again (they are not variable![3]). In fact, variables in LESS are constants. It is a common programming convention to use all caps for constants with underscores as word delimiters, and makes it very easy to visually locate the variables within your LESS files, but you should use whatever naming convention you and your team find most appropriate (many prefer to stick to CSS-like formats). Here's a basic example of variable usage:

```
@PRIMARY_COLOR: #faa344;

#content {color: @PRIMARY_COLOR;}
```

This, when compiled, emits the following:

```
#content {
  color: #faa344;
}
```

As you can see, LESS has its own ideas of how CSS should look: multiline indented with two spaces, and no vertical gaps between rules. Since the idea is that you would be developing primarily in LESS, the formatting of the output is of far less importance.

You can reuse your variables as many times as you like. LESS also understands the concept of *scope*, which means that you can declare the same variable in different contexts and have the value change only for that context. Any variable at the top level (outside of any selectors) is of *global scope*. Any variable declared inside a selector has that selector as its scope. A variable only exists within its scope and overrides any variable of wider scope. When referencing a variable, LESS will look within the scope local to the reference and then work its way up the chain to the global scope, using the first value it comes across. This might be easier to understand with an example.

This LESS:

```
@PRIMARY_COLOR: #faa344;

#content {
  @PRIMARY_COLOR: red;
```

---

[3] Exactly as in eXtensible Stylesheet Language (XSL), in which variables are not variable and are therefore named really, really badly.

```
    color: @PRIMARY_COLOR;
}

#footer {
    color: @PRIMARY_COLOR;
}
```

…compiles into the following:

```
#content {
 color: red;
}
#footer {
 color: #faa344;
}
```

The first declaration of @PRIMARY_COLOR is outside any selectors; it is in global scope. The second declaration is in the context of #content. At this point, it overrides the first declaration, since that declaration has wider (less specific) scope. The second declaration only lives for as long as its context lives, so as soon as we close the braces for #content that variable is discarded, and we are left with our initial declaration instead. Where the same variable is declared multiple times in the same scope, all declarations but the first are ignored.

You can output multiple variables in one property by space-separating them, like this for the LESS:

```
@VERTICAL_MARGIN: 10px;
@HORIZONTAL_MARGIN: 15px;

#content {
    margin: @VERTICAL_MARGIN @HORIZONTAL_MARGIN;
}
```

It outputs the following:

```
#content {
  margin: 10px 15px;
}
```

But there is no current way to concatenate strings together—leaving no space results in LESS adding a space on your behalf. To demonstrate:

```
@VERTICAL_MARGIN: 10px;
@HORIZONTAL_MARGIN: 15px;

#content {
    margin: @VERTICAL_MARGIN@HORIZONTAL_MARGIN;
}
```

In this code, we removed the space between the output variable, but the result is the same:

```
#content {
    margin: 10px 15px;
}
```

In addition to colors, variables in LESS can really represent anything we might use as or within a value in CSS, from strings of text to numbers.

Mixins

A *mixin* is a piece of code that is easy to reuse in another place. You could consider it similar to a function or method in JavaScript, or a way of inheriting properties from another CSS rule. Using mixins, it is possible to use a CSS rule within another. By using just the selector from a previous rule within another, all the properties from the referenced rule will be included.

This LESS:

```
.callToAction {
    color: #123;
}

#content {
    .callToAction;
}
```

...results in this CSS:

```
.callToAction {
    color: #123;
}
#content {
    color: #123;
}
```

It is worth noting that the original rule still exists in our outputted CSS. If you just intended this to be a reusable block of code that did not target any elements on its own, this would not be as efficient as you might like and would make for extraneous code in the output.

You can also use mixins in a similar fashion to functions or methods. This means you can pass values into a mixin and also have defaults for when nothing is passed. LESS calls these *parametric mixins.* To indicate that a mixin accepts parameters, you can follow it with brackets, with the names of the variables within the brackets. The variables should be comma-separated if there are more than one, and each should be followed with a colon and their default values if appropriate. For example, this LESS:

```
.box (@HEIGHT: 40px, @WIDTH: 40px) {
    height: @HEIGHT;
    width: @WIDTH;
}

#content {
    .box(20px,80px);
}
```

```
.callToAction {
    .box;
}
```

...compiles into this CSS:

```
#content {
  height: 20px;
  width: 80px;
}
.callToAction {
  height: 40px;
  width: 40px;
}
```

As you can see, this method has the added benefit of no longer outputting the mixin in our code! If we are aware of this, we can use this trick to make mixins that require no parameters to no longer appear in our output just by following their name with empty brackets, like so:

```
.callToAction () {
    color: #abc;
}

#content {
    .callToAction;
}
```

Which results in this CSS:

```
#content {
  color: #abc;
}
```

This method won't work with selectors more complicated than a single class name or ID, so you can't define a mixin with, for example, a tag name or descendent selector—it will cause an error. LESS is clever enough to know that any selector that contains no properties (or only variables) will not be outputted in the compiled CSS.[4]

Not specifying defaults, in effect, makes those arguments "required." If you reference a mixin that has no defaults set, and you don't pass values to it, this will cause an error.

Mixins are particularly useful for abstracting away experimental properties that are yet to be finalized in the specification. They are likely to have slightly different and convoluted syntaxes for different browsers and use vendor prefixes to separate them. Keeping these properties in separate modules makes them easy to amend as the specification and support changes, and have these changes reflected in the entirety of your code while minimizing human error and removing the need to write every vendor-specific version out each time you use it.

---

[4] Earlier versions of LESS let you include any selector that existed in the document, regardless of how many elements made up the selector.

Nested Rules

It is possible to nest rules within one another and for LESS to work its way up the chain of selectors to build the eventual selector for CSS. Again, an example:

```
#content {
    .callToAction {
        a {
            color: #321;
        }
    }
}
```

And the result:

```
#content .callToAction a {
  color: #321;
}
```

This is at the same time a blessing and a curse. By indenting and nesting, it is really easy to emulate the structure of our HTML, which can be a very intuitive way to work. However, the resulting selectors can be verbose and specific, which is unlikely to be the resulting CSS we had intended for. Here's a more complex example:

```
#content {
    .callToAction {
        a {
            color: #111;
        }
        p {
            color: #111;
        }
        div {
            color: #111;
        }
    }
}
```

And the result:

```
#content .callToAction a {
  color: #111;
}
#content .callToAction p {
  color: #111;
}
#content .callToAction div {
  color: #111;
}
```

Not only is this CSS more specific than it probably needs to be but it also could have been accomplished more efficiently with multiple comma-separated selectors, like so:

```
#content .callToAction a, #content .callToAction p, #content .callToAction div {
  color: #111;
}
```

This method also encourages you to write CSS specific to certain elements rather than reusable classes, which is an inefficient way of writing CSS. Unless you are using this method to group mixins or variables (covered later in the "Namespaces" and "Accessors" sections), or you are using a class name or ID as a namespace, we do not recommend using nested rules in this way.

It is possible to mix nested rules and properties, like so:

```
#content {
    position: absolute;
    p {
        color: red;
        a {
            color: blue;
        }
    }
}
```

And the result is the following:

```
#content {
  position: absolute;
}
#content p {
  color: red;
}
#content p a {
  color: blue;
}
```

You can also nest pseudo-classes, which is a great use for this feature. By simply including the colon and the pseudo-class, you can generate several lines in one go. The uncompiled LESS:

```
a {
    :hover {
        color:blue;
    }
    :visited {
        color:red;
    }
    :link {
        color:green;
    }
    :active {
        color:yellow;
```

```
    }
}
```

...and the resulting CSS:

```
a :hover {
  color: blue;
}
a :visited {
  color: red;
}
a :link {
  color: green;
}
a :active {
  color: yellow;
}
```

You can also use the & combinator to output the entire selector within your nested rules, and properties. This is particularly useful for chaining class names:

```
#content {
  .callToAction {
    color: red;
    &.disabled {
      color: gray;
    }
  }
}
```

Results in:

```
#content .callToAction {
  color: red;
}
#content .callToAction.disabled {
  color: gray;
}
```

However, if you try to use the & combinator to place the parent selector *after* the current selector, LESS will rearrange those selectors:

```
#content {
  body & {
    color:blue;
  }
}
```

It becomes the following:

```
#content body {
```

```
    color: blue;
}
```

This is almost certainly not your intent (you would expect the selector to be body #content). Provided that you understand the potential negative impacts of nested selectors, they can be very useful.

Operations

LESS allows us to perform basic mathematical operations on values and have those evaluated before outputting the CSS. The operations available are addition, subtraction, division, and multiplication (there is no modulus operator). Here's a quick example of these in action:

```
@BORDER_TOP: 1 + 1;
@BORDER_RIGHT: 1 - 1;
@BORDER_BOTTOM: 2 * 2;
@BORDER_LEFT: 6 / 2;

.callToAction {
    border-top:@BORDER_TOP;
    border-right:@BORDER_RIGHT;
    border-bottom:@BORDER_BOTTOM;
    border-left:@BORDER_LEFT;
}
```

The result is the following:

```
.callToAction {
    border-top: 2;
    border-right: 0;
    border-bottom: 4;
    border-left: 3;
}
```

It is important that the operator (+ or -) has a space before and after it (other whitespace characters cause errors), or else the results can be somewhat unpredictable when performing operations on variables. LESS can also apply these operators to units. Only one unit needs to be present in the equation, and LESS will assume that unit for all others. Trying to perform calculations with multiple units will cause an error and will fail to compile.[5] Here's an example:

```
@BORDER_TOP: 1px + 1px;
@BORDER_RIGHT: 1 - 1px;
@BORDER_BOTTOM: 2em * 2;
@BORDER_LEFT: 6 * 20%;

.callToAction {
    border-top:@BORDER_TOP;
    border-right:@BORDER_RIGHT;
```

---

[5] This is unlike the proposed calc() function in CSS3 (supported by the latest beta releases of Firefox—using the -moz-cal() vendor prefix—and planned to be supported by IE9), which is clever enough to mix units, since it is evaluated when the page is being rendered rather than beforehand. Read more about that here: http://www.w3.org/TR/css3-values/#calc.

```
    border-bottom:@BORDER_BOTTOM;
    border-left:@BORDER_LEFT;
}
```

The result is as follows:

```
.callToAction {
  border-top: 2px;
  border-right: 0px;
  border-bottom: 4em;
  border-left: 120%;
}
```

Note that % is treated as a unit, and does not act as a modulus operator[6] nor is it used to find a percentage of the other value in the calculation. Note also that LESS continues to append the unit even for values of zero (where it is unnecessary) when using its built-in compression, but an additional minification script could remove this.

You cannot perform operations on simple string values, but LESS is clever enough to perform calculations like this on colors (including HSL and HSLA colors), although it converts them to hex. Actually, the current version even converts RGBA and HSLA colors to hex when using them within calculations, losing the alpha channel altogether, so we recommend against this. The author has promised this will be fixed in the next release. It is not possible to perform calculations against a named color because LESS would treat it as a string of characters, not as a color—in fact with the addition operator, LESS attaches the named color after the first with a space, which is very unlikely to be your intended result. When using colors in calculations, LESS breaks them into their components, evaluates the calculation against each component, and then reattaches them. You can even use more than one color in a calculation, and LESS will evaluate the red, green, and blue channels independently (or hue, saturation, and lightness). It is also possible to use variables within operations. Again, here's an example:

```
@BORDER_TOP_COLOR: #aabbcc / 2;
@BORDER_RIGHT_COLOR: @BORDER_TOP_COLOR + #111;
@BORDER_BOTTOM_COLOR: rgb(13,26,39) * 2;
@BORDER_LEFT_COLOR: rgba(10,20,15,0.1) + @BORDER_RIGHT_COLOR;

.callToAction {
    border-top-color:@BORDER_TOP_COLOR;
    border-right-color:@BORDER_RIGHT_COLOR;
    border-bottom-color:@BORDER_BOTTOM_COLOR;
    border-left-color:@BORDER_LEFT_COLOR;
}
```

And the compiled code is the following:

```
.callToAction {
  border-top-color: #555e66;
  border-right-color: #666f77;
  border-bottom-color: #1a344e;
  border-left-color: #708386;
}
```

---

[6] The modulus operator is used to find the remainder after a division operation.

As you can see, the entire alpha channel for `@BORDER_LEFT_COLOR` has been lost. You need to be aware of this impediment when using operations with colors.

You can employ these methods to lighten or darken colors, and use a single primary variable to create shades of that color. This is a very powerful method for generating color schemes based upon only a few initial colors.

Color Functions

Newly introduced in LESS, some built-in functions exist for manipulating color:

- lighten(color, amount)
  - `lighten()` allows you to lighten a color by a percentage.
- darken(color, amount)
  - `darken()` allows you to darken a color by a percentage.
- saturate(color, amount)
  - `saturate()` allows you to further saturate a color by a percentage.
- desaturate(color, amount)
  - `desaturate()` allows you to further desaturate a color by a percentage.
- spin(color, amount)
  - `spin()` allows you to modify a color's hue in degrees (positive or negative).
- fadein(color, amount)
  - `fadein()` allows you increase a color's opacity by a percentage. Omitting the % symbol will still result in the argument being treated as a percentage, so 0.1 is the same as 0.1%. LESS will not increase an opacity past 100%.
- fadeout(color, amount)
  - `fadeout()` allows you decrease a color's opacity by a percentage. Omitting the % symbol will still result in the argument being treated as a percentage, so 0.1 is the same as 0.1%. LESS will not decrease an opacity past 0.

For each of these, LESS will convert the color to the HSL color-space before applying the transformation. It will then convert the color back to hex for the result, unless the opacity is less than 100%, in which case it will convert it to RGBA. Here's an example of these color functions in use:

```
@COLOR: #aabbcc;
@COLOR1: lighten(@COLOR, 10%);
@COLOR2: darken(@COLOR, 10%);
@COLOR3: saturate(@COLOR, 10%);
@COLOR4: desaturate(@COLOR, 10%);
```

```
@COLOR5: spin(@COLOR, 10);
@COLOR6: spin(@COLOR, -10);
@COLOR7: fadeout(@COLOR, 50%);
@COLOR8: fadein(@COLOR7, 25%);

a {
    color: @COLOR;
    :link {
        color: @COLOR1;
    }
    :visited {
        color: @COLOR2;
    }
    :hover {
        color: @COLOR3;
    }
    :active {
        color: @COLOR4;
    }
    .callToAction {
        :link {
            color: @COLOR5;
        }
        :visited {
            color: @COLOR6;
        }
        :hover {
            color: @COLOR7;
        }
        :active {
            color: @COLOR8;
        }
    }
}
```

And the result:

```
a {
  color: #aabbcc;
}
a :link {
  color: #cad5df;
}
a :visited {
  color: #8aa2b9;
}
a :hover {
  color: #a3bbd3;
}
```

```
a :active {
  color: #b1bbc5;
}
a.callToAction:link {
  color: #aab5cc;
}
a.callToAction:visited {
  color: #aac1cc;
}
a.callToAction:hover {
  color: rgba(170, 187, 204, 0.5);
}
a.callToAction:active {
  color: rgba(170, 187, 204, 0.75);
}
```

This is a great demonstration of how a single color can be used to generate an entire color scheme. There are also built-in functions to extract the individual HSL channels called (predictably) hue(), saturation(), and lightness(). You can use these functions to build colors based upon the channels of other colors. Any of these functions can be combined with others. Here's an example:

```
@COLOR1: #123;
@COLOR2: #456;
@COLOR3: #789;
@NEW_COLOR: lighten(hsl(hue(@COLOR1),saturation(@COLOR2),lightness(@COLOR3)), 10%);

a {
    color: @NEW_COLOR;
}
```

And the result, with our new color, is the following:

```
a {
  color: #8ea1b4;
}
```

Namespaces

It is possible in LESS to group properties together in nested mixins (namespaces) and reference those properties as groups by using the > character. This can be useful for encapsulating and keeping code tidy. As always, this is easiest to demonstrate with examples:

```
#box () {
    .square {
        width:80px;
        height:80px;
    }
}
```

```
.content {
    #box > .square;
}
```

...and the result:

```
.content {
  width: 80px;
  height: 80px;
}
```

This technique can be very useful, although it has been somewhat crippled since earlier versions of LESS, in which you could access individual properties and variables within namespaces. It is possible to nest namespaces as many levels deep as you like.

Commenting

LESS also enables C-style, single-line commenting as well as block commenting, however only CSS style comments are outputted in the compiled CSS unless you are using the built-in minification. Here's a quick example:

```
/*
A regular CSS block level comment:
*/
#content {
    color: black; //A single line C-style comment
}
```

And the result:

```
/*
A regular CSS block level comment:
*/
#content {
  color: black;
}
```

Importing

LESS supports the @import directive to directly include files within others. You can include CSS files or LESS files in this fashion. When including LESS files, the file suffix is not necessary. For this example, we'll need to demonstrate the contents of several files:

- style.less:

```
@import "style2";

#content {
    color: red;
}
```

- style2.less:

```
footer {
    color: red;
}
```

```
@import "style3.css";
```

- style3.css:

```
header {
    color: red;
}
```

Compiling style.less now results in the following:

```
@import "style3.css";
footer {
  color: red;
}
#content {
  color: red;
}
```

▪ **NOTE:** Notice anything? LESS is clever enough to realize that when we use @import with a CSS file rather than a LESS file we do not intend for it to combine these files and leaves our code as it was. But better than that, LESS understands that @import commands need to be at the top of a file, and has moved it on our behalf. Previous versions of LESS were even clever enough to realize that where multiple selectors have the same content and are directly adjacent to one another, it should comma-separate the selectors and group them together—this behavior appears to have disappeared, sadly.

This method is very useful for keeping features separate. Any variables or mixins declared in any of the LESS files are available to others, including that one. This makes it easy to create, for example, a single configuration file of variables used to drive the rest of the LESS code. It is important to remember that building that configuration file would result in an empty CSS file because there would be no standard CSS code within it. You must always compile the lowest-level file that includes the others to build the correct CSS. This means compiling that file even though there are no changes to it.

Conclusion

Using the included compiler is just one way you can create CSS files from their LESS counterparts. If you are using node.js, the node package can be used directly within your node.js applications.[7] For those who prefer a graphical user interface (GUI) to the command line, an application called Less.app is

---

[7] Read more about using LESS within node.js at http://lesscss.org/#-client-side-usage.

available for OSX at `http://incident57.com/less/`, which has the ability to watch folders or files, and automatically compile (see Figure 9-4).

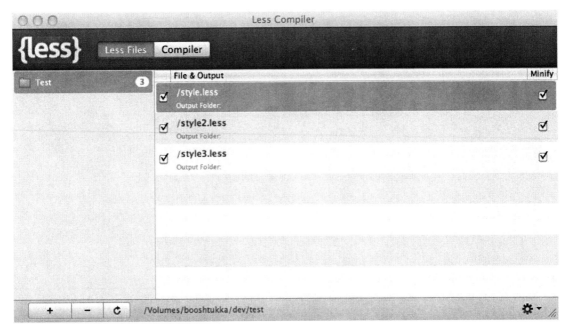

Figure 9-4. LESS.app version 2.3.1

There are also plugins for popular IDEs, text editors, and web frameworks such as Apache, Grails, PHP (`http://leafo.net/lessphp/`), and .NET (`http://www.dotlesscss.org/`). Using these plugins can make it possible to have LESS compiled for you at read-time (when the user tries to access the file), so you need not compile manually, and caching avoids performance worries.

Unfortunately, there are downsides to LESS. Although easy to learn, there are few developers out there who are familiar with LESS. You need to implement it strictly and educate your developers: any developer accidentally modifying CSS code directly will lose changes with the next compilation. The nested rules (for example) can make it difficult to control the specificity of selectors. And, worst of all, when trying to debug your CSS in Firebug or any other web inspector, the files you are inspecting (the outputted files) will not relate to your source files in any intuitive fashion (line number will not match, selectors may not appear the same, and so on) unless you are using LessPHP.

■ **TIP:** If you are using LessPHP, a Firebug add-on called Fireless (`https://addons.mozilla.org/af/firefox/addon/fireless-for-firebug/`) will enable you to debug your LESS code, provided you enable the LessPHP "debug_info" option.

Also, the code and behavior have been modified dramatically between versions, with no change log or documentation explaining what has changed or how to modify your existing code to cope with these changes. If you are using a port of LESS such as LESS.app, LessPHP, or .Less, the interface and code can differ greatly between versions because the port will need to be updated with each code revision and may take a while to catch up. Read "Evaluating Third-Party Preprocessors" later in this chapter for more information on how these critiques can apply to any third-party code you use in your development process.

That said, LESS is an attractive and fun way to write CSS. However, the issues we have mentioned make it very difficult for us to recommend it for a production system; if functionality and implementation changes so severely with no recorded justification and bugs creep into the system, it indicates there is no kind of regression testing taking place—this is not the sort of thing you want to be beta testing on a high-traffic website. Read more about LESS at the official website http://lesscss.org/.

Sass

Sass stands for Syntactically Awesome Stylesheets, which—as acronyms go—is certainly promising. Sass has been around longer than LESS and is already on its third revision. Because Sass is so mature, it seems a little unfair that we covered LESS first, especially since their syntaxes are now so alike. However, uptake of LESS has been faster due to its similarity to CSS and mixins. That said, the developers of Sass were quick to follow suit, and did so graciously and respectfully.

The original syntax of Sass is indented in a Haml-style.[8] In this syntax, whitespace, such as indentation and carriage returns, is important and implies ancestry and structure. Although Python developers love this (Python also considers whitespace part of its syntax), many other developers are used to the freedom of using whitespace as they please to format their documents. We will neatly sidestep that discussion, and instead say that as of SASS 3, the syntax has been replaced with something called Sassy CSS (SCSS).

SCSS is similar to LESS in that it is structured exactly like CSS, and every valid CSS file will also be a valid SCSS file. Visually, the difference between the old syntax (.sass files) and the new (.scss files) is that the newer has braces, whereas the older simply has indentation; and the newer ends rules with semicolons, whereas the older used carriage returns. Functionally, using Sass is very similar to using LESS, but the documentation for Sass is much more comprehensive, and there are many functions that are not available in LESS.

Sass, like the original version of LESS, is built in Ruby, so to install it you first need Ruby installed. If you are using Windows, you can get the installer from http://rubyinstaller.org/downloads/; if you have OS X it is already installed. Then, to install Haml (which includes Sass) type this in at the command line (see Figure 9-5):

```
gem install haml
```

---

[8] Haml is a concise templating language for HTML. Read more about Haml at http://haml-lang.com/. As of version 3.1 Sass will be available separately from Haml.

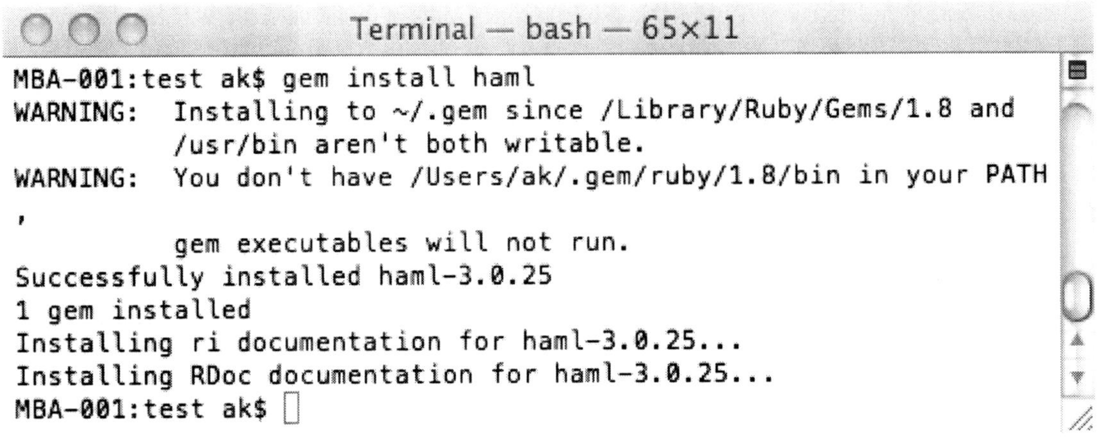

```
Terminal — bash — 65×11
MBA-001:test ak$ gem install haml
WARNING:  Installing to ~/.gem since /Library/Ruby/Gems/1.8 and
          /usr/bin aren't both writable.
WARNING:  You don't have /Users/ak/.gem/ruby/1.8/bin in your PATH
,
          gem executables will not run.
Successfully installed haml-3.0.25
1 gem installed
Installing ri documentation for haml-3.0.25...
Installing RDoc documentation for haml-3.0.25...
MBA-001:test ak$ 
```

Figure 9-5. Installing Haml (which includes Sass)

You're done. You may need to add Ruby to your PATH variable—if this were true, you would have been alerted to this when you ran the above command. The Sass command to compile files to CSS is called sass. Again, you can use it on a single file:

```
sass style.scss style.css
```

If you fail to provide the output file as an argument, the results will be simply outputted to the stdout (see Figure 9-6).

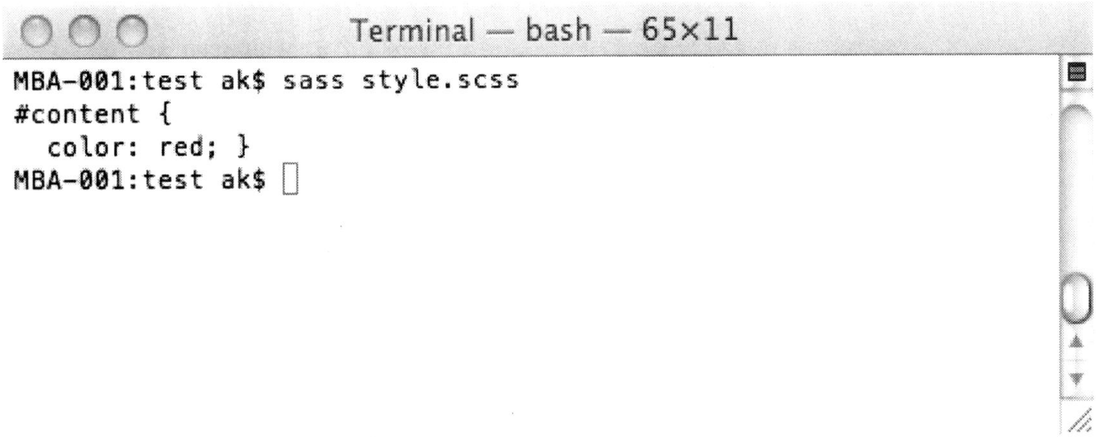

```
Terminal — bash — 65×11
MBA-001:test ak$ sass style.scss
#content {
  color: red; }
MBA-001:test ak$ 
```

Figure 9-6. Sass output to stdout

You can watch a file for changes to automatically generate the compiled CSS, with slightly different syntax:

```
sass --watch style.scss:style.css
```

Or you can watch an entire folder and output any changes in that folder to another, like this:

```
sass --watch path/sass:path/css
```

In this instance, the new files are named with the same names as the original files, but with the suffix changed to .css.

On the whole, Sass offers more functionality than LESS. Whereas LESS's documentation is simplistic and lacking, the documentation for Sass is comprehensive and well written. To that end, we refer you to their documentation at `http://sass-lang.com/docs/yardoc/file.SASS_REFERENCE.html` and will concentrate on many of the major features and differences, since to do otherwise would simply be duplicating their content. We will be focusing on the SCSS syntax, rather than the less CSS-like, older methods.

Variables

Variables use a slightly different syntax in Sass. Originally, creating variables used the following syntax:

```
!variable = value
```

Since the move to a more CSS-like syntax, this is deprecated. The new style is similar to LESS, but uses a dollar symbol as the prefix:

```
$variable: value;
```

Sass also gives you the ability to include variable values directly in the output (known as "interpolation"), which allows you to concatenate variables or even use them in selectors. This is achieved by surrounding the variable name with braces and prefixing it with a hash symbol. The following SCSS:

```
$id: product;
$property: color;
$value: green;

#content .#{$id} {
    #{$property}:#{$value};
}
```

...compiles to the following:

```
#content .product {
  color: green; }
```

This makes variables a lot more versatile in Sass than in LESS. By default, Sass also always formats the output on multiple lines, indented with two spaces, with the final closing brace on the last line rather than on a new line. Also unlike LESS, Sass understands Boolean (true or false) values for variables. This enables you to use conditional logic, which you can read about later in this chapter.

■ **TIP:** Sass actually supports four different output formats: compact, compressed, expanded, and nested. If you are using the command line, you can choose which to use with the `--style` switch, like so:

```
sass test.scss test.css --style compressed
```

The Sass compression is very good, and implementing this and @import directives can be more than enough to emulate a build script that concatenates and minifies.

In Sass, variables are actually variable rather than constant (which is why in our examples we are naming them in camel case rather than uppercase). You can change the value of a variable as many times as you like:

```
$color: red;
$color: green;
$color: blue;

#content {
    color: $color;
}
```

...compiles to:

```
#content {
  color: blue; }
```

Scoping of variables also works differently in Sass. Since there is no way to differentiate between creating and modifying a variable, once a variable has been created any attempt to create a variable with the same name in any scope more specific than the initial scope will modify the variable rather than create another. However, scope is still honored in that variables created at a certain scope will not be available at scopes less specific. This is easier to explain with an example:

```
$color1: red;

#content {
    $color1: green;
    $color2: blue;
    color: $color1;
    background-color: $color2;
}

.callToAction {
    color: $color1;
    //The following line is commented out, since it would cause a compilation error.
    //$color2 has not been created in the scope of this block.
```

```
    //background: $color2;
}
```

…results in:

```
#content {
  color: green;
  background-color: blue; }

.callToAction {
  color: green; }
```

In this instance, referencing $color2 within .callToAction would result in a compilation error, since $color2 has not been created in that scope (see Figure 9-7).

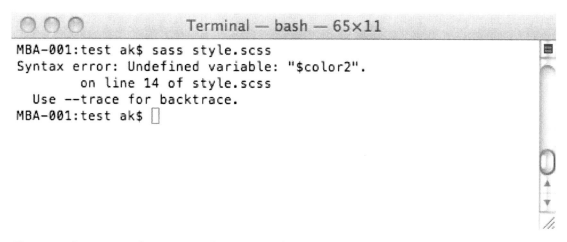

Figure 9-7. Sass reports clear errors with scoping problems

Note that if the command-line compiler encounters an error, Sass will create an empty file rather than ignoring the command altogether.

Nested Selectors

Nested selectors in Sass work exactly as in LESS, with one notable difference: Sass uses the & combinator correctly when placed *after* the current selector. This SCSS:

```
#content {
  a {
    .callToAction & {
      color: red;
    }
    &.externalLink {
```

```
            color: blue;
        }
      }
   }
}
```

... compiles to the following:

```
.callToAction #content a {
  color: red; }
#content a.externalLink {
  color: blue; }
```

Sass behaves as we would expect in this instance, whereas LESS would have output `#content a .callToAction` instead.

Both LESS and Sass will not output rules with no properties. They both happily output identical property and value pairs within the same selector, however:

```
#content {
    color: red;
    color: red;
}
```

...compiles to:

```
#content {
  color: red;
  color: red;
}
```

As you can see, it reformats the code, but does nothing to minimize unnecessary code. The same applies for the compressed version of the code, both with Sass and LESS.

Conditional Logic

Something sorely missing from LESS is conditional logic, and looping behavior (described in the next section), which Sass provides more than adequately. If and else clauses are supported. You would use braces to contain the SCSS to evaluate; and @if, @else and @elseif as the conditional commands. A very simple example is as follows:

```
$christmas: true;

@if $christmas {
    #content {
        color: red;
    }
} @else {
    #content {
        color: black;
    }
}
```

The resulting CSS is as follows:

```
#content {
  color: red; }
```

You can also use the if statements within selectors, just around individual properties. The standard operators are supported:

==	equal to
!=	not equal to
<	less than
>	greater than
<=	less than or equal to
>=	greater than or equal to
and/or/not	used to combine multiple parts of a condition

Here's a simple example:

```
$lines: 10;

#content {
  @if $lines < 10  {
    height: 20px;
  } @elseif $lines == 10 {
    height: 40px;
  } @elseif $lines > 10 {
    height: 60px;
  }
}
```

The result is the following:

```
#content {
  height: 40px; }
```

Although this can make the SCSS dramatically more complex and difficult to read, it also makes the variables, and Sass as a whole, much more powerful.

Looping

Sass supports two methods for looping: @for and @while. For simple iterations from one number to another, @for is the most appropriate. The syntax is simple and involves declaring a variable and defining the beginning and ending points of the loop. The variable can be used as normal during each iteration. Here's an example:

```
@for $counter from 1 through 3 {
    #product#{$counter} {
        color: green;
    }
}
```

The resulting CSS is the following:

```
#product1 {
  color: green; }

#product2 {
  color: green; }

#product3 {
  color: green; }
```

Sass also supports "from n *to* n" rather than "from n *through* n," which simply means that the variable must be less than, instead of equal to, the final digit. In our example, this would have given us two iterations rather than three.

The @while looping is for more complex iterations in which you might like to increment by more than one step for each iteration of the loop, for example. The loop will continue until the condition evaluates to false. Again, the syntax is simple:

```
    $counter: 1;

@while $counter <= 6 {
    #product#{$counter} {
       color: green;
    }
    $counter: $counter + 2;
}
```

Here's the result:

```
#product1 {
  color: green; }

#product3 {
  color: green; }

#product5 {
  color: green; }
```

These kinds of control directives are a very welcome addition to Sass (and are notably missing from LESS).

Commenting

Sass enables single-line, C-style comments, and behaves exactly like LESS in this respect.

Accessors

Sass gives you the ability to append a selector to a previous rule—if the selector only has one element—with the @extend keyword. Although the selector to be appended can be of any complexity, the rule it is being applied to must not have any nested selectors. The following code demonstrates this:

```
.box {
    width:80px;
    height:80px;
}

div#content.main {
    color: red;
}

#content #product {
    color: black;
}

.redBox {
    @extend .box;
    color: red;
}
#content div a.callToAction {
    @extend div#content.main;
    text-decoration: underline;
}
.productBox {
    //The following line would cause an error
    //@extend #content #product;
}
```

It compiles to the following:

```
.box, .redBox {
  width: 80px;
  height: 80px; }

div#content.main, #content div a.callToAction {
  color: red; }

#content #product {
  color: black; }

.redBox {
  color: red; }

#content div a.callToAction {
```

```
text-decoration: underline; }
```

You can extend several rules in one declaration. If we had uncommented the marked line, the error would have been as follows:

```
Syntax error: Can't extend #content #product: can't extend nested selectors
        on line 22 of style.scss
  Use --trace for backtrace.
```

Although complicated, this technique can be powerful. However, you must be careful if dealing with specificity issues, since Sass rearranges the order of your selectors when extending, and it is easy to place selectors in the file in places earlier than you may have intended.

Mixins

Mixins follow a slightly different format in Sass. Whereas in LESS, almost any simple selector can be used as a basic mixin, in Sass selectors are created with the @mixin keyword and a unique name, and referenced with the @include keyword, keeping the mixins and rules very separate. In some ways this could be considered less flexible, but it also encourages modular code, makes for code with clearer intent, and avoids some issues you could face otherwise (for example, mixins being output in the eventual CSS when unnecessary or trying to reuse blocks of CSS as mixins with complex selectors). Here's an example:

```
@mixin border {
    border: solid 1px black;
}

#content {
    @include border;
}
```

The output follows:

```
#content {
  border: solid 1px black; }
```

It is also possible to pass arguments to a mixin in Sass, just as in LESS, but omitting a required argument will cause a clearly identified error. Here's a real-life example:

```
@mixin borderRadius($radius) {
    -moz-border-radius: $radius;
    -webkit-border-radius: $radius;
    border-radius: $radius;
}

#content {
    @include borderRadius(5px);
}
#product {
    @include borderRadius(15px);
}
```

```
.callToAction {
   //The following line would cause an error
   //@include borderRadius;
}
```

It compiles to the following CSS:

```
#content {
  -moz-border-radius: 5px;
  -webkit-border-radius: 5px;
  border-radius: 5px; }

#product {
  -moz-border-radius: 15px;
  -webkit-border-radius: 15px;
  border-radius: 15px; }
```

If we had uncommented the marked line, the following error would have occurred (in the stdout) since there was no default value set for the $radius parameter:

```
Syntax error: Mixin borderRadius is missing parameter $radius.
        on line 15 of style.scss, in `borderRadius'
        from line 15 of style.scss
  Use --trace for backtrace.
```

Colors

Like LESS, Sass supports mathematical operations on colors. Sass understands all color formats, including named colors (LESS does not), and works correctly with alpha channels. Sass also exposes many color-specific functions, which are not available in LESS. First, there are *color accessors* that allow you to expose particular properties of a color variable:

- red(color)

  - red() returns the red channel of a color as an integer between 0 and 255.

- green(color)

  - green() returns the green channel of a color as an integer between 0 and 255.

- blue(color)

  - blue() returns the blue channel of a color as an integer between 0 and 255.

- hue(color)

- o hue() returns the hue of a color in degrees between 0 and 359.[9]
- saturation(color)
    - o saturation() returns the saturation of a color as a percentage.
- lightness(color)
    - o lightness() returns the lightness of a color as a percentage.
- alpha(color)
    - o alpha() returns the alpha channel of a color between 0 and 1.[10]

Although hue(), saturation() and lightness() are all available in LESS, the other color accessors are peculiar to Sass.

Using these individual pieces that make up complete colors enables you to build colors based on specific properties of another color, which can be a very advanced technique for building color schemes based on a few primary colors.

We will show a few quick examples with these properties in action. First, we will dissect a named color and use the component parts to build an RGBA color. Here's the SCSS:

```
$color: red;

$red: red($color);
$green: green($color);
$blue: blue($color);
$alpha: alpha($color);

#content {
    color: rgba($red, $green, $blue, $alpha);
}
```

Here's the compiled CSS:

```
#content {
  color: red; }
```

Interestingly, Sass opts to output this as a named color, which is actually the most efficient thing to do and least open to interpretation. It does this with all colors that can be resolved to named colors, which sometimes is more confusing when reading the outputted CSS, but you would be developing in SCSS so this should not present a problem except when debugging.

In fact, Sass will always convert colors to whatever it deems as the most efficient output. Where possible, it will output them as named colors. Failing that, it will use hex colors. Finally, if there is an alpha channel it will output RGBA. Here's another example:

```
$color: rgb(1, 2, 3);
```

---

[9] Calculating the hue of a color is very complicated and requires the use of some reasonably advanced mathematics. You can read more about hue at http://en.wikipedia.org/wiki/Hue.
[10] For reasons of backward compatibility with previous versions of Sass, the function opacity() is exactly the same as alpha().

```
#content {
    color: $color;
}

$color: rgba(1, 2, 3, 0.5);

#product {
    color: $color;
}

$color: hsla(90deg, 50%, 50%, 0.5);

.callToAction {
    color: $color;
}
```

Here's the output:

```
#content {
  color: #010203; }

#product {
  color: rgba(1, 2, 3, 0.5); }

.callToAction {
  color: rgba(128, 191, 64, 0.5); }
```

This is an interesting decision on the developers' part and important to be aware of. It is a commendable one as it usually makes for the most efficient output.

Sass also provides you with *color mutators*: functions that modify the value of a color variable. We will list each of them with a brief description:

- lighten(color, amount)

  o   lighten() allows you to lighten a color by a percentage.

- darken(color, amount)

  o   darken() allows you to darken a color by a percentage.

- adjust-hue(color, amount)

  o   adjust-hue() allows you to adjust the hue of a color by degrees. This is the same as spin() in LESS.

- saturate(color, amount)

  o   saturate() allows you to further saturate a color by a percentage.

- desaturate(color, amount)

  o   desaturate() allows you to further desaturate a color by a percentage.

- grayscale(color)
    - `grayscale()` will convert a color to its monochrome equivalent.
- complement(color)
    - `complement()` will convert a color to its complementary counterpart.
- mix(color, color, amount)
    - `mix()` will combine two colors together. If the amount property is supplied (as a percentage), it will use that much of the second color. If it is omitted, Sass will mix the two colors equally.
- opacify(color, amount)
    - `opacify()` will increase the opacity (or decrease the transparency/alpha) of a color by the specific amount (between 0 and 1). It will (sensibly) never increase the value past 1 or below 0.[11]
- transparentize(color, amount)
    - `transparentize()` is the opposite of `opacify()` and will increase the transparency/alpha of a color by the supplied amount (between 0 and 1). Like `opacify()`, Sass will never let an alpha channel exceed 1 or be less than 0.[12]

Although the equivalents of `lighten()`, `darken()`, `adjust-hue()`, `saturate()`, `desaturate()`, `opacify()`, and `transparentize()` are all available in LESS; the other color mutators are unique to Sass.

With these functions (and the color accessors we previously mentioned), very sophisticated color manipulation and calculation can be achieved. You could generate an entire color scheme or lighten/darken colors for the purposes of creating gradients, and so on. As always, here's a simple example:

```
$color: blue;

#content {
    background-color: $color;
    color: complement($color);
}
```

Here's the result:

```
#content {
  background-color: blue;
  color: yellow; }
```

---

[11] For reasons of backward compatibility with previous versions of Sass, the function `fade-in()` is exactly the same as `opacify()`.
[12] For reasons of backward compatibility with previous versions of Sass, the function `fade-out()` is exactly the same as `transparentize()`.

Importing

Sass supports @import, exactly as LESS does, with two minor differences. Sass will not move @import commands to the top of the file, which while hardly a glaring omission, is a shame since it results in invalid CSS where the @import rule will not be applied. Of course, if your intent is to directly include the CSS as part of your output, you only need to rename the file suffix to .scss (or .less for LESS files). If you use a command like the following:

```
@import "style.css";
```

Sass will convert it to the following:

```
@import url(style.css);
```

LESS will not do this. It is an unimportant change, since both syntaxes are acceptable according to the CSS 2.1 spec. However, the resulting CSS is larger by three characters. Since @import commands are not prolific in CSS (and we advise against them), we do not feel this is anything to be concerned with.

Conclusion

Sass has many other features, and if you intend to use it as part of your development process, you should read through the extensive and well-written documentation and become well versed with them.

There has been greater uptake with LESS than Sass—perhaps because it is simpler and has looked like CSS from the beginning—so finding staff, application support, and plugins that work well with it is likely to be easier. There is no denying that Sass is more powerful, however, and if you are choosing to use one of these preprocessors you should weigh up the pros and cons of each.

Although less prolific than LESS, methods for compiling Sass at read time with Apache exist, as well as plugins for most major extendable IDEs, and Ruby gems. Whatever your server setup, you will be able to incorporate Sass into it somehow should you wish to do so.

You can read more about Sass at http://sass-lang.com/.

Although there is a feeling of friction against moving toward either of these technologies (LESS or Sass) from many CSS developers because they think it would pose too big an undertaking, this is really an unfounded critique. Since they both support CSS-style syntax, it should be a simple task to rename your original CSS file as .less or .scss and add in new functionality as you see fit. The real criticisms should be the modifications to your build process, the difficulties in debugging, the dependency on a third party and the extra skills required. However, within your organization you may feel these issues are acceptable in return for the many benefits these technologies give you.

Evaluating Third-Party Technologies

Before using any kind of third-party code as part of your development process, a thorough investigation should be undertaken to ensure this code is appropriate and safe for use. Although it is easy to get excited about the capabilities of libraries, frameworks, or preprocessors, once they are implemented it can be costly and difficult to change them later on. It is therefore vital to research them thoroughly first, and make sure the team is onboard with the decision to use them.

Some things to consider are as follows:

- Are many developers actively working on the code?
  - If there are just one or two developers, this should be an immediate red flag. Few developers working on a piece of code means few sources of input, which in turn means a narrower view of use cases or potential issues. It also indicates risk, where a developer could lose interest or for some reason no longer be able to contribute to the code. The world of CSS moves (relatively) quickly, and technologies will need to be updated to accommodate that.

- Is the code mature (old)?
  - Code that has not seen much use is unlikely to be well tested. Although newer technologies tend to be the most exciting (and we certainly encourage trying the code out for ideas or inspiration), we would not recommend them in a production system or high-volume websites, where edge cases are likely to be numerous.

- Is the technology in widespread commercial use?
  - Again, code that is in use in more locations is likely to be safer and better tested. A result of popular technology is community, third-party documentation such as books and blog/web articles and enthusiasm in the industry (and therefore a greater pool of developers to hire from).

- Is the source code available?
  - As a final resort to a future scenario of the code stagnating and no longer being developed, available source code would allow your company to take future modifications in-house. This takes away the benefit of allowing third parties to test and develop code effectively on your behalf, but protects you from a degree of risk.

- Is there comprehensive documentation?
  - Good documentation is obviously useful for implementing and using the technology, but also demonstrates conscientious development, which is a good sign.

- Is there a test suite?
  - The existence of a test suite should indicate well-tested code and alleviate some worries with regard to regression bugs in future releases.

- Are there change logs?
  - When a new version of the code is released, it is likely to have an impact on older implementations. Clear change logs indicate exactly what has changed and what is likely to cause issues or affect your existing codebase. Old methods and syntaxes should be deprecated and not removed for at least a few revisions in order to give consumers of the technology a chance to update their code to the new interfaces.

If you are not answering yes to most of the questions with regard to the technology you are evaluating, you should think hard about whether implementing this technology would be a source of technical debt in the future, and if the problem you are trying to solve could not be better addressed with other methods.

Serving CSS with Server-Side Technologies

As we have mentioned before, all current browsers don't care what suffix your CSS files have.[13] As long as you serve the files containing your CSS with the right mime type (`text/css`), the browser will happily read it and go about its everyday business. This means that you can use your server-side technology of choice to give you the same kind of capabilities that the preprocessors do, and more. You could use PHP to connect to a database, populate variables from there, and insert them directly into code; or write your own ASP.NET color manipulation functions. As long as you reference a file that includes CSS and provide the correct mime type, this will work.

An example implementation is large websites with many sub-brands. Although the CSS is largely the same, the server can generate several versions of the CSS file with different color schemes populated from a database. The database could be populated via a CMS, resulting in a consistent automated layout from website to website, and color schemes that could be produced by publishing departments rather than developers.

You could also use this technique to provide different CSS in different situations. You could detect the department (e.g. finance, HR, IT, etc) a user works within, for example, and provide different CSS to them based upon a querystring or database entry. You could also provide the user CSS unique to them— although this technique is very difficult to cache server-side, and has performance and bandwidth implications. It would be better to offer the user CSS options or color schemes, and provide them one of a limited amount of CSS files (or querystring configurations) with shared URLs, so that the results can be effectively cached.

The same downsides that occur with LESS and Sass apply here, perhaps to a greater extent. When trying to debug your CSS, the line numbers will not tally with your source code, and selectors may look completely different between your source and resulting file. That said, the ability to use variables or databases to maintain your code can be a great way of allowing nontechnical people, such as your publishing or content team, to modify the aesthetics of your website, and custom code will give you a lot more control over the output. Another downside, of course, is that it is difficult to hire cheap or lower-end developers since the learning curve is steeper and they cannot become productive immediately.

As always, whether or not to implement this style of CSS generation depends upon your specific scenario.

Continuous Integration (CI)

As we have mentioned previously, it is possible to use build scripts to manipulate your CSS, usually for reasons of performance. Although you could run these scripts manually, it is useful to be able to run them in an automatic fashion for deployment to other environments. Typically an organization should have four primary environments (and maybe several of each):

- Development
    - Although CSS authors typically write and test CSS on their own machines, when they need to integrate their code with changes that others have made to test more effectively what they have built as part

---

[13] The same goes for other file types, such as images, JavaScript, or fonts.

of a project, they would deploy to a Development environment. This environment is usually unreliable because changes are being deployed to it very frequently, and as such is useful for the team to do high-level testing, but not for thorough or exploratory testing.[14]

- Integration or QA

    o This environment is deployed to less frequently, typically at predetermined intervals. Since the code does not often change, this is a good environment to do more thorough testing on. Often other teams that have been simultaneously modifying code your project has dependencies on will use this environment to test the connections between your code.

- Staging

    o Although the Development and Integration environments are rarely exact replicas of the live Production environment, the Staging environment should behave and be configured as closely to the Production environment as possible. Any deployments to this environment should be solid, reliable, and tested code; and it is at this point that User Acceptance Testing (UAT) should be carried out. This environment is also often one that is used by the publishing or content team to test their amendments to the site, before pushing them to the production environment.

- Production

    o This is the live site that your users are served their pages from.

When using version control, it is typical to push your changes to the main repository only when you are confident that they will work as expected. Once you have committed them, the first thing you are likely to want to do is to deploy them to the Development environment.

While it is possible to simply connect to the appropriate server, fetch the latest versions of your files from the source control repository and then manually run any build scripts, this is time-consuming and therefore not an efficient way to work.

Continuous integration (CI) systems deal with this shortcoming. A server might be set to automatically detect changes in the repository—either via polling after predefined intervals, or by hooks within the version control system. Whenever changes are detected, the server fetches the new versions of the files and then the project is built. When the project has been successfully built, it is then deployed automatically to the Development environment.

There are several advantages to this methodology:

- Any tests can be run after the project is built, but before deployment. This means that if you have tests that can be run client-side, you could build to a temporary environment, run the tests on the server automatically—potentially in many operating systems and browsers—and choose not to deploy to the Development environment if there is a problem or failed test. This is known as *breaking the build*. (You can read more about testing in Chapter 10.)

---

[14] "Exploratory testing" describes unscripted testing, where the tester relies upon their knowledge to "mess around" with the site looking for unexpected results or bugs.

- Any build scripts can be run automatically.

- All users are alerted to any build problem. If someone has broken the build, some kind of notification system can let all the other developers know, and a conversation can take place about who should fix it and how it should be fixed. Other developers should not commit to the repository until after the issue is resolved.

- The same system can be used to manually (or automatically) deploy to the other environments.

Often a traffic light system is used, in which a small application resides in the user's menu bar or system tray. It lights up green if the build is building successfully or red if it is broken.

If you have elected to incorporate build scripts for minifying or concatenating your code, CI can run these for you whenever it is set to deploy. However, you should try to include the ability to enable some kind of debug mode (as described in the next chapter)—at least in the Development environment—so that when tests fail or issues are found, they are easy to resolve.

Another test you might run is to see whether or not the resulting files of your site validate, or whether there are any build warnings. You would probably still choose to deploy in this scenario, but it would be pertinent to notify the developer who checked in the file that caused the warnings.

CI encourages all kinds of great habits in developers. If it is combined with automated testing, it can make code much more robust and save many wasted hours—as well as alerting developers and testers to problems earlier.

Clever Build Scripts

Rather than just minifying and concatenating a predefined list of files together, front-end engineer Jade Thomas has come up with her own methodology that solves many problems in one go. Choosing just to target WebKit with browser-specific vendor extensions in her CSS, the build script parses and duplicates these properties with all the other vendor-specific versions of the same property, giving an abstracted method of dealing with changes in the spec and adding more vendor-specific extensions as they come along. Next, a series of custom–defined vendor prefixes are set for versions of IE such as `-ie6-`, `-ie7-`, and so on (not `-ms-` because that already exists) that the build script can parse and output as the appropriate hacks for that browser.

But now, the clever part. Instead of outputting hacks, the build script actually outputs one file for each version of IE, and one file for all other browsers. These files can then be served to the appropriate browser with conditional comments, so that every browser gets only the code intended for it. A preprocessor such as LESS or Sass could emulate some of this behavior, but not nearly as well. The benefits of this method are significant:

- The original file works without being built (on WebKit)—this means when we debug we can still see what line the offending CSS is on.

- When vendor prefixes are supported in validation tools, our CSS would actually validate![15]

- No hacks in the output, ever.

---

[15] The latest version of the W3C CSS validator (`http://jigsaw.w3.org/css-validator/`) allows you to show vendor prefixes as warnings, rather than errors.

- Modified versions of the build script could output versions for IE without modifying line numbers, again making debugging easy.

- Each browser makes only a single HTTP request.

- Browser-specific code for each property lives side by side, making maintaining these files easy.

Sadly, there is no version or documentation for this technique available publicly, but we encourage you to consider emulating this behavior if your processes justify it.

Caching Considerations

When serving any kind of dynamic file, caching can become an issue. If you are providing files that are preprocessed, but otherwise static and served to many users, you just need to configure your web server to consider these files cachable (and you can still use versioning—described in the previous chapter—to effectively bypass the cache when necessary). If these files are processed at any point in reaction to the user, rather than before the fact, these files can also be cached via different mechanisms. However, it is better for your users that you proactively prepare any files like this before they are requested. This means that no single individual bears the brunt of the performance implications, and the servers undergo predictable (rather than inconsistent) stress.

Where files are modified on the fly (perhaps on a per-user basis), and too many potential variations exist for it to be reasonable to create these files in advance, caching becomes impractical from the server side (although the browser can still cache the content), so performance hits are unavoidable. To combat this, you can try to limit the potential variations, cache the variations that get the most traffic, or ensure that your web server has no problem with the extra load. In that situation, *Edge Side Caching* can help minimize the burden. Edge Side Caching is currently only usable within (X)HTML markup, but we mention it here for your interest and because it may be relevant to your chosen caching strategy.

Edge Side Caching uses a simple markup language called *Edge Side Includes (ESI)* to dynamically request only certain sections of the response and serve the rest as static content. This needs to be implemented and parsed by some kind of CDN or caching server so that the user hits it and is returned the correct response. Several organizations have implemented it, and it can be a very effective technique for performant websites.

▨ **NOTE:** See the list of vendors that support ESI at `http://en.wikipedia.org/wiki/Edge_Side_Includes`.

An ESI Language Specification was submitted to the W3C in August 2001, which has not been responded to. However, response and uptake of ESI has been positive, and if you want to use it, it is mature and simple enough to present minimal risk. A very simple piece of ESI markup would be something like this:

```
<esi:include src="http://yourcompany.com/uncachable.content"/>
```

Varnish[16] supports ESI, as does Akamai and many other CDNs and caching servers. You can read more about ESI at `http://www.w3.org/TR/esi-lang`.

Summary

This chapter explained some of the many ways you can have dynamic and self-building CSS files or responses. These techniques are not always appropriate and incur a productivity hit when hiring new staff, but in the right situations can make development a lot simpler and more pleasant. If they are appropriate for your website, and you have considered the downsides of these methods, you should not be worried about implementing them.

The next chapter concerns itself with debugging and testing, and will teach you what you need to know to find this balance and be certain you are making the best of your resources, as well as locating issues with your code and fixing them.

---

[16] Varnish is a great piece of software that dramatically improves the caching capabilities of many web servers. Read more about it at `http://www.varnish-cache.org/`.

■ ■ ■

CHAPTER 10

Testing and Debugging

So, you've got your website all set up and running, you've written your CSS, and everything worked exactly right the first time, right? Unlikely. With any type of scripting or programming there is a degree of trial and error involved in reaching your goals. This equally applies to CSS. When writing CSS, developers typically flick back and forth between the code and the browser (or browsers), writing or amending code, and refreshing to check the results. If there are any more complicated steps in between—building, uploading, compiling, and so on—the productivity of the developer is impacted with every edit.

Once the code is complete, it is necessary to ensure that it works as expected in all the browsers to be supported by the website. Testing like this takes time and effort—CSS often impacts large portions of a website—and everything that could be affected must be tested.

Whenever issues or bugs are found, they need to be fixed quickly, and with minimum impact and maximum confidence that they have not caused new issues (or re-created old issues) throughout the rest of the website.

This chapter will be concerned with tools and methods to help you achieve all this in the most productive manner and more. Many of the tools we will discuss have functionality we will not mention, since it is more of use to JavaScript or server-side developers; we will focus on the parts of interest to the CSS developer. You will learn about the following:

- Efficient and fast development

- Creating a "debug mode"

- Debugging and tools

- Automated testing

- Local manual testing

Fast Development

When you start out with web development, you tend to work on small static projects. These kinds of sites run equally well from a folder on your computer as from a server on the Internet. Development is simple and quick as you flick back and forth between your editor and your browser, with no worries of external dependencies, third-party code, or other developers and CMSs screwing with your CSS. However, in the world of high-traffic websites, it is safe to assume that your development practices are considerably more affected by your environment. There are likely to be several environments your code can exist on and extra steps necessary to deploy your code and test it. This goes against the grain for many CSS developers who are used to making small, iterative changes and testing these changes frequently. So, how can you get back the rapid development cycle and instant gratification you love so much?

The first step is to isolate the things that are impacting your productivity.

Build Scripts that Concatenate CSS

If you are using a build script that concatenates multiple CSS files together—and we certainly recommend that you do—this process can take a while and get in the way. Of course, for production code this is the correct thing to do, but for development environments the speed and performance gains of doing this are negligible, since the servers you are running from are likely to be on the same network that your development machine is on.

A good solution is to use a debug style sheet. Let's assume the build script runs as some kind of shell script that includes all the files we want to concatenate. There would probably be a configuration file that tells the shell script which files we want it to load and in which order. Our resulting file might be called "main.css". Instead of using that configuration file, you could consider using a CSS file, since you have the @import directive, which allows you to achieve the same thing but using multiple files. If you have a file called "main-debug.css", this could contain something like the following.

```
@import url(reset.css);
@import url(global.css);
@import url(login.css);
@import url(feature.css);
```

Using a few clever regular expressions, it's not hard to make our shell script read this file and use the @import directives to build "main.css". This gives us two significant benefits:

1. The list of files is maintained in just one place.

2. You can use "main-debug.css" to emulate the behavior of "main.css", but without needing to run the build script.

If you then modify your pages to accept a querystring of (for example) ?debugCSS=true and use this parameter to insert "-debug" in the file name for the included CSS, turning on and off this behavior becomes something simple. Now it is easy to modify the file and see the results immediately.

Build Scripts that Compress CSS

If you've followed our recommendations, you are also compressing your CSS. If the build script is compressing your CSS into a resulting file called, for example, "main.css", the same issues will present themselves as with concatenation. If you name the original files with "-debug" within the file name, you can use the aforementioned querystring trick to access the uncompressed file. Of course, if you are concatenating as well as compressing, the method of dealing with concatenated CSS that we mentioned in the previous section works equally well in this instance.

Pages That Don't Like to be Refreshed or Time Out Frequently

If you are working on sections of a website that require information to be posted to them or that have secure connections, it is possible that refreshing these pages will show you different content or redirect you to a different page. This means that every time you change the CSS used by these pages, you need to browse back to the page, possibly logging in again or going through some other time-consuming process.

However, there are methods to reload the CSS for that page, without reloading the rest of the page, assuming that the CSS hasn't been modified by JavaScript or is contained within the page itself. If you are using a browser with the ability to directly modify the HTML or an add-on with the same ability such as Firebug,[1] you can locate the link to the external file and modify the URL to include a querystring with a unique value. For example, if your code contains something like this:

```
<link rel="stylesheet" href="/css/main.css" />
```

You could modify it to be as follows:

```
<link rel="stylesheet" href="/css/main.css?12345" />
```

This should then make a new request for the file. Your URL might already include a querystring for some reason, such as the following:

```
<link rel="stylesheet" href="/css/main.css?hello=goodbye" />
```

Then you just need to append a new parameter on the end of it to force the refresh and leave the request unbroken:

```
<link rel="stylesheet" href="/css/main.css?hello=goodbye&12345" />
```

However, if you keep using this method, your appended strings will not be as unique as you might like! No matter how random your strikes on the keyboard, you will repeat yourself pretty quickly and begin returning files from the cache instead of new requests. To solve this, it is better to append the time and date, since those will always be unique. Entering these ourselves, though, is no fun, so you can use the console within Firebug, Web Inspector, IE Developer Tools, or Opera Dragonfly to run a little bit of JavaScript that does it for us, like this:

```
var date = new Date().getTime();
var links = document.getElementsByTagName('link');
for (var i=0,j=links.length; i<j; i++){
   var link = links[i];
   link.href += (link.href.indexOf('?') == -1 ? '?' : '&')+date;
};
```

This script will make these changes for every link tag it finds on the page. It is also possible to make this into a bookmarklet, which is a small snippet of code that can be run from the favorites menu of your browser (including IE) to achieve the same thing in a friendlier and quicker fashion.

▨ **TIP:** This block of code does have some limitations, but Antony has written a fuller-featured version at `http://zeroedandnoughted.com/bookmarklet-to-de-cache-css-and-images-version-2/`. His version will also refresh images and background images, and works within the current document and frames or iframes within it, but does not currently support files using the @import directive.

---

[1] Opera allows you modify the source of a page directly and then refresh from the cache. Although unintuitive to use, this useful behavior is available out of the box. Be aware though, that if you are running a file directly from your file system, it will modify the file itself.

Cached Files

Since caching files is not usually helpful during development, we would recommend disabling the caching mechanism in your browser while developing, but don't forget to re-enable it when checking performance.

Internet Explorer Bugs

Although not strictly impacting upon your productivity, developing within Internet Explorer is enough to make most developers want to give in and take up a career in plumbing instead. We recommend working in a standards-compliant browser first and then fixing everything in older versions of IE and other browsers second. This ensures you reach a good working point quickly and will help maintain your sanity. Of course, it helps to be aware of the limitations of the browsers you intend to support so that you don't build things that you will not be able to make display correctly in them. We talk about this more in Chapter 3.

Debugging

On occasion, there will be an issue with your code that is hard to pin down. Possibly one rule will be overriding another, or a file that is being included could be affecting something unexpected. If a selector does not seem to be being applied, setting a background color to something strong like red, green or blue with `!important` is often enough to prove that the selector is working,[2] but if it is a property you are having issues with, it is unlikely to be this simple to resolve. However, there are tools to help us deal with this. The following is a list of some tools either built-in to browsers or available as add-ons. Many others are available.

Firebug (Firefox)

Firebug was the first really useful front-end web debugger. The first public version (0.2) was released in January 2006, and it has come on in leaps and bounds since then, inspiring and pushing browser vendors to develop and provide their own equivalent tools. Since Firebug is an extension for Firefox, many other extensions exist that plug into it, and further enhance its functionality such as add-ons to monitor cookies, HTTP headers, and more. Although Firebug (and the other developer tools discussed later in this chapter) provides methods to monitor and debug all aspects of front-end web development, we will concentrate on the CSS, HTML, and HTTP portions.

Firebug can be "snapped" to the main window of our browser, but we will look at it in its "popped out" windowed view. First, the HTML view (shown in Figure 10-1).

---

[2] Using colored borders has the same result, but modifies the size and positioning of the element.

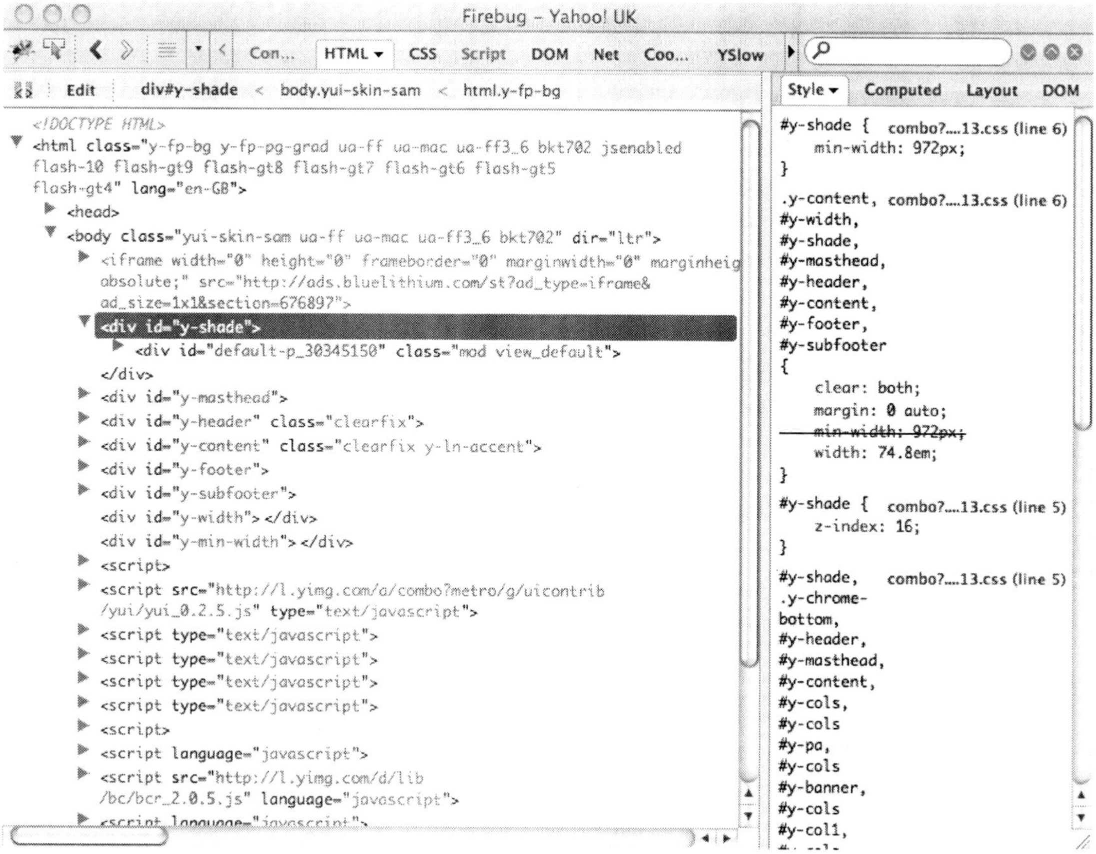

Figure 10-1. The HTML view of Firebug

This view encompasses all kinds of useful information and functionality. In the main window, it shows the HTML document for the current page, and allows you to expand and contract any node with child nodes. Some possible actions in this view are the following:

- Hovering the mouse over an element will highlight that element in the page.

- Hovering the mouse over an image will show the image in a small window with its dimensions (none of the other browser tools do this).

- Clicking an element will select that element.

- Next to the Edit button in the toolbar, the ancestry of the selected element is shown as breadcrumbs. Clicking any of these will highlight that parent element instead.

- Clicking any element attribute will allow you to rename that attribute; clicking any attribute value will allow you to change the value of the attribute.

- Pressing the Tab key while editing attributes allows you to cycle to the next attribute name or value (Shift-Tab will cycle to the previous one), and when you reach the last value for that element, tabbing again will allow you to enter a new attribute and value.

- Clicking a text node will allow you to amend the text in that node.

Performing any of these actions results in immediate changes to the Document Object Model (DOM) and the page, and you can see these changes straight away.

■ **TIP:** You can also select elements within the webpage by right-clicking them and choosing Inspect Element (which will automatically show Firebug). Alternatively, you can click the icon next to the Firebug logo and then click the element—this is useful since as you hover over elements blue borders are shown around them, which demonstrates the layout and space taken up by elements in a rapid visual fashion.

Clicking the Edit button in the toolbar will allow you to edit the HTML for that element (including the outer HTML) in its entirety, in a built-in, simple text editor (see Figure 10-2). Again, these changes will take effect immediately. Clicking the Edit button again will return you to the previous view.

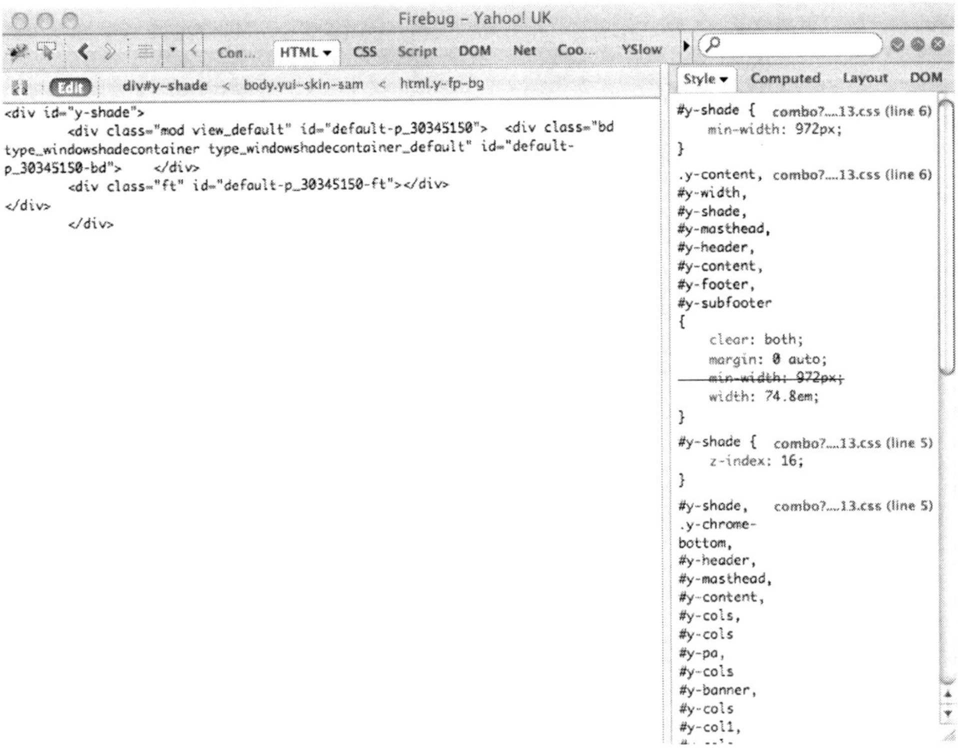

Figure 10-2. Edit mode in the HTML view of Firebug

On the right side, all the author CSS selectors that apply to the highlighted element are displayed, in descending specificity from top to bottom. Inherited values are shown below. Next to each rule is a link to the style sheet it is declared in, with the line number shown in brackets. On the line beginning with "Inherited from" is a link—hovering over the link will highlight matched elements in the page, and clicking it will highlight these in Firebug and switch focus to them in the HTML.

For any of these rules, you can click any property or property value to change it and immediately see those changes in the page. When hovering over them, a circle with a line through it is shown on the left of the property; clicking this will disable that property for that rule. Tabbing out of the last property value for a rule will allow you to enter a new one, or you can double-click anywhere on the selector or next to properties to achieve the same thing. When entering new properties, Firebug adds the colon and semicolon for you, so omit those or they will be treated as part of the parameter name or value.

Any property that is overridden in another selector of greater specificity is visually struck through.

By default, this view does not show the user agent CSS (rules that are applied by Firefox itself). By clicking the down arrow next to Style you can choose to show them and therefore where they are applied in the cascade. User agent CSS is shown with "<system>" in red alongside the rules to make the differentiation clear. The Computed tab will show the computed values of any CSS applied to the element (for example, the actual pixel font size) broken into sections for text, background, box model, layout, and other (you can read more about computed values in Chapter 3). If you want to quickly add a property to just one element, you can right-click the selector and choose "Edit Element Style..."—this is the equivalent of adding a style attribute to the element, which we do not recommend, of course, but is useful for rapid testing.

▓ **TIP:** Other useful options are accessible in Firebug by clicking the down arrows next to the Active tab such as methods for viewing and editing :hover or :active states of links, which would be difficult to access otherwise.

The Layout tab exposes the size, padding, border, and margin for the selected element, as well as the position and z-index (see Figure 10-3). Hovering over any of them will show them visually in the page, and clicking any of the values allows you to edit them and see the changes immediately. These changes will only affect the selected element, as they will manifest themselves as inline styles on the element in the HTML.

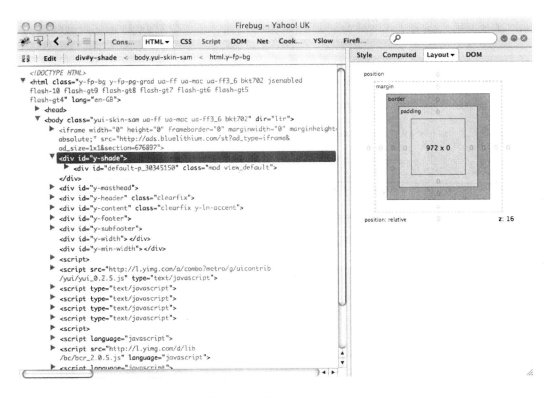

Figure 10-3. The Layout tab in the HTML view of Firebug

■ **TIP:** Any time in Firebug you find yourself amending a numerical value, you can use the up and down keys on your keyboard to quickly increment and decrement the values in integers (one whole number at a time) while maintaining the unit value (px or em).

We'll ignore the DOM tab since it concerns itself primarily with JavaScript.

The CSS view shows the entire contents of each CSS file and is editable in the same fashion as the Style sidebar in the HTML view (see Figure 10-4). It also includes an Edit button to use the built-in text editor. In this view, the selectors are also editable, which they are not in the HTML view. This view can be useful as a holistic view of the entire file, but the HTML view is more useful in general.

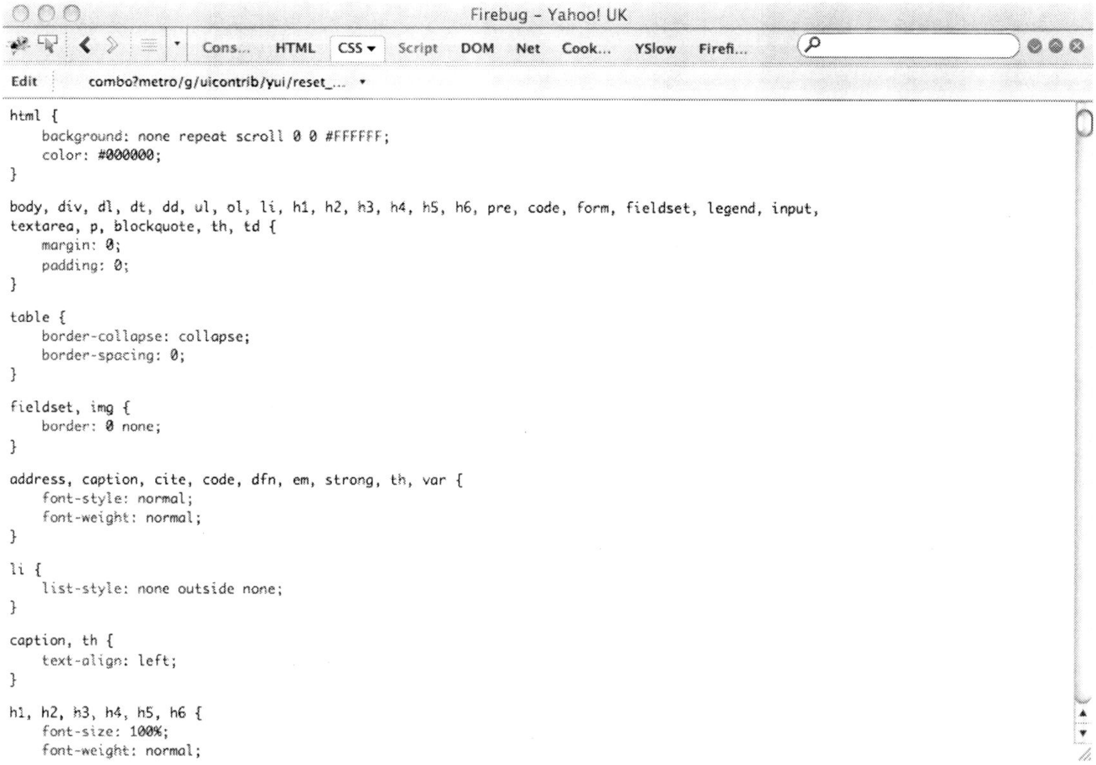
Firebug - Yahoo! UK
Cons... HTML CSS Script DOM Net Cook... YSlow Firefi...
Edit combo?metro/g/uicontrib/yui/reset_...
html {
background: none repeat scroll 0 0 #FFFFFF;
color: #000000;
}
body, div, dl, dt, dd, ul, ol, li, h1, h2, h3, h4, h5, h6, pre, code, form, fieldset, legend, input,
textarea, p, blockquote, th, td {
margin: 0;
padding: 0;
}
table {
border-collapse: collapse;
border-spacing: 0;
}
fieldset, img {
border: 0 none;
}
address, caption, cite, code, dfn, em, strong, th, var {
font-style: normal;
font-weight: normal;
}
li {
list-style: none outside none;
}
caption, th {
text-align: left;
}
h1, h2, h3, h4, h5, h6 {
font-size: 100%;
font-weight: normal;

Figure 10-4. *The CSS view of Firebug*

The Net view shows all of the resources that were loaded when the current page was requested. A wealth of information is available here (see Figure 10-5). On a line level, you can see at a glimpse any resources that took an unusually long time to load and that blocked other resources. You can filter by the type of file with the buttons along the top (obviously, as a CSS developer you would be most interested in All for the complete view, or CSS and Images for drilling down).

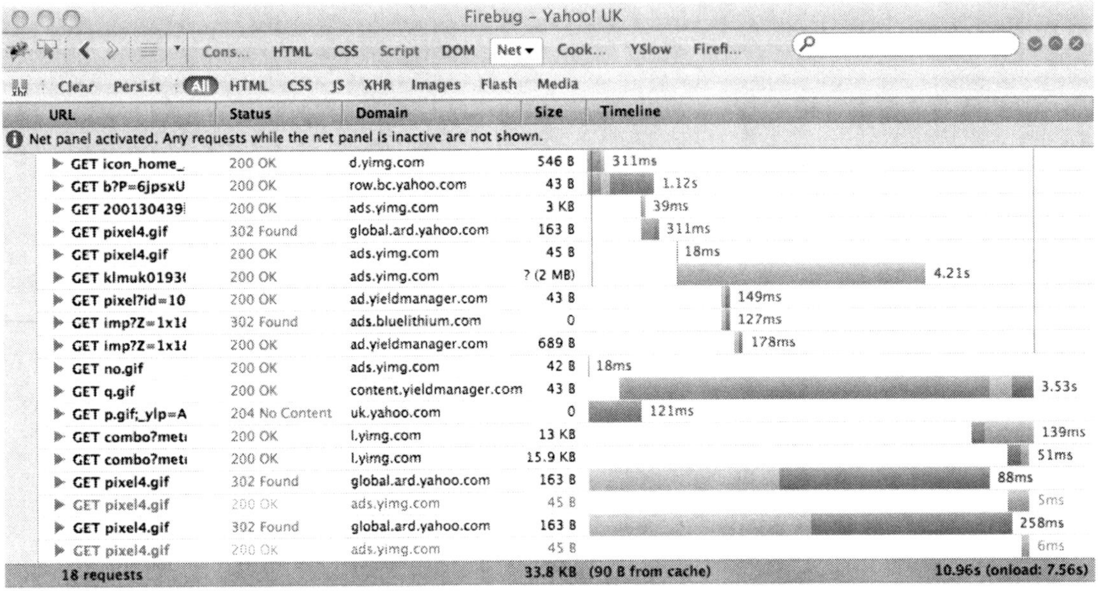

Figure 10-5. The Net view of Firebug

Hovering over any timeline (see Figure 10-6) for a resource will show more details for that particular request (this was covered in great detail in Chapter 8). Sometimes this view will show Blocking (or Queuing in older versions) before Sending, which means the browser has used up all its available simultaneous connections to that domain, and is waiting for other resources to download before downloading this file. These details are invaluable in discovering which factors are responsible for poor performance on your website.

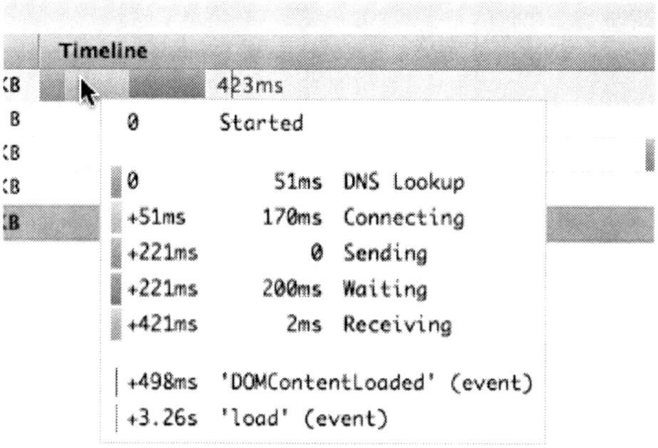

Figure 10-6. Hovering over a timeline in the Net view of Firebug

Expanding any resource item shows more details for that particular request (see Figure 10-7). The first tab, Params, shows any information that was posted, or included as a querystring in the request. The second tab shows the HTTP Headers, which are useful for:

- Locating the caching headers to ensure they are working correctly

- Inspecting any cookies sent with the request, which is a performance issue for CSS files and should be avoided

- Checking that the response is being compressed (Content-Encoding), which is a performance enhancement

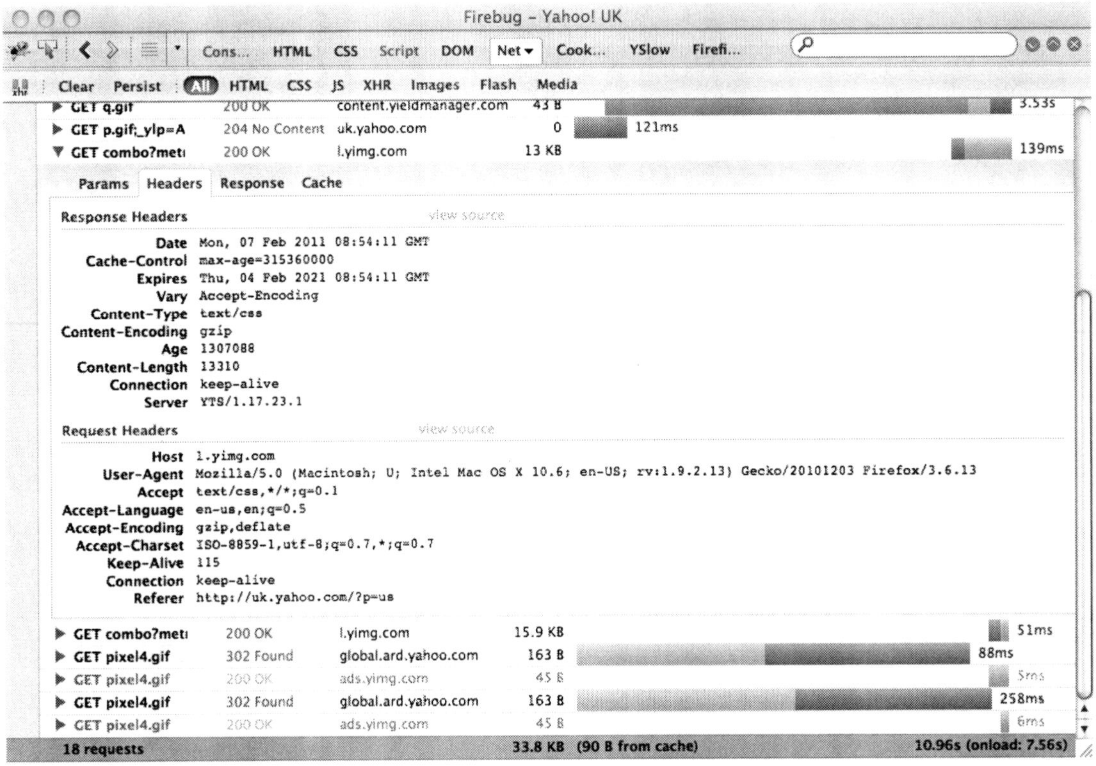

Figure 10-7. Viewing details of a request in the Net view in Firebug

The rest of the tabs show us the actual response in various guises.

You can get Firebug for Firefox from `http://getfirebug.com/`. Although it is cross-platform and works in Windows, OS X, and Linux, it is currently only available for Firefox on these operating systems. A cross-browser version of Firebug is in development, with a planned release in 2011.

A version of Firebug called Firebug Lite is available at `http://getfirebug.com/firebuglite,` which can be accessed with a bookmarklet to provide many of the same features of Firebug in other browsers, the most notable omission being the Net tab.

Some of the best available extensions for Firebug (which may make Firefox less stable) are:

- Firecookie for managing cookies

- Firediff to view changes that have been made to the page within Firebug

- Firefinder to see which elements would be selected by an entered CSS selector (or XPath expression)

- Codeburner shows reference material for HTML and CSS

- Pixel Perfect to overlay images to help line up elements with provided screen images

- CSS Usage to isolate unused selectors

- YSlow to give recommendations on how to improve performance of your pages

Since many of the other tools on this list basically emulate Firebug, we shall only go into greater detail where their functionality differs.

Web Developer (Firefox or Chrome)

Although not really a competitor to Firebug or a debugging tool per se, Web Developer (http://chrispederick.com/work/web-developer/) gives some additional functionality and deserves a mention on this list (see Figure 10-8).

Figure 10-8. Web Developer extension in Firefox

The ability to rapidly disable/enable caching, JavaScript, cookies, CSS, and images often demonstrates itself to be a valuable timesaver. Conveniently validating CSS and HTML is useful, and switching between predefined window sizes to test multiple resolutions is also an effective way of increasing productivity and saving time.

Developer Tools (Internet Explorer 8)

Developer Tools is provided with Internet Explorer 8 in an effort to bring the browser up to par in the debugging stakes. Visually it aims to emulate Firebug, but the features available do differ. It can also be docked to the main window, or have a window of its own.

Developer Tools includes several pieces of functionality that Firebug does not, and in fact goes far toward emulating the capabilities of Firebug and Web Developer in tandem. The disabling/enabling of JS, CSS, and images is two clicks away; the same goes for caching and cookies. It is easy to validate HTML and CSS, and you can generate an "image report"—a list of all images on the current page and their respective file sizes, dimensions, alt attributes and so on—which is very useful for SEO and accessibility concerns.

Figures 10-9 to 10-11 were taken on a Windows XP machine, put in "ugly mode" (with all the shiny plastic turned off) to make it slightly faster. Other than that, they should match what you experience.

The left pane of the HTML tab (see Figure 10-9) is similar to Firebug's, but without the ability to add new attributes. To add new attributes it is necessary to use the Attributes tab in the right pane, with the added benefit of a drop-down menu to auto-complete entries. It is possible to edit the HTML in a built-in text editor, but not that of individual pieces or elements. Also, the edited HTML is only that inside the body tag; it is not possible to edit any HTML outside of that.

Figure 10-9. HTML view of Internet Explorer 8 Developer Tools

The rules in the right pane's Style tab can be expanded and contracted, but the selectors themselves cannot be edited, which mirrors Firebug's behavior. Entire selectors can be enabled/disabled in this view (they cannot in Firebug) as well as individual properties. It is not possible to add new properties/values in this view.

The Trace Styles panel shows the result of all CSS applied to the current element, without the selectors (all nondefault properties).

The Layout panel behaves exactly as Firebug's, but without the useful hover behavior (see Figure 10-10). You can click to edit most of the values. It also shows Offset values (which Firebug does not), which may be useful to you.

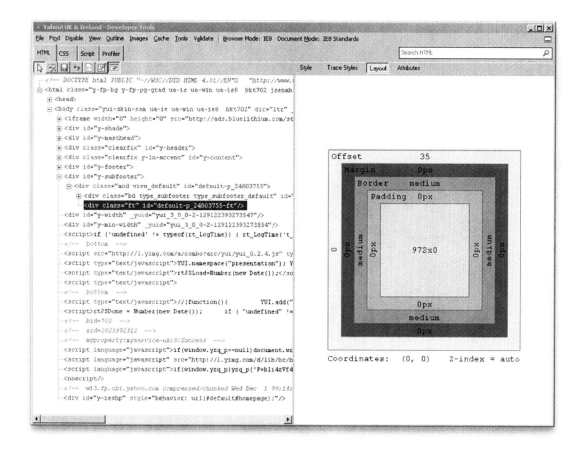

Figure 10-10. The Layout tab of the HTML view of Internet Explorer 8 Developer Tools

The CSS tab almost exactly emulates that of Firebug, with the entire (reformatted) contents of individual style sheets visible and editable (see Figure 10-11). The selectors are editable in this view, and you can enable/disable entire selectors with a check box, which is not currently possible with any of the other tools on this list apart from Opera Dragonfly.

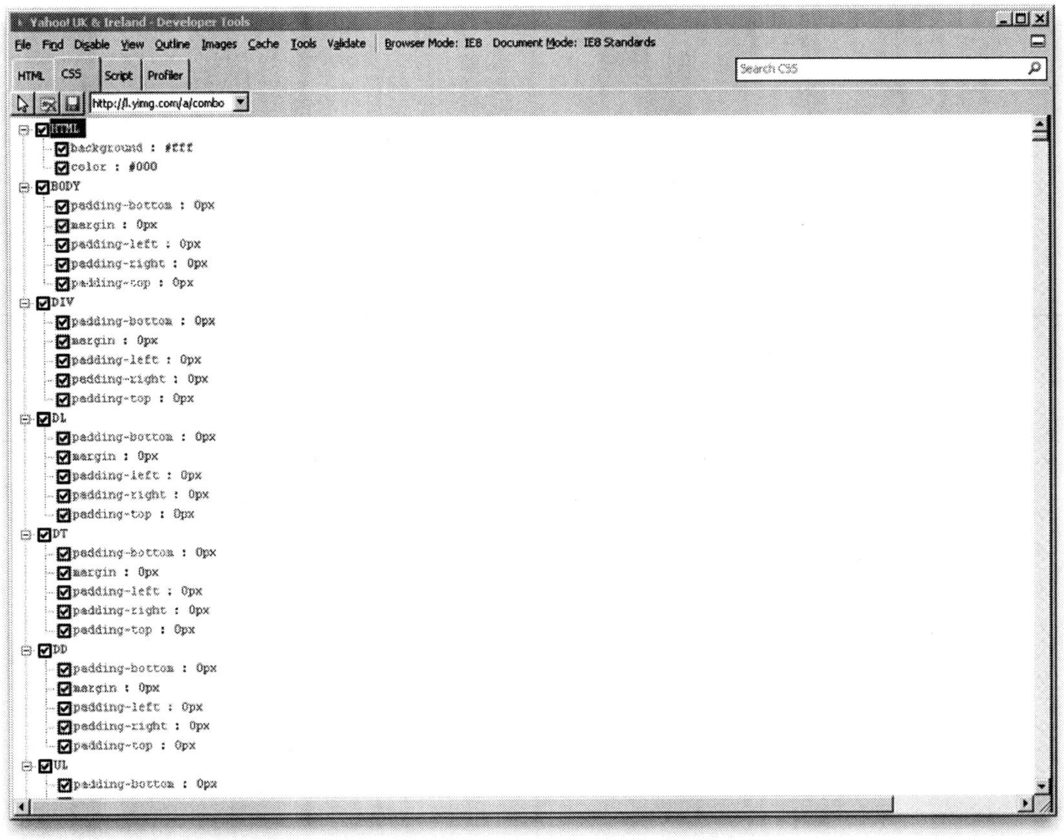

Figure 10-11. The CSS view of Internet Explorer 8 Developer Tools

There is no equivalent of the Net tab. Although you can more than make up for this with Fiddler or Charles (mentioned later in this chapter), requiring different tools to achieve this reduces your efficiency and productivity.

All in all, this tool is far more useful than what was provided previously, but is still not visually appealing and feels incomplete. It can be a *quantum tool*; there are many instances when using the Developer Tools actually slows down IE dramatically, or causes it to crash.

Internet Explorer 9's Developer Tools (although still in beta) are looking like a great improvement, and now include an equivalent of the Net tab, but they are changing so much from version to version that it would be unproductive to cover them in detail here.

Web Inspector (Safari)

If you enable the Develop menu in Safari, you can access Apple's version of these tools: the Web Inspector[3] (see Figure 10-12). Generally, all the same functionality available in Firebug is available here, although it feels less mature. However, in places, the fact that Firebug is open source and the Web Inspector has money behind it becomes very clear. In particular, the Resources tab (the equivalent of Firebug's Net tab) feels a lot more polished, although you need to toggle back and forth between the request and the Resources view to see all the details.

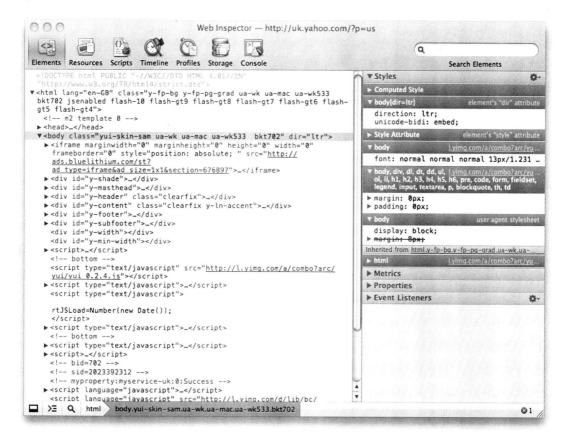

Figure 10-12. Safari's Web Inspector

Safari now supports extensions, but none for the Web Inspector exist at the time of writing. WebKit is progressing in leaps and bounds, though, and it seems at some point it will overtake Firebug both in terms of functionality and usability.

---

[3] A wiki for WebKit's Web Inspector is available at https://trac.webkit.org/wiki/WebInspector.

> ■ **NOTE:** Interestingly, the Web Inspector is in fact written in HTML, CSS, and JavaScript, which means you can inspect the code behind the Web Inspector itself.

Developer Tools (Chrome)

Chrome's equivalent can be found by going to View > Developer > Developer Tools. Because WebKit engine is behind both Safari and Chrome's Inspectors, they are almost identical. Chrome's, however, is a newer version since Google releases versions of Chrome more frequently (see Figure 10-13).

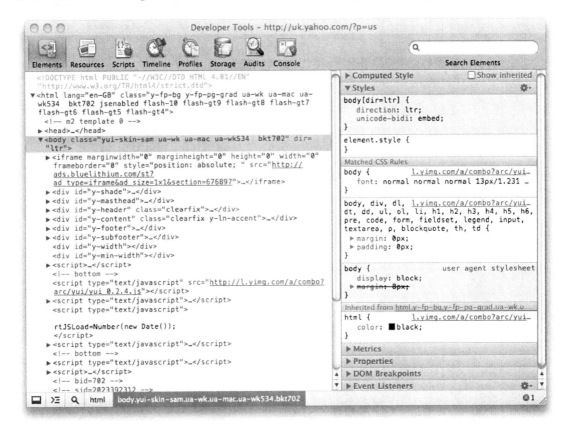

Figure 10-13. Chrome's Developer Tools

The display of CSS is the most obvious difference. Chrome shows the braces around the properties, so it looks a little friendlier and less cluttered, but this means the rules are not expandable/contractable.

▪ **TIP:** In both the Web Inspector for Safari and the Developer Tools for Chrome, it is possible to double-click the selectors and amend them directly, which is something that cannot be achieved (at the time of writing) in the Style pane in Firebug or other tools.

Internet Explorer Developer Toolbar

For IE 6 and IE 7, Firebug Lite is often the way to go if you are able to use it with your site. However, the Developer Toolbar, which can be downloaded from `http://www.microsoft.com/downloads/en/details.aspx?FamilyID=95e06cbe-4940-4218-b75d-b8856fced535` (it is probably simpler to search for it than type that into a browser!), does offer some useful features.

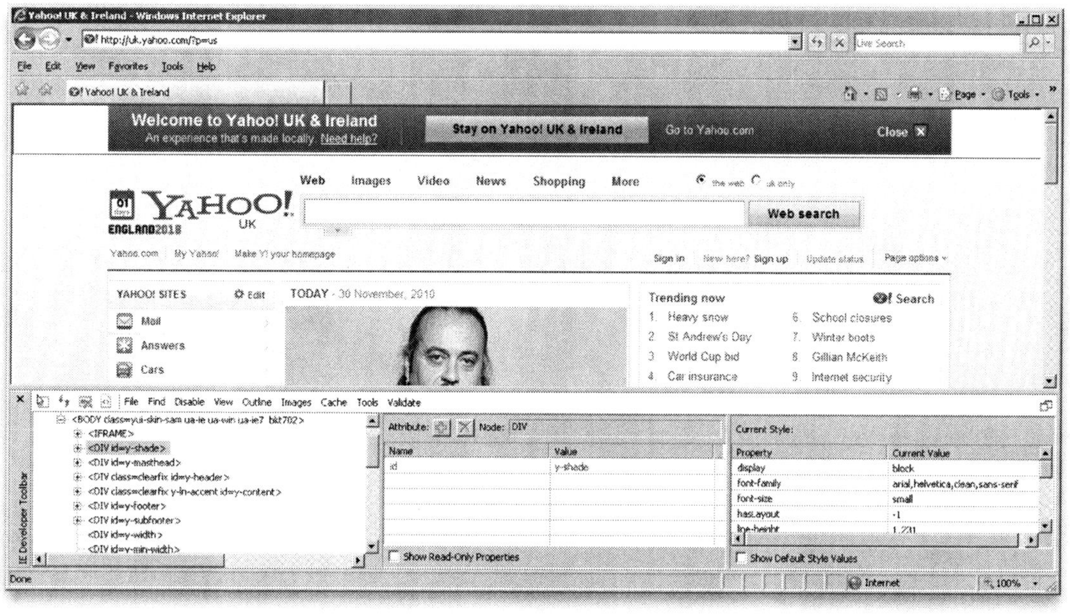

Figure 10-14. Internet Explorer Developer Toolbar

Some of the functionality offered by the Firefox Developer Toolbar is available; read-only views of applied styles to elements are also available, but in no real way does the toolbar compete with the other items on this list. However, it does offer some useful debugging options if you have no other option.

Opera Dragonfly

Opera Dragonfly is the offering from Opera that gives us the debugging features we would otherwise turn to Firebug for (see Figure 10-15). Since it is served directly from Opera as an offline application, the latest

319

version is always downloaded seamlessly. When this book is released, Dragonfly 1.0 will be available, so we used an experimental version to emulate the capabilities of version 1.0 as much as possible[4].

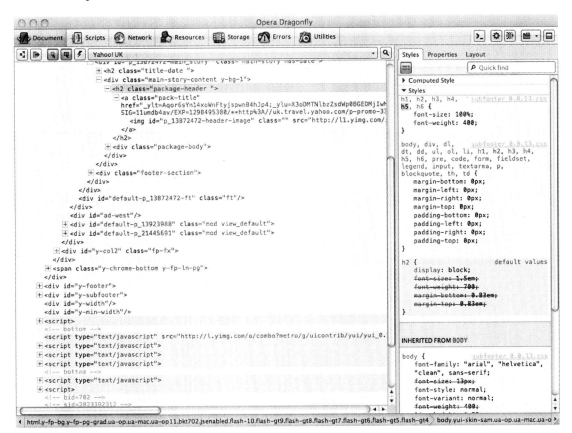

Figure 10-15. *Opera Dragonfly*

Opera Dragonfly is younger than the other offerings on this list, and it is still in the alpha stages of development at the time of writing. It offers built-in features such as a color picker, screen magnifier, and stored colors manager that the others do not offer without add-ons. Some other touches are nice, too, like the horizontal and vertical rules that extrude from a highlighted element to help with alignment.

The fact that it is in development is apparent in some of the immediate bugs that can be easily found, but it is certainly one to watch and is in fast iterative development.

That all of the major browser vendors now provide these tools is a great thing and demonstrates an understanding of developers' requirements and an intention to provide for them. They are all useful and give us capabilities in each browser that can make dramatic changes to your workflow. However, it is

---

[4] Instructions on enabling the experimental version can be found at
http://my.opera.com/dragonfly/blog/getting-opera-dragonfly-ready-for-opera-11/#enable.

difficult to recommend any over Firebug, which feels the most mature, the most capable, and the most expandable, regardless of the browser you prefer.

Proxy Tools

Whereas the Firebug Net tab or equivalent offers us the ability to view HTTP requests and their component parts, *proxy tools* intercept the traffic at a lower level and give us more functionality than their cut-down browser counterparts. Many products exist to achieve this, but few compete with Charles and Fiddler for their debugging abilities.

Fiddler

Fiddler 2 is a free Windows program developed by Eric Lawrence from Microsoft, and initially released in 2003 (see Figure 10-16). Its maturity makes it a very robust and polished product. It uses the .NET Microsoft development framework (version 2.0 or greater; Fiddler 1.3 is available for users of version 1.1), so you will need to install it to be able to use Fiddler. It is available from `http://www.fiddler2.com/`.

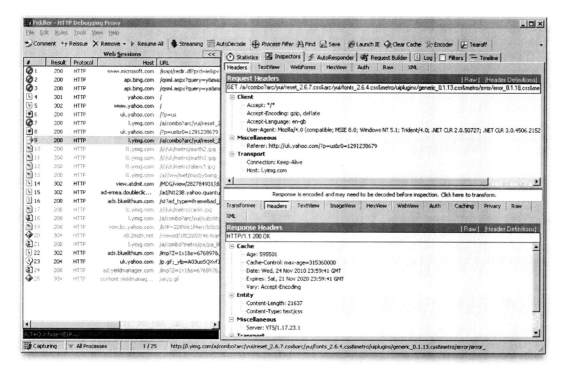

Figure 10-16. Fiddler

There are far too many components of Fiddler to cover in this book, but we will mention the most common features that are useful to the CSS developer. Essentially, Fiddler sits between your browser and the servers your browser is requesting information from. This allows it to inspect any traffic (including secure traffic) passing between these two points.

The screen is separated into two vertical panes: the first shows the traffic passing through Fiddler, and the second allows you to inspect that traffic further. Under the File menu you can choose to enable or disable the capturing of traffic (whether or not to show requests in the left pane).

■ **TIP:** You can also quickly toggle the capturing of traffic by pressing F12.

When Fiddler is capturing traffic, every request will show in the left pane with the order it was requested in, the HTTP status code, the protocol, the host (domain), URL, body (the size of the content), caching details, Content-Type, and the process that requested it (for example, iexplore). Highlighting that request will show further information in the right pane.

Many websites make a lot more HTTP requests than we expect them to, and will very quickly fill up the left pane (and also the memory of your computer). The Filters tab on the right allows you to specify exactly the kinds of requests you want to show and be captured, which will help you to focus on the requests you care about, rather than them getting lost in the noise.

The Statistics tab gives very detailed information about the time the selected request took and goes so far as to give performance estimates for different Internet speeds and geographical locations, which can be very useful for locating performance issues.

The Inspectors tab is one of the most useful and provides all the header information, as well as multiple ways to view the response data. For the request, you can see the headers, textual data, form data, the request in hexadecimal, authentication information, the raw data, and any XML provided with the request. For the response, you can see the headers, textual data, image data, the response in hexadecimal, a basic web preview, authentication information, caching information, privacy data (for example, cookies being created/modified/removed), and the raw response. If the response is compressed, Fiddler will warn you, detect the algorithm for you, and present you with the decoded data.

Primarily these comprehensive views are useful to the CSS developer in checking for unexpectedly large files, that compression is working correctly, that the expected data is being returned, and that the data is being cached correctly.

The AutoResponder tab is possibly the most useful function that Fiddler provides. A common issue when debugging is that a CSS file or HTML response in one environment does not match other environments, or some other factor is interfering with our expected result. To be absolutely certain that a CSS change will fix the problem in our target environment can be very difficult. Ideally, we want to know the exact results if we replace one file on our production environment, for example. The AutoResponder allows you to do exactly this. You can provide a URI to match to (for example, `http://www.mycompany.com/css/style.css`) and a response. Fiddler provides typical responses for various HTTP status codes, but it also allows you to choose a file on your local machine. Doing this allows you to replace individual files on any server with your own, which is a fantastic way to develop for a client-side developer because they no longer need concern themselves with the server or the underlying infrastructure, but can work on specific files independently with confidence.

The provided URI format is not as simple as it might seem and can be prefixed with "EXACT:", "regex:" and others for different pattern types. It is also not possible to redirect an entire folder (for example, to match `http://www.mycompany.com/css/` and redirect to a local folder like `c:/projects/mycompany/css`) but keep the file name intact, so that `http://www.mycompany.com/css/1.css` redirects to `c:/projects/mycompany/css/1.css`, `http://www.mycompany.com/css/2.css` redirects to `c:/projects/mycompany/css/2.css` and so on.

To decrypt HTTPS traffic, Fiddler installs a certificate on your computer, which is a potential security risk but a necessary approach. You can enable this in Tools > Fiddler Options. Since Fiddler provides all of the data to your browser, it is also able to "throttle" this traffic, and simulate slower Internet connections.

Charles

Although not as mature as Fiddler, Charles is quickly becoming a contender (see Figure 10-17). Available on Windows, OS X, and Linux, Charles exceeds the feature set provided by Fiddler and is often easier to use. It is not free, but neither is it expensive and you can download a free 30-day trial at http://www.charlesproxy.com/.

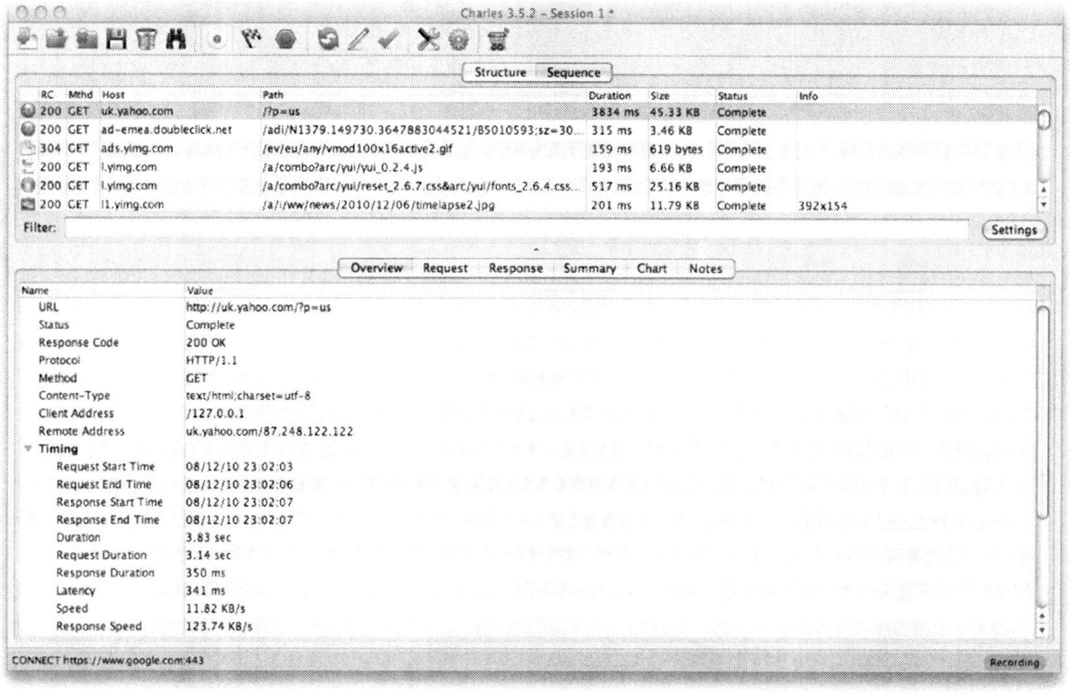

Figure 10-17. Charles

The cross platform nature of Charles is a big advantage; you need only learn its interface once and those lessons will serve on whichever operating system you choose to use. The interface is more attractive and less intimidating than that of Fiddler, and it builds upon some of the functionality available therein.

To enter recording mode (what Fiddler thinks of as capturing mode), a big red circle button at the top of the window can be toggled on and off. When in recording mode, Recording shows in the bottom-right corner of the window, and Charles will intercept all HTTP data requested via web browsers. During the initial installation, Charles will offer to install a plugin for Firefox in order to be able to intercept the data coming from there.

TIP: To inspect HTTPS traffic it is necessary to add the hosts under Proxy > Proxy Settings > SSL and install a certificate. Instructions for this are available at `http://www.charlesproxy.com/documentation/using-charles/ssl-certificates/`.

There are two main methods of viewing the data. The first is in Structure view, which breaks everything down by host so that it is easy to see which requests came from which. The other view (demonstrated previously) is the Sequence view, which is similar to Fiddler's default view, and shows each individual request in order. In this view, a textbox makes it simple to enter strings to filter by. Any items that do not contain the entered string are hidden from view, which is a fast and intuitive way to interrogate the data. It's also possible to use regular expressions in this text.

In either view, highlighting an individual request shows further information in a tabbed pane—to the right in Structure view, and beneath in Sequence view. The first tab is Overview, which is similar to the Statistics tab in Fiddler.

The next tabs are Request and Response, which represent the request and response data, respectively. Depending on the data, other tabs may show at the bottom for these views, including Headers, Text, Hex, Compressed, HTML, Query String, Cookies, Raw, and JSON. The information is named and presented in a more intuitive format than Fiddler, which is likely more useful to a CSS developer. HTML is color coded in that view, although unfortunately there is no CSS-specific view.

The Summary tab shows basic details for the highlighted request and any requests triggered as a response to that one. For example, highlighting an HTML request will show all the assets specified by that page. This is useful for a high-level view, but the Chart tab is more detailed and similar to the equivalent in WebKit's Web Inspector or Firebug's Net tab. This tab also offers other views to the default Timeline view, such as Sizes for a visual comparison of all the requested files relating to the original request, Duration for the length of those requests, and Types to visually demonstrate the types of files requested and how many of each there are.

Bandwidth throttling can be enabled and disabled by toggling a checkered flag icon at the top of the screen. The settings for this can be set in Proxy > Throttle Settings, and there are several useful presets as well as the ability to enter your own custom values.

Hidden under the Tools menu are the real gems that Charles offers. Map Remote allows you to redirect any remote request to any other remote destination, which is useful for mapping one environment's resources to another—perhaps to use one particular CSS file or folder on one server, or to replace a file or folder on another. Map Local is the equivalent of Fiddler's AutoResponder, but is more capable with friendlier methods of matching and the ability to redirect entire folders as well as files. The Rewrite option allows us to rewrite the contents of the request or the response—for matching locations—in almost every conceivable manner, including replacing strings in the body or adding new headers.

TIP: To inspect traffic from other devices, put them on the same network as a machine running Charles and manually set that machine as the proxy server on the device.

Aside from the extra functionality Charles provides, it also feels more polished. Touches like Charles being intelligent enough to break the URL apart when you paste in a URL and populate all the fields with the respective pieces on your behalf make this feel like a good, solid piece of software. Some of the deeper functionality embedded in Fiddler exceeds the capabilities of those in Charles, but for a CSS developer Charles feels more appropriate.

Testing

Testing is an important step in the process of making a robust site that performs well, and looks and works consistently between browsers. Unfortunately, effectively testing CSS—which is the presentational layer of the website—is a very difficult thing to achieve. Whereas testing the other layers of the site can all be done in an automated fashion—JavaScript can have unit tests, server-side code can have unit tests, HTML can be parsed and validated—CSS depends on how the browser renders it, and needs to be checked visually by a human being.

It is theoretically possible to have a screenshot of how the page should be rendered and, as part of an automatable process, to compare this screenshot with actual screenshots in different browsers. An acceptable margin of error could be defined, and depending on the difference between the two screenshots, the test could pass or fail. However, it is a fact that a website cannot and will not look the same on different browsers. Differences in browser handling of various properties, font rendering, and even image rendering ensure that regardless of how small, inconsistencies will always exist. The comparison of two files can never take into account which inconsistencies matter and which are acceptable, so this method of testing would never be completely accurate.

However, automatable techniques to aid in this process do exist. Whereas typically a tester would be required to visit every page that required testing, in every supported browser, you can instead use techniques to generate screenshots on your behalf, which can be looked at by the tester in quick succession and easily compared to a master example by overlaying the two. First though, it is necessary to be aware of what comprises a pass or a fail in this instance.

Graded Browser Support

Since it would not be practical to support every browser perfectly, it is necessary to come up with a matrix showing which browsers are supported and to what degree. The contents of this matrix vary greatly from site to site. Typical sites' traffic is predominantly made up of the latest version of Internet Explorer. More technical sites are likely to have a higher percentage of visitors using browsers that could be considered more advanced—which are essentially all current browsers, and to a lesser extent the current version of Internet Explorer. When dealing with high-traffic websites, it is likely that even older browsers, which make up a small portion of the traffic, still represent a significant number of users. Deciding which browsers you support is dependent on the traffic to your website, which should be tracked and reportable to help you make that decision.

A good example matrix that is kept up-to-date is Yahoo!' Graded Browser Support, which can be viewed at `http://developer.yahoo.com/yui/articles/gbs/`. The current version at the time of writing is shown in Figure 10-18.

	Win XP	Win 7	Mac 10.6.†	iOS 3.†	iOS 4.†	Android 2.2.†
Safari 5.†			A-grade			
Chrome † (latest stable)	A-grade					
Firefox 4.†		A-grade (upon GA release)	A-grade (upon GA release)			
Firefox 3.6.†	A-grade	A-grade	A-grade			
IE 9.0		A-grade (upon GA release)				
IE 8.0	A-grade	A-grade				
IE 7.0	A-grade					
IE 6.0	A-grade					
Safari for iOS				A-grade	A-grade	
WebKit for Android OS						A-grade

Figure 10-18. Yahoo! Graded Browser Support

Your decided matrix may vary dramatically from this one. For example, many sites are now seeing reasonable levels of traffic from Opera or Safari on Windows, or Chrome on OS X—some are seeing low levels of traffic from IE 6.

We discuss Graded Browser Support in great detail in Chapter 6. Once you have decided on your accepted browser matrix, it is necessary to ensure that you (and the testers) have the ability to use all the browsers you intend to test upon.

Running Multiple Versions of Internet Explorer

Most browsers (mobile devices excepted) are simple to install side by side, as long as you have access to a Windows install and an OS X install (and possibly Linux, too). This can be achieved through virtual machines (software that allows the user to run other operating systems within their current operating system), although you cannot legally run OS X on non-Apple hardware. Browsers other than IE have a fast update rate, in that the users of these browsers often quickly upgrade to the latest versions. However, to test multiple versions of Internet Explorer, other measures are required.

Although it is possible to have a separate virtual machine for every version of IE (and indeed, this is what the testers should do) it is overkill for the CSS developer. A piece of software called Multiple IEs solved this problem for a long time, allowing the installation of IE versions 3 to 6 concurrently.[5]

There were some caveats with this approach, mainly due to stability, filters, and cookie handling, but it was more than adequate for a quick visual check of a page in older versions of IE.

Development has ceased on Multiple IEs, but Core Services have developed a Windows application called IETester (see Figure 10-19). IETester essentially provides the same functionality as Multiple IEs,

---

[5] Although Multiple IEs is no longer under active development, it can be found at `http://tredosoft.com/Multiple_IE` if you are interested.

but in a single window with tabs, which can represent any version of IE from 5.5 onward. Although it is an alpha release (and has been since 2008), development is still active on the product, and stability is adequate for testing purposes. It can be unstable—there are several known issues—but for the CSS developer it provides a useful and capable replacement for the multiple virtual machines that would otherwise be required to provide the same features.

Figure 10-19. IETester

IETester can also be configured to use IE 9, but this requires Windows Vista Service Pack 2 or 7 (or later). You can download it from `http://www.my-debugbar.com/wiki/IETester/HomePage`.

■ **NOTE:** An app called ies4osx also allows you to run versions of IE under OS X, but it requires Darwine (a Windows emulator) or similar, and is buggy and nontrivial to install. With that said, if you'd like to play with it you can download it from `http://www.kronenberg.org/ies4osx/`.

Emulating Other Devices

It is not always practical to own every device you need to test your website on, and sometimes getting access to your development environment from those devices can be a pain. To that end, here is a quick list of emulators you can use to mimic those devices on a desktop computer:

- *Apple iOS SDK:* `http://developer.apple.com/devcenter/ios`
    - This tool allows you to emulate iPhones, iPads, and iPod Touches. It is not free however, and only runs under OS X.

- *Android:* `http://developer.android.com/sdk`

- *Opera Mini Simulator:* `http://www.opera.com/developer/tools/`

- *Firefox Mobile:* `http://www.mozilla.com/en-US/mobile/download/`

- *Perfecto Mobile:* `https://vf.perfectomobile.com/np-cas/login`
    - This tool allows you to remotely test on real mobile devices and networks. This link is for the Vodafone version, which is free for registered Vodafone developers.

Automatically Generating Screenshots

Since testing CSS typically requires a human being, the best way you can make this process more efficient is to have a piece of software generate screenshots on your behalf. Many tools are available that can help with this. Let's take a look at three of the most common.

Selenium

Selenium is an integration testing tool that is in widespread use (see Figure 10-20). Selenium is currently at version 2, which gives important improvements over the original. It was initially developed as an internal framework for ThoughtWorks, but has since become a fully fledged system in its own right with many contributors. A Firefox plugin, called Selenium IDE, allows you to create tests to (for example):

- Browse to `http://mycompany.com`

- Wait for the page to load

- Check that the text inside a specific div contains the phrase "our company is amazing"

- Click a specific anchor

- Check that the text inside a specific div contains the phrase "click here to contact us"

The plugin can either record your actions in the browser or be used to build these tests up piece by piece. Recording is especially useful to get an idea of how the actions are built and how they work. The actions are stored within a "test case," and you can have multiple test cases within a "test suite." These tests can be run from within the IDE, and each action will turn green or red, depending on whether it passed (executed successfully or was true) or failed, respectively.

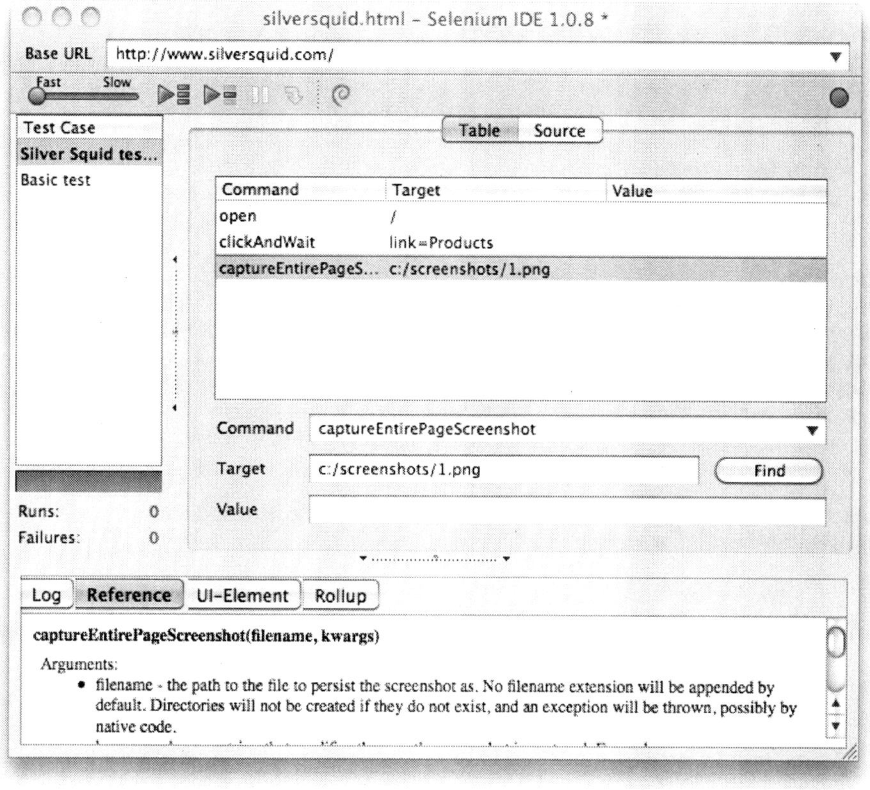

Figure 10-20. Selenium IDE

From a CSS developer's perspective, the most useful command that Selenium provides is captureEntirePageScreenshot, which does exactly what it says it does. Using this command, it is easy to automate the creation of a series of screenshots within Firefox.

However, testing just Firefox is not as useful as testing our entire supported browser matrix. To that end, Selenium IDE's big brother Selenium RC can be used to run these tests against multiple browsers, resolutions, color depths, and operating systems. Selenium RC also supports more commands than Selenium IDE; for example, captureScreenshot captures just the view within the current viewport. The tests can quickly become very large and slow to complete, which could be an issue if you are using them within a continuous integration (CI) environment (see Chapter 9), but this can be overcome with Selenium Grid, which allows you to attach many servers together and run all the tests in parallel.

Once you have created your screenshots and approved them, it would be possible to compare the approved versions with subsequent screenshots, and to pass or fail tests based upon this—but this is likely to be a fragile test as we have previously mentioned.

Although Selenium IDE feels clunky and limited in functionality, the suite of tools available is free, mature, and very capable. If you have the need for the other functionality provided (which you are likely to), Selenium is a great tool to help you achieve this. You can read more about it at http://seleniumhq.org/.

329

Although Selenium is as close to an industry standard integration testing tool as you are likely to find, several alternatives exist, some of which are listed here:

- Watir: http://watir.com/

- Sahi: http://sahi.co.in/

- Windmill: http://www.getwindmill.com/

Browsershots

Assuming that the only thing you are interested in is screenshots, *Browsershots* is a much simpler one-shot test. By browsing to http://browsershots.org/, you can enter a URL, tick the boxes for the browsers and operating systems you want to test, and then submit the form. Your request will be put in a queue, and when complete you will be returned a series of screenshots. Browsershots can take a long time to complete, but it is free. Alternatively, for around $30 per month, you can get priority processing and skip many in the queue. While it is a great tool for performing a large number of tests in one go, it has several drawbacks:

- It is hosted, meaning the pages you test must be accessible to the outside world, which may not be acceptable to your organization

- It would be very difficult and fragile to try to automate the process

- It is very slow

If you have no alternative, Browsershots is a useful tool to have in your arsenal.

Browsercam

Browsercam (http://www.browsercam.com/) is a more capable and functional equivalent to Browsershots, with the ability to also perform interactions for a fee. It also provides a remote access service so that you can pick the operating system and browser you want and connect directly to a machine with that configuration to try things out on. From the perspective of simply generating screenshots, it has the same downsides as Browsershots and is also expensive, although it is faster.

Summary

This chapter demonstrated some of the many tools that can help you with debugging, as well as understanding how to decide which browsers to test and the best way to run those browsers. It also shows you some of the best ways that automation can help with the testing of CSS.

In the next chapter, we will be putting all our knowledge into practice and we will provide guides on and examples of how to build your own CSS framework.

CHAPTER 11

■ ■ ■

Creating Your CSS

In this chapter and the appendices, we put all previous chapters to practical use. We intend to take everything that you have learned throughout the book and give you real-life examples that you can modify for your own use. While we do not intend to dictate your processes and how you should build your own guidelines, we will provide you with templates you can use for discussions within your team to build your own. We will also go through the process of making a framework from start to finish that you can then adapt to the needs of your website.

In Appendices 1, 2, 3, and 4, you will find an example CSS Coding Standards document, an example Accessibility Guidelines document, an example Browser Support Guidelines document, and an example Development Process document, respectively.

In this chapter you will learn the following:

- How to deconstruct a design into assets and templates for a site

- Which factors to consider when creating a CSS framework

- How to document a CSS library of design assets

Igloo Refrigerator Parts Inc. Website

Let us introduce you to the design of the fictitious Igloo Refrigerator Parts Inc. company. Here you are shown the homepage (see Figure 11-1) and an interior top-level section page (see Figure 11-2), as provided by the design team.

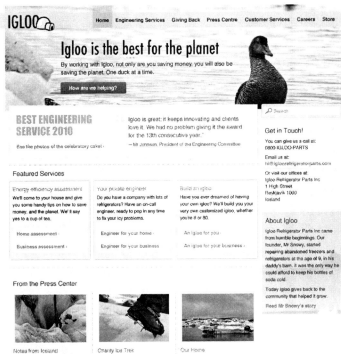

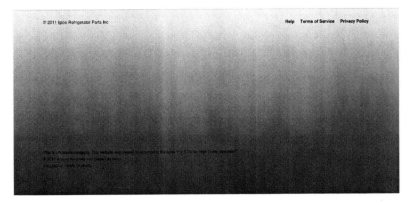

Figure 11-1. The homepage design of the Igloo Refrigerator Parts website

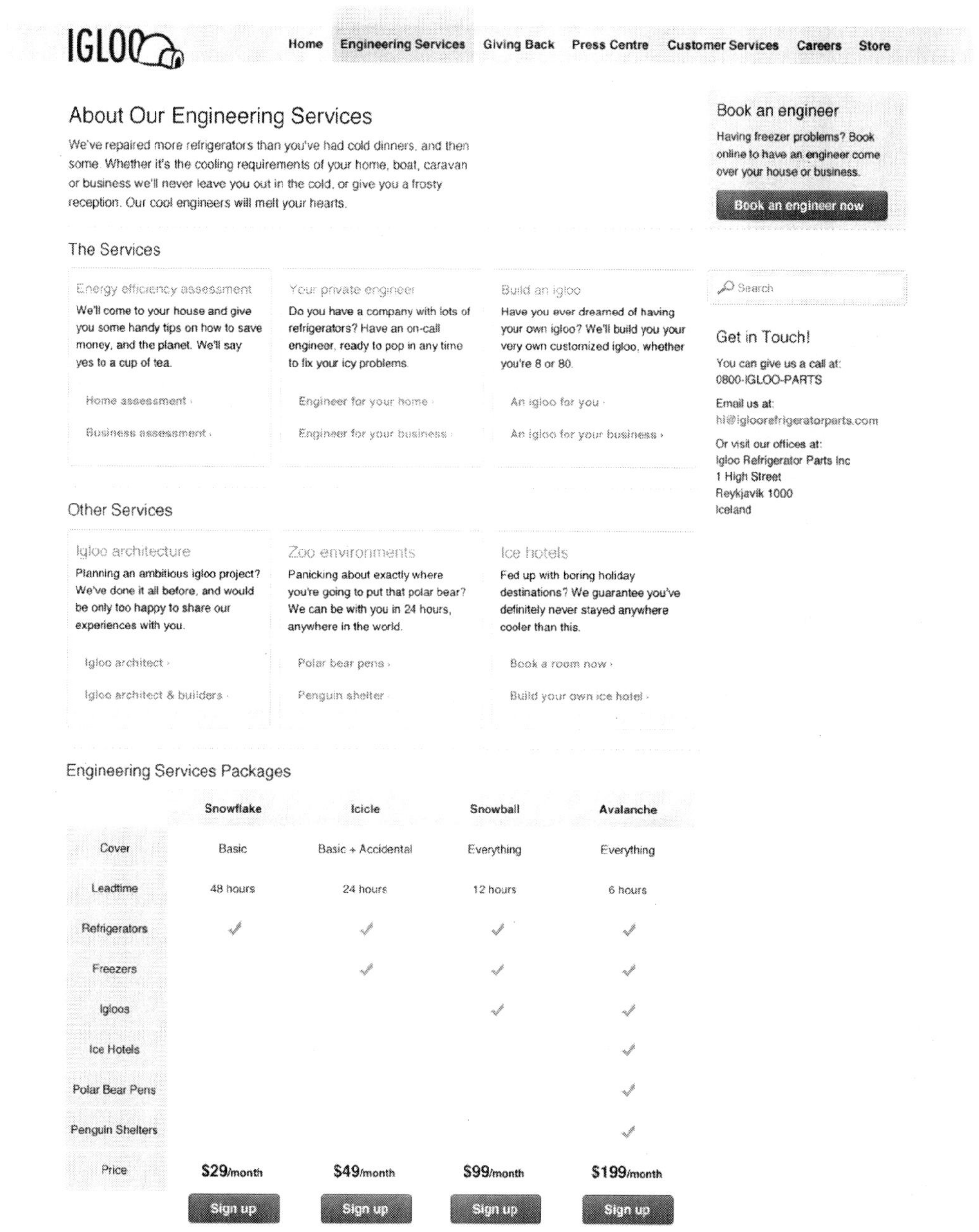

Figure 11-2. An example content page of the Igloo Refrigerator Parts website

The design team has made an effort to create a design that is in line with the business needs and goals, making sure that the user experience and interaction is as clear and simple as possible, that the message is conveyed seamlessly, and that the user completes his journey happily.

As often happens in large organizations, many stakeholders have probably had a say into how the design should look, or what content should be included in certain areas of the website. Knowing that several people with different responsibilities and objectives have had influence in this outcome, it is the job of the CSS author and developers in general to make sure that what has been created is feasible, that it is coded as cleanly as possible, and that everything is built so that you end up with a final product that is not only usable and accessible, but that is also maintainable.

The next step is to analyze this design and see whether there are any issues that we might have to resolve before moving on to building it.

Analyzing the Design

When analyzing a design before building it, there are certain important questions that should always be answered:

- What is (and is not) acceptable to appear differently in different browsers?

- What issues might you encounter when implementing the solution?

- What other questions do you need to discuss with the designers that might become larger problems if left unaddressed?

After answering these questions, a good exercise is to identify common elements that are used across the pages (this might have already been done by the design team if a design library is in place; you can read more about design libraries in Chapter 5). This will make it easier for you to avoid redundancy in your code: if you notice a component is being used repeatedly, in different locations of the page, you will know that you should not make the CSS for it too specific so that you can allow for it to be reused. If you notice another component has two (needed) variations, you will know that you should create base CSS for the default state of the component, which can then be easily extended with another class (as inspired by Object Oriented CSS (OOCSS), which you can read more about in Chapter 4).

In answer to the first question, after a discussion with the designers, you have been told that it is not acceptable for the logo to look different cross-browser.

As for the second half of that question, it is acceptable for the following elements to look different cross-browser (but as similar as possible for browsers with level A support):

- Rounded corners on boxes

- Drop shadows on buttons

- Drop shadows on text

Some of the concerns and queries that your team has raised with the solution are the following:

- How will the text on the homepage's banner be handled? It is using *Futura Condensed*, which is not a web-safe font, and is only available via font-face through web font services (see Chapter 5 for more details on these).

- The design does not provide hover states for the navigation items or links. You will need to feed this back to the design team so that together you can reach a solution.

An example of a question that you should pose within your own team is whether or not it is acceptable to use advanced selectors (such as the :nth-child() selector) to remove margins and borders on first/last elements. Is the performance hit that comes with advanced selectors worth it? Should you go with the simpler solution of targeting these elements via a class? And if you do use advanced selectors, will you be providing a JavaScript fallback for browsers that do not support them?

This last question should also be consulted with the design team because if you do not supply a fallback, some browsers will display a different design. Remember to explain the pros and cons of the proposed solution not only to developers but also to the business, as the designers will prefer to have the solution implemented as similar as possible to their original artwork, regardless of whether you will have more work implementing it.

The Grid

The underlying grid of the design should be specified in the Design Guidelines, and is not something that the front-end developer will usually create. Being aware of this grid, at least at a basic level, will make it easier to build the CSS and will make your results more accurate. Grids are covered in more detail in Chapter 5.

In our example website, the grid is based on the Blueprint default grid, which is composed of 24 columns, with 30 pixels width and 10 pixel–wide gutters (see Figure 11-3). Knowing this, you will know that if an element spans 4 columns, it will be 150 pixels wide (this result is achieved by adding 4*30px, the width of the columns, to 3*10px, the width of the gutters).

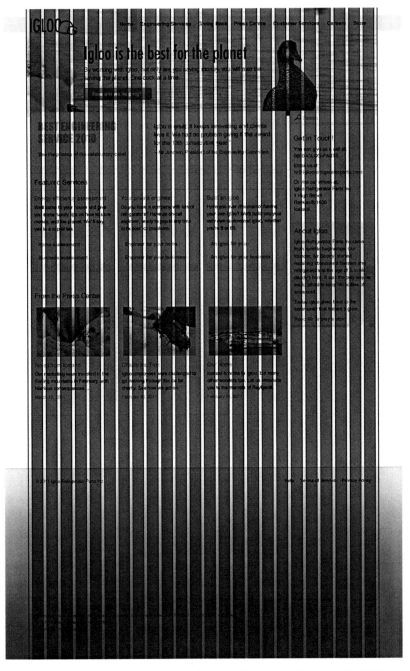

Figure 11-3. Igloo Refrigerator Parts design with its underlying grid visible

Reusable Components

As mentioned previously, it is important to identify reusable blocks before starting to write the markup and CSS. And this is especially important if there isn't a design library or component library set in place that you can follow.

In the two pages you have been provided, you have identified seven different boxes or content blocks that will be reused throughout the various different pages of the website (see Figure 11-4):

- Rounded pale ("Contact")

- Rounded with background image ("About")

- Gradient with links list ("Services")

- Call-to-action banner ("Book an engineer")

- Search

- Table

- Pale with 3 columns ("Press")

Get in Touch!

You can give us a call at:
0800-IGLOO-PARTS

Email us at:
hi@igloorefrigeratorparts.com

Or visit our offices at:
Igloo Refrigerator Parts Inc
1 High Street
Reykjavik 1000
Iceland

About Igloo

Igloo Refrigerator Parts Inc came from humble beginnings. Our founder, Mr Snowy, started repairing abandoned freezers and refrigerators at the age of 9. In his daddy's barn. It was the only way he could afford to keep his bottles of soda cold.

Today Igloo gives back to the community that helped it grow.

Read Mr Snowy's story

Energy efficiency assessment

We'll come to your house and give you some handy tips on how to save money, and the planet. We'll say yes to a cup of tea.

Home assessment ›

Business assessment ›

Book an engineer

Having freezer problems? Book online to have an engineer come over your house or business.

Book an engineer now

Search

	Snowflake	Icicle	Snowball	Avalanche
Cover	Basic	Basic + Accidental	Everything	Everything
Leadtime	48 hours	24 hours	12 hours	6 hours
Refrigerators	✓	✓	✓	✓
Freezers		✓	✓	✓
Igloos			✓	✓
Ice Hotels				✓
Polar Bear Pens				✓
Penguin Shelters				✓
Price	$29/month	$49/month	$99/month	$199/month
	Sign up	Sign up	Sign up	Sign up

Notes from Iceland

Our marketing team travelled to the Kerling mountains in February, with hilarious consequences...

March 10, 2011

Chanty Ice Trek

Igloo employees were challenged to go trekking through the ice for charity. See how we got on.

February 28, 2011

Our Home

Iceland is home to Igloo, but many other wonders too. Let us introduce you to the marvels of Reykjavik.

February 14, 2011

Figure 11-4. The different types of boxes.

This list gives you a bird's-eye view of the design and an important outline for you to use as you start your work. It also makes it easy to detect blocks and elements that are very similar and that can be merged into one single module so the CSS and the designs can be further simplified. In the case of our example, on the content page (refer to Figure 11-2), you can see that the first row of services boxes and the second row are very similar, except that the second row's headings are larger (see Figure 11-5).

Figure 11-5. The only difference between the box on the left and the box on the right is the size of the headings

Ideally, the decision of making this a single box by homogenizing the heading sizes would not be made by the implementation team, but would have to be signed off by a designer. Still, it is important to be aware of these small variations that may creep into the designs and make them more complex (the design team and brand manager will also be looking out for them as part of their roles). It is unlikely that the variations in your case are as simple as the previous example, but it is important that you be aware that sometimes the design solution can and should be changed to keep both design and code simple.

The Color Palette

The design presents us with ten colors used frequently throughout:

- Main text
- Help text (search)
- Unvisited links
- Navigation background
- Navigation selected
- Boxes backgrounds (blue and yellow)
- Dotted lines
- Gradient box border
- Table background

There are also four gradients used: on the box with links list, on the buttons, on the table headings, and on the footer background.

Other colors are used (for example, on the Awards promotional banner), but they are mainly one-offs that should not clutter the basic color palette.

While analyzing the colors used, make sure you have the correct values necessary to work with by either talking directly to the design team or consulting your organization's design guidelines. It is important that, for example, whenever you are dealing with simple text, you use the same correct color rather than ending up with 12 different very similar (and incorrect) variations.

Accessibility Concerns

Ideally, the designer or design team will have tested the designs so that the color combinations provide enough contrast for colorblind users. In the Accessibility Guidelines (see Appendix 2), it is recommended that the designs are tested with a tool such as Color Oracle, which provides a quick and easy way of simulating what a colorblind user would see.

Foreground and background colors should have also been tested using a contrast checker, such as Jonathan Snook's Colour Contrast Check (again, mentioned in the Accessibility Guidelines).

A quick analysis of the design surfaced one issue: the contrast between the text on the footer and the background does not appear to be sufficient. In cases such as this, if the suspicions prove to be correct, you can discuss the best solution with the design team: perhaps simply changing the text color to white would solve it.

For now, we are analyzing possible complications based on only the design at hand. Other accessibility considerations should have been discussed while developing this design solution, and others can only be addressed while creating the code.

If there are accessibility concerns that you can spot immediately, it is better to solve them before getting hands-on with the code.

Communication Is Important

It is easy for developers to feel completely separate from designers and for communication to be kept to a minimum. This is not ideal. Both designers and developers are working toward the same goal: having a great website that people will feel compelled to visit and use and that will help the company achieve its goals. While developers might not feel comfortable advising designers on design, it is reasonable to ask from a diligent CSS author that he feeds back, advises, and even educates not only designers but also everyone involved in the creation of a website on best practices, standards, and the implications of doing things a certain way. This is not a one-way street: the same diligent developer should be open to new ideas brought by other sections of the business and should strive to find solutions to problems that might not necessarily be easy to solve in code but that are ultimately best for the users.

One type of element that tends to spark confusion is the headings, so they are a good example of how communication between people who make the designs and people who build the pages is so crucial. If a designer keeps in mind that the heading level used in a particular situation is not dependent on how large we want the type to be, but rather on the actual hierarchy of the content, it will be easier for him to develop a solution in which headings (and their sizes and scales relative to their position on the page) are better thought through and more carefully considered.

Creating the CSS

After the important step of analyzing the overall design, it is time to start creating the HTML and CSS for the website. As this book focuses on the CSS side of things, we assume you will be following web standards and making your markup accessible, and (as much as is possible) clean and semantic.

Remember: clean and efficient CSS can only come from clean and efficient markup, although it is in the moments of difficulty, where more complicated and messy puzzles need to be solved, that true expertise comes to light. If you head to this book's accompanying website at `http://procssforhightrafficwebsites.com`, you can inspect its markup at will.

We will continue to use the Igloo Refrigerator Parts Inc. website as our example. Even though it isn't an overly complex website, we will provide you with tips on how to think about and write your CSS that can be applied to any website and process.

The main goals of this exercise are to discuss and amend the design; provide you and your team with CSS that will allow you to create more pages without the need to edit the CSS files (except on occasions where a different type of design element might need to be added to the library); and show you how to create efficient and maintainable code, and create and augment its associated design library.

The creation of the CSS for Igloo Refrigetor Parts Inc's website follows the organization's CSS Standards Guide (Appendix 1), CSS Accessibility Guidelines (Appendix 2), Browser Support Guidelines (Appendix 3), and Development Process (Appendix 4).

We will begin every CSS file with our charset declaration:

```
@charset "UTF-8";
```

This helps us avoid having to escape characters later, which saves characters and makes our code easier to read.

Commenting

Following the CSS Standards Guide (see Appendix 1), we will use CSSDOC comments (see Chapter 2 for more details on CSSDOC) at the beginning—*file comment*—and for separating the sections of the style sheet—*section comments*. In the file comment, we will include a description of the style sheet and information about the project, the team who originally created the style sheet and copyright. We will also use this comment to include a list of main colors used throughout the CSS (as listed previously). Here is what this comment looks like:

```
/**
 * Igloo Refrigerator Parts Inc Corporate site
 *
 * Main CSS file for the IRP Inc's corporate site
 *
 * @project          IRP Inc Corporate
 * @author           Design Team at IRP Inc
 * @copyright        2011 Igloo Refrigerator Parts Inc
 *
 * @colordef         #333; main text
 * @colordef         #999; help text (search)
 * @colordef         #1299b4; unvisited links
 * @colordef         #cdf2f8; navigation background
 * @colordef         rgba(18,153,180,.2); navigation selected
 * @colordef         #a1e0e9; navigation selected fallback
 * @colordef         #e1f4f7; box background blue
 * @colordef         #fffbeb; box background yellow
 * @colordef         #cecac5; dotted lines
 * @colordef         #b0daea; gradient box border
 * @colordef         #fffbeb; table background
 */
```

Following the file comment, we will state whether this file has any dependencies. In our case, we will import a reset style sheet (reset.css), so we will include the following comment:

```
/**
 * Dependencies
 *
 * Importing reset file: reset.css
 */
```

Followed by the table of contents, for easier reference of the contents of the style sheet. Remember, it is more practical if this table of contents is succinct, so it doesn't have to be updated very often.

```
/**
 * Table of contents
 *
 * Structure
 * Generic typography and lists
 * Global elements
 * Links
 * Forms
 * Tables
 * Visual media
 * Components
 * Reusable
 * One-offs
 */
```

This structure is also an indication of which section comments we will need to include in the style sheet. It is a good idea, however, to already have a bare bones template, which should include an example file comment and the ideal structure of the CSS file, followed by the section comments. This will make it easier for developers creating new style sheets to start working. Here is an example of a section comment, where the description is optional:

```
/**
 * Reusable
 *
 * Modular classes that can be applied to other elements
 *
 * @section reusable
 */
```

Apart from introductory and sectioning comments, some of the most useful comments that you can add to your style sheets are the ones that explain why a certain action was taken. In our example, we have commented on every Internet Explorer filter used, so that future editors of the file know the reason for them. Here is an example:

```
#masthead {
        margin-top: -20px;
        *margin-top: 0; /* IE 7 and below: Navigation is partially hidden on IE 7 without this
property. */
```

```
padding-top: 20px;

}
```

In this case, we needed to reverse the negative top margin property from the "masthead" section, so that its contents aren't cropped in IE 7. By adding the asterisk before the property name, only IE 7 and below will correctly parse the second property (you can read more about this in Chapter 3).

You might want to include a note on which CSS hacks are acceptable to use within the main style sheet in your CSS Standards Guide. Sometimes, when the number of hacks applied is small, it is more efficient and performant to not have these stains separated from the main CSS. You may argue that, in the future, if you want to remove these hacks this will make it a harder task, but it is unlikely that these simpler documented hacks will pose any problems if left untouched.

You can also (and, in fact, you should) mark up the hacks with a common language so they are easy to search for in the future. We will use "HACK_" and then details of the hack. Our updated code follows:

```
#masthead {
        margin-top: -20px;
        *margin-top: 0; /* HACK_IE_LTE_7: Navigation is partially hidden on IE 7 without this
property. */
padding-top: 20px;

}
```

The exact syntax of this code is detailed in Appendix 3, and you can read more about commenting in Chapter 2.

Units

In our CSS we will use a combination of relative and absolute units: ems for font sizes and pixels for other measurements. The reasoning behind this decision is that fonts sized in relative units can be resized in most browsers, but also using ems for values such as an element's width will make the whole layout expand, even when the user has set a preference for only resizing text.

To make the calculations simpler, we have included in the body element the property `font-size: 62.5%`. This will make the default browser font size 10 pixels (it is usually 16 pixels). Knowing this, we can then infer that 1 em equals 10 pixels, 1.1 em equals 11 pixels, and so on.

Baseline Styles

We want to start with a clean slate, so we will create a reset style sheet (you might want to call this "base.css" rather than "reset.css") that will make most HTML elements work similarly cross-browser by resetting some of the properties that tend to be less consistent (such as margins and padding). But we do not want to reset everything, so we will take advantage of some of the user agent style sheet defaults rather than adding those to our code later on (you can read more about user agent style sheets in Chapter 3).

Starting with Eric Meyer's reset style sheet (you can read more about this and other reset style sheets in Chapter 4), we will remove the following elements from the initial declaration: `fieldset`, `dt`, and `dd`. Despite the margins and padding on these elements being inconsistent in some browsers, they are good enough as a basic styling, and we know that, in this case, they will not be used often.

The next step is to customize the body selector, so that it meets our needs. In his original reset, Eric only applied `line-height: 1` to the body element. In our case, we will need a bit more than that:

```
body {
        background: #fbfdfc url(i/bkg.jpg);
        color: #333;
        font-family: "Helvetica Neue", Helvetica, Arial, sans-serif;
        font-size: 62.5%;
        line-height: 1;
}
```

We will also add basic style for elements such as `blockquote`, `ins` and `abbr`. We will leave the default typography to the main style sheet, applying generic font-related properties only to the body element at this point.

Structure

Our website's design follows a simple two-column layout with a full-width header section at the top (which incorporates the navigation) and full-width footer at the bottom. The underlying grid (refer to Figure 11-3), as mentioned previously, is based on a 24-column layout, where each column is 30 pixels wide separated by 10 pixel–wide gutters. Container elements can span across 6, 9, 12, 18, and 24 columns.

Taking note of these measurements is a fairly simple but extremely important step in starting to build your framework. These are values that will emerge in your style sheets over and over again, so it is vital that you have the correct ones, rather than mere approximations.

The same applies to values such as margins and padding. In the case of our design, the standard box has a padding value of 14px 11px. It is unlikely that good designers would create solutions where, for example, list items present different bottom margins. Consistency is important, and consistency in the mockups will have to be translated into consistency in the code.

Let's begin to write our CSS. In the "Structure" section of our bare bones template, we will add the styles for the main content wrapper:

```
.wrapper {
        width: 950px;
        margin: auto;
}
```

We have used a class in this instance because we will be using this wrapper more than once per page. Because some of the areas of our design have a full-width background, with the content area centered in the middle, we will use this generic class to style inner container div or section elements, while keeping the main area wrapper full width. Here is the footer markup:

```
<footer>
        <div class="wrapper">
                <ul>
                        <li><a href="#">Help</a></li>
                        <li><a href="#">Terms of Service</a></li>
                        <li><a href="#">Privacy Policy</a></li>
                </ul>
                <p class="copy">© 2011 Igloo Refrigerator Parts Inc</p>
        </div>
</footer>
```

Following this generic class, we will add styles for the other main containers such as the top header element, the main (#main) and secondary column (#sec) areas, and the footer element. We will, however, leave the widths of the #main and #sec selectors for later...

Because we want our elements to be as flexible as possible, we will create accessory classes that can be appended to any container, giving it one of the possible widths we want to allow page builders to use. For these, we will use presentational classes. This is fine as long as there is a justification for it; in our case, how else would we name a class that means an element that spans across 6 columns other than "span-6" or "col-6"? If we had included the width per element (for example, a width for the "main" and "sec" container, and so on), we would not be providing enough flexibility for page creators—be they developers or content editors—to create new pages rapidly. If this is exactly what you need to achieve, then we advise you to not use these nonsemantic class names—this is a compromise that we are willing to accept for a higher level of flexibility. Here are the classes we will make available for container widths:

```
.span-6,
.span-9,
.span-12,
.span-18 {
        margin-right: 10px;
}
.span-6 {
        width: 230px;
}
.span-9 {
        width: 350px;
}
.span-12 {
        width: 470px;
}
.span-18 {
        width: 710px;
}
```

These classes follow the example that known frameworks set, in which every width selector also includes a right margin. When you need to have floated containers, you can use the classes "fRight" or "fLeft" (mentioned following). To remove the margin of the last container in a row, you will have to add the class "last" to it, which only contains the property margin-right: 0 (you can read more about reusable classes later in this chapter).

When building a generic and public framework, such as 960.gs or Blueprint (you can read more about these frameworks in Chapter 4), you need to make sure your code is catering for as many variations possible. When creating a custom framework, however, there is no need to go to such extremes. You know the design it will be used for, you know the possible variations, and you will probably even know what you don't want it to do. You can think of this framework as a tool that will allow you to create as many page variations as you need, no more and no fewer. Rather than being everything to everyone, this framework is exactly what is necessary, which means no wasted or unused code or bandwidth.

For our website, we will not need more than the container widths listed previously. In your particular case, you might want more complex variations.

Typographic Defaults

After defining the main structural elements and creating reusable classes for varying layouts, we will add basic typographic styles for all the elements we need to cater for. The difference between this and the reset style sheet is that in this section only selectors with font-related properties are included.

By having a basic style for every element, you make sure content creators can build new pages that will always present at least the correct hierarchy of elements and follow the design guidelines. We will style all six heading levels (h1 to h6), paragraphs (p), list elements (li), definition lists (dt and dd), quotes (blockquote) and preformatted text (pre). The design has a very consistent heading hierarchy, so we know that even when some level headings are within specific containers they will have the same font-size, line-height, and margin values. There are some variations, but they should not be addressed in the default style section and should only be added at a component level, applying only the necessary changes and taking advantage of inheritance to make the variations minimal and avoid redundancy.

As we have mentioned previously, we will use ems to define the font-size values in our website, but we will use pixels to define heights, widths, margins, and padding. This will allow for font resizing even in older browsers, keeping the layout consistent and avoiding unwanted horizontal scrollbars.

Here is the style for the first three level of headings:

```
h1, h2, h3, h4, h5, h6 {
        font-weight: normal;
}
h1 {
        font-size: 2.4em;
        margin-bottom: 10px;
}
h2 {
        font-size: 1.8em;
        margin-bottom: 12px;
}
h3 {
        font-size: 1.5em;
        margin-bottom: 10px;
}
```

And here is the style for our paragraphs and list elements:

```
p, li, dt, dd {
        font-size: 1.3em;
        line-height: 1.4;
        margin-bottom: 12px;
}
```

The line-height value is unitless, so that it can adapt itself to the size of the text. In this case, the computed font-size value will be 13px, and the computed line-height value will be 18.2px (you can read more about computed values in Chapter 3). If the font size is increased, for example to 1.5em, the computed values will be 15px and 21px, respectively—the line-height value grows proportionaly with the font-size.

We have consciously left the ul, ol, and dl elements out of this basic styling: the default user agent style serves the needs of the design, so there is no need to reset these styles or override them.

You can go even further, by adding styles for headings that follow certain elements. For example:

```
p + h1,
p + h2,
p + h3,
p + h4,
p + h5,
p + h6 {
        margin-top: 24px;
}
```

The possibilities are endless: you can include styles for headings that follow certain list types or images, or for paragraphs that follow the same elements, or list types that follow certain heading levels, and so on.

For our website, we will also add styles for the p and cite elements when placed within a blockquote element:

```
blockquote p {
        font-size: 1.3em;
        font-style: italic;
        margin-bottom: 8px;
}
blockquote p:before {
        content: """;
}
blockquote p:after {
        content: """;
}
blockquote cite {
        display: block;
        font-size: 1.3em;
}
blockquote cite:before {
        content: "–";
}
```

The previous code should be self-explanatory. We have used the :before and :after pseudo-elements to add the quotation marks to the beginning and end of the paragraphs within the blockquote. Since we have already declared the charset of the file to be UTF-8, there was no need to escape these special characters. We did not use the CSS3 version of these pseudo-elements (::before and ::after, respectively) so that Internet Explorer 8 could understand them: we want to show the same design to as many browsers as possible.

We haven't included forms and table styles in this section for two reasons. Our form elements will inherit most of their styling from the user agent style sheet, with only some added styles for positioning and custom button design. Table styles can be quite involved on their own, so keeping a separate section in the style sheet where tables are treated as a special type of component can make this basic styles section cleaner and easier to scan and refer to.

You can read more about typographic considerations in Chapter 5.

Global Elements

After adding the basic styles, we will create the styles for the global elements. These are elements that are present on every (or almost every) page of the website. In our case, these are the header area, the main

347

navigation, and the footer. For some, we will be required to override some of the basic styles we have created, as in the case of the navigation list:

```
nav ul {
        list-style: none;

}
nav li {
        display: inline;
        font-size: 1.4em;
        font-weight: bold;
        margin-top: -35px;
        margin-bottom: 0;
}
```

For the list items in the main navigation, we have had to override the default user agent `list-style` value, apply different margin values from the basic styles, and increase the font size. We will leave link styles for the "Links" section so that we have a centralized area where we can make sure all link states are being catered for. You do not have to follow this structure in your own style sheets, but our experience shows that having all the links in the same place makes it easier for different developers to find them in the document whenever they need to be edited or augmented.

Depending on the design at hand, this section may have more or fewer elements that you will need to include. You might find it easier to separate global elements in their own sections and then have different sections for the main navigation, secondary navigation, footer, and so on.

Components and Reusable Classes

In our example, we have classified components as reusable blocks of content that have specific styles applied. By adding the class or ID of the component to a container element, the elements inside it can be made to inherit these styles. This makes the CSS more reusable and modular. Rather than styling these blocks for each instance where they appear, they are location-agnostic, movable chunks. We will use the serviceBox as our example component (refer to Figure 11-6).

Before creating the serviceBox, however, we have first created a basic box component:

```
.box {
        background: #fffbeb;
        padding: 14px 11px;
        -moz-border-radius: 4px;
        -webkit-border-radius: 4px;
        border-radius: 4px;
}
```

This class can be applied to any container and it will be styled with the correct rounded corners value, padding, and background. With the "serviceBox" class we will expand the "box" class. This follows the concepts of OOCSS, where classes can be reused and expanded by other classes, making for a more modular style sheet. You can read more about OOCSS in Chapter 4.

The next step is to create the serviceBox class:

```
.serviceBox {
        background: #fff url(i/box-grad.jpg) repeat-x left bottom;
        border: 1px solid #b0daea;
```

```
        overflow: hidden;
        height: 1%;
}
```

As shown in the design, the serviceBox has a different background, a border, and appears in rows of three. The width and margins of the "serviceBox" element will be determined by a parent container div, with the correct "span" class applied (in this case, span-6). We have included the height property with a value of 1% so that IE 6 will clear the container, as it does not understand the overflow: hidden property (which is used to clear the container in other more compliant browsers). The content within this box is always a heading, a paragraph, and a list of links. Knowing this, we can further style the contents inside it:

```
.serviceBox ul {
        list-style: none;
        margin-left: 0;
}
.serviceBox li {
        border-top: 1px solid #eef9fb;
        margin: 0;
        width: 100%;
}
```

We have taken advantage of the fact that the heading is using the same style as the ones defined in the basic styles section of our file, so we don't need to add any styles for it here. We now only need to add the rounded corners to the list elements. Because this is not a style that will change with the hover or active state of the link, we can add it in this section:

```
.serviceBox li:first-child a {
        border-top: none;
        -moz-border-radius: 4px 4px 0 0;
        -webkit-border-top-left-radius: 4px;
        -webkit-border-top-right-radius: 4px;
        border-radius: 4px 4px 0 0;
}
.serviceBox li:last-child a {
        -moz-border-radius: 0 0 4px 4px;
        -webkit-border-bottom-left-radius: 4px;
        -webkit-border-bottom-right-radius: 4px;
        border-radius: 0 0 4px 4px;
}
```

Notice that the WebKit-specific properties were added individually for older versions of WebKit. WebKit only supports the shorthand in its most recent versions in the border-radius property. Some older browsers will not see this style, but they wouldn't understand the border-radius property, either, so it is a fair compromise. And we have styled our serviceBox component! As mentioned previously, we will add the link styles in the appropriate section of our style sheet.

Components are reusable, but here we make the distinction between components and reusable classes in that reusable classes have a more presentational aspect to them, and tend to only cater for a single property/value combination. Components are mainly created to hold a particular type or combination of content.

In our main style sheet, we have created five different reusable classes. The first reusable class is one that is likely to be familiar to most front-end developers: clearfix. This class can be applied to any element that needs to be "self-clearing" (cleared without an element specifically created to do this). We also include the Internet Explorer 7 and below version of this little trick:

```
.clearfix:after {
        content: ".";
        display: block;
        height: 0;
        clear: both;
        visibility: hidden;
}
.clearfix { /* HACK_IE_LTE_7: IE 7 and below don't support the :after pseudo-element (above).
*/
        *zoom: 1;
}
```

Next, we create two classes that will allow developers and content creators to easily left- or right-align elements:

```
.fLeft {
        float: left;
}
.fRight {
        float: right;
}
```

Following this, we will add the "last" class that can be applied to the final element in a row. This will remove the right margin, which would otherwise be applied, so that it neatly fits the available width:

```
.last {
        margin-right: 0;
}
```

And finally, we include an accessibility class that will allow content creators to hide pieces of text that are only to be read by screen readers:

```
.accessibility {
        position: absolute;
        text-indent: -9999px;
}
```

One-offs

Invariably there will be elements that need to be created and styled that do not follow the design of anything else we've added to our framework. We call these *one-offs*. You might prefer to call them "exceptions," "uniques," or any other name you feel is appropriate.

In the case of the Igloo Refrigerator Parts Inc. website, we have identified (so far) two special cases: the banner on the homepage, and the "Best Engineering Service Award" box, also on the homepage.

For the banner, we will create a class that can be appended to the #masthead component, including the correct background image, and text sizes:

```
.planet {
        background:url(i/hp-banner01.jpg) no-repeat center 20px;
}
.planet h2 {
        font-size: 4.8em;
        margin-bottom: 0;
}
.planet p {
        font-size: 1.6em;
        padding-bottom: 6px;
}
```

This class is basically an extender of the #mastead ID and is dependent on it. Because its style is so particular and does not apply to anything else, it is placed under the "One-offs" section of the style sheet.

For the award box, we will also take advantage of the default styling of some elements, but we will need to alter many properties:

```
#bestEngAward {
        border: 1px solid #fce8b8;
        background: #fff;
        padding: 23px 20px;
}
#bestEngAward h2 {
        color: #fcb61a;
        font: 3em/1.1 Impact, "Helvetica Compressed", "Helvetica Inserat", Arial Narrow,
Tahoma, Geneva, "MS Sans Serif", sans-serif;
        margin-bottom: 20px;
        text-transform: uppercase;
}
#bestEngAward p {
        margin-bottom: 0;
        width: 100%;
}
#bestEngAward p a:link, #bestEngAward p a:visited {
        border: none;
}
#bestEngAward p a:after {
        content: " ›";
}
#bestEngAward blockquote {
        background: url(i/blockquote.gif) no-repeat;
        color: #0f6080;
        margin: 0 25px 0 0;
        padding: 3px 0 0 40px;
        width: 321px;
}
#bestEngAward blockquote p {
        font-size: 1.6em;
        font-style: normal;
        margin-bottom: 3px;
}
```

```
#bestEngAward blockquote p:before {
        content: "";
}
```

In order to style them differently, we had to overwrite properties of the h2 and p elements, link styles, and the style of the blockquote element and its children. This code would have been a lot more verbose were the initial styles overly specific: we either could have not taken advantage of inheritance to declare only the minimum amount of properties, or we would have had to overwrite selectors that were too specific.

Be careful: as websites grow, the number of one-offs is likely to grow exponentially. Designers should be sensitive to this scenario and make sure that elements are not created that are very similar to existing ones. This will not only make the CSS more complex and rendundant but also make the design solution more diluted. Make sure the element you are creating is not already present in some way in your style sheet or that it cannot expand an existing component with a couple of properties.

Compromises

As conscious CSS authors, we know what the best practices are; we are aware of and follow web standards; and we are on top of the latest CSS techniques, which are usually created with the intent of making CSS more efficient and developers more productive. We know all of this. But as CSS authors that work on large-scale websites—visited by millions of users on infinite number of different devices and settings—we also know we need to make some compromises.

The Igloo Refrigerator Parts Inc. website is not an exception. We have already mentioned some of the compromises made, such as using nonsemantic class names to increase flexiblity or resorting to user agent style sheets defaults for basic styling of some of the elements.

Another example of a compromise we have made is the use of an image to be able to display a custom, non–web-safe font on the banner on the homepage. The original design uses Futura Condensed Medium, which very few users are likely to have installed in their computers. The options for this scenerio were the following:

- Use an image

- Use an image replacement technique

- Use Cufón or sIFR (you can read more about them in Chapter 5)

- Use Fontdeck as a web font service, since it provides this font

Since this font is only used in one instance, simply replacing the text with an image and using the alt attribute to identify the text within the image proved to be the quickest, simplest, and cheapest solution, and one that doesn't hamper accessibility. Our favorite solution would have been utilizing a service such as Fontdeck if the font was needed in more places, but the extra download, and the added expense, were not justifiable in this scenario.

In the case of the font used in the "Best Engineering Service Award" box, *Impact*, we know that this is a font that is commonly installed by default in Windows and Mac computers. The best solution in this instance is, then, to create a font stack that, where the font is not installed, the second, third, or even fifth font in the stack are still acceptable (the final font stack is Impact, Helvetica Compressed, Helvetica Inserat, Arial Narrow, Tahoma, Geneva, MS Sans Serif, and sans-serif). See Figure 11-6.

Figure 11-6. Comparison between the text rendered in the preferred font, Impact (top), and rendered in a font that appears later in the font stack, in this case Arial Narrow (bottom)

These are very simple examples of where you might have to make compromises, but as long as you weigh all the options and opt for the most accessible one that is sensible in terms of efficiency and maintenance, you should be on the right track. Remember, you (and the team involved in the creation of the design) are likely to be the only ones who will know things don't look exactly right; the users won't compare the rendering of the site across different platforms.

Cross-browser Consistency

The subject of *cross-browser consistency* is neatly tied into the subject of compromises, discussed previously. When we analyzed the design before starting the CSS, we were informed that the only element that needed to be perfect cross-browser was the company's logo. Other elements should look the same in browsers with A-level support (see Appendix 3 for Browser Support Guidelines) as much as possible.

To make sure the logo looks consistent even in IE 6, which does not support alpha-transparent PNG images, we have resorted to the Fireworks hack, where we export the logo with alpha-transparency as an 8-bit file; this gives us alpha-transparency in browsers that support it and index transparency in IE 6. The difference is almost impercetible, so it was deemed acceptable. You can read more about this trick in Chapter 8.

```
header h1 a:link, header h1 a:visited {
        background: url(i/logo.png) no-repeat;
        border: none;
        width: 132px;
        height: 46px;
        display: block;
        text-indent: -9999px;
}
```

We could have achieved the same effect with the following code, using a different image and a hack instead to give us more control over the display in IE 6:

```
header h1 a:link, header h1 a:visited {
        background: url(i/logo.png) no-repeat;
        _background: url(i/logo.gif) no-repeat; /* HACK_IE_6: IE 6 doesn't support alpha
transparent PNGs */
        border: none;
        width: 132px;
        height: 46px;
        display: block;
        text-indent: -9999px;
}
```

In this instance, this level of control was not necessary, but we have resorted to some hacks (or filters) *within* the main style sheet to overcome other browser discrepencies. We know what you are thinking: you should not use hacks. We certainly do not recommend this technique where more than a handful of hacks are needed. When only a couple are needed, though (for an entire website), we have to be pragmatic: we are dealing with high-traffic websites, where HTTP requests need to be minimized, and serving the browser an extra file just for a particular browser is never ideal. As long as it is a global decision, and that developers are informed about which hacks they are permitted to use, we do not feel this is an approach that you should absolutely disregard. It impacts performance positively and it makes it easier for values to be updated at the same time for both cases: compliant and noncompliant. How many times have you forgotten to update the file path for background images in IE-only style sheets or the correspondent min-height/height value?

The most noticeable browser-rendering differences that were not catered for (but that were considered acceptable variations) in the CSS are present in Internet Explorer 6 and 7.

- The main navigation does not render perfectly (IE 6 and 7) (see Figure 11-7)

- Attribute selectors used to target the search input are not supported, affecting the styling of the search box (IE 6 and 7). See Figure 11-8.

- When the :empty pseudo-class is not supported, empty table cells present a background (IE 6, 7, and 8). See Figure 11-9.

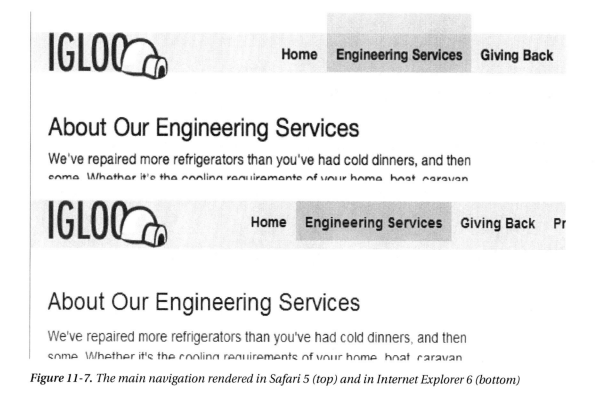

Figure 11-7. The main navigation rendered in Safari 5 (top) and in Internet Explorer 6 (bottom)

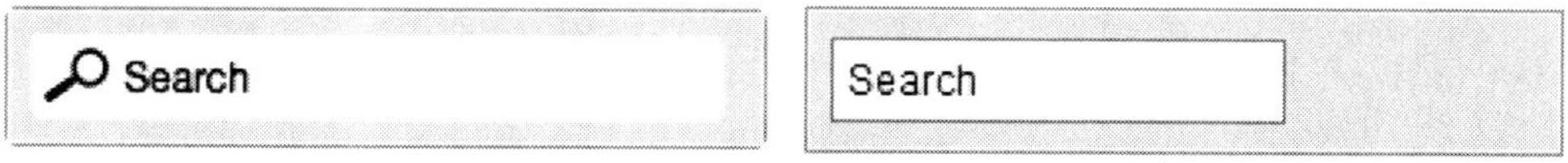

Figure 11-8. The search box does not show the background image (Firefox 3.6, left) in Internet Explorer 7 (right)

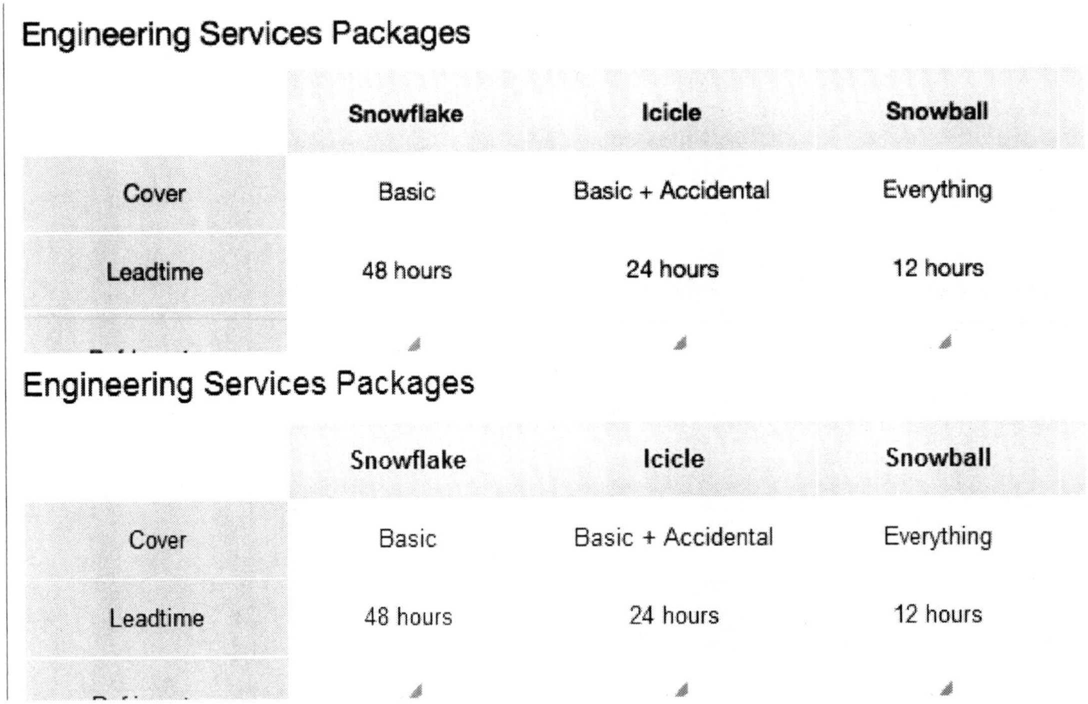

Engineering Services Packages

	Snowflake	Icicle	Snowball
Cover	Basic	Basic + Accidental	Everything
Leadtime	48 hours	24 hours	12 hours

Engineering Services Packages

	Snowflake	Icicle	Snowball
Cover	Basic	Basic + Accidental	Everything
Leadtime	48 hours	24 hours	12 hours

Figure 11-9. Firefox 3.6 (top) renders empty table cells correctly. Internet Explorer 8 (bottom) does not, since it does not understand the `:empty` *pseudo-class*

Other decorative details that do not show at all in some browsers are the following:

- Rounded corners

- Transparency of the selected link in the main navigation

- Drop shadows on buttons

In our experience, these are details that most designers are comfortable to have render differently in different browsers. The time that it would take to make these work consistently in older noncompliant browsers and the impact that these techniques would have on the style sheets' (and markup's) maintainability are not justifiable, knowing that there are simpler solutions that still look right.

However, some measures were taken to provide the nicest possible solution for older browsers:

- Rather than using CSS3 gradients for some backgrounds, simple GIF images were used.

- Instead of using advanced selectors to target first and last elements that would have otherwise broken the layout in older browsers (for lack of support), classes were used.

- Where transparent colors were used, solid fallback colors were provided that mimic as closely as possible the result that would have displayed had transparency been supported.

Sometimes we need to shy away from more complex and advanced features if we know that in doing so we will be providing a nicer experience to more visitors to our site. We do not recommend that you go to extremes; as you can see from the lists above, there are newer and easier ways of doing things that would have taken hours or days just a few years ago. But sometimes, by simply using an image instead of a CSS gradient, the experience will be exponentially improved for some users, who will appreciate the effort.

Accessibility and Links

Accessibility must be something that is constantly in the back of our minds in the creation and development process of a website. In terms of front-end development, it must start from the very foundations, the markup, what gives the content meaning, and then build its way up to the other layers—style and behavior.

The Igloo Refrigerator Parts Inc. website makes sure that it is as accessible as possible by doing the following:

- Ensuring the website's content is clear and understandable with all styles disabled, and also with CSS enabled and images disabled.

- Making sure foreground and background color combinations have enough contrast for colorblind users.

- Testing the website for font size increases of two steps up and down (see Figure 11-10).

- Providing not only hover and active link states but also focus link states, for keyboard users.

- Including a "Skip to content" link, right at the top of the page. This will make it easier for users to jump straight into the content.

- Providing hooks, in the form of body classes and IDs, which users can use to create user style sheets.

- Wherever possible, using microformats, which turn content into more machine-readable formats. This helps screen readers, as well as assistive devices and search engines.

- Including a sensible print style sheet.

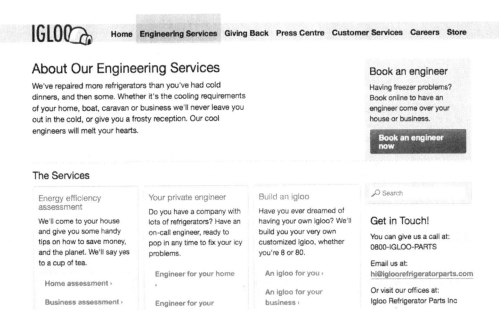

Figure 11-10. Although slightly less elegant, the layout survives neatly a font size increase of two steps.

Other steps can be added to your list, such as making sure the mobile version of the website is stripped of secondary elements (but still providing a link for the user to view the full website) and making sure that all image file sizes are as small as possible.

All these measures should exist in a CSS Accessiblity Guidelines document (see Appendix 4).

We have included the topic of links in accessibility because they are one of the most important elements to take into account when making our websites accessible and are frequently forgotten. In our style sheet, we have joined all the link styles into a single section so it is easier to compare different link styles and to guarantee all necessary link states are styled.

You can read more about accessibility in Chapter 6.

Documentation and Design Library

Once the reusable elements are defined, the next step is to keep them in a repository that can be accessed by designers, developers, and content editors.

Ideally, each reusable snippet should be documented visually and accompanied by the HTML markup necessary to use it on a page, as well as Photoshop files for the designers to easily drop into their designs, examples, class names, IDs, and anything else that might be useful. This repository should be accessible to everyone, searchable, and versioned.

For example, if we were to document the serviceBox, it would be useful to show the different measurements used in creating it (see Figure 11-11).

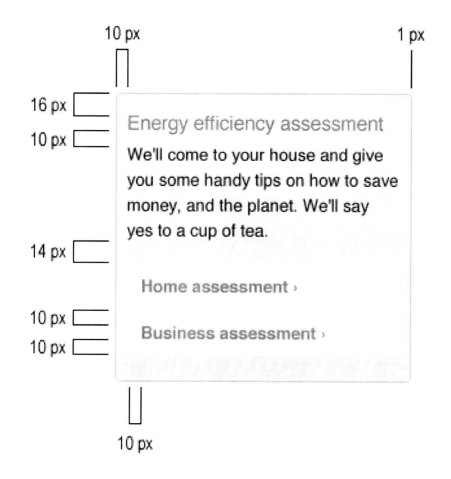

Figure 11-11. *A documented reusable block.*

When developers need to use this box in a page, they will copy and paste the following HTML markup:

```
<div class="box serviceBox">
        <h3>Title</h3>
        <p>Description of title</p>
        <ul>
                <li><a href="#">Action link</a></li>
                <li><a href="#">Action link</a></li>
        </ul>
</div>
```

In this case, we can specify that this particular block should not be used by itself; it should always be used in rows in multiples of three, where the last block in each row should include the class of "last" (a reusable class that can be used to remove the right margin on the last element in a row, regardless of context), and preceded by a heading (h2). We can also specify the amount of copy that each block should include, how many links it should contain, and whether it has any dependencies on surrounding code (not in this instance).

Even though our recommendations are geared toward developers, it is also useful to include, along with the code and specification, a Photoshop file (or other type of layered file such as Illustrator or Fireworks) that can be used by designers.

Bear in mind that this library easily becomes useless if not kept up to date. Assigning someone with the task of updating it on a regular schedule is of utmost importance.

Summary

Finally, we have a site ready and built with a CSS backbone that is ready for as many pages as we want to throw at it. In this chapter we took you through dissecting the design and the conversations you might have had to ensure agreement between design, the business, and the developers. We considered which elements were reusable, structure and grids, global elements, one-offs, and accessibility. We also demonstrated the likely points of contention and compromise between browsers and how you might tackle them. Our resulting CSS was clear, concise, and uncomplicated. The selectors are not difficult to override, and it is easy to locate particular pieces in the code. Most importantly, it is fast, with the minimum reasonable file size and few HTTP requests.

We looked at building the design library, which is paramount to achieving efficiency and consistency in these designs and future amendments to the sites. As much as possible, we tried to follow our own advice and give justification where we did not. It's all about increasing efficiency and reducing redundancy.

In the four appendices you will find supporting documents for the process and rules we have implemented with our fictitious organization, which are intended to be as practical and useful to you as possible.

We genuinely hope that you have enjoyed this book and that you will take away with you a good understanding of how CSS can make a really big difference to your website, from many angles such as productivity, cost, brand perception, user experience, and performance. Let's all work together to build scalable, accessible, clever interfaces that look beautiful and work intuitively. Every team has its own way of doing things, and as long as everyone is agreed on the same system, that is absolutely fine. We would love to hear about your own experiences.

Thanks for reading. Now go write some code!

APPENDIX 1

■ ■ ■

CSS Standards Guide

This guide serves as an example and is not exhaustive. The goal is to show you what type of content can be made into a guideline that all CSS authors must adhere to. The degree of detail into which you go in your guide, or how you divide different documents (for example, you might prefer to join this and the Browser Support Guidelines into a single document) is up to you.

The pages referred to here as links do not actually exist. They are an indication of other types of documents you might want to create and make available in a central company-wide repository.

Each guideline should include a justification to save on further discussion. Any points that have been decided against should still be recorded with the conclusion so that they are not needlessly discussed again. Each item should be numbered so that it can easily be referred to within the document or cross-document.

Igloo Refrigerator Parts Inc. CSS Standards Guide

1. Introduction and conventions

2. Implementation

3. General rules

4. Comments

5. Formatting

6. Naming

7. Typography

8. Color

1. Introduction and Conventions

These CSS Guidelines are applicable to all websites created and managed by Igloo Refrigerator Parts Inc. and under the igloorefrigeratorparts.com domain.

The keywords used in this guide have the following significance:

- **MUST**: This rule must be followed at all times with no exceptions.

- **MUST NOT**: This rule means an absolute prohibition with no exceptions.

- **SHOULD**: This rule should be followed at all times unless there is an acceptable reason not to that has been justified.

- **SHOULD NOT**: This should be avoided at all times unless there is an acceptable reason that has been justified.

- **MAY**: This rule gives permission to implement a particular measure under certain circumstances.

For accessibility guidelines, please read the *Accessibility Guidelines*.

You can access the necessary templates and files to start a new project from the "Templates and Assets" section.

Please refer to the *Browser Support Guidelines* for information on browser support, QA, and tips on how to avoid some common rendering bugs.

2. Implementation

2.1 All CSS **SHOULD** be loaded externally because it enables caching control and makes the HTML smaller.

2.2 External CSS **MUST** be referenced via the link element, which **MUST** be placed in the head section of the document as close as possible to the top, but after the title element. This will improve performance and not impede SEO.

2.3 External style sheets **MUST NOT** be imported using @import because it impairs caching and blocks rendering. Debug files are the only exception to this rule.

2.4 Document head CSS **SHOULD NOT** be used where a style rule is only required for a specific page. To do so makes these rules uncacheable and inconsistent.

2.5 All linked style sheets **MUST** exist (you **MUST NOT** use placeholders). Missing files create unnecessary requests, which may impede performance, and 404 errors, which may impede SEO.

2.6 CSS files **SHOULD** live in the "css" directory of the website. Images pertaining to the CSS **SHOULD** live in a directory named "i" within the "css" directory. This makes the "css" directory location-agnostic.

2.7 All CSS files **MUST** be referenced via @import statements in a debug file, although there **MAY** be multiple debug files (one global file and one file per section). This aids debugging.

2.8 Served CSS files **MUST** be concatenated and minified via YUI Compressor in production. The debug files **MUST** be used as the source for the list of CSS files. This improves performance and improves maintainability.

2.9 You **SHOULD** use CSS sprites where appropriate. This improves performance because it reduces HTTP requests. This is particularly important when targeting low bandwidth devices.

2.10 You **MUST NOT** use CSS expressions because browser support is poor and they are not performant.

2.11 You **MUST NOT** use CSS behaviors (HTC files) because browser support is poor and they create a JavaScript dependency.

2.12 You **SHOULD NOT** use data URIs because they are larger than their file equivalents and break caching control.

3. General Rules

3.1 You **SHOULD** use UTF-8 character encoding. This helps to avoid localization errors.

3.2 You **MUST NOT** use inline CSS. To do so makes these rules uncacheable and inconsistent.

3.3 You **MUST NOT** use `!important`. It may prevent the good use of user style sheets and makes it hard for other authors to override that CSS declaration.

3.4 You **SHOULD NOT** create rules using the universal selector (*) as it may have unexpected effects, break inheritance and hamper performance.

3.5 You **MUST NOT** create rules where the universal selector (*) is used in conjunction with other selectors as it will break inheritance and hamper performance.

3.6 You **SHOULD** avoid the use of advanced, complex selectors, or CSS3 selectors when a simple class or ID would suffice. Complex selectors can impede performance.

3.7 You **SHOULD** start with less-specific rules ("p") and add specificity (from right to left) as need arises (".aside p"). This aids in overriding the rules when necessary and keeps rules simple.

3.8 Every HTML tag that will be used **MUST** have at least a simple CSS element selector with basic style applied to it or there must have been a conscious decision to use the browser defaults (for example, in form elements). This ensures consistency between browsers.

3.8 You **SHOULD NOT** specify units for values of 0 (zero). These are unnecessary.

3.9 You **MUST** only use CSS animation for visual decoration, not for functionality. Support for them cannot be depended on.

3.10 You **SHOULD** test your style sheets for redundant or duplicated selectors.

3.11 Shorthand properties **SHOULD** be used wherever possible. Be aware that they will override the individual properties.

3.12 You **SHOULD NOT** modify built files (minified and concatenated files). This can cause confusion, and your changes will be lost.

3.13 Everything other than fonts **SHOULD** be sized with pixels.

3.14 Every page **SHOULD** have an ID on the body tag that references that page, so that it can be targeted specifically. For example:

```
<body id="home">
```

3.14 Every page **MUST** have a class on the body tag that references the language and country combination for the language of the page, so that it can be targeted specifically. For example:

```
<body class="en-us">
```

4. Comments

4.1 File (the initial comment at the top of the CSS file) and section comments **SHOULD** follow the CSSDOC (`http://cssdoc.net/`) format. CSSDOC provides a standardized way of making comments. A CSSDOC comment block (DocBlock) has the following structure:

```
/**
 * Short description
 *
 * Long description
 *
 * @tags (optional)
 */
```

4.2 A CSS file **MUST** include a file comment at the top, including the following information: title of the document, short description, long description (optional), project it relates to, author, copyright, and color information (optional). For example:

```
/**
 * Christmas theme
 *
 * CSS theme for the Christmas version of the Igloo Refrigerator
 * Parts Inc website
 *
 * This theme should only be used between the dates of November
 * 7th and January 7th
 *
 * @project    IRP Christmas Site
 * @author     Design Team at IRP Inc
 * @copyright  2011 Igloo Refrigerator Parts Inc
 *
 * @colordef   #111111; main text
 * @colordef   #999999; headings
 * @colordef   #9f0000; unvisited links
 * ...
 */
```

4.3 All related blocks of CSS **SHOULD** be prefixed with a section comment in this format to aid visual scanning and searchability of the CSS document:

```
/**
 * Typography
 *
 * @section typography
 **/
```

Visit the "Templates and Assets" section to access a bare-bones CSS template with comment examples.

4.4 You **SHOULD NOT** mention version numbers or dates in the comment because the version control system will maintain this information and it is likely to get outdated if it is managed manually.

4.5 You **SHOULD** maintain a table of contents of the sections in the file. For example:

```
/**
 * Table of contents
 *
 * Structure
 * Generic typography and lists
 * Global elements
 * Links
 * Forms
 * Tables
 * Visual media
 * Components
 * Reusable
 * One-offs
 */
```

4.6 Values that require calculations **SHOULD** have an inline comment showing the necessary steps to arrive at that value. For example:

```
#main {
        margin-left: 220px; /** aside width + 20px of margin */
}
aside {
        width: 200px;
        float: left;
}
```

4.7 Properties that need to be updated in different files **SHOULD** be properly commented. For example, when modifying the min-height property, the height property in IE 6–only style sheets needs to be updated at the same time. A comment alongside both properties should reflect this.

5. Formatting

5.1 The opening brace of a rule **SHOULD** be on the same line as the last selector, with a single space between the selector and the brace. Each property/value pair **SHOULD** be declared in a separate line with one tab of indentation. The closing brace of a rule **SHOULD** be on a separate line. Each property **SHOULD** have a single space between the colon and the property value, and end in a semicolon. Here's an example:

```
#content {
        color: red;
        font-size: 1em;
}
```

5.2 Multiple selector rules **SHOULD** declare one selector per line. Exceptions **MAY** apply for reset style sheets or other multiple selector rules with many short selectors.

5.3 Vendor-specific properties **SHOULD** be included after all the other properties to create clear visual distinction. The specified W3C name **MUST** be declared after the vendor-specific alternatives (for example, border-radius must be declared after -moz-border-radius and -webkit-border-radius).

6. Naming

6.1 Class and ID names **MUST** be lowercase. Class and ID names **SHOULD** contain one word only. If necessary, separate words **MUST** be separated via camel case, as such: highlightModule. Where using camel case and acronyms, if the acronym is at the beginning it should be in lowercase (for example, wwwLink); otherwise uppercase (linkWWW).

6.2 Class and ID names **MUST** only use alphanumeric characters and hyphens. They **MUST NOT** include underscores, forward or backward slashes, or asterisks; or begin with a numeric character.

6.3 Class and ID names **SHOULD** be semantic whenever possible and not presentational. For example, instead of "red" you **SHOULD** name a warning message style as "warning." You **SHOULD** always try to use well-recognized class and ID names, such as "nav," "aside," or "footer."

6.4 You **SHOULD** use microformats or equivalents such as Microdata or RDFa if appropriate uses exist.

6.5 Namespaces **MUST** be separated from the rest of the class or ID name with a hyphen. For example: "igr-blogWidget", where "igr" is the namespace.

7. Typography

7.1 You **MUST** choose the font stack carefully (complying with the *Branding Guidelines*).[1] Start with the ideal font; followed by a font that is more likely to be installed on users' systems; followed by a font that is installed in most users' systems; and finally one of these default `fonts: sans-serif`, `serif,` or `monospace`.

7.2 Where you are displaying text in uppercase, you **MUST** convert the text via the `text-transform` property. This helps with changes of design at a later date.

7.3 Fonts **SHOULD** be sized using ems, but **MAY** be sized in % or keyword values. They **MUST NOT** be sized in pixels, because this breaks the ability to zoom text only.

8. Color

8.1 When using hex colors, you **MUST** put them in lowercase because this aids gzipping efficiency.

8.2 You **MAY** use the following named colors in lowercase: black, white, red, blue. The named colors are easier to read.

8.3 You **SHOULD NOT** use named colors other than those defined in 8.2 because their values are open to interpretation by developers.

8.4 Elements with an image background **MUST** have a defined fallback background color. This makes the page easier to use while images are loading and avoids a jarring change of color.

---

[1] We will not provide you with example branding guidelines because they are out of the scope of this book. We assume your organization will already have them.

8.5 When using RGBA colors, you **MUST** declare a fallback hexadecimal color before it so that browsers that do not support RGBA still show a color. You **SHOULD NOT** use RGBA colors where non-alpha-transparent colors would suffice.

8.6 You **MUST NOT** use colors for foreground text that are the same color as the background to hide text. This would result in search engines penalizing search results.

CSS Coding Standards References

Many example coding standards exist. Here are some that we drew inspiration from that you may find useful, too:

- BBC Future Media Standards & Guidelines Cascading Style Sheets (CSS) Standard v1.3 `http://www.bbc.co.uk/guidelines/futuremedia/technical/css.shtml`

- BBC Future Media Standards & Guidelines Use of Colour and Colour-Contrast Standards v1.7 `http://www.bbc.co.uk/guidelines/futuremedia/accessibility/colour_contrast.shtml`

- BBC Future Media Standards & Guidelines Text Links Standards v2.1 `http://www.bbc.co.uk/guidelines/futuremedia/accessibility/links.shtml`

- BBC Future Media Standards & Guidelines Browser Support Standards v3.72 `http://www.bbc.co.uk/guidelines/futuremedia/technical/browser_support.shtml`

- Drupal CSS Coding Standards `http://drupal.org/node/302199`

- WordPress CSS Coding Standards `http://codex.wordpress.org/CSS_Coding_Standards`

- Stoyan Stefanov's CSS Coding Conventions `http://www.phpied.com/css-coding-conventions/`

- Isobar North America Code Standards `http://na.isobar.com/standards/`

APPENDIX 2

■ ■ ■

Accessibility Guidelines

The guidelines your organization uses to ensure the accessibility of your website may live separately from your coding standards. They would be much more comprehensive than the example shown here because they should also cover markup, JavaScript, and content. We have repeated some items from the coding standards document so that the two documents work as separate entities.

Igloo Refrigerator Parts Inc. CSS Accessibility Guidelines

1. Introduction and conventions

2. General rules

3. Typography

4. Links

5. Color

1. Introduction and Conventions

These Accessibility Guidelines are applicable to all websites created and managed by Igloo Refrigerator Parts Inc. and under the `igloorefrigeratorparts.com` domain.

The keywords used in this guide have the following significance:

- **MUST**: This rule must be followed at all times, with no exceptions.

- **MUST NOT**: This rule means an absolute prohibition, with no exceptions.

- **SHOULD**: This rule should be followed at all times unless there is an acceptable reason not to that has been justified.

- **SHOULD NOT**: This rule should be avoided at all times unless there is an acceptable reason to that has been justified.

- **MAY**: This rule gives permission to implement a particular measure under certain circumstances.

For coding standards, please read the *CSS Standards Guide*.

You can access the necessary templates and files to start a new project from the "Templates and Assets" section.

Please refer to the *Browser Support Guidelines* for information on browser support, QA, and tips on how to avoid some common rendering bugs.

2. General Rules

2.1 The site **MUST** satisfy Priority 1 WCAG checkpoints (http://www.w3.org/TR/WCAG10/full-checklist.html).

2.2 The site **SHOULD** satisfy Priority 2 WCAG checkpoints.

2.3 The site **SHOULD** satisfy Priority 3 WCAG checkpoints.

2.4 You **MUST NOT** use !important. It may prevent the good use of user style sheets and makes it hard for other authors to override that CSS declaration.

2.5 You **MUST** place a consistent class on the body element for every page on the site to give user style sheets a hook. For example:

```
<body class="iglooRefrigeratorSite">
```

2.6 You **SHOULD** avoid any flickering content.

2.7 You **SHOULD** check the site with a screen reader such as JAWS (http://www.freedomscientific.com/products/fs/jaws-product-page.asp), NVDA (http://www.nvda-project.org/) or Mac OS X Voiceover (http://www.apple.com/accessibility/voiceover/).

2.8 You **MAY** use alternate style sheets, but if you do, you **MUST** provide an in-page method of switching rather than relying on the browser.

2.9 You **MUST NOT** rely on hover states or animations to convey information.

3. Typography

3.1 The default font size **MUST NOT** be less than 12px.

3.2 The websites **MUST** be tested for font size increases and decreases of at least two steps (in each direction).

3.3 Fonts **SHOULD** be sized using ems, but **MAY** be sized in % or keyword values. They **MUST NOT** be sized in pixels because this would break text-only zooming in some browsers.

3.4 Where you are displaying text in uppercase, you **MUST** convert the text via the text-transform property. This avoids screen readers spelling out words as if they were acronyms.

4. Links

4.1 Links **SHOULD** always have a style defined for their visited, hovered, active, and focused states in the following order: :link, :visited, :hover, :active, :focus.

4.2 You **MUST NOT** underline text that is not a link because this is confusing to the user.

4.3 Links **SHOULD** have large clickable areas.

5. Color

5.1 The color of visited links **SHOULD** be different from the color of unvisited links. This color difference **MUST** be evident to colorblind users.

5.2 Color contrast between text and backgrounds **MUST** have at least 125 brightness difference and at least 400 color difference. Use Jonathan Snook's Colour Contrast Check (`http://snook.ca/technical/colour_contrast/colour.html`) to confirm.

5.3 You **MUST NOT** use any color combinations that will be indistinguishable by people with a form of colorblindness.

5.4 You **MUST NOT** convey information with color alone.

5.5 Navigation **MUST** be identifiable by means other than color.

5.6 Elements with an image background **MUST** have a defined fallback background color. This makes the page easier to use while images are loading and avoids a jarring change of color.

5.7 You **SHOULD** test the website's color combinations with a colorblindness simulator, such as Color Oracle (`http://colororacle.cartography.ch/index.html`).

■ ■ ■

Browser Support Guidelines

The guidelines for browser support may live separately from your coding standards. All these guidelines should link to each other and live on a wiki. Some items may be repeated from other documents so that the guide can stand alone as a single entity.

Igloo Refrigerator Parts Inc. Browser Support Guidelines

1. Introduction and conventions

2. General rules

3. Avoiding common bugs

4. Hacks and filters

5. Devices

1. Introduction and Conventions

These Browser Support Guidelines are applicable to all websites created and managed by Igloo Refrigerator Parts Inc. and under the `igloorefrigeratorparts.com` domain.

The keywords used in this guide have the following significance:

- **MUST**: This rule must be followed at all times with no exceptions.

- **MUST NOT**: This rule means an absolute prohibition with no exceptions.

- **SHOULD**: This rule should be followed at all times unless there is an acceptable reason not to that has been justified.

- **SHOULD NOT**: This should be avoided at all times unless there is an acceptable reason to that has been justified.

- **MAY**: This rule gives permission to implement a particular measure under certain circumstances.

For coding standards and accessibility considerations, please read the *CSS Standards Guide* and *Accessibility Guidelines*, respectively.

You can access the necessary templates and files to start a new project from the "Templates and Assets" section.

2. General Rules

2.1 You **MUST** test the website against the Graded Browser Support chart available on the Graded Browser Support page.[1]

2.2 You **MUST** test the website with the following setting combinations: CSS on/images on, CSS on/images off, and CSS off/images off because they cover most realistic scenarios.

2.3 The site **MUST** be legible and functional on each and every device.

3. Avoiding Common Bugs

3.1 You **SHOULD NOT** set both width/height and padding on the same element because this may cause layouts to break if a browser renders the page in quirks mode.

3.2 Absolutely positioned elements **SHOULD** have both horizontal and vertical positioning defined to avoid inheritance issues.

3.3 Floated elements **SHOULD** have a set width because some browsers will behave unpredictably otherwise.

3.4 You **SHOULD** set a value for `height` in IE 6 where `min-height` is set for other browsers because this browser does not understand `min-height`.

3.5 When positioning an element relatively, you **SHOULD** ensure that you trigger hasLayout; `position:relative` does not trigger hasLayout (see 4.7).

4. Hacks and Filters

4.1 You **MUST NOT** use conditional comments that could potentially target future browsers. For example, you **MUST NOT** target IE, but you **MAY** target IE 6 or lower.

4.2 Hacks and filters **SHOULD** be avoided. When they cannot be avoided, they **MUST** be properly documented; you **SHOULD** provide a link to the documented solution, as well as the common name for the bug, as follows:

```
/** HACK_IE_LTE_6: "display: inline" fixes the Double Float Margin bug on IE5/6. More on this
bug/solution: http://www.positioniseverything.net/explorer/doubled-margin.html */
```

4.3 When using hacks and filters for Internet Explorer, they **MUST** be prefixed with a comment following the syntax shown here:

```
HACK_IE_LTE_7:
```

---

[1] We do not include this document here because we typically recommend using the Yahoo! Graded Browser Support as a start. You should modify it based upon your reporting tools and the browsers your users use.

This comment means a hack for IE versions previous to or equal to 7:

`HACK_IE_7:`

This comment means a hack for IE version 7. This methodology makes it easy to search for these hacks in the future.

4.4 You **MUST NOT** use hacks to target browsers other than those in this list:

- The underscore hack
    - To target IE 6 and below, prefix the property name with an underscore.
    - Example: `_property: value;`
- The star hack
    - To target IE 7 and below, prefix the property name with an asterisk.
    - Example: `*property: value;`
- The backslash 9 hack
    - To target IE 8 and below, suffix the value with backslash 9.
    - Example: `property: value\9;`

4.5 To target multiple versions of IE, you **MAY** combine the hacks described in 4.4. For example:

```
 property: value\9; /* HACK_IE_8: Comment… */
*property: value;   /* HACK_IE_7: Comment… */
_property: value;   /* HACK_IE_LTE_6: Comment… */
```

4.6 In cases where the hack you need to use is not mentioned in 4.4, you **MUST** have it agreed and added to this document before you may use it.

4.7 You **SHOULD NOT** use `zoom:1` for normal purposes, but only to fix hasLayout in IE that cannot be fixed with a cleaner solution.

4.8 You **SHOULD** use CSS validation as the first step to fixing possible bugs.

5. Devices

5.1 You **MUST** test the website against the Mobile Graded Browser Support chart available in the Mobile Graded Browser Support page.[2]

5.2 Background images **SHOULD** be applied to elements with a class that is unique to that device, not elements with no class applied, because those images may be downloaded unnecessarily.

---

[2] We do not include this document here because we typically recommend using jQuery Mobile's Mobile Graded Browser Support (http://jquerymobile.com/gbs/) as a starting point. You should modify it based upon your reporting tools and the browsers your users use.

5.3 You **SHOULD** support print style sheets. The main style sheet **SHOULD** be aimed at "all" so no devices are left out.

5.4 In print style sheets, lists that use background images for bullets **SHOULD** have the default bullets reinstated, as most browsers won't print background images by default.

5.5 Navigation elements aren't usually necessary for printed media and **SHOULD** therefore be hidden via CSS.

5.6 Wherever possible, floated containers **SHOULD** be unfloated for print style sheets.

5.7 In print style sheets, font sizes **SHOULD** be set in pt.

5.8 There **SHOULD** be an indication of the link's `href` attribute on external links. Visit A List Apart for a good technique on how to do this: "CSS Design: Going to Print" (`http://www.alistapart.com/articles/goingtoprint/`).

5.9 You **SHOULD** make sure that tables and images are not cropped on page breaks.

APPENDIX 4

■ ■ ■

Development Process

Your development process guide should live separately from your coding standards on a wiki. These processes can (and should) change frequently so there needs to be a single point of authority for the team to reference.

Igloo Refrigerator Parts Inc. Development Process

This document describes the process we intend to use within our organization. This process can be amended from team to team, but this guide should serve as a baseline for new projects. This document should live on a wiki and discussions around improving it should be encouraged. Each project should amend the document for its purposes, to be more accurate to its intended process.

The development process spans the time between receiving the requirements and deploying to production.

The Team

The team for this project is defined as the following:

- Project manager
- Server-side developer x 2
- Front-end developer x 2
- Tester

Iterations

The project is broken into two-week sprints (or iterations). This length is intended to be long enough to avoid the cost and time implications of each sprint, but short enough to react quickly to change. Every iteration will begin on a Monday and end on the second Friday after. Before the project begins, we must already have a list of requirements and designs from the business. These should not change, but they might, and this process is intended to accommodate that.

The first sprint is known as iteration zero. During iteration zero, anything blocking the team from performing their roles will be dealt with. This may include setting up environments and builds, adding users or licenses to the tools, buying software and hardware, and so on. At the end of this iteration the team will have the following:

- A good understanding of the requirements
- A prioritized list of stories that represent the entirety of the project

- An idea of the intended architecture of the system

- Everything the members of the team need to start development

- A working continuous integration environment with necessary build scripts and debug methods

Stories

During iteration zero, the requirements will be broken into stories in the current tense, such as the following:

- The login web service exists

- The user can log in

The stories will be each given acceptance criteria, which are what is used to define a story as complete. The tester, who should be skilled in edge cases and security holes, will help with these. During this process, other requirements might be discovered. Nonfunctional requirements[1] should also be considered, since stories may arise from them, too. Example acceptance criteria might be the following:

- The login web service exists

  - The service **MUST** accept two parameters: username and password

  - The service **MUST** ignore any further parameters

  - Where the username and password match an entry in the database, a logged-in cookie **MUST** be set and the user redirected to the secure page

  - Where the username and password do not match an entry in the database, the user **MUST** be redirected back to the original page and an error shown

These stories will be tracked in JIRA and GreenHopper. The stories will also be placed in a prioritized order. No two stories will have the same priority.

Structure and Version Control

We will be using SVN. Our (front-end) folder structure will be as follows:

```
/
    css/
        build/
            [Build files]
        i/
            [CSS imagery]
        [CSS files]
        all-debug.css
    i/
        [Imagery]
```

---

[1] Non-functional requirements are those that describe how a system should be rather than what it should do. Examples include uptime, performance, reliability, and usability.

```
js/
        [JS files]
[HTML files]
favicon.ico
```

All CSS files will be built in the `css` folder. There can be as many as are needed to keep development easy. Every CSS file will be referenced in `all-debug.css` in @import statements. Here's an example:

```
@charset "UTF-8";

@import url(reset.css);
@import url(main.css);
```

A build script[2] (in the `build` directory) will be runnable manually that will parse this file, concatenate all the referenced files (prefixed with the @charset) and save those as `all-concat.css`. Finally, it will minify that file with YUI Compressor and save it as `all.css`. In development, the HTML files will point at `all-debug.css`, but in production they will point at `all.css`. `all-concat.css` may be useful for debugging the build process. An SVN hook on the `css` directory will automatically trigger this build script whenever a CSS file is committed to SVN.

Planning Meeting

At the beginning of every sprint following iteration zero, at 10am, the team will have a planning meeting, which is facilitated by the project manager. First, the project manager will calculate the resources he has available. We will only need the totals for the server-side and front-end developers. We assume that each member of the team has six hours available to work per day to allow for meetings, replying to emails, and so on. We will take into account planned holidays or days off. We will subtract three hours from this total for the meetings on the first and last day of this iteration. As an example, this would give us totals of:

- Server-Side Developer

  o 2 * ((6 * 10) -3) = 114 hours

- Front-End Developer

  o 2 * ((6 * 10) -3) = 114 hours

Next, the highest-priority story will be broken down into tasks. The tasks are for developers, so they need to make sense for the developers. Each task will be marked as a server-side or front-end task, and each will need an estimate in time against it. The estimate should be equally divisible by three hours—if it is less than three hours, multiple tasks may be combined together. Estimates should be rounded up. When estimating the appropriate time for the task, the two appropriate developers should have a conversation until they both agree on the estimate, though other members of the team may contribute to the discussion. The tasks should (like the stories) be in priority order. Here are example tasks:

- Story: The login web service exists

  o Front-End: Create HTML—3 hours

  o Server-Side: Create server-side form validation—3 hours

  o Front-End: Create front-end form validation—6 hours

---

[2] An example build script is available on the website of this book.

o   Front-End: Create CSS—6 hours

o   Server-Side: Set cookie—3 hours

o   Server-Side: Check details against database—6 hours

o   Server-Side: Implement redirections—3 hours[3]

The project manager should be tallying this against his total resource available. Once this story has been estimated, the remaining resource available is 99 front-end development hours, and 99 server-side development hours. This story and its tasks should now be moved in our tool (GreenHopper) to the iteration. Next, the team will do the same for the highest priority story of those remaining and will continue this process until there are no more hours available. Finally, another story will be estimated and considered to be the stretch for the project, i.e. we may not achieve this, but if we get to it, we will.

Stand-up Meeting

After the first Planning Meeting the team can begin development. Every day there will be a stand-up meeting at 10 am, which is facilitated by the project manager. Any member of the team late to this meeting will receive a mark against them. After three marks, that member must buy the entire team donuts at the next meeting! Representatives of the business will be encouraged to attend these meetings, but should not contribute. During the meeting, everyone will gather around a screen showing the current state of the project in JIRA. This will make it immediately clear what everyone is working on. The project manager should highlight any tasks that seem to be taking very long to complete, any developers that have no tasks in progress and isolate anything that is blocking the team from completing any work (as well as creating actions to address these).

Day-to-Day Development

Outside of the meetings, the developers should take the highest-priority task from the queue and mark it as in progress. They should do nothing but work on that task until it is complete. When it is complete, they should add a comment letting the tester know how to test that task and then move on to the next available task.

The tester should sign off any task that is complete and mark it as done. If it fails the testing for whatever reason, the tester should add a comment explaining how it failed testing and move it back into the task queue. Only the developer that worked on that task should pick it up.

When all the tasks for a story are marked as done, the tester and project manager should work together to check all the acceptance criteria for that story. If everything is acceptable, the story will be marked as complete.

During the iteration, nothing within the sprint should be changed or added. Whenever possible, however, it is acceptable for new stories to be added to the backlog or for the stories outside of the current sprint to be reprioritized.

Tidy-up Meeting

On the last day of each sprint are two meetings. The first, the tidy-up meeting that is be facilitated by the project manager, will happen at 3 pm. During this meeting, any incomplete tasks and stories will be moved back into the backlog, and the project manager will work out the sprint velocity. This is the

---

[3] Note that the CSS will be the last thing to happen. This is to allow for changes in design as late as possible in the process. Design is the most likely thing to change, and although we should try to avoid this, we should also be prepared for it.

number of hours of estimated work that were actually completed in the previous sprint. Over time, this value can be used to calculate the average number of hours that are actually achieved, which will help with more accurate estimations in future iterations.

Retrospective

The second meeting on the last day of each sprint is the retrospective, which is facilitated by the project manager. The retrospective is intended to be a conversation about how well the iteration went and any problems that occurred and how they could be addressed. It should also be used to recognize any team members who have done well in the previous iteration. If the team has achieved a high velocity, when possible we will take the team to a nearby bar or restaurant and have the meeting there as a reward.

The format of the retrospectives shall be as follows:

- First, the team (minus the project manager) will spend one minute writing down things they think went well in the previous iteration on post-it notes.

- The project manager will go through these, putting similar items together into piles. The more items in a pile, the more positive the team feels about these particular items. Each of them should be discussed, and the appropriate members congratulated.

- Next, the team (minus the project manager) will spend one minute writing down things they think went badly in the previous iteration on post-it notes.

- The project manager will go through them, and for every item an action must be recorded to address it. Each action must have a person responsible for actioning it (typically the project manager) and must be complete by the next retrospective.

- If the process needs to change, we will change it!

- Finally, the team should have a general informal chat about how everything is going. This is a great time to bring up general gripes or non-work-related issues and for the team to bond.

The last retrospective of the entire project will be the Project Retrospective. This will take the same form as any other retrospective, but will be based around the entire project rather than only the previous iteration. The project manager may like to present his findings to a wider audience than his team, to recognize them and share any changes to their process they may have implemented that might help the organization as a whole.

Scheduling

Here's a quick recap of the scheduling for the iterations:

- Monday
  - 10 am Planning Meeting
- Tuesday-Friday
  - 10 am Stand-up
- Monday-Thursday
  - 10 am Stand-up

- Friday
  - o 10 am Stand-up
  - o 3 pm Tidy-up Meeting
  - o 4 pm Retrospective

Warranty

The entire process will be repeated until there are no more stories, or the project is deemed complete. At this point, the project is released to an environment for quality assurance (QA), which involves more in-depth testing to ensure the project is ready for release. Then, the project is immediately released to production and is considered to be under warranty for three months.

Finally, the team will move onto the next project, although it must have availability to address any further bugs found for the duration of the warranty period.

Index

■ E

CPSIA information can be obtained at www.ICGtesting.com

225104LV00004B/2/P